PRIEST
AF683749
EST
V
AUGUSTA, ME 04330
622-3789

The Interpretation and Application of Statutes

The Interpretation and Application of Statutes

Reed Dickerson
Professor of Law, Indiana University

Little, Brown and Company
Boston 1975 Toronto

COPYRIGHT © 1975 BY F. REED DICKERSON

ALL RIGHTS RESERVED. NO PART OF THIS BOOK MAY BE REPRODUCED IN ANY FORM OR BY ANY ELECTRONIC OR MECHANICAL MEANS INCLUDING INFORMATION STORAGE AND RETRIEVAL SYSTEMS WITHOUT PERMISSION IN WRITING FROM THE PUBLISHER, EXCEPT BY A REVIEWER WHO MAY QUOTE BRIEF PASSAGES IN A REVIEW.

LIBRARY OF CONGRESS CATALOG CARD NO. 75-2504

Permissions to reproduce previously
copyrighted materials appear on page xv.

Published simultaneously in Canada
by Little, Brown & Company (Canada) Limited

PRINTED IN THE UNITED STATES OF AMERICA

To Jane

Citations to Crawford, Hart & Sacks, and Sutherland

Because of the large number of citations to E. Crawford, The Construction of Statutes (1940), H. Hart, Jr. & A. Sacks, The Legal Process: Basic Problems in the Making and Application of Law (tentative ed. 1958), and J. Sutherland, Statutes and Statutory Construction vol. 2A (4th ed. D. Sands, 1973), I have switched in these instances from full citation to the short forms "Crawford," "Hart & Sacks," and "Sutherland." This note supplies the rest.

Contents

Table of Cases xiii
Permissions xv
Preface xvii

1. Is There a Problem? 1
2. Four Constitutional Assumptions 7
   A. Introduction 7
   B. First Assumption: Legislative Supremacy 7
   C. Second Assumption: Exclusiveness of Statutory Vehicle 9
   D. Third Assumption: Reliance on Accepted Means of Communication 10
   E. Fourth Assumption: Necessity of Reasonable Availability 11
3. Basic Concepts: The Ascertainment of Meaning (Cognition) and Judicial Lawmaking Through the Assignment of Meaning (Creation) 13
   A. What Is Involved in Applying a Statute? 13
   B. The Cognitive Function: The Nature of Ascertainment 21
   C. Drawing the Line: Judicial Creativity as a Test 22
   D. Are Statutes Unique? 28
   E. Ascertainment of Meaning, and Application 29
   F. A Note on the United Kingdom 32
4. Basic Concepts: The General Concept of Meaning 34

A. The Meaning of "Meaning" 34
B. Actual Meaning, Literal Meaning, and True Meaning 38
C. Legal Meaning 39
D. Express Meaning and Implied Meaning 40
E. Referential Meaning: Ogden and Richard's Triangle 42

5. Basic Concepts: Legislative Uncertainty and the Diseases of Language 43
A. Introduction 43
B. Ambiguity 43
C. Overvagueness and Overprecision 48
D. Overgenerality and Undergenerality 51

6. Basic Concepts: Legislative Certainty and the Purposive Element 54
A. Clarity in Statutes 54
B. The Hart Attack 55
C. The Fuller Reply 56
D. Does Legislative Certainty Depend Only on Purpose? 58
E. The Limiting Force of Context 64
F. Summary 66

7. Basic Concepts: Legislative Intent 67
A. Introduction 67
B. The Radin Onslaught 68
C. What Is "Intent"? 69
D. The Specific Arguments 71
E. The Limitations of Legislative Intent 79
F. Objective Versus Subjective Interpretation 83
G. Summary 85

8. Basic Concepts: Legislative Purpose 87
A. Relation to Legislative Intent; Terminology 87
B. The Limitations of Legislative Purpose 89
C. Ascertainment of Legislative Purpose 92
D. Judicial Bootstrap Pulling 93

E. Legislative Purpose as an Aid to Interpretation 95
F. Drafting Policy 97
G. Discrepancies Between Purpose and Intent 98
H. Summary 101
9. Basic Concepts: The Statute and Its Context 103
A. Introduction 103
B. The Statute 104
C. Its Context 105
1. The Backdrop of Culture 105
2. The General Nature and Workings of Context 108
3. Sharing the Elements of Context (Availability) 116
4. "Taking into Account": The Reliance Factor 120
5. Compromising the Ideal 122
D. Intermediate Summary 124
E. Changes in Context: Aging Statutes; Reenactment 125
F. Geographical Differences in Context: Borrowed Statutes 131
10. The Uses and Abuses of Legislative History 137
A. Introduction 137
B. Is Legislative History Part of Context? 138
1. In General 138
2. Taking Into Account 142
3. Availability 147
4. Relevance and Reliability 154
5. The General Case Against Legislative History 162
6. Adding Special Statutory Provisions 165
C. Use of Legislative History in Making New Law 168
D. Improving Legislative History 170

E. Is Use or Improvement of Legislative History Worth the Effort? 174
F. Postenactment Developments 179
G. "Travaux Préparatoires" 183
H. Conclusions 195

11. Strict Interpretation and Liberal Interpretation; the Spirit or Equity of a Statute 198
A. Narrow or Broad Interpretation 198
B. Strict Interpretation and Liberal Interpretation 205
C. The Equity or Spirit of a Statute; Casus Omissus 213

12. How To Read a Statute (Summarizing the Cognitive Function) 217
A. The Perception of Meaning: In General 217
B. The Importance of Attitude 218
C. The Role of Logic 219
D. Resolving Uncertainty 221
E. The Main Materials of Ascertainment 223
F. The Canons of Interpretation 227
G. Summary 236

13. How To Apply a Statute (Summarizing the Creative Function) 238
A. The General Problem 238
B. Supplementing the Very General (Type 1) 240
C. Removing Uncertainty of Meaning (Type 2) 242
D. Furthering Legislative Purpose (Type 3) 250
E. Using an Analogy Beyond the Scope or Purpose of a Statute (Type 4) 251
F. Correcting Erroneous Interpretations (Type 6); Prospective Overruling 252

14. Legislative Control of How Courts Read and Apply Statutes 262
A. Introduction 262

B. Typical Interpretation Act Provisions 263
1. Codifying an Existing Usage of Words, a General Principle of Communication, or a Tacit Assumption 263
2. Changing the Meaning of Existing Statutes 267
3. Establishing a Rule of Law for Deciding Cases Where Statutory Meaning is Unresolvably Uncertain 268
4. Terminating a Judicial Rule of Law for Applying Statutes 269
5. Establishing a New or Different Usage of Words or a New or Different Rule of Communication 270
6. Enacting Specific Rules to Supplement Recurrent General Rules 276
7. Enacting Legislative Boilerplate 277
8. Determining the Boundaries of Effective Legislation 279
C. Summary 280

Appendix A. Meanings of Terms 283
Appendix B. A Catalogue of Popular Misconceptions 288
Appendix C. Referential Meaning: The Static Aspects 291
Appendix D. Modern Treatises on Statutory Interpretation 296
Index of Names 297
Index of Subjects 301

Table of Cases

Addison v. Holly Hill Fruit Products, Inc. (U.S.), 99 n.26
Aerated Bread Co. v. Gregg (Eng.), 125 n.55
A. P. Green Export Co. v. United States (Ct. Cl.), 137
Agar v. Orda (N.Y.), 204, 212, 239 n.3
Amtorg Trading Corp. v. Miehle Printing Press & Mfg. Co. (2d Cir.), 202, 212, 213, 239 n.2, 250
Baker v. Jacobs (Vt.), 203, 212, 215
Bell v. Pedigo (Mo.), 258 n.48
Brown v. Barry (U.S.), 207
Brown v. Board of Education (U.S.), 257
Bryan v. Board of Education (Ky.), 180 n.97
Caminetti v. United States (U.S.), 181
Carroll v. Kittle (Kan.), 258 n.47
Cathcart v. Robinson (U.S.), 131, 132
Chapman v. Brown (D. Hawaii), 80
Church of the Holy Trinity v. United States (U.S.), 80
Citizens to Preserve Overton Park, Inc. v. Volpe (U.S.), 164 n.65
Commissioner v. Acker (U.S.), 78 n.32, 143, 240 n.7
Commonwealth v. Welosky (Mass.), 127, 128 nn.66, 70, 129 n.71
Coral Gables, Inc. v. Christopher (Vt.), 206 n.20
D. A. Schulte, Inc. v. Gangi (U.S.), 87
Douglass v. County of Pike (U.S.), 127 n.62, 253 n.35
Eyston v. Studd (Eng.), 213 n.39
Gatewood v. Matthews (Ky.), 272 n.12
Girouard v. United States (U.S.), 133 n.81, 182 n.105, 239 n.5, 254, 255
Great Northern Ry. v. Sunburst Oil & Ref. Co. (U.S.), 256 n.43
Green v. American Tobacco Co. (Fla.), 31 n.65
Green, A. P., Export Co. v. Gregg (Eng.), 125 n.55
Haeger Potteries, Inc. v. Gilner Potteries (D.C. Cal.), 203
Hawkins Construction Co. v. Matthews Co. (Neb.), 235 n.58
Heydon's Case (Eng.), 82, 201, 212, 213
Hilder v. Dexter (Eng.), 156 n.49
Hochgertel v. Canada Dry Corp. (Pa.), 235 n.57
Hoffman v. Misericordia Hospital (Pa.), 215 n.49

Hutton v. Phillips (Del.), 231, 232
I.C.C. v. J-T Transport Co. (U.S.), 224 n.15
Johnson v. United States (1st Cir.), 93, 214, 215
Lake County v. Rollins (U.S.), 229, 231 n.43
Lee v. Showman's Guild of Great Britain (Eng.), 60 n.25
Markle v. Mulholland's, Inc. (Ore.), 235 n.58, 260 n.53
McDaniel v. Baptist Memorial Hospital (W.D. Tenn.), 216 n.49
Melby v. Anderson (S.D.), 135
Miranda v. Arizona (U.S.), 261 n.57
Naftalin v. King (Minn.), 259
O'Brien v. Atlas Finance Co. (Ark.), 260 n.53
Ott v. Johnson (Ind.), 84 n.53
Pine Hall Coal Co. v. United States (U.S.), 160 n.57
Proffitt v. State (Colo.), 258 n.47
Rhodes Pharmacal Co. v. Continental Can Co. (Ill.), 204 n.17
Riggs v. Palmer (N.Y.), 108 n.14, 199, 200
River Wear Commissioners v. Adamson (Eng.), 231 n.44, 232 n.46
Roschen v. Ward (U.S.), 58, 221
Russman v. Luckette (Ky.), 258 n.45
Saxon v. Georgia Assoc. of Independent Ins. Agents, Inc. (5th Cir.), 81 n.45, 82 n.47
Schulte, D. A., Inc. v. Christopher (Vt.), 206 n.20
Schwegmann Bros. v. Calvert Distillers Corp., 148, 162
Shepard v. Alexian Brothers Hospital, Inc. (Cal.), 216 n.49
State v. Gannites (R.I.), 258 n.49
Swarb v. Lennox (E.D. Pa.), 258 n.48
Tidewater Oil Co. v. United States (U.S.), 3 n.5, 138 n.6
Town of Menominee v. Skubitz (Wis.), 198
United States v. Alpers (U.S.), 234 n.53
United States v. American Trucking Assocs., Inc. (U.S.), 230
United States v. Johnson (U.S.), 21 n.31
United States v. Public Utilities Commn. (U.S.), 120 n.43, 148
United States v. Turley, 201 n.7, 210 n.33
Warring v. Colpoys (D.C.), 255, 257
Widell v. Holy Trinity Catholic Church (Wis.), 258 n.46

Permissions

I should like to acknowledge the permissions kindly granted to quote the selections indicated below.

C. Cherry, On Human Communication (2d ed. 1966). Quoted with permission of the author and MIT Press.

E. Crawford, The Construction of Statutes (1940). Quoted with permission of the author and the Thomas Law Book Company.

P. Ekelöf, Teleological Construction of Statutes, in 2 Scandinavian Studies in Law (1958). Quoted with permission of The Stockholm Institute for Scandanavian Law.

F. Gény, Method of Interpretation and Application of Private Positive Law (2d ed. 1963). Quoted with permission of The Louisiana State Law Institute and West Publishing Company.

G. Gottlieb, The Logic of Choice (1968). Quoted with permission of the author.

H. Hart, Jr. & A. Sacks, The Legal Process: Basic Problems in the Making and Application of Law (tentative ed. 1958). Quoted with permission of the author.

P. Heymann, Ice Cream at Harvard Square, But No Vehicles in the Park—A Study of Purposes (third-year paper, Harvard Law School 1960). Quoted with permission of the author.

P. Mishkin & C. Morris, On Law in Courts (1965). Quoted with permission of The Foundation Press, Inc.

E. Nida, Message and Mission (1960). Quoted with permission of Harper & Row, Publishers, Inc.

C. Ogden & I. Richards, The Meaning of Meaning (10th ed. 1956). Quoted with permission of Harcourt Brace Jovanovich, Inc.

E. W. Patterson, Jurisprudence: Men and Ideas of the Law (1953). Quoted with permission of Penelope P. Ideson (acting for the trustees of the Edwin W. Patterson Testamentary Trust) and The Foundation Press, Inc.

R. Pound, Jurisprudence, vol. III (1959). Quoted with permission of West Publishing Company.

B. Shartel, Our Legal System and How It Operates (1951). Quoted with permission of Michigan Legal Publications.

B. Whorf, Language, Thought, and Reality (1956). Quoted with permission of MIT Press.

Preface

Philosophy is a battle against the bewitchment of our intelligence by means of language.
— L. Wittgenstein, Philosophical Investigations 47 (1953)

Commenting in 1966 on the First Programme of England's Law Commission, Lord Wilberforce suggested that statutory interpretation was a "non-subject,"[1] an evaluation that helps to explain why many readers of this book may be disappointed by the apparent diffuseness of its analysis. What usually passes as a single legal subject is, rather, a conjunction of at least two widely different disciplines (one of which is not uniquely legal) brought together by the special responsibilities of courts operating in a system in which their lawmaking function with respect to statutes remains subordinate to that of the legislature.

The main purpose of this book is not to present easy rules of thumb for disposing of the usually unique mysteries of uncertain statutes, an objective that is unattainable, but to set forth, consistently with existing constitutional restrictions, a coherent account of "statutory interpretation" that clarifies the great bulk of what has been taking place under that banner. Although terminology and specific doctrine have been sharpened, the important contribution, if any, of the book is its attempt, as an exercise in jurisprudence, to develop a general philosophy that realizes more fully the implications of basic assumptions with which few lawyers, I believe, would today disagree. If there is a significant break with existing case law, I trust that it lies more in the supporting reasons than in the results themselves. In this area, the courts' intuitive grasp of sound results often outruns

1. 227 Parl. Deb., H.C. (5th ser.) col. 1294, November 16, 1966.

their ability to rationalize them in concepts that lie comfortably with the basic presuppositions of our legal order. [2]

Although I have not hesitated, where it seemed appropriate, to break with tradition, neither have I hesitated, where it made the better sense, to return to it. In each instance, I have tried to be guided by principle and practicality rather than by what is merely legally fashionable. For the latter indiscretion, I may suffer heavy scorn. In the meantime, I am sustained by the hope that I have at least succeeded in getting part of a serious accumulation of doctrinal rubbish into the legal dustbin. This alone would be worthwhile.

In seeking to achieve coherence where coherence may now be lacking, I have strayed from purely descriptive accounts of conventional doctrine to recommend adjustments in concepts and terminology necessary to more effectively realizing underlying social goals, without, however, rejecting the basic principles of or trends in the existing system. Unfortunately, these adjustments are sufficiently unconventional that, were statutory interpretation under the jurisdiction of the Surgeon General, he would very likely insist that this book carry the warning UNLESS USED WITH CARE THE CONTENTS OF THIS BOOK MAY BE DANGEROUS TO YOUR PROFESSIONAL HEALTH.

Whereas the book may be used freely to enlighten the reader, an advocate should use it sparingly in court. Although it is not substantively radical, the necessity of sharpening concepts and clarifying terminology has produced a number of reformulations that are sufficiently unorthodox that, should they be used intact before a tradition-bound judge, the practical results might be disastrous. Thus, while trying to improve his own understanding, a lawyer who believes that the judge will react more favorably to arguments couched in conventional legal jargon should feel free to stay within the bounds of local tradition. On the other hand, the lawyer for whom the traditional formulations may be unfavorable can afford to be a little bolder. Even for the former, there is always the possibility that the judge has already been corrupted by some of the ideas here advanced.

Case law has been included mainly for its illustrative value. Many, if not most, interpretative cases are unauthoritative as

2. ". . . [O]ne who essays an analysis of the judicial process in the application of statute law finds more conflict in legal literature than inconsistency in the judicial decisions." H. Jones, Statutory Doubts and Legislative History, 40 Colum. L. Rev. 957, 959 (1940).

precedent beyond the specific statutory provisions with which they respectively deal,[3] mainly because they are only occasionally relevant. The need to find case law in this area is accordingly less. Thus, persons interested in collecting the minutiae of local case law will have to look elsewhere. On the other hand, where case law is important, I have either cited it or referred to conventional secondary sources, again without trying to be exhaustive. Because the main mission is to present a broad theory of statutory interpretation, I have not undertaken to discuss every doctrinal aspect or local variation of the subject.

Along the way, I have been helped so widely that full acknowledgment is now out of the question. Fortunately, I can record my thanks to my former colleague Professor Jerome Hall for his initial suggestions. I am grateful also to the Ford Foundation and to Professor James Willard Hurst of the University of Wisconsin for making it possible for me to spend a year at Harvard University digging into the principles of language and communication. This provided a welcome opportunity to consult with Professors Lon Fuller and Henry M. Hart, Jr. and to attend the latter's stimulating course on the Legal Process.

I owe a heavy debt also to Sir Leslie Scarman, recent chairman of England's Law Commission,[4] for letting me work, during the spring of 1966, in temporary tandem with the Commission team then tilling the field of statutory interpretation. I am especially grateful to Norman S. Marsh and Maurice Abrahams, both of the Commission, who in generous return for my few, small contributions to its report rewarded me with legislative riches from the United Kingdom and other parts of the world and an opportunity to participate in the seminar on statutory interpretation held at All Souls College, Oxford, May 20 and 21, 1966. In the Office of the Parliamentary Counsel, Sir John Fiennes, Henry P. Rowe, and Godfrey Carter provided many a helpful lead. Also helpful were my conversations with Professor H. L. A. Hart of Oxford University and Professor R. W. M. Dias of Cambridge University. Maurice Abrahams, Edward O. Craft, and Professors James Willard Hurst and Charles B. Nutting read the manuscript and made valuable suggestions.

At Indiana University, my colleagues, Professors Morris S.

3. E. Driedger, The Construction of Statutes vii-viii (1974); Sutherland §45.15.

4. Now Mr. Justice Scarman, Court of Appeal.

Arnold, Patrick Baude, and Arthur R. Hogue reviewed some historical and constitutional matters and students Jonathan F. Buchter, Philip R. Cockerille, and Stanley C. Kent contributed valuable legal research. Law librarians Betty LeBus, Jurij Fedynskyj, and Cheryl Jones were always ready to lead me, almost by the hand, to an elusive volume. In patience and compassion, they were outrageously profligate.

To my many helpers, then, enthusiastic thanks.

R.D.

Bloomington, Indiana
November 1974

The Interpretation and Application of Statutes

1

Is There a Problem?

The hard truth of the matter is that American Courts have no intelligible, generally accepted, and consistently applied theory of statutory interpretation.

— H. Hart, Jr. & A. Sacks, The Legal Process 1201 (tentative edition 1958)

It would be hard to think of a field of law that needs clarifying more than that of "statutory interpretation." I suppose that every specialist feels this way about his own area of interest and that he hopes, privately, that he is the one whom Fate has selected to enlighten the bewildered. While waiting to feel its wise touch on my own shoulder, let me explain briefly why I believe that this important legal area has fallen on evil days. Horack's reference to "the disintegration of statutory construction," [1] while hardly reflecting any personal despair, aptly describes the current intellectual morass.

One evidence of the need to rework the field is the difficulty and even impossibility of conversing sensibly on statutory interpretation without elaborate precautions to establish or stabilize terms, concepts, and premises. The plainest discrepancies abound even in the language used to talk about statutory interpretation. The term "statutory interpretation" itself is used to refer, on the one hand, solely to the cognitive process of ascertaining meaning

1. F. Horack, Jr., The Disintegration of Statutory Construction, 24 Ind. L.J. 335 (1949); Cooperative Action for Improved Statutory Interpretation, 3 Vand. L. Rev. 382 (1950). For an extended survey of the competing approaches to statutory interpretation, see the series of articles by J. Witherspoon on The Administrative Discretion to Determine Statutory Meaning in 35 Tex. L. Rev. 63 (1956); 38 Tex. L. Rev. 392, 572 (1960), and 40 Tex. L. Rev. 751 (1962).

and, on the other hand, to the entire process by which a court discharges its responsibility of applying statutes to specific controversies. It is hard to tell which sense is being used on which occasion.

The inadequacies of terminology also plague such other basic terms as "meaning," "plain meaning," "intent," "purpose," "express," "implied," "strict interpretation," "liberal interpretation," "equitable interpretation," "ambiguity," "vagueness," "generality," "remedial," "penal," "retroactive," and "context." There are others.

For true problems of meaning, some of the current difficulty inheres in unavoidable limitations of communication and human thought. Language itself is vulnerable to a number of partly but not wholly curable diseases such as ambiguity and overvagueness.[2] Also, the application of general language to concrete problems requires difficult judgments in characterizing or classifying the relevant kinds of facts. Nature in the raw can be comprehended only when it is seen through a cultural screen or grid, or as a cultural map, appropriate to the relevant objectives.[3] On how to draw an appropriate map of human experience reasonable minds can differ. More than language-deep, current confusion extends even to primary concepts and basic premises.

Some current concepts perform no useful function and thus distract attention from the significant ones. The current idea of "extrinsic" materials, for example, is not helpful, because it fails to distinguish between extrinsic materials that are part of legislative context and extrinsic materials that are not. Ideas of "strict interpretation" and "liberal interpretation" likewise perform no legitimate function and should be got rid of. Faulty conceptualization arises also in the failure to keep intellectually alive the differences between immediate legislative purpose and ulterior legislative purpose, and between the subjective aspects of legislative intent or purpose and their corresponding objective aspects.

One basic error has been a failure to take adequate account of the well-established constitutional principles that, while making the legislature the supreme lawmaker, limit the methods by which it can effectively communicate its will to its several legislative audiences. This failure has made it hard to know, for example,

2. See ch. 5.
3. See ch. 9, pp. 105-106.

the extent, if any, to which the courts may look beyond statutory language for indications of legislative purpose or intent.

Another basic error has been a failure to recognize and take into account the implications of the fact that the judicial functions involved in applying statutes to particular controversies require not only attention to the problems of communication involved in finding out what statutes mean but the exercise of judicial statecraft involved in adapting imperfectly expressed statutes to the settlement of those controversies. Combining these functions in a single, undifferentiated concept of "legislative interpretation," while tending to overplay the difficulties of immediate application or to disguise the creative aspects of judicial administration by overplaying problems of communication, has made it hard to define or explain the respects in which courts are constitutionally limited in dealing with statutes and the respects in which they may be expected to exercise wise discretion. Consequently, statutory interpretation has become a hodgepodge of principles of communication and legal guides for getting justice done in particular cases. Under such conditions, confusion is inevitable.

If one of the two basic steps in reading and applying statutes is to solve the relevant problems of meaning, surely a court should pay appropriate deference to the established principles of communication. Ironically, the profession that confronts perhaps the most sophisticated problems of meaning lacks the sophisticated understanding of the principles of communication necessary to solve them. The semantic naiveté of lawyers is nowhere more clearly shown than in their abuse of stipulative definition ("In this Act, the term 'supplies' includes land").

The inadequate attention paid to matters of communication is reflected in many ways, most basically in the typical lawyer's imperfect understanding of the respective roles played by express language, on the one hand, and by context, on the other. Although context is now universally recognized as a vital conditioning element in all forms of communication, little has been done to make clear what it consists of and how it operates. [4] As a result, it is hard to make sense out of the current uses of the materials of federal legislative history, all of which are commonly and unquestioningly assumed to be part of legislative context. [5]

4. On context, see ch. 9.

5. E.g., Tidewater Oil Co. v. United States, 409 U.S. 151, 157, 93 S. Ct. 408, 413 (1972).

Traditional overemphasis on the literal aspects of meaning has provoked today's reactionary underemphasis on them. This has been accompanied by a misunderstanding of and an overemphasis on extrinsic materials, as if the court in quest of legislative meaning had to reject the former kind of aid while selecting the latter. In currently overemphasizing the relevance and weight of extrinsic materials, legal writers have tended to overstate the range of discretion that a court may properly exercise when applying statutes. This has encouraged the widespread tendency to place the courts at the apex of the function of making law as well as at the apex of the function of administering justice. A wholesome resistance to the excesses of literalism need not exaggerate the uncertainties of language nor distort the proper role or range of judicial discretion.

One unfortunate by-product of failing to separate the factual aspects of communication from the legal aspects of statutory supplementation and repair necessary to application is the tendency to view all canons of statutory interpretation as cut from the same cloth, whether rule-of-law, rule-of-usage, presumption, factual tendency, or fatuous rationalization. [6] Instead, careful examination will show that these canons make up a grab bag of items differing in kind, validity, and usefulness. Another by-product is the tendency to assume that the canons of interpretation, taken as a multitude of specific rules of law, can be used to unlock specific problems of meaning, when the nub of the problem is to maintain a proper point of view.

Worst of all, confusion has so penetrated the core of statutory interpretation that it is impossible, without careful overhauling, to integrate the generally avowed principles and rules of statutory interpretation into a comprehensive, coherent, and communicable philosophy preferable to the present miscellany of alternative rationalizations that courts use to dignify results.

What is most needed, therefore, in interpreting and applying statutes is a philosophy of what "statutory interpretation" in its broad, bastard sense is all about. If we threw out the term "statutory interpretation" altogether and referred, instead, to the "ascertainment of statutory meaning" or to "judicial lawmaking," as circumstances made appropriate, it might become clearer that what is needed with respect to the former is not an interpretative key ring jingling with specific rules designed to unlock a

6. See ch. 12, pp. 227-236.

miscellany of specific meanings but a wholesome perspective based on appropriate attitudes and general approaches. Beyond this, little can be done except to describe an occasionally useful convention of language.

If the foregoing appraisal is sound, the first need in developing an adequate theory of how to read and apply statutes is to perfect and standardize the terminology used to talk about statutes. The results of trying to do so throughout the book are summarized in appendix A.

The second need is to purge statutory interpretation of its spurious concepts and erroneous assumptions. (The latter are listed in appendix B.) Attempts to do this are made at the many places throughout the book where they might otherwise be likely to intrude.

The third need is to take better account of the relevant constitutional limitations. These are outlined in chapter 2.

The fourth need is to take better account of the difference between the cognitive process of ascertaining legislative meaning and the creative process of judicial lawmaking through the assignment of meaning. This difference, which is referred to at many points, is specially considered in chapter 3.

The fifth need is to become more fully aware of the basic principles of communication as they operate in the context of legislation. These are considered in chapters 4-9.

The sixth, and most important, need is to integrate the useful concepts into a coherent and communicable general philosophy respecting the courts' role in interpreting and applying statutes, in the light of the basic problems of communication and the relevant constitutional limitations.[7] The effort will be worthwhile so long as we do not slip into the beguiling dream that persevering will ultimately lead us to a never-never land of convenient and comfortable rules. This sixth need is the main preoccupation of this book.

But before beginning our search for the holy legislative grail,

7. "Current textbooks do little more than to mix these various recipes without any serious attempt to reconciling them." W. Friedmann, Law and Social Change in Contemporary Britain 244 (1951). "Though it would not dispel all the doubts which are inherent in the situation, it would help give objectivity to the process of interpretation and assurance to drafting of statutes, if we could have general acceptance by the bench as well as the Bar of a few basic principles of statutory construction." R. Jackson, The Meaning of Statutes: What Congress Says or What the Court Says, 34 A.B.A.J. 535, 538 (1948).

let us consider the risk that the expectation of developing a unified, systematic theory of statutory interpretation is pure mirage. Indeed, Thornstedt has told us that "the various fields of law are so entirely different from one another that it is not likely that any given method will be useful in all of them." [8] Friedmann makes the same general point, but he subdivides the legislative landscape differently. [9] Neither tells how to mediate jurisdictional disputes among such legislative areas.

Fortunately, the general point on which Thornstedt, Friedmann, and others agree need not detain us here. It is true that, if "interpretation" in its broadest sense covers at least two widely differing disciplines, as many authorities now seem to assume, we need at least two major philosophies, one relating to "interpretation proper" and the other to judicial lawmaking, and we may well need to differentiate also on other bases.

On the other hand, the fact that the total domain of statutory interpretation and application is so heterogeneous that it precludes a single, simple set of working rules does not automatically preclude a set of broad integrative principles that leave room for necessary divergences. It may still be possible, then, to tie the basic elements and subelements together into a coherent, constitutional, and functional whole.

8. The Principle of Legality and Teleological Construction of Statutes, in 4 Scandinavian Studies in Law 1960, at 211-212. Thornstedt distinguishes (1) areas in which there is "systematic, exhaustive, and detailed legislation," (2) areas in which "different special cases are governed by a great number of isolated rules but important questions involving general principles are left unsolved," and (3) areas "where statutory rules have the character of a programme rather than a detailed regulation." Id. at 212.

9. W. Friedmann, Law and Social Change in Contemporary Britain 252-253 (1951). Friedmann accepts a "pseudo-logical" approach for "routine" cases, a "social policy" approach for legislation "dictated by an easily definable social purpose," and a "free intuition" approach for legislation whose social purpose remains murky, supplemented by distinctions based on the kind of statute involved. Id. at 251-252.

2

Four Constitutional Assumptions

It is sometimes more important to emphasize the obvious than to elucidate the obscure.

— Attributed to Oliver Wendell Holmes

A. Introduction

The analysis offered by this book rests on several constitutional assumptions. However obvious they may seem, they need to be expressed and kept continuously in the foreground, because without necessarily intending to reject them courts often act as if they were false.

B. First Assumption: Legislative Supremacy

The first assumption is that the general powers of government are constitutionally allocated among the three central branches in such a way that, although it does not enjoy an exclusive power to make substantive law, the legislative branch exercises lawmaking power that takes precedence over the lawmaking powers respectively exercised by the executive and judicial branches.[1]

The facts that this separation of powers is not absolute, and

1. E.g., see L. Jaffe, Judicial Control of Administrative Action 28, 32 (abridged student ed. 1965); C. Breitel, The Courts and Law Making, in Legal Institutions Today and Tomorrow 1, 26 (M. Paulsen ed., 1959); Q. Johnstone, An Evaluation of the Rules of Statutory Interpretation, 3 U. Kan. L. Rev. 1, 8 (1954); R. Jackson, The Meaning of Statutes: What Congress Says or What the Court Says, 34 A.B.A.J. 535, 536 (1948).

that the allocation is complicated rather than simple, [2] in no wise detract from the simple assertion that, within the domains of lawmaking in which they are constitutionally permitted to operate and within the differing means by which they make their pronouncements, any conflict between the legislative will and the judicial will must be resolved in favor of the former. It is assumed, therefore, that within these boundaries the judicial branch must remain appropriately deferential to the properly promulgated views of the legislature. Although the courts, too, make general law, they do this in the absence or supplementation of statute. No reservation need be made for the courts' power to declare a constitutionally offensive statute invalid.

In England, where the constitution remains unwritten, legislative supremacy grew out of ideas that were encouraged by the revolution of 1688. [3] Before that, the lines between the branches of government had been widely blurred. In the fourteenth century judges were also legislators and, consistently with what the sovereign permitted, what they failed to accomplish as legislators they could often accomplish as judges. Even after judges ceased to sit as legislators in the upper house, gaps between what was expressed and what seemed to be the legislative purpose were bridged by notions of "equitable interpretation."

The revolution of 1688 fostered the idea that Parliament's powers over fundamental human rights relating to liberty and property, though preeminent, were limited. Notions of "liberal" or "strict" construction evolved as judicial devices for encouraging or inhibiting legislative action. However, efforts to cushion or deflect what the courts considered legislative misjudgment or overreaching spurred Parliament to greater specificity. Unfriendly judicial interpretation thus encouraged a legislative prolixity that, in milder form, persists even today. [4]

2. Crawford 10-14.

3. This brief historical sketch is drawn largely from J. Corry, Administrative Law and the Interpretation of Statutes, 1 U. Toronto L.J. 286, 293-298 (1936). For other historical materials on statutory interpretation, see R. Dias, Jurisprudence 93-99 (3d ed. 1970); A. Hogue, Origins of the Common Law 229-230 (1966); F. Horack, Jr., Statutory Interpretation — Light from Plowden's Reports, 19 Ky. L.J. 211 (1932); O. Phillips, A First Book of English Law 118-119 (6th ed. 1970); T. Plucknett, A Concise History of the Common Law 292-298 (3d ed. 1940); M. Radin, Early Statutory Interpretation, 38 Ill. L. Rev. 16 (1944); S. Thorne, A Discourse Upon the Exposicion & Understandinge of Statutes (1942), reviewed by Plucknett in 60 L.Q. Rev. 242, 246-248 (1944).

4. D. Mellinkoff, The Language of the Law 176-178 (1963).

With the weakening of the Crown and the reinforcement of notions of separation of powers developed by Montesquieu and other political thinkers, Parliament emerged generally supreme, certainly so by the nineteenth century.[5] Despite the development, in most jurisdictions, of the courts' power to blow the constitutional whistle on legislative overreaching and despite their assertedly exclusive power to interpret, the supremacy of the legislature in formulating social policy appears to be universally accepted today, an assumption unchallenged by the not-so-universal assumption that within circumscribed areas the courts, too, make law.

In the United States, legislative supremacy is expressly written into the federal[6] and state constitutions.[7]

C. Second Assumption: Exclusiveness of Statutory Vehicle

A second constitutional assumption is that the legislative will can be communicated as effective law only if the legislature promulgates its views in the way prescribed by the applicable constitution. The exclusive means by which a legislature may create new law is enacting a statute or its procedural equivalent.[8] This it cannot do by writing a letter, by passing a simple or concurrent resolution not submitted to the executive for his approval, or by any other method not involving the legislative steps specified by the constitution. Although the United States Constitution is not express on the point, the limitation appears to be nailed down, through negative implication, by the enactment procedure prescribed by article I, section 7. As for the states,

5. M. Radin, A Short Way with Statutes, 56 Harv. L. Rev. 388, 392 (1942).

6. U.S. Const. art. I, §1.

7. New Jersey's constitution is typical: "The legislative power shall be vested in a Senate and General Assembly." Art. II, §1. It also includes a provision commonly found in state constitutions: "No person . . . belonging to . . . one branch shall exercise any of the powers properly belonging to either of the others, except as expressly provided in this Constitution." Art. III, §1.

8. ". . . [T]he constitutional power granted to Congress to legislate is granted only if it is exercised in the form of voting on specific statutes." M. Radin, A Case Study in Statutory Interpretation: Western Union Co. vs. Lenroot, 33 Calif. L. Rev. 218, 223 (1945). And see Crawford 58-59; Sutherland §1.02.

almost half of their constitutions provide, in effect, that "no law may be enacted except by bill," [9] and the same limitation seems to inhere, by negative implication, in the enactment procedures prescribed by the others. [10]

If this second assumption is correct, it means that not even the most reliable document of legislative history, such as a conference committee report, may have the force of law. Certainly, it may not be given weight equal to that of the statute to which it relates. If it has weight, it must be because it is part of proper legislative context (if it can meet the applicable standards), or because it is used for a purpose other than ascertaining the meaning of the statute.

D. Third Assumption: Reliance on Accepted Means of Communication

A third constitutional assumption is that, as a communication from the legislature to one or more legislative audiences, a statute is subject to the accepted standards of communication in effect in the given environment. [11] This tacitly underlies the applicable constitution and is therefore part of it. Any other assumption would unjustifiably magnify the risk that legislative supremacy would in fact be subverted, because it is the very nature of language, which is founded on accepted usage, to comply with that usage most of the time.

Thus, a court seeking to discharge its constitutional duty of deference to the expressions of legislative will made in the constitutionally prescribed way is obliged to ascertain the meaning of

9. E.g., Cal. Const. art. IV, §15; Colo. Const. art. V, §17; Ill. Const. art. 4, §8; Mich. Const. art. IV, §26; Mo. Const. art. 3, §21; N.Y. Const. art. 3, §13.

10. The basic principle that legislatures are confined to the statutory medium is not contradicted by constitutional provision for public initiative.

11. ". . . [Courts] cannot permit the legislative process, and all the other processes which depend upon the integrity of language, to be subverted by the misuse of words. . . . [T]hese policies of clear statement may on occasion operate to defeat the actual, consciously held intention of particular legislators, or of the members of the legislature generally. . . . [T]hey constitute conditions of the effectual exercise of legislative power. But the requirement should be thought of as constitutionally imposed." Hart & Sacks 1412-1413. See also F. de Sloovère, Textual Interpretation of Statutes, 11 N.Y.U.L.Q. Rev. 538, 541 (1934).

those expressions according to accepted standards of communication. Although constitutionally implied, such standards are not themselves matters of law. That, as matters of fact, they are sometimes hard to ascertain and apply does not absolve a court of the duty of making a conscientious effort to do so. Indeed, it is not constitutionally free to change or interfere with those standards, even for what it conceives to be a wholesome social purpose.

Radin tells us that the "legislature has no constitutional warrant to demand reverence for the words in which it frames its directives,"[12] and in the exaggerated terms of "reverence" for particular language we must agree. On the other hand, it seems clear that, so long as the legislature uses language according to accepted standards, it is justified in assuming that the courts should read it according to the same standards. The legislature cannot adequately discharge its responsibility of shaping the future unless the integrity of the accepted communication process is maintained.

This premise should be kept constantly in mind, because courts have often felt free to recognize and resolve uncertainties of meaning contrary to the preponderance of factual probabilities or plausibilities of meaning. That they may have been motivated by what they have believed to be the public good is not, in the light of the constitutional separation of powers, adequate justification.

E. Fourth Assumption: Necessity of Reasonable Availability

A fourth constitutional assumption is that a legislature is required to make the laws that it enacts reasonably available to the persons who are affected by them. Although the United States Constitution and some state constitutions are silent on the subject, the notion of providing a reasonable opportunity to know what the law is inheres in the constitutional requirement that the legislature must communicate its commands and pronouncements by means of a specified kind of vehicle developed and launched in a specified way. It would make no sense to

12. M. Radin, A Short Way with Statutes, 56 Harv. L. Rev. 388, 406 (1942).

assume, on the one hand, that the Constitution is deeply concerned with the creation of such a vehicle and, on the other hand, that it is unconcerned with whether the vehicle reaches its intended destination.

The constitutions of at least three states provide that a law may not take effect until it has been published.[13] More than half of the others provide, in cases not involving emergency, that it may not take effect until a specified period has elapsed.[14] A constitutional opportunity for the persons affected to adjust to the new law necessarily implies a constitutional policy of providing a reasonable opportunity to know what the new law provides. The effectiveness of the law is thus conditioned, not on actual knowledge of the law, but on a reasonable opportunity to acquire that knowledge. Because this standard cannot be met unless the opportunity to know extends to all aspects of the legislature's communication, no material extrinsic to the statute can properly be treated as part of the total legislative communication unless it meets the minimum standards of availability to which the statute itself is constitutionally subject. This it can do only as part of proper legislative context; otherwise it runs afoul our second constitutional assumption, already discussed.

13. Ind. Const. art. 4, §29; Wis. Const. art. VII, §21; Utah Const. art. 6, §25. "All Acts shall be published in the official journal without delay after passage." La. Const. art. III, §27. See also Md. Const. art. III, §30. The proposed Botswana Interpretation and General Provisions Bill, 1973, §8(2), provides that an act "comes into operation immediately on the expiration of the day next preceding the day on which it is published in the Gazette."

14. E.g., Alaska Const. art. II, §18; Md. Const. art. III, §31; N.D. Const. art. II, §67; Ore. Const. art. IV, §28; Tenn. Const. art. II, §20.

3

Basic Concepts: The Ascertainment of Meaning (Cognition) and Judicial Lawmaking Through the Assignment of Meaning (Creation)

. . . *[W]hether the process of judicial legislation should be called finding or making the law is undoubtedly of great practical moment.*
— M. Cohen, Law and the Social Order 121 (1933)

A. What Is Involved in Applying a Statute?

Because the legislature is, within constitutional limits, the supreme lawmaking body, and because statutes are the sole constitutional vehicles for communicating its official will, the first function of the persons to whom they are addressed, including the courts, should be to find out what they mean and honor the meaning so found. Although it is popularly assumed, and occasionally stated, [1] that the duty of the courts with respect to statutes is this and nothing more, what is the legal reality?

The main function of a court is to adjudicate particular con-

1. E.g., J. Thomas, Statutory Construction When Legislation Is Viewed as a Legal Institution, 3 Harv. J. Legis. 191, 194 (1966). In E. Driedger, The Construction of Statutes (1974), only the court's function of ascertaining meaning is discussed.

troversies between particular disputants. [2] In each case, it must support its action by reciting legal rules that mesh adequately with the existing legal order. If there is no pertinent statute, the court must fashion or adjust a rule of law to fit the situation at hand. [3] It may not throw up its hands and pass.

If there is a relevant statute, the statute may resolve the issue almost automatically, [4] as where the court is used mainly as a collection agency. In other instances, the statute may be generally relevant without providing a clear answer or any answer at all. Here, too, the court must decide the case. And so, if the statute is invincibly obscure or substantively incomplete, the court must perfect the rule that the statute announces or fashion or adjust one in the light of how the court relates its role to that of the legislature. [5]

Lumping the court's functions with respect to statutes under the single term "interpretation," by suggesting in some contexts

2. ". . . [T]he function of making authoritative determinations of the meaning of statute law is exercised by the courts in the settlement of cases." C. Nutting, The Relevance of Legislative Intention Established by Extrinsic Evidence, 20 B.U.L. Rev. 601, 605 (1940).

3. C. Breitel, The Courts and Law Making, in Legal Institutions Today and Tomorrow 1, 5 (M. Paulsen ed., 1959); The Lawmakers, 65 Colum. L. Rev. 749-750 (1965).

4. ". . . [W]hen a Legislature has had a real intention . . . on a point, it is not once in a hundred times that any doubt arises as to what its intention was." J. Gray, The Nature and Sources of the Law 172 (2d ed. 1921).

5. The lawmaking function of courts with respect to statutes is now generally recognized. E.g., C. Allen, Law in the Making 499-500 (7th ed. 1964); J. Gray, The Nature and Sources of the Law 173 (2d ed. 1921); Hart & Sacks 1225; R. Keeton, Venturing to do Justice 78 (1969); B. Shartel, Our Legal System and How It Works 328 (1951); C. Breitel, The Courts and Law Making, in Legal Institutions Today and Tomorrow 1, 2 (M. Paulsen ed. 1959); J. Cohen, Judicial "Legisputation" and the Dimensions of Legislative Meaning, 36 Ind. L.J. 414 (1961); W. Cook, Scientific Method and the Law, 13 A.B.A.J. 303, 308 (1927); J. Corry, Administrative Law and the Interpretation of Statutes, 1 U. Toronto L.J. 286, 291 (1936); J. Frank, Words and Music: Some Remarks on Statutory Interpretation, 47 Colum. L. Rev. 1257, 1267, 1269-1270 (1947); F. Horack, Jr., Cooperative Action for Improved Statutory Interpretation, 3 Vand. L. Rev. 382, 388, 394 (1950); H. Jones, The Plain Meaning Rule and Extrinsic Aids in the Interpretation of Federal Statutes 2, 3 (1939); Q. Johnstone, An Evaluation of the Rules of Statutory Interpretation, 1 U. Kan. L. Rev. 1, 9 (1959); A. S. Miller, Statutory Language and the Purposive Use of Ambiguity, 42 Va. L. Rev. 23, 30 (1956); L. Tunks, Assigning Legislative Meaning: A New Bottle, 37 Iowa L. Rev. 372 (1959). On the courts' creative function generally, see C. Breitel, The Lawmakers, 65 Colum. L. Rev. 749, 765-772 (1965). And see ch. 13.

a single, undifferentiated function, tends to confuse the respective contributions of the legislature and the court and thus to subvert the preeminence in policy formulation that the legislature is constitutionally entitled to enjoy. Whether the statute is clear or obscure, whether or not it adequately resolves the current issue, and whether it can be applied as it came from the legislative oven or must be remolded, the court should first examine it in its proper context to discover, if possible, what it most probably means. Then, after measuring the legislative contribution, the court, where necessary, may add its own contribution.

Although the two steps provide a single disposition of a case, they remain separate and distinct contributions, drawing their strength from different sources and operating under different, though merging, principles. The first step we will refer to, in Ross's term, [6] as the "cognitive function" or the "ascertainment of meaning"; the second we will refer to as the "creative function" or "the assignment of meaning." [7]

This dichotomy will be resisted by old-line traditionalists (most of whom, today, reside in the United Kingdom) [8] who assert that the only step in the adjudication of statutory issues is that of ascertaining legislative meaning. They apparently believe that a statute, however defective, contains within it at least a latent answer to every question falling within its orbit and that the judiciary's responsibility remains one only of discovery. This approach is supported on the level of form by the prevailing terminology of "meaning" or "interpretation," under which all judicial functions relating to the interpretation or application of statutes currently tend to be subsumed. Although the approach has been widely repudiated, many judicial opinions are still written as if it were sound.

At the other extreme is a smaller and more vociferous group, apparently spawned by Gray,[9] that often seems to be saying that

6. A. Ross, On Law and Justice 138 (1959).

7. Gény recognizes the distinction by dividing judicial "interpretation" (in its loose, overall sense) into "interpretation proper" and "free interpretation." F. Gény, Method of Interpretation and Sources of Private Positive Law 182, 208 (2d ed. 1963). He also respectively describes them as "receptive" and "productive." Id. at 212.

8. There appears to be at least one in the United States. See J. Thomas, Statutory Construction When Legislation Is Viewed as a Legal Institution, 3 Harv. J. Legis. 191 (1966).

9. J. Gray, The Nature and Sources of the Law 124-125 (2d ed. 1921), but cf. 179.

legislative pronouncements have no meaning and thus little significance until the court breathes life into them in the act of applying them to concrete situations.[10] Chief Justice Hughes's half-truth that "a federal statute finally means what the Court says it means"[11] is only an echo of Bishop Hoadly's famous pronouncement, "Whoever hath an *absolute authority* to *interpret* any . . . laws, it is *he* who is truly the Law-giver . . . and not the person who first wrote . . . them."[12] Curtis's[13] and Morris Cohen's[14] more recent expressions appear to be in the same vein.

In a superficial examination of this approach, words might appear as little more than empty vessels into which the court may pour any desirable judicial meaning. Whether these writers undertake to deal with language in general or only its trouble areas they do not always make clear. The matter is clouded by a seeming disregard of the instances in which expressed meaning can be and is quite plain.[15]

Much recent writing in this field thus sounds as if the only significant thing that happens in a lawsuit involving a statute is the transmutation of legislative dross into judicial gold. There is little or no consideration of what the legislative dross may consist of; the focus is almost entirely on what the court has added. Although such a view might have made sense in the early fourteenth century, when English statutes stood no higher than the case materials that courts molded as useful precedent,[16] today's typical statutory provision, which gets enacted and obeyed with

10. "[A]fter all, it is only words that the legislature utters; it is for the courts to say what those words mean. . . . [A]ll the Law is judge-made law. . . . The courts put life into the dead words of the statute." Id. Who puts life into the dead words of the courts?

11. C. Hughes, The Supreme Court of the United States 230 (1928). On the other hand, Lord Devlin's statement in his Samples of Law Making 2 (1962) that "The law is what the judges say it is," which refers to the state of the law as distinct from the actual meaning of a statute, is quite acceptable.

12. Quoted in J. Gray, The Nature and Sources of the Law 172 (2d ed. 1921). (Emphasis in original.)

13. "Words in legal documents . . . mean, in the first instance, what the person to whom they are addressed makes them mean." C. Curtis, It's Your Law 65 (1954).

14. M. Cohen, Law and the Social Order 131 (1933).

15. See ch. 6.

16. See, generally, S. Thorne, A Discourse Upon the Exposicion & Understandinge of Statutes (1942); J. Corry, Administrative Law and the Interpretation of Statutes, 1 U. Toronto L.J. 286, 293-294 (1936).

only sporadic help from the courts, appears to have a life of its own.[17] Certainly, statutory language is not so frail that it must be bolstered, at every point, by judicial exegesis.

The consequences of such an unbalanced legal view have been aggravated by legal theorists who have turned the lawyer's case-law focus on sick language into a permanent principle of statutory interpretation. Until he became more counselor than advocate, the typical lawyer was preoccupied with the kind of statutory pathology that gets special attention in court. Such a preoccupation leads easily to the conclusion that all language is as inherently inadequate as the statutory fragments that become the subjects of legal opinions.[18]

Why is it necessary today to constantly reaffirm that in the interpretation of statutes it is as important to read the statute as it is to read about it? The reason is clear. As an officer of the court, the lawyer not only has been educated in a court-oriented law school but is court oriented in much of his general practice. But this hardly justifies an overall preoccupation with the judicial function that treats it, as Hurst has said, "as if it were the whole . . . legal order."[19]

The tendency to neglect the specifics of statutes in favor of judicial commentary corrupts students, lawyers, and even judges. Driedger has expressly noted what others have observed informally: A lawyer is likely to read a statute only superficially. Typically, he glances at it over his shoulder as he runs to see

17. E. Patterson, Jurisprudence 199 (1953). "Attorneys whose law school training has buried them in the case method . . . tend to forget that most words in most statutes never become the subject of a lawsuit." F. Newman & S. Surrey, Legislation — Cases and Materials 645-646 (1955).

18. See also ch. 6. p. 54. It is ironic that this mistrust of language tends to dissipate as the legal mind turns from statutory language to the language of legislative history, judicial language, or legal writing generally. If a statute is, by itself, too shallow a vessel to carry the legislative message, how can we confidently rely on the impromptu statement of a legislator on the floor of the legislature? In the language used in a judicial opinion? In the statement of a law professor in a law review article? Or is communication in the law an art reliably practiced only by judges, politicians, and law professors?

19. J. Hurst, The Law in United States History, 104 Proc. Amer. Phil. Soc. 518, 522 (1960). "Until recently not the least notable characteristics of American law were, on the one hand, the excessive output of legislation in all our jurisdictions and, on the other hand, the indifference sometimes almost to contempt with which that output was regarded by lawyers, law teachers, and text writers." R. Pound, Sources and Forms of Law, 22 Notre Dame Law. 1, 36-37 (1946).

what the courts have said about it.[20] That judges are not immune to the temptation to concentrate elsewhere is shown by the disproportionate reliance they place on what courts have already done, even with respect to matters of the most tenuous relevance. Indeed, one state supreme court judge recently admitted, privately, that he had applied a statute on breaches of the peace for twenty years before he got around to reading it!

This does not deny that a statute includes, in a real sense, the judicial gloss that courts have added to it. It does deny that a court is justified in treating the statute as if it consisted only of that gloss and the words as if they had furnished only the historical occasion for adding it.

A realistic analysis of the judicial role in relation to statutes must mediate between these two extremes by recognizing that a court has two different, intimately related, and equally important responsibilities: (1) to read the statute in its proper context to ascertain whether and how its meaning relates to the controversy at hand (thus establishing the court's legislative terms of reference), and (2) where the meaning of the statute as so ascertained does not resolve the controversy, to apply, adjust, or create an appropriate judicial rule to resolve it. No approach that focuses on one of these functions to the neglect of the other can make sense out of what courts have been or should be doing in relation to statutes.

Recognition of the vital distinction between the courts' cognitive function and their creative function is not new. It has been recognized by many legal writers.[21] What would be new would

20. E. Driedger, A New Approach to Statutory Interpretation, 29 Can. Bar Rev. 838, 839-840 (1951).

21. E.g., C. Allen, Law in the Making 499-500 (7th ed. 1964); R. Keeton, Venturing to do Justice 78, 82 (1969); C. Breitel, The Courts and Law Making, in Legal Institutions Today and Tomorrow 1, 16-18 (M. Paulsen ed., 1959); K. Llewellyn, The Common Law Tradition: Deciding Appeals 382 (1960); B. Shartel, Our Legal System and How It Operates 328-329, 387 (1940); J. Cohen, Judicial "Legisputation" and the Dimensions of Legislative Meaning, 36 Ind. L.J. 414, 416 (1961); J. Corry, Administrative Law and the Interpretation of Statutes, 1 U. Toronto L.J. 286, 291 (1947); A. Cox, Judge Learned Hand and the Interpretation of Statutes, 60 Harv. L. Rev. 370, 375 (1947); F. Horack, Jr., Cooperative Action for Improved Statutory Interpretation, 3 Vand. L. Rev. 382, 388-389, 394 (1950); Q. Johnstone, An Evaluation of the Rules of Statutory Interpretation, 3 U. Kan. L. Rev. 1, 9 (1954); H. Jones, Extrinsic Aids in the Federal Courts, 25 Iowa L. Rev. 737, 760 (1940).

be to take adequate account of its implications. To do this is one of the main purposes of this book.

The distinction between the cognitive and the creative bears at least a superficial resemblance to that sometimes made, though now generally disregarded, [22] between "interpretation" and "construction." Whether the resemblance is more than superficial is uncertain, because the latter distinction is not entirely clear. As explained by Crawford, [23]

> Construction, . . . to be technically correct, is the drawing of conclusions with respect to subjects that are beyond the direct expression of the text, from elements known and given in the text, while interpretation is the process of discovering the true meaning of the language used. Thus, the court will resort to interpretation when it endeavors to ascertain the meaning of a word found in a statute, which when considered with the other words in the statute, may reveal a meaning different from that apparent when the word is considered abstractly or when given its usual meaning. But when the court goes beyond the language of the statute and seeks the assistance of extrinsic aids in order to determine whether a given case falls within the statute, it resorts to construction. . . . If legislative intent is not clear after the completion of interpretation, then the court will proceed to subject the statute to construction.

If this means distinguishing between reliance solely on matters internal to the statute and reliance on matters including those external to it, the two distinctions would appear to differ. Only if "interpretation" related to matters solely within the statute and its proper context while "construction" related also to matters external to both would the two distinctions coincide.

On the other hand, the distinction between the cognitive and the creative corresponds closely to that between "genuine interpretation" and "spurious interpretation." [24] The important difference is that "spurious interpretation" refers only to judicial lawmaking that masquerades as interpretation, [25] whereas "judicial lawmaking" refers also to the franker varieties of judicial creativity.

Although the line between the ascertainment of legislative

22. Sutherland §45.04.
23. Crawford 241.
24. R. Pound, Spurious Interpretation, 7 Colum. L. Rev. 379 (1907).
25. "Such 'interpretation' suggests the story of the waiter who, on an order for beefsteak, brought in mutton and explained that it was a mutton beefsteak." III R. Pound, Jurisprudence 488 (1959).

meaning and judicial lawmaking through the assignment of meaning cannot be precisely drawn in specific instances, the judge must make a conscientious attempt to draw it to avoid frustrating the pronouncements of the legislature [26] and (in some situations) unfairly upsetting the reasonable expectations of the legislative audience. [27] Legislative supremacy in the creation of law cannot be maintained unless cognition precedes creation, [28] and this sequence cannot be honored unless the two are conceptually differentiated. That differentiation is hard and the area of uncertainty wide offers no exemption from what appears to be a clear

26. If the court makes law before ascertaining its legislative terms of reference, it may inadvertently derogate from those terms.

27. The problem of unfair surprise is dealt with at a number of places throughout this book (e.g., ch. 13, p. 249).

28. The principle that with respect to statutes judicial cognition should precede judicial creation has been occasionally recognized, although not in those terms nor in constitutional terms. The principle is either alluded to or strongly implied. "Legislative primacy means . . . that construction must first be effected with full commitment to legislative intent and purpose. . . ." C. Breitel, The Courts and Law Making, in Legal Institutions Today and Tomorrow 1, 26-27 (M. Paulsen ed., 1959). See also R. Keeton, Venturing to do Justice 94 (1969). ". . . [T]hose who say the court must recognize that it is making law . . . sometimes come too quickly to a point at which they cease to search for the legislature's meaning. . . ." A. Cox, Judge Learned Hand and the Interpretation of Statutes, 60 Harv. L. Rev. 370, 375 (1947). ". . . [B]efore the court can resort to any other source for assistance, it must first seek to find the legislative intention from the words, phrases and sentences which make up the statute subject to construction." Crawford 256. "The taking of attitudes in interpretation of legislation has value only after all genuine criteria for getting at the real meaning have failed to give a solution." F. de Sloovère, Textual Interpretation of Statutes, 11 N.Y.U.L.Q. Rev. 538, 548 (1934) (see also 552). "First I establish the *meaning* of the statute as accurately as I can and try to solve the problem at issue *on this basis alone*. After that I proceed to consider it in accordance with *the teleological method*." P. Ekelöf, Teleological Construction of Statutes, 2 Scandinavian Studies in Law 1958, at 75, 102. (Emphasis in original.) "When a court strives to ascertain the legislative purpose, the judges should try to eliminate as far as possible their own personal views of policy." J. Frank, Words and Music: Some Remarks on Statutory Interpretation, 47 Colum. L. Rev. 1259, 1265 (1947). ". . . [W]hen all else fails, a process which can be described as 'assigning legislative meaning' is appropriate." L. Tunks, Assigning Legislative Meaning: A New Bottle, 37 Iowa L. Rev. 372 (1952).

The time sequence is also implicit in the conditional form of statement. See C. Breitel, The Courts and Law Making, in Legal Institutions Today and Tomorrow 1, 5 (M. Paulsen ed., 1959); The Lawmakers, 65 Colum. L. Rev. 749-750 (1965); F. de Sloovère, Textual Interpretation of Statutes, 11 N.Y.U.L.Q. Rev. 538, 552 (1934).

constitutional mandate. Besides, as Gény has pointed out, [29] law that results from cognition is of a higher order than law that results from judicial creation and thus may not be so freely changed by the courts.

Failure to adequately differentiate between these widely differing functions has, on the one hand, stunted the growth of an adequate theory of legal communication and, on the other, prevented the development of an adequate theory of judicial lawmaking with respect to statutes. [30]

B. The Cognitive Function: The Nature of Ascertainment

Ascertaining the meaning of a statute is essentially an act of recognition or discovery. Because communication is built on habit patterns, it would be easy to conclude that discovery requires only passive receptivity. As with Pavlov's dogs, the reader's mental or emotional salivation begins as soon as the words reach their mark. Communication, or the basis for communication, is established almost instantaneously. To this extent, it is an immediate, largely automatic [31] response to a complex of visual or auditory stimuli.

29. F. Gény, Method of Interpretation and Sources of Private Positive Law 215-216 (2d ed. 1963).

30. "What Austin calls spurious interpretation and genuine interpretation are so commonly confused by institutional writers that it is seldom brought home to the student of law that there is a difference. So long as the bulk of a legal system is in the form of case law, this is no great matter. When the growing-point shifts to legislation and judicial lawmaking, being interstitial, is confined within relatively narrow limits, the confusion becomes a serious matter because it obscures the real and legitimate lawmaking power of the courts and brings about neglect to study the principles of judicial law finding and lawmaking." III R. Pound, Jurisprudence 483-484 (1959).

31. C. Cherry, On Human Communication 12, 61 (2d ed. 1966); C. Ogden & I. Richards, The Meaning of Meaning 15 (10th ed. 1956). ". . . [I]n most communication, interpretation is automatic. . . ." F. Horack, Jr., The Disintegration of Statutory Construction, 24 Ind. L.J. 335, 338 (1949). ". . . [W]e *understand* the meaning of a word when we hear or say it; we grasp it in a flash. . . ." L. Wittgenstein, Philosophical Investigations 53 (G. Anscombe, transl. 1953). (Emphasis in original.) And see ch. 9, p. 107, and ch. 12, pp. 217-218. ". . . [T]he meaning of a sentence is to be felt rather than proved. . . ." Justice Holmes, in United States v. Johnson, 221 U.S. 488, 496, 31 S. Ct. 627 (1911).

Yet something more than passivity is needed; certainly, the reader cannot assimilate a communication without at least the interest necessary to focus attention on it. More important, practicality requires that much of the message be left to inference and tacit assumption. This imposes a corresponding, though usually modest, burden on the reader.

There is more: Because communications are often imperfectly framed or inadequately transmitted, a corresponding part of the message is lost unless the reader, by logical induction and deduction, makes a compensating effort to search the relevant and sometimes competing elements to find the most plausible basis for a reliable, though more attenuated, inference of intended meaning.[32] This often takes some doing, especially with complex communications such as statutes. In such instances, successful communication depends on aggressive, imaginative attitudes, both in the author and in his audience. Here, Llewellyn's metaphor of "quarrying" is very appealing.[33]

For statutes, the incentive to quarry is strong. In addition to whatever interest the statute has for the parties to the controversy or the intellectual tastes of the particular judge, the court has a responsibility to resolve the controversy that it may not evade. Because this responsibility requires deference to the legislature, the court is justified in initiating its own solution[34] only if a legally adequate answer cannot be found, through the normal processes of cognition, within the statute and its proper context.

C. Drawing the Line: Judicial Creativity as a Test

The problem now to be discussed is this: Where does the cognitive process of ascertaining legislative meaning leave off and the creative process of judicial lawmaking through the assignment of meaning begin? Certainly, it does not coincide with

32. ". . . [S]ubjective intention must always be determined by inferences from objective manifestations." C. Nutting, The Relevance of Legislative Intention Established by Extrinsic Evidence, 20 B.U.L. Rev. 601, 607 (1940). See generally ch. 7.

33. K. Llewellyn, The Common Law Tradition: Deciding Appeals 374 (1960).

34. On judicial lawmaking, see ch. 13.

any distinction between passivity and activity by the legislative audience.

Although it is impossible to answer this question precisely in particular instances, especially when it falls within the penumbra of uncertainty surrounding the word "meaning" itself, establishing the line is well worth the effort because it marks the boundary between what the court must do and what it may do, between matters essentially of fact and matters involving at least some judicial discretion. The fact that the line is hard and sometimes impossible to draw does not lessen the significance of the vastly different polarities that it ultimately separates.[35] Making the effort is necessary to developing the most critical element in the reading and administration of statutes: an appropriate judicial attitude.

Jones agrees that what we broadly call "statutory interpretation" consists not only of quarrying meaning from a statute but of adding, in appropriate cases, an element of judicial creativity.[36] Under his analysis, however, judicial lawmaking takes over where the legislature's ability to foresee left off.[37] As an example, he cites the case where new kinds of objects that the legislature could not possibly have envisaged came into existence after the statute was enacted, thus suggesting that a statute's semantic reach is no greater than the actual legislative intention behind it. This line of demarcation seems inaccurate. The reach of a statute should be measured, rather, by the range of subjective connotations that it establishes in the mind of the typical reader. Clearly, such a set of connotations (meanings) may easily outrun actual intent[38] and *a fortiori* the capacity of the legislature to specifically foresee.[39] It would be more acceptable,

35. B. Shartel, Our Legal System and How It Operates 344 (1951).

36. H. Jones, Statutory Doubts and Legislative Intention, 40 Colum. L. Rev. 957, 970 (1940). See also K. Llewellyn, Remarks on the Theory of Appellate Decision and the Rules or Canons About How Statutes Are to be Construed, 3 Vand. L. Rev. 395, 400 (1950).

37. H. Jones, Statutory Doubts and Legislative Intention, 40 Colum. L. Rev. 957, 971-972 (1940).

38. A. Ayer, Language, Truth and Logic 86 (2d ed. 1947). "The mere fact that the thought of such a thing as *x* hadn't occurred to me does not imply anything about what I did or did not intend." G. MacCallum, Jr., Legislative Intent, 75 Yale L.J. 754, 772 (1966). And see ch. 7, pp. 76, 80.

39. "It is common error to believe that thought is a complete slave of our will and never produces anything but what we intend." J. Kohler, Judicial Interpretation of Enacted Law, in Science of Legal Method 187, 188 (1921).

therefore, to say that judicial lawmaking takes over where legislative meaning leaves off.

Llewellyn's "quarrying" metaphor may falsely suggest that the thing sought, though hidden from initial view, is already in existence, fully developed, waiting only to be uncovered, whereas even the concept of ascertainment of meaning allows some leeway to the interpreter. Is there not, therefore, an element of creativity in the ascertainment of meaning distinguishable from the element of creativity that inheres in judicial lawmaking?

Judge Frank has intrigued us with a possible analogy between the interpretation of statutes and the interpretation of music.[40] Although he tends to identify the interpretation of statutes solely with judicial lawmaking, it is interesting to speculate on the value of such an analogy. Leaning heavily on the composer and musicologist Krenek, he accepts the latter's assertion that there is no single way of interpreting a musical composition and that the interpreter may choose among a number of equally valid interpretations.[41] This requires the interpreter to pour much of himself into the performance.

I have trouble making sense out of Frank's interpretation of Krenek's views. On the one hand, he seems to say only that the composer is unable to prescribe all the elements of the actual performance and that his efforts result, therefore, in a work that can be completed only at the moment of performance by the performing artist.[42] Here, "interpretation" is supplementation. On the other hand, he seems also to say that there is some principle requiring the performer to deviate from the specified directions of the composer if he is to avoid "unbearable caricature."[43] Here, Frank assumes a discrepancy between the literal instructions of the composer and his transcendent purpose,[44] only the latter of which is the key to unlocking the aesthetic meaning of the music. But nowhere does he explain to what source the interpreter looks, beyond the manuscript, for a revelation of the

40. J. Frank, Words and Music: Some Remarks on Statutory Interpretation, 47 Colum. L. Rev. 1259 (1947).

41. Id. at 1261.

42. Id. at 1264.

43. Id. at 1261.

44. Frank fails to spell out the specific discrepancy between the literal notes and marginal instructions on tempo, volume, accent, and expression, on the one hand, and the composer's musical purpose, on the other.

composer's purposes. Or does a musical composition, like a federal statute, have a discoverable "legislative history"? [45]

The mystery deepens when we read that the interpreter " 'should put himself in the place of the composer, trying to reconcile the impulses of his (own) imagination with the principle' that he must 'obey the prescription of the composer as well as he can.' " [46] What prescription?

Whatever range of choice the performer may have, it does not include the privilege of changing the notes themselves. This alone makes him overwhelmingly subservient to the composer. In only the most incidental and peripheral sense is he a creative artist. Furthermore, the interpretation of written words is not a performance of another's composition, where the performer is a necessary link in the chain of communication that ends with the audience. (Certainly, the audience itself is not the performer.) Finally, the emotive contributions of a performer have no counterpart in a nonemotive communication not involving a performer.

Going beyond conventional musical analogy, writers like Morris Cohen, [47] Curtis, [48] and Miller [49] seem to say that the courts' reading of statutes parallels, instead, the free improvisations of the jazz artist, for whom the spare lines of the subject composition are only a point of departure. [50] Such an approach bypasses the great bulk of musical literature, which leaves little or no room for notes of the performer's own devising.

What Frank tries to parallel is clear: the well established distinction and frequent discrepancy between the literal meaning of a statute and its legislative purpose. But he fails to develop a convincing analogy with music.

45. Some musical compositions apparently do. H. Leventhal, How the Problem Looks to the Judiciary, in Professionalizing Legislative Drafting: The Federal Experience 25, 28 (R. Dickerson ed., 1973).

46. J. Frank, Words and Music: Some Remarks on Statutory Interpretation, 47 Colum. L. Rev. 1259, 1265 (1947).

47. M. Cohen, Law and the Social Order 131 (1933).

48. "[Words] mean, in the first instance, what the person to whom they are addressed makes them mean." C. Curtis, It's Your Law 65 (1954).

49. A. S. Miller, Statutory Language and the Purposive Use of Ambiguity, 42 Va. L. Rev. 23, 30 (1956). However, Miller makes clear that he addresses his views only to statements that are vague or very general. Id. at 39.

50. This analogy seems best adapted to the judicial supplementation of general statutes such as the Sherman Act.

Getting back to the law, where Frank had a surer grasp, we may also wonder whether, in selecting words such as "reasonable," "fair," and "equitable"[51] and statutes such as the Sherman Act[52] as examples of legalisms that raise problems of meaning, he was not confusing vagueness, the judicial leeway that results from uncertainty at the semantic margin, with generality, the judicial leeway that inheres in a general delegation of legislative authority to the courts. The choice between implementing alternatives does not necessarily involve a choice between competing meanings. Thus, most of the judicial creativity generated by the Sherman Act has been the creativity of supplementation, not the creativity incidental to cognition.

Perhaps a happier analogy to a court's function of disposing of an authentic problem of meaning would be that of the restorer who makes a substitute for a small piece missing from the body of an ancient vase. Here, he is guided by the adjacent contours and, if he is skillful, the result blends well enough to attract little or no attention and the vase can be enjoyed as an integrated whole. His job is harder if the vase has been decorated, but the difficulty is small if the decoration follows a discernible pattern.

What, if any, is the element of creativity here? If the perception necessary to project observed contours and patterns can be called "creativity," it is creativity of the lowest order. Whatever it is, it still falls under the general heading of "cognition" or "ascertainment of meaning."[53]

On the other hand, suppose that the craftsman has only the piece that was missing in the first example and the decoration is free and nonrecurrent. Suppose that he wishes to incorporate it into a projected vase with which it will be aesthetically and culturally compatible. Suppose that, drawing on his imaginative understanding of the relevant cultural context, he produces such a vase. Has he been "creative?" If so, it is creativity of a significantly higher order without, however, attaining the level of a Benvenuto Cellini. Is it creativity of so low an order that it may still be classed as "cognition," or should it be classed as creativity

51. J. Frank, Words and Music: Some Remarks on Statutory Interpretation, 47 Colum. L. Rev. 1259, 1266 (1947).

52. Id.

53. ". . . [It is like] the broken tooth, the severed rib, the dislocated vertebra. . . . At best, what is involved is skilled craftsmanship." J. Cohen, Judicial "Legisputation" and the Dimensions of Legislative Meaning, 36 Ind. L.J. 414, 416 (1961).

comparable to that involved in resolving a controversy under the Sherman Act?

Because in the first example the craftsman is moved only to portray the original vase under conditions that make success highly probable, it seems appropriate to liken his efforts to the cognitive process involved in the ascertainment of meaning. On the other hand, when he is forced to rely on a high degree of speculation, as in the second example, he is limited to creating something "in the general style of" the original, one that he can offer only as one of many ways the original may have looked.[54] Because they produce an end product representing only his preference among a number of defensible alternatives, the craftsman's efforts seem more analogous to an act of judicial lawmaking than to the resolution of a question of meaning.

If these analogies are valid (none should be pressed to extremes), we may conclude that whenever a court can say with reasonable confidence, "This reading of the statute is one that the typical reader views as most probably intended by the legislature," it has ascertained the meaning of the statute in the general sense explained above. Such a conclusion, being one of fact, is reached for the most part according to the cognitive aspects of communication principles not peculiar to the law.

We may conclude also that, whenever a court can say only "We cannot be reasonably sure which, if any, of a wide range of compatible readings was probably the intended one," or "What we perceive to be the meaning of the statute does not adequately resolve the current controversy," the meaning that it thereupon assigns to the statute involves the kind of disciplined creativity that is more appropriately classed as "judicial lawmaking."[55] The problem of choosing among a number of plausible alternatives, not calling for an act of discovery, is not one of fact, but of judicial responsibility discharged according to principles peculiar to the law.

This distinction is important because in the former situation the legislative audience has the same opportunity to weigh the probabilities as the court. Not so in the latter.

Other useful analogs are, of course, available. The mathematically minded may find helpful parallels in the field of vector

54. In such a spirit, the Cloisters in New York City presents architectural sculpture from the Abbey of Saint Guilhem-Le-Desert "in a setting suggested by" the Cloisters of Saint Trophime at Arles and the Abbey of Montmajour.

55. For a discussion of this disciplined creativity, see ch. 13.

analysis. But it is unnecessary at this time to pursue these and other possibilities that, like the analogies discussed, build on what Hart and Sacks [56] and Judge Breitel [57] have called "reasoned elaboration" or "creative elaboration" and Julius Cohen, [58] "legisputation."

Even where the resolution of an uncertainty of meaning can be confidently ascribed to ascertainment, there is an incidental element of lawmaking, though not of creativity, when the result is officially declared by a court. Although it may merely reflect strong factual probabilities, the court is in a very limited sense making law when it replaces legislative probability with judicial certainty. Because the statute is given no new or changed thrust, this is incidental judicial lawmaking in its blandest form. Most important, it is not the kind of lawmaking that threatens unfair surprise.

D. Are Statutes Unique?

In general matters of communication, are statutes unique? The existing literature of statutory interpretation suggests strongly that they are. [59] This is underlined by the inbred quality of the literature, in which it is the practice to cite other legal authorities and refer only occasionally to nonlegal sources.

If the interpretation of statutes is a single, undifferentiated function of getting justice done in specific controversies in the light of the relevant statutes (probably the prevailing view), the subject is certainly *sui generis*. If, on the other hand, the broad river of statutory interpretation results from the confluence of two streams that draw on widely different sources, the one that constitutes "cognition" or the "ascertainment of meaning" need not be treated as unique. [60] It may be fruitfully appraised as the

56. Hart & Sacks 162-179, 1417.

57. C. Breitel, The Courts and Law Making, in Legal Institutions Today and Tomorrow 1, 2 (M. Paulsen ed., 1959).

58. J. Cohen, Judicial "Legisputation" and the Dimensions of Legislative Meaning, 36 Ind. L.J. 414, 416 (1961).

59. E.g., J. Frank, Words and Music: Some Remarks on Statutory Interpretation, 47 Colum. L. Rev. 1259, 1272 (1947); E. Levi, An Introduction to Legal Reasoning, 15 U. Chi. L. Rev. 501, 540 (1948).

60. "The interpretation of statutes is merely one aspect of the interpretation of writings generally." F. Frankfurter, Foreword to A Symposium on Statutory Construction, 3 Vand. L. Rev. 365 (1950).

application, in a legal context, of the general principles of communication, which exist independently of the law.

Even so, there may be identifiable elements in the ascertainment of meaning that have only an infrequent counterpart outside the law. This does not refer to words and expressions, such as "tort" and "certiorari," that are peculiar to the law, because as technical-area signs of which communication theory takes general account they have their counterparts (such as "isotopes" and "appendectomy") in other specialized fields. It refers, instead, to the special social, substantive, constitutional, equitable, and procedural assumptions that comprise the broad legal context in which the normal principles of communication are considered to operate and of which those principles take implied account. These include the many tacit assumptions relating to the nature, goals, methods, and constitutional limitations of the prevailing legal system; that is, the general social and legal context in which statutes are necessarily read. On the other hand, the fact that law is formally prescriptive rather than descriptive may not be as substantively significant as some observers have contended.[61]

E. Ascertainment of Meaning, and Application

From time to time the relationship of cognition (the ascertainment of meaning) to application has been discussed, even with respect to situations not involving questions of judicial lawmaking. For example, de Sloovère, following in the general footsteps of Austin, has divided the process of statutory interpretation in its broadest sense into three steps: (1) finding the applicable statutes, (2) interpreting them, and (3) applying the meaning so found to the case at hand.[62]

The difference between steps (2) and (3), according to de Sloovère, involves not only a distinction between "interpretation" and "application" but different rules for their execution. Interpretation, he says in effect, determines the general thrust of the statute by selecting a "single meaning" that can be said to be "the" meaning of the statute.

61. See ch. 12, p. 220.

62. F. de Sloovère, Textual Interpretation of Statutes, 11 N.Y.U.L.Q. Rev. 538, 553-558 (1934).

This second step in "interpretation" apparently consists largely of the resolution of verbal and syntactical ambiguities on the basis of contextual considerations. If these fail, the court may then resort, still under the banner of "interpretation," to principles of judicial attitude such as those governing strict or liberal interpretation. With these functions, de Sloovère's concept of interpretation apparently ends. Excluded are problems of vagueness: Does the "single meaning" so selected apply to the particular situation under consideration? These problems he classes as problems not of "interpretation," but of "application." They are governed not by the general principles of interpretation, but by principles of judicial attitude such as those that apply in step (2) when textual and contextual guides fail.

However, de Sloovère's concept of "interpretation," being confined largely to the resolution of ambiguities, takes care of only one kind of uncertainty. Why the uncertainties of ambiguity should involve a question of meaning, while those of vagueness should not, is hard to explain. [63]

Jones has disputed de Sloovère's views on two additional grounds. [64] First, he finds it unrealistic to divorce application from the ascertainment of meaning, because to determine whether the particular situation falls within the statute ("application") involves determining whether the statute covers the

63. For the difference between ambiguity and vagueness, see ch. 5. So far as the inclusion or exclusion of the particular fact situation depends on textual and contextual considerations, it involves, almost by definition, a problem of ascertaining meaning. The problem of ascertaining the direction of the statute's verbal thrust and that of ascertaining its specific outer boundaries are equally problems of meaning and should be resolved as such, Thus, in de Sloovère's concept of "application," textual and contextual considerations would seem to be as relevant in the resolution of problems of vagueness as they are in the resolution of problems of ambiguity.

Moreover, in his concept of "interpretation," it seems preferable, under the analysis of the preceding chapters, to class the residual techniques for resolving otherwise unresolvable problems of meaning, not as cognitive techniques for ascertaining meaning (he includes these as legitimate techniques of "interpretation"), but as creative techniques for judicial lawmaking.

64. H. Jones, The Plain Meaning Rule and Extrinsic Aids in the Interpretation of Federal Statutes, 25 Wash. U.L.Q. 2, 8-9 (1939). ". . . [T]he processes of interpretation and application are telescoped together in a manner that defies separation." J. Corry, Administrative Law and the Interpretation of Statutes, 1 U. Toronto L.J. 286, 291 (1947). That this may be true functionally in many cases does not mean that a useful distinction cannot be made conceptually.

particular situation ("interpretation"). Instead of two different activities, we have one activity described in two different ways.

This criticism assumes that a lawyer, and expecially a court, can function only in specific controversies. However, as every legislative draftsman knows, significant doubts as to the general connotations of a statute can arise and be resolved without reference to specific situations or events. Also, lawyers preoccupied with case law should not forget that in some states a court may give a formal advisory opinion, even on a general question of law, without focusing on a specific controversy. [65] There was also the time when Secretary of State Jefferson, at the behest of President Washington, directed a series of questions to the Supreme Court concerning the meaning of current treaties, and of these questions none related to a specific factual situation. [66] Although the Supreme Court properly and respectfully declined, it did not do so on the ground that questions of this kind are meaningless or inherently unanswerable. Legislative draftsmen, who never view problems of meaning in their own products from the point of view of justiciable controversies, would hasten to agree.

Second, Jones doubts that the psychological process of interpretation and application involves the two-step process of determining, first, the connotations of the words used and, second, the relevant specific denotation. On this I can only respectfully disagree.

Even a court that confines its determinations to specific controversies administers a statute in several steps. First, it forms a general view of the statute's thrust and scope. This includes an estimate of the factual conditions, or protasis, of the relevant rule. Second, it determines, in generalized form, what it considers the facts of the particular controversy. (The order of these two steps may be reversed, and their reciprocal interplay may result in successive reformulations.) Third, it determines how fully the generalized facts of the particular controversy fall within the parameters of the statute. So far as the court must, for example, resolve ambiguities, there is judicial interpretation in de Sloovère's intermediate sense preliminary to, and independent of, application. Although this may lead immediately to

65. E.g., Green v. American Tobacco Co., 154 So. 2d 169 (Fla. 1963). And see Sutherland §3.29.

66. III The Correspondence and Public Papers of John Jay 486-489 (H. Johnston ed., 1891).

application and any accompanying interpretative problems traceable to the looseness of the statute's factual norms, it may lead, instead, to the announcement of a general dictum. Application may thus furnish an occasion for interpretation without being identical to it. The possibility of interpretation without application reflects the fact that legislative intent necessarily relates to classes of situations (connotations) rather than the particular situations (denotations) that populate those classes. For the legislative draftsman there is no alternative.

Conversely, application can occur without interpretation, because the applicability of a statute to some situations is obvious on mere reading. That this is normally so is evident even from case law.

Although the terms "interpretation" and "application" are thus neither synonymous nor necessarily co-existent, the distinction between them loses most of its significance if we repudiate de Sloovère's attempt to differentiate between them for the purpose of applying different sets of rules to problems that are essentially those of meaning. De Sloovère's main error was not in distinguishing interpretation from application, but in applying to the problem of specific denotation principles of ascertainment different from those applicable to the problem of general connotation. Ascertainment of meaning, which includes the interpretative problems incidental to application, is the central concept, whereas application independent of ascertainment has little significance in the present inquiry. Accordingly, the latter calls for little further consideration.

Where application involves creation, the implied constitutional mandate that cognition precede creation, mentioned earlier, is reason enough to distinguish ascertainment of meaning from application.

F. A Note on the United Kingdom

A person who, after reading this chapter, examines the two British Law Commissions' recent report on statutory interpretation [67] may be struck by the fact that nowhere does the report expressly recognize the courts' creative function in the applica-

67. The Law Commission and the Scottish Law Commission, Statutory Interpretation (1969).

tion of statutes. In so sophisticated a report, what is the significance of the omission? Was it oversight? Was it a repudiation of the view that "statutory interpretation" includes judicial creation? [68]

The answer to the last two questions seems to be no. The authors of the report were fully aware of the distinction and there is no indication that they would repudiate it. The simple fact is that in current British judicial thinking all judicial action with respect to statutes is still officially subsumed under the term "interpretation," presumably in its authentic, cognitive sense. Although it is now conceded that British courts make common law, it is not yet acknowledged that they make law in supplementation of statutes. The authors were therefore reluctant to couch their report in terms that most British readers would have considered dangerously revolutionary.

68. The same questions arise also with respect to E. Driedger, The Construction of Statutes (1974), a Canadian treatise.

4

Basic Concepts: The General Concept of Meaning

Theories of meaning have no gospel that will save lawyers the pain of thinking.

— E. Patterson, Jurisprudence: Men and Ideas of the Law 29-30 (1953)

A. The Meaning of "Meaning"

The philosophers of language are fond of pointing out the uncertainties in the meaning of the word "meaning" itself. Ogden and Richards wrote a book about it. [1] Morris avoided the term because it fails to take account of distinctions necessary to analyzing language and communication. [2] Cherry damned it as a "harlot among words," because its many meanings are hard to distinguish. [3] Is such righteous, eloquent condemnation justified? Ogden and Richard's devastating examination of its use by philosophers suggests that it is.

In the metalanguage (language used to talk about language), the word "meaning" or "means" may relate to the concept of reference, that is, to what specific language denotes or connotes, or both. In such a connection, it may relate to what the author intended the specific language to refer to, what the particular

1. C. Ogden & I. Richards, The Meaning of Meaning (10th ed. 1956).

2. C. Morris, Introduction to the Theory of Signs, vol. 1, no. 2, International Encyclopedia of Unified Science 43-44 (1938).

3. C. Cherry, On Human Communication 114 (2d ed. 1966).

reader believed it referred to, or what the hypothetical typical member of the audience to which the language was addressed would believe it referred to. It may also relate to mere synonymity.

In the object language (language used to talk about matters other than language), the word "meaning" or "means" may relate to importance or worth ("Her father means a lot to her"), to evidentiary value ("Smoke often means fire"), to portent ("This means war!"), to wanted explanation ("What is the meaning of this commotion?"), or to simple intent ("He did not mean to say that"; "I meant to call you, but I forgot"). There may be other related senses in which the word is used. The word "interpretation" has a cluster of meanings that generally correspond. Additional senses ("When you feel mean, remember what Dr. Mean said about the golden mean") are here irrelevant.

Fortunately, difficulties of lexicography do not necessarily cause difficulties of use. That a word may be used in many senses does not damn it as ambiguous unless those senses are usually inadequately separated by the contexts in which they respectively appear. This distinguishes a bundle of homonyms from semantic ambiguity. [4]

Because a discussion of the meaning of a statutory provision takes place (by definition) in the metalanguage, we may summarily exclude as possibilities any sense in which the word "meaning" or "means" is used in the object language. Even in the metalanguage, we can safely rule out some potential senses. For example, the occasion for discussing the syntactical equivalence that constitutes synonymity is so rare that it may for present purposes be ignored. All that remain are the referential senses involving denotation or connotation.

Thus, in the typical question "What does the statute mean?" the word "mean" normally relates to the problem of ascertaining the combined impact of a congeries of connotations. This referential use, in turn, presupposes a particular point of view. Instead of the question "In which general sense is the word 'mean' used?" the significant uncertainties are more likely to lie in the question "Whose point of view is to be taken as the base line: the author's, the particular reader's, or the typical reader's?"

4. See ch. 5, pp. 44–45.

Even these alternatives can be reduced. Because laws are almost always addressed to general audiences and not specific persons, and because the law necessarily relies on objective criteria, there is little occasion to ask what the statute means to a particular member of such an audience. The question is more likely to be whether meaning is to be determined from the point of view of the author of the document (the legislature) or from that of a typical member of the audience to which it is addressed. Here we hit rock bottom: Both concepts are vital to a consideration of the problems of communication, legal or otherwise. [5]

On the one hand, we are interested in the intended meaning of the author in the sense that the process of communication makes no sense unless some intention can be attributed to him. Intended meaning, therefore, remains the ultimate object of search even though no method has yet been devised by which this meaning can be directly known. [6] Because the author's subjective intent is knowable only through inferences drawn from his use of external signs, and because communication through external signs is possible only by virtue of established conventions, [7] actual subjective intent is knowable, if at all, only by inference from those conventions as conditioned by context. [8]

The conventions of language, on the other hand, inhere in the cultural patterns shared by the author and his audience. [9] Because we must generally assume that the author has not performed the futile act of trying to communicate by unfamiliar signs, the only reliable general key to meaning lies in the language habits of that audience. This notion of a predominating, observable pattern of usage it is convenient to personify in the "typical member of the audience to which the communication is addressed." [10] Although like the "reasonable man" he is in a sense fictional, he is nonetheless useful. What the statute means to such a person is what the word "means" means in the question

5. Sutherland, §45.08, seems to treat these ideas as competing alternatives rather than complementary.

6. C. Cherry, On Human Communication 112 (2d ed. 1966). And see ch. 7.

7. Id. at 69. ". . . [T]he fixed meaning represents, not a state of consciousness fixed by a name, but a recognition of a habitual way of belief: a habit of understanding." J. Dewey, Logic: The Theory of Inquiry 56 (1938).

8. See ch. 7.

9. " 'Culture' . . . is both a condition and a product of language." J. Dewey, Logic: The Theory of Inquiry 56 (1938). And see ch. 9, pp. 105-106.

10. E.g., H. Jones, The Plain Meaning Rule and Extrinsic Aids in the Interpretation of Federal Statutes, 25 Wash. U.L.Q. 2, 22 (1939).

"What does the statute mean?" and that is the only thing it can mean.

The assumption here is that for the most part language is a complex of social habits and that the determining factor in fixing the meaning of words is the way in which they are habitually used in the particular cultural milieu. [11] True meaning, therefore, is always a matter of fact and it is to be found, not by asking people how they believe they use language, [12] but by observing how they actually use it. [13] And yet these things remain, at best, imperfect means to our main goal: to find the most reliable external basis for inferring actual subjective intent.

To say that the word "meaning" has an unequivocal thrust in the present context is not to say that it has no element of vagueness. It only asserts that for present purposes there is little doubt as to which sense of "meaning," however imprecise, is being used.

Is the word "meaning" precise, if limited to a single sense? Probably not. One purpose of this analysis, for example, is to investigate the question whether it is appropriate to consider it as referring only to the connotations and denotations immediately and directly invoked by the specific language used when it is read in proper context, or whether it includes those contained in a paraphrase of the language necessary to say more clearly what the total statement reliably suggests that the author was trying to say but only imperfectly expressed.

It should be unnecessary to dwell on the important difference between mere convention and usage. Although all language is conventional in the sense that words have no inherent meanings,

11. "The process of logical analysis of a language can be regarded as the exhibition of a set of conventions for the use of symbols, abstracted from the regularity of linguistic habits in some postulated speech community. . . ." M. Black, Language and Philosophy 28 (1949).

12. "There is no more reason why a person who uses a word correctly should be able to tell what it means than there is why a planet which is moving correctly should know Kepler's laws." Quoted from The Analysis of Mind (p. 198) in B. Russell, My Philosophical Development 147 (1959).

13. *"A symbol refers to what it is actually used to refer to. . . ."* C. Ogden & I. Richards, The Meaning of Meaning 103 (10th ed. 1956). (Emphasis in original.) ". . . [T]he meaning of a word is its use in the language." L. Wittgenstein, Philosophical Investigations 20 (G. Anscombe, transl. 1953). "One learns the game by watching how others play." Id. at 27. "One cannot guess how a word functions. One must *look at* its use and learn from that." Id. at 109. (Emphasis in original.)

its effectiveness in communicating meaning depends on the establishment of its conventions as observable usage. The difference is between use and habitual use.

B. Actual Meaning, Literal Meaning, and True Meaning

Even if the word "meaning" has in the general context of statutes the unequivocal thrust attributed to it in the last section, it is desirable to observe several additional distinctions.

The word "meaning," when used without qualification, normally refers to the true meaning of language in the sense of the total impact that it makes when it is read in its proper context by a typical member of the audience to which it is addressed. This use of "meaning" is to be distinguished, on the one hand, from that of "literal meaning" and, on the other, from that of "actual meaning."

Literal meaning is the meaning carried by language when it is read in its dictionary sense unaffected by considerations of particular context. Although literal meaning sometimes coincides with actual or true meaning, as where language is read out of context or where its meaning is unaffected by the context in which it is or should be read, more often that context yields a meaning significantly different from its literal meaning. In such a case, "the meaning" of the language is its true or actual, rather than its literal, meaning.

True meaning should be distinguished also from actual meaning. Whereas actual meaning is the meaning carried by the language when it is read in a particular context, true meaning is the meaning carried by the language when it is read in the light of its proper context. Although the context in which the language is actually read may also be the proper context, they are not necessarily the same. So far as the differences in context create or permit differences in meaning, actual meaning diverges or may diverge from true meaning. Again, the difference is not so much that the two meanings are necessarily different as that they may be different. Use of the word "true" in this context is not intended to suggest that language has inherent or natural meaning or even that particular language read in proper context always has a single ascertainable meaning.

In resting trueness of meaning on propriety of context, this second distinction makes it important to understand the notion of proper context, discussed more fully in chapter 9. Briefly, it is the context, shared by the communicant and his audience, that is presupposed by the communication. Because all communications are a function not only of particular language but also of particular context, reading the words against another context is likely to yield a meaning significantly at variance with the intended one.

Because interpretation is by definition concerned with the ascertainment of true meaning, and because true meaning often differs from literal meaning or actual meaning or both, reliance on either of the latter without reference to proper context is likely to subvert effective communication.

There are instances in which the words of the document themselves effectively orient the reader to its proper context. In such a case, the typical reader to whom it is addressed cannot normally read the document out of its proper context. Here, actual meaning, literal meaning, and true meaning tend to be the same. Only in these instances does the so-called "plain meaning rule," [14] so far as it identifies true meaning with literal meaning, make sense. However, the adequacy of such a document for this purpose cannot always be known with assurance without knowing the context in which it was written.

C. Legal Meaning

Legal meaning is the meaning declared by a court with respect to a problem of meaning that it is responsible for adjudicating. Where true meaning exists, the legal meaning is presumably the same. The fact that it sometimes differs is witnessed by the occasions on which courts have overturned earlier interpretations. [15]

Statements such as Chief Justice Hughes's that "a federal statute finally means what the Court says it means," [16] while providing a practical insight, tend to obscure the fact that even where legal meaning differs from true meaning, the latter remains valuable as a potential basis for overruling. Otherwise,

14. See ch. 12, pp. 229-233.
15. E.g., see ch. 13, pp. 252-261.
16. C. Hughes, The Supreme Court of the United States 230 (1928).

there would never be a basis for saying that a court's reading of a statute was wrong.

The importance of the distinction between legal meaning and true meaning will be considered further in chapter 13.

D. Express Meaning and Implied Meaning

One of the most pervasive distinctions made in the law is that between express meaning and implied meaning. Because the present inquiry is limited to considerations of true or actual rather than fictitious meaning, "implied" refers only to the implied-in-fact. The implied-in-law, by definition a fictitious implication, is a rule of law and therefore irrelevant here.

How does the expression of meaning differ from the implication of meaning? Although legal usage has hardly been consistent, a communication is "express" so far as it is directly conveyed by language taken in its relevant dictionary sense. The affirmative thrust of express meaning thus derives from the established meanings of the individual words and phrases used, even as limited by context. Thus, "express meaning" is not necessarily the same as "literal meaning," which is dictionary meaning unlimited by context. Express meanings lose none of their expressness by being read in restrictive contexts. This means merely that the connotations permitted by the particular context normally fall within the usually wider range of connotations that constitute the relevant dictionary or other lexical meaning.

Express meaning includes the meaning that is attached by usage to a particular phrase even when that meaning is not revealed by the individual words that comprise the phrase. Thus, "Eau de Cologne," taken as a phrase, has the express meaning of diluted perfume, even though the words "eau" and "Cologne," taken separately, carry an aggregate express meaning that is significantly different.

Implied meaning, on the other hand, is meaning carried other than by express language taken in its dictionary sense. Thus, whereas the express meaning of a word or phrase includes any meaning, permitted by the context, that usage attaches to it when it is read in or out of context, the implied meaning of a word or phrase is any difference in meaning that it conveys when it is read in context. Implied meaning, therefore, is meaning that exists

only by virtue of specific context. Implications may attach to sentences, paragraphs, or whole documents.

A negative implication [17] is an implication that denies outside the area of express coverage what is expressly asserted within it. This implication, asserted in the maxim *expressio unius est exclusio alterius,* has also been called, variously, "reverse implication," "negative pregnant," "co-implication," "preemption," and "*argumento a contrario.*" The adjective "negative," although descriptive of most instances of this kind of implication, and the one most often used, seems inappropriate to describe the occasional converse instance in which an express negation implies, outside its express coverage, a corresponding positive assertion.

In contrast with express meanings, implied meanings are often lexically difficult to ascertain because they are based on configurations of language and context that are likely, in significant particulars, to be unique. The received meanings are thus more subtly inductive or intuitive.

Implied meanings, like express meanings, are based on tacit assumptions reliable enough to generate identifiable expectations in the particular audience. The main difference is that for express meanings the underlying usages attach to identifiable words, phrases, and syntactical relationships, whereas for implied meanings they attach to kinds of contexts, which are not so readily identified. Even so, the usages of context are generally identifiable. If a boy asks his mother, "May I go for a swim and then to the movies?" and she replies, "You may go for a swim," the boy will have no difficulty, from the juxtaposition of particular answer and particular question, in identifying the kind of context in which it is ordinarily inferred that permission to engage in the omitted activity is withheld. Usage in such a case thus relates to a general pattern of internal context and not to particular words or expressions.

Because the patterns of internal and external context tend to be more nearly amorphous than those of words and phrases, implied meanings are less reliably ascertained than express meanings. This is especially true of negative implications, partly with respect to their existence but more especially with respect to their extent.

From this discussion, it should be clear that implications of

17. See also ch. 5, p. 47; ch. 12, pp. 234-235.

meaning[18] are not implications in the sense used in formal logic.[19] The logical implications of a set of express statements are the unstated propositions that cannot be contradicted without making assumptions that contradict one or more of the express statements. Although logical implications are usually also implications of meaning, the converse is not true. Implied meanings, being those that the typical member of the audience to whom the communication is addressed would in fact take as being asserted even though they are not asserted expressly, are not necessarily deducible from the express statements. This is exemplified in the instance of negative implication supposed above. The conclusions that it is permissible to draw from implied meanings are, however, logical implications.

E. Referential Meaning: Ogden and Richard's Triangle

It has become traditional in law books dealing with problems of meaning to include a triangular diagram, first appearing in Ogden and Richards' famous book *The Meaning of Meaning,*[20] that shows the relationship between symbols, thoughts, and things. Although the diagram is useful in showing that words are linked to things only through the mind, more recent analysis suggests that, in important collateral respects, it is incomplete and possibly misleading.[21] Because any attempt to modernize it involves identifying and interrelating a number of separate aspects, not all of which are immediately relevant to this book, I have relegated my own attempt to appendix C.

18. These are called "ulterior meanings" in G. Williams, Language and the Law — IV, 61 L.Q. Rev. 384, 400 (1945).

19. Logical implications are discussed id., 384, 398.

20. 10th ed. 1956, at 11.

21. E.g., G. Williams, Language and the Law — IV, 61 L.Q. Rev. 384, 392 (1945).

5

Basic Concepts: Legislative Uncertainty and the Diseases of Language*

Laws suffer from the disease of language.
— Bernard Berenson
(in conversation)

A. Introduction

Although the inadequacies of language are often exaggerated by legal writers, [1] language remains subject not only to inherent limitations but to serious and not easily curable diseases. The main diseases of language are ambiguity, overvagueness, overprecision, overgenerality, and undergenerality. Fortunately, the inadequacies and diseases of language, however baffling, are no cause for professional despair.

B. Ambiguity

Perhaps the most serious disease of language is ambiguity in the traditional sense of equivocation. Language is equivocal when it has "different significations equally appropriate" or is

* This chapter is an edited and expanded version of the author's article, The Diseases of Legislative Language, 1 Harv. J. Legis. 5 (1964) (used with permission).

1. E.g., "an inexact, clumsy tool." A. S. Miller, Statutory Language and the Purposive Use of Ambiguity, 42 Va. L. Rev. 23 (1956). And see ch. 6, p. 54.

"capable of double interpretation,"[2] that is, has two or more competing thrusts. A good example is the word "residence," which unless particular context resolves the doubt can refer equally to the place where a person has his abode for an extended period, or to the place that the law considers to be his permanent home, whether or not it is his place of abode.

To avoid the so-called "one word one meaning" fallacy, it is commonly assumed that all words are ambiguous in the equivocation sense because almost every word is used in various senses and thus has more than one meaning.[3] Does the existence of multiple dictionary meanings make a word equivocal and therefore ambiguous? The answer lies in the difference between an ambiguous word and a group of homonyms.

Groups of homonyms are easily confused with ambiguous words, because both have multiple thrusts of meaning. But the two are not the same.[4] On the one hand, the intended sense of a word designating a bundle of homonyms is almost inevitably revealed in use, whatever the peculiarities of context. The homonym's capacity for sense sifting is built in and automatic. Examples of these multi-purpose words abound: "If the bear escapes, the owner shall bear the cost." "If he can, the buyer shall return the empty can." This kind of multiplicity of meanings, often considered a defect of language, may actually be a benefit. At least, it makes possible an economy of symbols.

With the ambiguous word, on the other hand, the uncertainties of alternative reference are not resolved by mere use in context. In the statement, "His rights depend on his residence," it is not clear whether they depend on place of abode or on legal home. That, clothed in its broadest context, the uncertainty may in fact be resolved (as where the word "residence" appears in a divorce statute in which for jurisdictional reasons it seems probable that the legislature intended to refer to legal home) does not turn an otherwise ambiguous word into an innocuous bundle of homonyms. Intermediate are families of use patterns that, while related, are individually identifiable.

Whereas homonyms present no significant danger, the ambigu-

2. III Oxford English Dictionary E263 (1933).

3. E.g., J. Frank, Words and Music: Some Remarks on Statutory Interpretation, 47 Colum. L. Rev. 1259, 1263 (1947); F. Waismann, Language Strata, in Essays on Logic and Language, 2d Series, 11 (Flew ed., 1953).

4. On this difference, see S. Stebbing, A Modern Introduction to Logic 21 (6th ed. 1948); R. Dickerson, Legislative Drafting 62 n. 3 (1954).

ous word carries the threat, in specific use, of competitive thrusts of meaning that are almost never desirable or justifiable. Because of its potential for deception or confusion, the draftsman should not use an ambiguous word in a context that does not clearly resolve the ambiguity. Indeed, he should avoid the ambiguous word (e.g., "residence") whenever his intended meaning (e.g., legal home) may be adequately expressed by an unambiguous word (e.g., "domicile"). References to the "purposive use of ambiguity," sometimes found in legal literature, are usually directed to the purposive uses of vagueness or generality, [5] discussed below.

Because the line between homonyms and ambiguity depends on their respective potentials for deception and confusion in use, differences in degree sometimes make it hard to tell on which side of the line a particular word falls. But mere naming is not the important thing. What is important is that the draftsman determine whether, in the particular context, there is likely to be a significant uncertainty of reference. If there is, he should resolve it by using another word or by taking the precaution of adjusting the context or adding explanatory language.

Whatever the degree of uncertainty, if any, about the intended sense of a word, and whether it represents homonym or ambiguity, the interpreter will want in every case to recognize and separate the potential alternative meanings and, if there is uncertainty of reference in the particular context, to resolve it.

In a recent criticism of H. L. A. Hart's theories respecting the "standard instance" of words, Fuller puts this situation: [6]

> Let us suppose that in leafing through the statutes, we come upon the following enactment: "It shall be a misdemeanor, punishable by a fine of five dollars, to sleep in any railway station." . . . Suppose I am a judge, and that two men are brought before me for violating this statute. The first is a passenger who was waiting at 3 A.M. for a delayed train. When he was arrested he was sitting upright in an orderly fashion, but was heard by the arresting officer to be gently snoring. The second is a man who had brought a blanket and pillow to the station and had obviously settled himself down for the night. He was

5. E.g., F. Horack, Jr., In the Name of Legislative Intention, 38 W. Va. L.Q. 119, 131 (1932); A. S. Miller, Statutory Language and the Purposive Use of Ambiguity, 42 Va. L. Rev. 23, 39 (1956).

6. L. Fuller, Positivism and Fidelity to Law — A Reply to Professor Hart, 71 Harv. L. Rev. 630, 664 (1958), discussed further in ch. 6.

arrested, however, before he had a chance to go to sleep. Which of these cases presents the "standard instance" of the word "sleep"?

Does not this phrasing of the question imply that in general the verb "sleep" refers to a single concept, whereas in fact it represents a family of separately discernible use-patterns (possibly a set of homonyms) including at least the following?

(1) To be in an unconscious state of natural repose.
(2) To spend the night, with appropriate accoutrements, for the purpose of being in such a state.

If so, the question cannot be answered until it is determined which sense was intended in the statute. Here, there is little difficulty in concluding that the statute is using sense (2). There is also little difficulty in concluding that the tramp falls within the standard instance of sense (2), whereas the upright (!) snorer does not. The recognition or selection of the appropriate sense, therefore, necessarily precedes any consideration of its standard instance or marginal uncertainties.

The ambiguities discussed so far are called "semantic ambiguities." [7] Their uncertainties of meaning, not inevitably resolved by context, are traceable to the multiplicities of dictionary meanings, which exist independently of context. That their evils are felt, nevertheless, only in specific context makes it desirable to distinguish them from a second kind of ambiguity.

By far the most prevalent kind of ambiguity is syntactic ambiguity. Syntactic ambiguities are uncertainties of modification or reference within the particular statute. [8] Simple examples include squinting modifiers ("The trustee shall require him

7. On the detection and resolution of semantic ambiguities, see D. MacKaye, The Logic of Language, ch. 5 (1939).

8. On the detection and resolution of syntactic ambiguities, see L. Allen, Symbolic Logic: A Razor-Edged Tool for Drafting and Interpreting Legal Documents, 66 Yale L.J. 833 (1957); Interpretation of California Pimping Statute, 60S M.U.L.L. 114 (1960); J. Montrose, Mock Turtle: A Problem in Adjectival Ambiguity, 59D M.U.L.L. 28 (1959). "Circuit and isomer diagrams may make explicit the ambiguity involved, but they do not assist in the resolution of the ambiguity. . . . Allen considers that the arrow diagram is a procedure 'for the systematic detection of such syntactic ambiguity'. . . . It is submitted, however, that the construction of a diagram is possible only after the ambiguity has been detected. It is of course true, as Allen has pointed out, that the attempt to construct a diagram helps in the discovery of an ambiguity." J. Montrose, Syntactic (Formerly Amphibolous) Ambiguity, 62J M.U.L.L. 65, 69, 70 n. R3 (1962).

promptly to repay the loan")[9] and modifiers preceding or following a series ("charitable corporations or institutions performing educational functions").[10] These are usually ambiguities in the original etymological sense of alternatives limited to two.

A third, and likewise prevalent, kind of ambiguity is contextual ambiguity. Even when the words and syntax of a statute are unequivocal, it may still be uncertain which of two or more alternatives was intended. An internal contextual ambiguity may result, for example, from an internal inconsistency: When one provision plainly contradicts another, which is intended to prevail? Contextual ambiguities may also be external. Thus a statute may bear a similarly ambiguous relationship to another statute with which it is inconsistent. Or there may be doubt whether a particular tacit assumption has been made.

Perhaps the most troublesome contextual ambiguity, and one of the most frequent, is the uncertainty whether a particular implication arises. This is often true of "negative" implications,[11] covered by the maxim *expressio unius est exclusio alterius*. Sometimes the maxim applies and sometimes it does not, and whether it does or does not depends largely on context. Unfortunately, context tends in its particulars to be unique, and therefore does not always supply a clear answer. Even so, a person who has watched the currents and eddies of usage develops an eye for these things. The ascertainment of implied meaning, like that of express meaning, is largely the recognition of familiar language patterns and use situations.

For semantic and syntactic ambiguities, it is important to remember that their characterization as such normally depends on their demonstrated potentiality for giving trouble in particular uses rather than on their producing an actual ambiguity in a particular instance. As with some unesteemed kinds of women, classification is by established reputation rather than by specific performance. Thus, the word "residence," taken in isolation, is properly classed as "ambiguous," even though in a particular context the notion of domicile clearly emerges. Similarly, a

9. Does "promptly" modify "require" or "repay"?

10. Does "charitable" modify "institutions"? (Or, does "performing educational functions" modify "corporations"?)

11. This is also called "coimplication." L. Allen, Symbolic Logic: A Razor-Edged Tool for Drafting and Interpreting Legal Documents, 66 Yale L.J. 840 (1957). For its other names, see ch. 4, p. 41.

squinting modifier may be syntactically ambiguous in the isolation of a particular phrase or sentence, but unambiguous in its broadest context. Because the typical reader usually sees the details of a statute before he feels its total impact, what first appears to be an ambiguity may disappear on a more careful, comprehensive reading. If so, the ambiguity is apparent rather than actual. If not, the ambiguity is actual and can be resolved only by judicial fiat; that is, by an act of judicial lawmaking.

The difference between apparent ambiguity and actual ambiguity is important. The draftsman's highest responsibility is to see that the final text, when read in its proper context, [12] contains no unresolved ambiguity. It is also highly desirable, though not so critical, that he see that the effectiveness of the statute is not impaired by unnecessary uncertainties of reference that, although resolvable, risk misreading at the hands of unperceptive courts or, at best, require time and effort to resolve. It is also desirable that he avoid the needless use of terms and configurations of syntax that, whatever their immediate impact, are known to carry the general risk of real or apparent ambiguity.

Fortunately, once an actual, apparent, or potential ambiguity has been recognized, it can almost always be avoided or minimized. Beyond human fallibility, there is no reason why a legal instrument need be ambiguous. Although ambiguity is ipso facto bad, it is also avoidable.

C. Overvagueness and Overprecision

It is unfortunate that many lawyers persist in using the word "ambiguity" to include vagueness. [13] To subsume both concepts under the same name tends to imply that there is no difference between them or that their differences are legally unimportant. Ambiguity is a disease of language, whereas vagueness, which is sometimes a disease, is often a positive benefit. [14] With at least this significant difference between the two concepts, it is helpful to refer to them by different names.

12. See ch. 9.

13. E.g., H. Jones, Extrinsic Aids in the Federal Courts, 25 Iowa L. Rev. 737, 739 (1940).

14. C. Curtis, It's Your Law 65 (1954); R. Dickerson, Some Jurisprudential Implications of Electronic Data Processing, 28 Law & Contemp. Prob. 53, 62 (1963).

Whereas "ambiguity" in its classical sense refers to equivocation, "vagueness" refers to the degree to which, independently of equivocation, language is uncertain in its respective applications to a number of particulars. [15] Whereas the uncertainty of ambiguity is central, with an "either-or" challenge, the uncertainty of vagueness lies in marginal questions of degree. This uncertainty is said to result from the "open texture of concepts." [16]

Language can be ambiguous without being vague. If in a mortgage statute, for example, it is not clear whether the word "he" in a particular provision refers to the mortgagor or the mortgagee, the reference is ambiguous without being in the slightest degree vague or imprecise. Conversely, language can be vague without being ambiguous. An example is the word "red."

Most words that denote classes or categories (these words include most of the words of which statutes are composed) have elements of vagueness. Terms such as "near" and "intentional" have wide margins of uncertainty, whereas terms such as "male" and "natural child" have narrow ones. A few terms of general reference, such as "the first day of the calendar month," have no significant margins of uncertainty. Most nonvague terms, on the other hand, are terms of unique reference, such as "the current President of the United States."

As with ambiguity, vagueness may be semantic in that it attaches by uncertain usage to particular words and phrases, as in the examples just given, or it may be contextual. Contextual vagueness, which likewise is either internal or external, arises, for example, where one relevant provision prevails generally over another but the extent of prevalence remains uncertain. Similarly, where it is clear from context that an express grant of authority is intended to be exclusive and thus to carry a negative implication, it is likely to remain uncertain how far the implied withholding of authority to act extends in the broad reaches beyond the express coverage of the statute.

Unlike ambiguity, vagueness is often desirable. [17] How desirable it may be in a particular instance depends on whether and

15. For the interesting development of a "vagueness profile," see M. Black, Language and Philosophy 25-58 (1949).

16. F. Waismann, "Verifiability," in Essays on Logic and Language 117, 120 (Flew ed., 1951).

17. C. Curtis, It's Your Law 65 (1954); R. Dickerson, Some Jurisprudential Implications of Electronic Data Processing, 28 Law & Contemp. Prob. 53, 62 (1963).

how far the legislative client believes it desirable to leave the resolution of uncertainties to those who will administer and enforce the statute. (This is apparently what the advocates of "purposive ambiguity" have been trying, inartistically, to say.) [18] Fortunately, through a careful choice of terms and definitions and a partial control of context, the legislative draftsman has wide control over the areas and degrees of vagueness. Even though he may be unable to avoid it altogether, he can usually reduce it to the point where the residual uncertainties are no longer significant for the legislative client's purpose. Ideally, the legislative draftsman should try to make the statute no more nor less vague than is indicated by his client's desire to leave the resolution of uncertainties of meaning to the discretion of those who will administer or officially interpret the statute. [19]

That the uncertainty of vagueness is not peculiar to natural language, but inheres in all symbolism used in scientific observation involving classification or measurement, has been well stated by Black: [20]

> The ideal standard of precision which those have in mind who use vagueness as a term of reproach, when it is not a shifting standard of a relatively less vague symbol, is the standard of scientific precision. But the indeterminacy which is characteristic of vagueness is present also in all scientific measurement.

From this, it should be clear that the kind of uncertainty in marginal usage that we call "vagueness" does not result simply from the cognitive incapacities or variant purposes of the particular observer but reflects the objective condition that is being observed. That vagueness has an objective as well as a subjective aspect is confirmed by the relative statistical consistency with which even vague words are used. To sharpen appraisal, Black has developed a "consistency profile" for charting and measuring the varying degrees of vagueness and certainty in particular words or expressions. [21]

18. E.g., A. S. Miller, Statutory Language and the Purposive Use of Ambiguity, 42 Va. L. Rev. 23 (1956).

19. ". . . [H]is words should be as flexible, as elastic, indeed as vague, as the future is uncertain and unpredictable. . . . A lawyer's words should be no more precise than his client's control of the future is both practicable and desirable." C. Curtis, It's Your Law 64 (1954).

20. M. Black, Language and Philosophy 27 (1949).

21. Id. at 42-58.

Any attempt to locate and measure vagueness implies a standard. A subjective standard would be the observer's own range of uncertainty. The objective standard used by Black, on the other hand, is an appropriate sampling of the users of the language each of whom has been induced to draw the line that, despite his own uncertainty, seems to him the most appropriate. These alternatives pose a difficult dilemma for the judge, whose desire for scientific objectivity may have to be compromised, for reasons of practicality, with a subjective test. Under any objective test, an appropriate concept of the "users of a language" is critical because "the process of selecting a group of users and of discovering the consistency profile of a symbol are complementary and interact upon each other." [22]

D. Overgenerality and Undergenerality

A third concept, often confused with vagueness and sometimes even with ambiguity, is that of generality. A term is "general" when it is not limited to a unique referent and thus can denote more than one. It would be hard to imagine a statute that did not contain at least one general term.

The confusion of generality with ambiguity [23] is most likely to occur with respect to heterogeneous classes that include different referents that it is often useful to distinguish. For example, the general term "grandmother" is not ambiguous merely because it includes a paternal grandmother as well as a maternal one. Similarly for the general term "brother-in-law," which includes both a wife's or husband's brother and a sister's husband. The difference between such hetero-generality and ambiguity is that the former permits simultaneous reference, whereas the latter permits only alternative reference. Which is present usually depends on the context in which the term is used. In the sentence, "A grandmother sometimes has heavy responsibilities," the word "grandmother" is general. In the sentence, "My grandmother sometimes has heavy responsibilities," it may well be ambiguous, if both grandmothers are living.

22. Id. at 51.

23. E.g., "If therefore a group of events is described in a statute, there must be at least two which will fit that description, and since events are unique, any description of a group is almost by definition ambiguous." M. Radin, Statutory Interpretation, 43 Harv. L. Rev. 863, 868 (1930).

Generality, like vagueness, is not necessarily a disease of language. It is an indispensable tool of communication. The diseases, rather, are overgenerality and undergenerality. The classes denoted in a statute should be neither broader nor narrower than those appropriate to carrying out the legislature's objectives.

Generality is more easily confused with vagueness than with ambiguity.[24] That most general terms are also vague in their marginal applications makes it easy to overlook that the leeway permitted by vagueness is not the same as the leeway permitted by generality. The word "many," for example, is both vague and general. So also the word "automobile." The generality of the latter is exemplified by its capacity for simultaneously covering both Fords and Chevrolets without a tinge of uncertainty. Its vagueness is exemplified by the uncertainty whether it covers three-wheeled vehicles that bear a strong resemblance also to motorcycles.

The most important difference between ambiguous or vague language and general language is that ambiguity and vagueness constitute uncertainties of meaning, whereas mere generality does not. As a means of granting leeway to those who will administer or officially interpret the statute, it is preferable (where there is a choice) for the draftsman to rely on the generality of language rather than its vagueness, simply because, other factors remaining neutral, certainty is normally preferable to uncertainty. Vagueness, on the other hand, is a proper (though second-choice) vehicle for granting leeway where the legislative client's uncertainty as to specific results is matched by the marginal uncertainty in the language and context of the statute.

This difference is important in any statute that delegates broad quasi-legislative power. In the Emergency Price Control Act of 1942, the price administrator was authorized to set "generally fair and equitable" maximum prices on the great bulk of purchasable commodities in instances where it would "effectuate the

24. "Russell's definition of vagueness . . . as constituted by a one-many relation between symbolizing systems is held to confuse vagueness with generality. . . . The finite area of the field of application is a sign of its *generality,* while its vagueness is indicated by the finite area and lack of specification of its boundary." M. Black, Language and Philosophy 29, 31 (1949). (Emphasis in original.)

purposes of this Act." [25] As with all such statutes, problems of vagueness inevitably arose as to the outer reaches of the powers granted and the duties imposed. However, for actions falling within the general sweep of the norms so established, exercises of the power represented the exercise of discretion by the agency and not results prescribed by any meaning discoverable from the statute.

So far as meaning prescribes result, there can be for the interpreter only one theoretically "most plausible" result (however much reasonable men may differ), and it is found by the cognitive function of ascertaining the statutory meaning. On the other hand, so far as an agency or a court has discretion to select this or that reasonable result, both of which fall within the statute, the principles governing the selection among acceptable alternatives are, by definition, principles other than those relating to the ascertainment of meaning.

25. Act of January 30, 1942, ch. 26, §2a, 56 Stat. 24.

6

Basic Concepts: Legislative Certainty and the Purposive Element*

Words . . . "mean" nothing by themselves. . . .
— C. Ogden and I. Richards, The Meaning of Meaning 9 (10th ed., 1956)

A. Clarity in Statutes

Somewhat like physicians, lawyers concerned with litigation or the literature of litigation are generally preoccupied, so far as statutes are concerned, with the pathology of the legislative process. Although this preoccupation with sick [1] or intentionally uncertain statutes reflects for the most part sound pedagogy and normal practice, it tends to warp the scholar's and the lawyer's views of language in general and of legal language in particular.

That the warping has been only partial is witnessed by the presence in almost every discussion of statutory interpretation of an express or implied, though sometimes grudging, admission that, despite the vicissitudes of ambiguity, overvagueness, and overgenerality, most language is clear in at least some of its applications. [2] Beyond this generally perfunctory recognition,

* This chapter is an edited and expanded version of the author's article, Statutory Interpretation: Core Meaning and Marginal Uncertainty, 29 Mo. L. Rev. 1 (1964), © 1964 by the Curators of the University of Missouri (used with permission).

1. I.e., ambiguous, overvague, or overgeneral. See chapter 5.

2. "Inside, well on the inside, of the area of their meaning there will be little or no doubt or obscurity or even disagreement." C. Curtis, It's Your Law 62

however, little direct attention has been given to the areas of clear meaning, mainly because it is the legislative squeak that gets the judicial oil.

On the other hand, a full-blown theory of the interpretation of statutes, even though preoccupied with resolving significant uncertainties of meaning, cannot deal adequately with uncertainty without taking account of the basis for certainty in meaning and the bearing that the certain has on the uncertain. Except for an utterance composed wholly of gibberish (which would not be language), the character of a specific uncertainty of meaning is shaped, at least in part, by the relevant certainties. Thus, an ambiguity [3] presupposes at least two particular alternatives each of which, taken alone, is free of ambiguity and not so vague as to be meaningless. Similarly, a margin of vagueness presupposes a nonmarginal area that, if free of ambiguity, is clear because it is, by hypothesis, nonvague. In each case, the uncertainty thus relates to the presence or absence of factors having a close affinity with those operating in the area of certainty.

Because little attention has been paid to the elements that make clear language clear or how the elements of a particular uncertainty draw their character from what in the relevant context is clear, a recent exchange of views between H. L. A. Hart [4] and Fuller [5] carries special significance.

B. The Hart Attack

Hart's thesis is that communication is possible only because the general words through which it is conducted have a core meaning or "standard instance in which no doubts are felt about its application." [6] Around each vague word there is a margin of uncertainty called the "penumbra." The distinction between core

---

(1954). "Words . . . are after all not portmanteaus. We cannot quite put anything we like into them. And we may not disregard them in statutes." M. Radin, Statutory Interpretation, 43 Harv. L. Rev. 863, 866 (1930).

3. In the traditional, limited sense of equivocation.

4. H. Hart, Positivism and the Separation of Law and Morals, 71 Harv. L. Rev. 593 (1958).

5. L. Fuller, Positivism and Fidelity to Law — A Reply to Professor Hart, 71 Harv. L. Rev. 630 (1958).

6. H. Hart, Positivism and the Separation of Law and Morals, 71 Harv. L. Rev. 593, 607 (1958).

and penumbra is important to Hart's larger thesis that the core is the stronghold of the "isness" of the law, whereas the penumbra is the arena to which issues of the nature and role of "oughtness" in resolving uncertainties resulting from imprecision of legislative meaning are confined. Hart's and Fuller's central dispute concerns the respective roles of "isness" and "oughtness" in the law.

Although the larger issue is not the immediate concern of this discussion, it provides the setting in which the issues respecting the concept of "standard instance" or "core meaning" must be seen. Most important is the question: Does "oughtness" affect meaning in the core area? Fuller's deepest concern about Hart's theory of standard instance or core meaning lies in the assumption that it precludes recourse to the purpose of the statute in cases falling within the core,[7] thus sealing off the value-systems with which the law should be in constant and intimate touch.

On core meaning, Hart supposes this situation:[8]

> A legal rule forbids you to take a vehicle into the public park. Plainly this forbids an automobile, but what about bicycles, roller skates, toy automobiles? What about airplanes? . . . If we are to communicate with each other at all, and if, as in the most elementary form of law, we are to express our intentions that a certain type of behavior be regulated by rules, then the general words we use — like "vehicle" in the case I consider — must have some standard instance in which no doubts are felt about its application. There must be a core of settled meaning, but there will be, as well, a penumbra of debatable cases in which words are neither obviously applicable nor obviously ruled out.

C. The Fuller Reply

Fuller finds several bases for repudiating such a concept. His first objection is that meaning is not conveyed by a mere sequence of single words individually received and separately appraised. Because meaning attaches, rather, to sentences, paragraphs, or whole pages of text (which are likely to be unique), he argues:[9]

7. L. Fuller, Positivism and Fidelity to Law — A Reply to Professor Hart, 71 Harv. L. Rev. 630, 662-666 (1958).

8. H. Hart, Positivism and the Separation of Law and Morals, 71 Harv. L. Rev. 593, 607 (1958).

9. L. Fuller, Positivism and Fidelity to Law — A Reply to Professor Hart, 71 Harv. L. Rev. 630, 663 (1958). (Emphasis in original.)

> Surely a paragraph does not have a "standard instance" that remains constant whatever the context in which it appears. If a statute seems to have a kind of "core meaning" that we can apply without a too precise inquiry into its exact purpose, this is because we can see that, however one might formulate the precise objective of the statute, *this* case would still come within it.

His second objection is that, even if we accept a word-by-word approach to meaning, Hart fails to give a "real account of what does or should happen" with respect to core meaning. [10] Fuller also says that even within the alleged core meaning of the word "vehicle" Hart's insistence that it obviously includes automobiles would produce a dubious result in a case in which some citizens wanted "to mount on a pedestal in the park a truck used in World War II," if the court paid no attention to what the statute was intended to accomplish. [11] Thus, he objects to Hart's assumption that it is possible to interpret a word in a statute without knowing the aim of the statute.

> . . . [W]e do not proceed simply by placing the word in some general context . . . Rather, we ask ourselves, What can this rule be for? What evil does it seek to avert? [12]
>
> . . . Surely the judicial process is something more than a cataloguing procedure. [13]

It is thus through the mediation of purpose that core meaning is affected by considerations of "oughtness."

Fuller's third objection is that Hart's theory fails "to recognize that a rule or statute has a structural or systematic quality that reflects itself in some measure into the meaning of every principal term in it." [14]

Finally, he says that the theory of meaning implied in Hart's article appears to have been rejected by three of the principal authorities on modern logic: Wittgenstein, Russell, and Whitehead.[15]

If Hart is propounding a word-by-word approach as a full-blown theory of meaning, Fuller's criticism is largely justified.

10. Id.
11. Id.
12. Id. at 665.
13. Id. at 666.
14. Id. at 669, n. 40.
15. Id. at 669.

Certainly, a communication is more than the sum of its verbal and syntactical parts and, in the integration of total meaning, the legislative purpose manifest in the context of particular use is the only intelligible unifying force. This is well illustrated by *Roschen v. Ward.*[16] Although in that case the express words of the relevant statute required no more than the presence of a physician or an optometrist at each place where eye glasses were sold, its clear purpose showed that it obligated him in each case either to examine the customer's eyes or to determine that an examination was unnecessary.

D. Does Legislative Certainty Depend Only on Purpose?

The question nevertheless remains whether Fuller's view of the role of purpose rules out all notions of "standard instance" or "core meaning." Although he denies core meaning to the word "vehicle," he can see "without thinking" what the statute "is aiming at in general," with the result that he has no difficulty in concluding that in every case "a noisy automobile must be excluded."[17]

Such an assurance invites these questions: By what means is the legislative purpose so obviously manifested? Is Fuller's own certainty as to purpose unrelated to any element of certainty in the individual words of the statute? Are the words of a statute devoid of content when uttered out of context?[18]

To this last question Whorf's belief that dictionary meanings derive from the patterned "potentials of linkage" seems pertinent.[19] Even in the lonely isolation of their dictionary cells, words reflect the patterns of their many appearances in specific contexts.[20] Dewey, although conceding that "no term has logi-

16. 279 U.S. 337, 49 S. Ct. 336 (1929).

17. L. Fuller, Positivism and Fidelity to Law — A Reply to Professor Hart, 71 Harv. L. Rev. 630, 663 (1958).

18. "Words are meaningless in isolation. . . ." C. Allen, Law in the Making 490 (7th ed. 1964).

19. B. Whorf, Language, Thought, and Reality 67 n. 4 (1956).

20. ". . . [E]ven when read out of specific context particular words and phrases retain much of the flavor of their usual associations." R. Dickerson, The Difficult Choice Between "And" and "Or," 46 A.B.A.J. 310, 311 (1960).

cal force save in distinction from and relation to other terms," adds: [21]

> This statement is not contradicted by the fact that all familiar words carry some meaning even when uttered in isolation. . . . [T]heir meaning is potential rather than actual until they are linked to other words. If the words *sun, parabola, Julius Caesar,* etc., are uttered, a line of direction is given to observation or discourse. But the objective of the direction is indeterminate until it is *distinguished* from alternative possible terminations, and is thus *identified* by means of relation to another term.

Thus, although "terms as such are logically conditioned by propositions," [22] they have content even apart from their specific contexts. This is true even of syntactical links such as the word "unless," which Flesch has characterized as the most difficult word in the English language. [23] That this content-out-of-context is likely to be very general, rather than specific, is well illustrated by Fuller's word "improvement," which presumes that a standard of value must be supplied by context before the word can take on specific concretion. [24] Clarity of meaning is thus a function of the regularity and consistency of particular patterns that, although they arise out of particular uses, persist even beyond them.

Moreover, single words are not the only linguistic elements to which ascertainable and measurable usages attach. For example, the term "parol evidence rule" has a generally understood range

21. J. Dewey, Logic: The Theory of Inquiry 349 (1938). (Emphasis in original.) How often we read that "words have no meaning in themselves." C. Allen, Law in the Making 490 (7th ed. 1964); P. Ekelöff, Teleological Construction of Statutes, in 2 Scandinavian Studies in Law 1958, at 75, 95; C. Ogden & I. Richards, The Meaning of Meaning 9 (10th ed. 1956); A. Ross, On Law and Justice 113 (1959); Sutherland §45.04. Such statements are often ambiguous. If they mean that words taken in isolation are meaningless, they are simply not true; words have dictionary meanings. On the other hand, if they mean that words have no intrinsic meanings (e.g., F. Horack, Jr., The Disintegration of Statutory Construction, 24 Ind. L.J. 335, 337 (1949)), they cannot be challenged. Cf. statement in R. Dias, Jurisprudence 129 (1970), that "words have no proper meaning." This seems to deny the force of accepted usage.

22. Id. Is it not also true that propositions as such are conditioned by terms?

23. R. Flesch, The Art of Plain Talk 167 (1946).

24. Cf. L. Fuller, Positivism and Fidelity to Law — A Reply to Professor Hart, 71 Harv. L. Rev. 630, 664-665 (1958).

of meaning even though it is not a rule of evidence and even though it does not apply solely to oral utterances.[25]

Usage also shapes the ways in which words can be related to one another. The conventions of word arrangement make it possible, for example, to distinguish the meaning of "man bites dog" from the meaning of "dog bites man." A combination of words and phrases can thus produce a meaning that, while unique in the aggregate, is at least partly a function not only of their established meanings but of the established meanings of particular syntactical relationships. Fuller himself recognizes that "implicit systematic or structural elements in language often enable us to understand at once the meaning of a word used in a wholly novel sense, as in the statement, 'Experts regard the English Channel as the most difficult swim in the world.' "[26]

Some syntactical usages are well recognized and expressly recorded. Others are latent and subtle. The latter were apparently what Whorf had in mind when he said:[27]

> A covert linguistic class may not deal with any grand dichotomy of objects, it may have a very subtle meaning, and it may have no overt mark other than certain distinctive "reactances" with certain overtly marked forms. It is then what I call a CRYPTOTYPE. It is a submerged, subtle, and elusive meaning, corresponding to no actual word, yet shown by linguistic analysis to be functionally important in the grammar.

A third kind of specific usage that colors or supplements meaning includes the relevant assumptions that are left tacit because by usage they are not only agreed on but may be taken for granted.[28] Perhaps the simplest example is the one suggested by Scriven.[29] When the writer of a document dates it "1/4/75," intending to refer to January 4, 1975 (rather than to April 1,

25. "It is often fallacious in considering the meaning of a phrase consisting of two words to find a meaning which each has separately and then infer that the two together cover the combination so arrived at. The two together may, as here, have acquired a special meaning of their own." Lee v. Showman's Guild of Great Britain, [1952] 2 Q.B. 329, 338 ("unfair competition").

26. L. Fuller, Positivism and Fidelity to Law — A Reply to Professor Hart, 71 Harv. L. Rev. 630, 668, n. 40 (1958).

27. B. Whorf, Language, Thought, and Reality 70 (see also 92) (1956).

28. L. Fuller, Basic Contract Law 666-670 (1947).

29. In Definitions, Explanations and Theories, in II Minnesota Studies in the Philosophy of Science (Herbert Geigl and others, eds.) 99, 133 (1958).

1975), he is tacitly assuming that his addressee, like himself, is operating under the usual American, rather than British or military, system of indicating dates. In general, tacit legislative assumptions are established usages, common to the legislators and the legislative audience to which the particular statute is addressed, that are both relevant to the legislative message and taken account of by it. As integral parts of the shared environment, they are matters of which a court is likely to take judicial notice.

Although, as Hart suggests, a word, phrase, or syntactical relationship may have a single, relatively standardized and therefore determinable usage, it is much more likely to have a cluster of such usages. So far as these usages are interrelated, they comprise a family of usages and, if they relate to different aspects of the same general referent, they may be treated, not as separate words, but as inflections or other use-variants of the same word. [30] On the other hand, so far as the usages are unrelated, they constitute a bundle of homonyms, each of which, when identified, carries a standard instance or core meaning and may be treated for most purposes as a separate word. [31]

Such an identifiable use-pattern, consisting of specific language and the particular pattern of "actions into which it is woven," constitutes, in Wittgenstein's terminology, a "language-game" that is played according to the rules that custom has established for it. [32] These rules, in turn, comprise the core meaning of the particular use-pattern.

Moreover, even when the cluster of usages is taken as a whole (i.e., when the word is read apart from any particular use-pattern), it carries a core meaning. For a family of related usages, a single, broader core meaning attaches so far as they relate to the same general referent. For a family of unrelated usages or a bundle of homonyms, the "core meaning" consists simply of the aggregate of the core meanings of the separate use-patterns. Accordingly, the core meaning of a word taken out of context is in most cases like a quiver of individually unique arrows each of which shares, in addition to the same quiver, one or more aspects, such as the same size, weight, color, or shape,

30. E.g., "run," "have run," "ran," "was running," etc.

31. E.g., "Well," the judge asked, "how well did the contractor build the well?" See also ch. 5, pp. 44-45.

32. L. Wittgenstein, Philosophical Investigations 5, 20, 27, 80, 109 (G. Anscombe, transl. 1953).

with some, all, or none of the others. As an alternative, Fuller has likened such a word to a number of keys on the same ring.

The distinction between the vague and the certain, even with respect to single words, seems to be taken for granted by most philosophers of language. This is hardly surprising, because the vague implies the nonvague and, if it is proper to characterize some words in isolation as having wide areas of vagueness, it is likewise proper to characterize others as being relatively precise and certain. Although significant vagueness, like significant ambiguity, is realized only in specific use and, although a word or phrase is highly flavored by the particular context in which it appears, it is useful to classify words and phrases according to their potentialities for giving or avoiding trouble. Use in many specific legal contexts makes it possible, for example, to classify the word "reasonable" as potentially vague, and the word "children" as potentially ambiguous. This makes possible a science of lexicography and the writing of dictionaries.

Here is Black's account of how certainty and uncertainty can be predicated even of words taken in isolation: [33]

> The process of logical analysis of a language can be regarded as the exhibition of a set of conventions for the use of symbols, abstracted from the regularity of linguistic habits in some postulated speech community, and proceeding by a series of successive approximations involving the use of "simplified" or "model" entities.
>
> The vagueness of symbols in any such abstract system is a symptom of the degree of deviation of the "model" language from the empirically discoverable linguistic habits in the corresponding speech community.

Black's concept of an "empirically discoverable linguistic habit" seems to approximate Hart's concept of "standard instance" or "core meaning." Here, again, the definiteness of the habit, and thus the clarity of the meaning that it generates, depends on who are assumed to be the "users of the language." [34] These, in turn, define the relevant speech community. (It may be important to know whether a statute is addressed to the general public or to

33. M. Black, Language and Philosophy 28 (1949). Vagueness results not only from the cognitive incapacities or variant purposes of particular users but, more important, from minute, objective differences in degree in what is being observed.

34. Id. at 29.

an elite technical group.) It is not surprising that in concrete situations the line between the certain and the significantly uncertain, between core and penumbra, is usually blurred.

Some notion of standard instance is implicit in the almost universal assumption that there is a practical limit to the meaning that a specific configuration of words is capable of bearing. The factors of usage that set an outer limit to the penumbra are those that determine the existence and extent of the core. The revelation of legislative purpose is similarly circumscribed, because (1) so far as it is revealed by the enacted language itself, it is no more certain than the language by which it is revealed, and (2) so far as a purpose is revealed by elements (verbal or nonverbal) other than the enacted language, constitutional requirements as to how statutes must be enacted intervene to inhibit the wholesale extension of that language. Because total specific context tends to be unique, what do these relatively standardized inhibitions consist of except the established use-patterns of specific words, phrases, syntactical relationships, and tacitly shared assumptions?

On the other hand, Hart's approach, taken alone, reflects the limitation in Charles W. Morris's behavioristic approach to meaning.[35] It ignores that the total meaning conveyed by a unique configuration of symbols uttered in a unique context may be more than the sum of a series of separate conditioned responses and that, in many cases, an act of induction or deduction (i.e., of "interpretation") is required of the reader, an act shaped by the necessary presumption that the total communication is intended to express a rational and integrated legislative purpose or congeries of related purposes.

In this process, the concept of standard instance with its penumbra plays two important roles. First, it furnishes the basic data upon which any later act of induction or deduction necessarily depends. Second, it has a composite limiting effect on the ultimate range of meanings possible even in a loose context.

Even if, in the interpretation of statutes, we must agree with Fuller that the "judicial process is something more than a cataloguing procedure," it is partly a cataloguing procedure. Single words carry, even into context, an important one-way significance: Their established ranges of connotations set maximum

35. C. Morris, Signs, Language, and Behavior (1949). See discussion in M. Black, Language and Philosophy 169-177 (1949).

limits on what the total communication can mean to the audience addressed. That they do not fix minimum limits reflects the normal functioning of context.

E. The Limiting Force of Context

Fuller is fully justified in criticizing Hart for saying that the word "vehicle" necessarily covers all automobiles regardless of circumstances, including the circumstances of a narrower legislative purpose disclosed by proper context. To say that standard instance is immune to the forces of context is to deny what is perhaps the central and most useful function of context: to limit otherwise overgeneral language. Context makes it possible, for example, to include in a federal statute a very general word such as "person" without incurring the slightest risk that it will be read as including persons wholly beyond the jurisdiction of the United States.

However, the limitations so imposed by context do not affect the general lexical meaning of an otherwise broad word. In the sentence, "A special statute is undesirable in this case," there is no inconsistency in saying that the word "statute" means statute in its usual broad sense, even though the sentence as a whole refers to only one kind of statute. The general meaning of a word is not necessarily the same as the meaning of the particular sentence or paragraph in which it appears. No legitimate purpose is served by a contextual theory of meaning that treats the word "statute" as changing its meaning simply because it carries a modifier. The significant question in most cases is not the meaning of any constituent word but the meaning of the entire sentence or provision, as conditioned for that "language-game" by the standard instances and penumbras of the words "special," "statute," "undesirable," and "case," the syntactical usages reflected, and the contextually implied, and therefore tacit, legislative assumptions. For this reason, the concept of the general stability of standard instance or core meaning need not be abandoned merely because of the concomitant limitations of context.

Nor is the concept of standard instance or core meaning necessarily denied by variations in shades of meaning provided by variations in specific context. As with all classifications, lexical samenesses exist only because the existing differences are insignificant in the light of the purpose at hand, and thus may be disregarded.

If the concept of standard instance or core meaning is limited to particular words, phrases, syntactical relationships, and their use-patterns, and if its composite effects are subject to the normal conditioning of context, including the legislative purposes revealed by total context, there is wide scope for the play of the value-systems reflected in expressed legislative purpose, at least so far as context serves to limit the full potentialities of standard instance. On the other hand, they cannot extend lexical meaning beyond the outer reaches of standard instance and its penumbra of uncertainty.

That context not only limits the sweep of otherwise overgeneral language but also selects among homonyms and other use-patterns and often resolves grammatical ambiguities, both without changing the general potential force of established usage, refutes any notion that the vital effect that context has on total meaning rules out any concept of standard instance or core meaning. On the contrary, it presupposes it. For this reason, the mere recognition of the force of context found in Wittgenstein, Russell, and Whitehead does not repudiate the notion of standard instance or core meaning as such. At most it refutes Hart's apparent assertion that standard instance and core meaning are invulnerable to the limiting force of context.

Russell's strictures on the "cult of common usage"[36] seem directed, not at the concept of common usage, but at what blind enthusiasm has claimed for the vaguenesses and overgeneralities that comprise much of what passes as "plain English." It seems generally agreed among the philosophers of language not only that common usage in a particular speech community generates the conditioned responses upon which even unique communications are built but also that such linguistic habits are empirically and objectively discoverable. On this assumption are founded all notions of clear meaning. Nor is this assumption undermined by the fact, made so evident by Wittgenstein,[37] that even within the same speech community the same word plays as many roles as there are identifiable use-patterns that employ it.

36. See The Cult of Common Usage, in B. Russell, Portraits from Memory and Other Essays 154 (1956), reprinted in The Basic Writings of Bertrand Russell 137 (1961).

37. L. Wittgenstein, Philosophical Investigations 5, 20, 27, 80, 109 (G. Anscombe, transl. 1953).

F. Summary

A full-bodied theory of interpretation should recognize (1) that the common usage that makes clear language clear is not limited to individual words taken in isolation, (2) that by usage, combinations of words often carry meanings independent of the meanings of their constituent parts, (3) that usage extends also to observed patterns of syntax and to shared tacit legislative assumptions, (4) that the same word, expression, syntactical pattern, or tacit assumption may have multiple common usages, (5) that each such usage relates to a particular speech community, and (6) that patterns of context are to a limited extent reflected in the dictionary meanings of words. Crowning these facts is the integrating force of legislative purpose.[38] Hart's views as expressed on the occasion of this exchange with Fuller may not have been wrong so much as they failed to include other equally important aspects of communication. A practical consequence of taking these elements into account during the pulling and hauling of contending parties is to assign a burden of persuasion.

These observations, of course, do not detract from the validity of Fuller's main points: (1) that a legislative communication is presumably both an integrated whole and inherently purposive, (2) that knowledge of this fact not only is helpful in resolving many uncertainties of meaning, but conditions the normal play of established usage, and (3) that where the immediate legislative purpose is clearly revealed by the pertinent statutory language read in proper context its meaning is clear.

Although Fuller has effectively punctured any notion that standard instance or core meaning is impervious to context and the value-systems inherent in manifest legislative purpose, a concept of standard instance or core meaning is indispensable to setting outer limits on potential meaning and, indeed, even to the revelation of legislative purpose itself. If so, Hart is right in supposing standard instance or core meaning, but wrong in dissociating it from the limiting implications of legislative purpose. It is unfortunate, too, that he did not delineate more fully its extent and significance, because therein lies the source of legislative clarity.

38. See ch. 8.

7

Basic Concepts: Legislative Intent

> . . . [*T*]*he psychic transference of the thought of an artificial body must stagger the most advanced of the ghost hunters. . . .*
>
> — J. Gray, The Nature and Sources of the Law 170 (2d. ed 1921)

A. Introduction

One of the most fundamental, and at the same time elusive, concepts in the interpretation and application of statutes is that of legislative intent.

The appeal of the concept is strong. In the division of responsibilities represented by the constitutional separation of powers, the legislature calls the main policy turns and the courts must respect its pronouncements. In such a relationship, it would seem clear that so far as the legislature has expressed itself by statute the courts should try to determine as accurately as possible what the legislature intended to be done.

Unfortunately, this objective is not easily realized, because people are not always successful in communicating their thoughts. Difficulties of this kind are familiar in all aspects of human experience and no parade of examples is needed to document the fact. And yet, these difficulties do not signify that communication is impossible.

All this seems to be supported by common sense and personal experience. On the other hand, is there not reason to suspect that "common sense" is not always reliable? Scientists tell us, for example, that the "solidity" that we experience in objects such as tables and typewriters is not a characteristic that nuclear physicists experience when they examine the materials from which such objects are made. And so, they also tell us, we cannot always take for granted what seems obvious to the eye, ear, or touch. [1] Many students of legislation have come to a similar conclusion for "legislative intent."

B. The Radin Onslaught

One of the most exhaustive analyses of legislative intent has been provided by Radin. [2] Although made more than four decades ago, its impact is still felt. Briefly, he says that it is unrealistic to talk about legislative intent, because the notion of "the lawmaker" is fictional; there is no such person. Nor is it realistic to talk about the intent of the heterogeneous collectivity known as "the legislature." In most cases, only one or two persons drafted the bill, many persons voted against it, and those who voted for it may have had differing ideas and beliefs. Even if the participating legislators had the same intent, we have no means of knowing it except "by the external utterances or behavior of these hundreds of men." Even if a unanimous legislative intent were knowable, it would be powerless to bind the courts, because the legislators' function is not to impose their respective wills, but to "pass statutes." Even if legislative intent had binding force, it could hardly control the final interpretation in advance, because the legislature could not have intended to cover a particular factual situation that did not yet exist. Finally, legislative intent is irrelevant under any rule of interpretation that limits the interpreter to the text of the statute. [3]

The folly of any attempt to conjure up a legislative intent has been asserted so often that many respectable scholars refuse to recognize the concept. [4] So deep is their antipathy that the very

1. S. Stebbing, Furniture of the Earth, in Philosophy of Science 69, 73 (A. Danto & S. Morgenbesser eds., 1960). The fallacy of this point is, of course, that it denies meaning to a well established word ("solid"), whereas the significant problem is simply to redescribe what the word customarily refers to. Id. at 74. And see A. Ross, On Law and Justice 114 (1959).

2. M. Radin, Statutory Interpretation, 43 Harv. L. Rev. 863 (1930).

3. Id. at 870-872.

4. E.g., L. Fuller, The Morality of Law 86 (1964); ". . . [T]he psychic transference of the thought of an artificial body must stagger the most advanced of the ghost hunters. . . ." J. Gray, The Nature and Sources of the Law 170

phrase "legislative intent" has become a legislative impropriety that some of them feel it necessary to avoid. Even those who let the expression pass their lips are careful to protect their professional respectability by pointing out that they use it to refer, instead, to some objective expression or the more acceptable concept of legislative purpose.[5] Because so many professional commentators apparently agree, it is strange that the concept of a subjective legislative intent keeps cropping up. If it is truly a ghost, we should banish it once and for all.

C. What Is "Intent"?

In the present context, "intent" refers usually to the actual intent of some human being, or group of human beings, respecting what he or they intended to say. It reflects the user's expectation that the reader or hearer will take the language as referring to what the user had in mind. It is, therefore, the specific message that the user intended to convey.

"Intent" is also used in the sense of the intent objectively manifested by the language used. Because language has meaning independent of the actual intent of the user, the meaning actually carried may imply an intent that differs from the user's actual intent. It will be useful, therefore, to distinguish actual intent from manifest intent.

Actual intent, which is necessarily a conscious activity, must be distinguished also from what Fuller has called "tacit legislative assumptions," the underlying propositions that the user of language takes for granted without taking express account of them and, perhaps, even without even being aware of them.[6] These assumptions, in turn, have their objective counterparts in whatever may be fairly inferred from the language actually used. Such an inference may be one that the user neither intended nor took for granted.

(2d ed. 1921); R. Keeton, Venturing to do Justice 81 (1969); W. Bishin, The Law Finders: An Essay in Statutory Interpretation 1, 2 (1965); J. Corry, Administrative Law and the Interpretation of Statutes, 1 U. Toronto L.J. 286, 290 (1936).

5. E.g., F. Frankfurter, Some Reflections on the Reading of Statutes, 47 Colum. L. Rev. 527, 538 (1947); F. Horack, Jr., The Disintegration of Statutory Construction, 24 Ind. L.J. 335, 340-341 (1949).

6. See ch. 9, p. 121.

With these distinctions in mind, we may now inquire whether actual subjective intent "exists" and, if so, whether it is relevant to and useful in the interpretation of statutes.

MacCallum, in his penetrating analysis of legislative intent, points out that a legislator may have many intents with respect to a statute.[7] He lists as possibilities the intent to enact a statute, the intent to enact this statute, the intent to enact the particular words in question, the intent to enact their meaning, the intent to enact his understanding of their meaning, the intent to further some ulterior purpose,[8] and the intent to further his own legislative career. For present purposes, only these are immediately relevant: the intent to enact this statute, the intent to enact these words, the intent to enact their meaning, and the intent to enact the legislator's understanding of their meaning.

Because the legislator in question voted for it, the intent to enact this statute may be taken for granted. Also, it is hard to see any significance in an intent to enact words apart from their meaning. Two significant intents remain: the intent to enact the meaning of these words (as normally read) and the intent to enact them as the legislator interprets them.

Because the significant intent is that of a person who is familiar with the text and supports it, it is suggested that the two intents coalesce psychologically into a single intent: the intent to enact these words as the legislator understands them, coupled with the tacit assumption that his understanding is the same as that of a typical member of the legislative audience. To assume differently is to assume that his purpose is to deceive or confuse (which, fortunately, is the rare exception).

Even if reference to "legislative intent" in the subjective sense is sometimes questionable, little objection can be found to the expression "manifest intent" (which by definition is objectively determinable), except that it appears to be a mere synonym for "meaning to the typical reader." To avoid possible confusion, it may be preferable to confine the term "legislative intent" to actual or supposed subjective intent, and to use the term "meaning" to designate what is suggested by the relevant language of the statute when read in its proper context.

7. G. MacCallum, Jr., Legislative Intent, 75 Yale L.J. 754, 756 (1966). Cf. R. Nunez, The Nature of Legislative Intent and the Use of Legislative Documents as Extrinsic Aids to Statutory Interpretation: A Reexamination, 9 Cal. West. L. Rev. 128 (1972).

8. Ulterior purpose is considered in ch. 8.

There is also a possible difference between the intent to achieve an immediate result by means of a statute (what the authors intend to do) and the accompanying intent to express that result in the statute (what the authors intend to say). Here again, the two intents coalesce into an intent to convey a particular idea, coupled with the tacit assumption that what the authors intend to say reflects adequately what they intend to immediately accomplish.

D. The Specific Arguments

Radin's first point is that there is no single person whom we can call "the legislator" and whose mind we can successfully investigate to discover the legislative intent behind a statute.[9] The point is indisputable. However, it does not say that there is no such thing as legislative intent; it says only that we cannot find it in the mind of some person comparable to the author of a private communication.

The second point is that it is futile to look for legislative intent in the minds of a large and heterogeneous group such as a legislature.[10] What about those who voted against the bill? This poses no problem under majority rule, where once the statute has been enacted the views of the minority are for the most part irrelevant. What about those who voted for the bill but did not read it or did not read the particular provision in question? What is their legislative intent? Again, the answer seems plain: They intended to adopt or acquiesce in either (1) the intent manifested by the bill and the other objective indicia of intent, which is directly determinable, or (2) the actual intent of those conversant with the bill, which is not.[11] Because such a

9. M. Radin, Statutory Interpretation, 43 Harv. L. Rev. 863, 870 (1930). In appraising Radin's thesis, I have been much helped by J. Landis, A Note on "Statutory Interpretation," 43 Harv. L. Rev. 886 (1930).

10. Id.

11. "In the enactment of statutes there is delegation, too, with respect to sponsorship and draftsmanship. . . . The legislature expects that statutes will be drafted by others, not only by its own arms . . . but also by agencies and individuals outside the legislature. In such situations the intent, purpose, and draftsmanship of others is adopted as its own by the legislature. On this theory there is no statute without a legislative intent or purpose. It is a glib superficiality to suggest otherwise." C. Breitel, The Courts and Lawmaking, in Legal Institutions Today and Tomorrow 1, 27 (M. Paulsen ed., 1959).

derivative intent can only support what must be independently determined, its content has only subordinate interest. (If valid, Radin's legislative misgivings might lead us also to question the "judicial intent" of a nine-man court.)

This narrows the search to the actual intent of the particular legislators who undertook to sponsor, mold, and understand the bill. In a few cases, the significant legislative intent might be that merely of the draftsman, whose handiwork the legislature adopted. Although this would be unusual for an entire bill, the draftsman often includes individual provisions to which no legislator pays particular attention even though several may have carefully scrutinized the bill as a whole. Here, it would seem appropriate to say that the legislative intent of the participating legislators is to adopt or acquiesce in the legislative intent manifested by the bill when viewed in its proper legislative setting or to adopt or acquiesce in the actual intent of the draftsman.

However, an adoption approach suffices only when the intent adopted is that of an individual author. Where there is a group of authors, the problem of institutional intent is simply transferred from the legislature as a whole to the group as a whole.

The usual case is that in which the statute or provision was developed or scrutinized by a handful of legislators operating as a subcommittee of a standing committee. Even here, says Radin, there may be frequent differences of opinion or understanding. For an actual legislative intent that we may attribute by adoption or acquiescence first to those who voted for the bill, second to the legislature as a whole, and ultimately to the chief executive who signed it, whose intent do we seek? Is this not an insuperable difficulty?

But to talk of actual "legislative intent" even here is not entirely fatuous. Among such a group there can be a general consensus,[12] even though the views of the participants vary in many details. Variant views have not deterred legislative and quasi-legislative bodies from sharing general objectives and from using their intent to accomplish these objectives as a basis for future operations. That a general consensus is a consensus and nothing more, leaving unresolved particular issues on which the participants disagree, does not mean that that consensus is not

12. On consensus, see T. Newcomb, R. Turner, and P. Converse, Social Psychology ch. 8 (1965).

operating in the area where it does exist.[13] The errors seems to be in assuming that, if there is an ascertainable legislative intent, it necessarily resolves the question at hand, and conversely that, if it does not resolve the question at hand, it must not have existed.

Moreover, in ascertaining the message that the language used was intended to convey, the intentions and opinions of some actively participating legislators are usually more significant than those of others. Thus, the expressions of the sponsor of the bill normally reveal a legislative intent more significant than that revealed by those of a more casual legislative adherent. In this context, the significant legislative intent may well be the actual intent of the former.

If this analysis is correct, the mere multiplicity of legislators is insufficient reason for ruling out the possibility of an actual legislative intent. At most it blurs the already difficult problem of determining the actual intent of particular individuals.

The possibility of an effective general consensus suggests the further possibility of a real (not fictitious) corporate legislative intent consisting, not of the shared intent of a group of improbably like-minded legislators, but of the composite thrust of many individual intents, no one of which need wholly coincide with the composite.[14] Such an institutional intent is best likened to the resultant of a set of vectors. Although even an organic group, as

13. "It is surely not necessary for persons to agree in *all* cases in order for them to agree in *some* cases." G. MacCallum, Jr., Legislative Intent, 75 Yale L.J. 754, 770 (1966). (Emphasis in original.)

14. ". . . '[C]ollective intent' in the light of modern psychology is not as unrealistic a concept as it is made out to be by jurists. . . ." H. Silving, A Plea for a Law of Interpretation, 98 U. Pa. L. Rev. 499, 510 (1950), citing Sigmund Freud as recognizing, in Massenpsychologie Und Ich-Analyse, "the reality of psychological experiences of groups or masses." See also G. MacCallum, Jr., Legislative Intent, 75 Yale L.J. 754, 763-766 (1965).

Work with groups has shown that they have characteristics and exhibit features that differ from the aggregate of the characteristics and features of the individual members of the group. See R. Brown, Social Psychology ch. 13 (1965); L. Doob, Social Psychology 219 (1952). For example, when individuals are presented with a problem their individual solutions are "less risky" than those proposed by a group made up of the same individuals. The conclusion has been drawn that this "shift of the risk" is solely a function of the existence of groups. M. Wallach, N. Kagan, & D. Bem, Group Influence on Individual Risk Taking, 65 J. Abnorm. & Soc. Psy. 75 (1962). See also M. Sherif, Group Influence Upon the Formation of Norms and Attitudes, in Readings in Social Psychology 77 (T. Newcomb & E. Hartley eds., 1947).

such, has no separate psyche, its activities display the characteristics of intentional behavior guided by an aggregate motivation that it is useful to recognize and take into account. Such a group intent differs from the constituent individual intents, it is significant, and, through reasonable inference, it can be broadly identified. If there is something approaching an institutional state of mind, why not recognize it in a legislature? [15]

For this concept, the term "legislative intent" is apt, because it is one that usage has already firmly attached. Asserting that "there is no such thing as legislative intent" because a legislature, as an abstraction, cannot intend anything, is like asserting that there is no such thing as ptomaine poisoning because food ptomaines are not in themselves poisonous. Whatever their origins, words mean what they are normally used to refer to. [16] Here, fortunately, usage remains close to semantic origins, because legislative intent is ultimately rooted in individual intents.

This leads us to Radin's third point: Even if there were perfect unanimity of understanding and intent, we could discover that intent only through the utterances of hundreds of men. [17] But why a wealth of evidences of intent would make the problem harder rather than easier is not clear. If we assume complete agreement, it should be necessary only to determine the intent of a single legislator. With the utterances of others as a cross check, we could more easily select the most reliable and revealing utterances. The factual supposition is, of course, fanciful.

Because the mere multiplicity of utterances does not seem to pose a serious problem, Radin's main point may have been, instead, the impossibility of knowing even an individual's actual intent. We have, of course, no means of peering into an individual's consciousness. Unfortunately, the argument proves too much: Communication itself is impossible, inside and outside the law. It is interesting, indeed, to speculate on Radin's own "legislative intent." By his apparent standards, it cannot be inferred from the language of his article. On the other hand, it is comforting to know that despite this baffling problem the philosophers of

15. ". . . [L]egislatures are enough like men in important respects to be counted as having intentions." G. MacCallum, Jr., Legislative Intent, 75 Yale L.J. 754, 765-766 (1966).

16. See note 1 *supra*.

17. M. Radin, Statutory Interpretation, 43 Harv. L. Rev. 870 (1930).

language still presume to communicate. Wittgenstein, for one, apparently does not find this a serious problem.[18] And so, Radin's logical tour de force can claim the same kind of practical success as the well-known, "irrefutable" proof that bumble bees cannot fly.[19]

Radin's fourth point is that, even if there were an ascertainable legislative intent, it would be powerless to bind the court, because the function of legislators is not to "impose their will" but to "pass statutes."[20] The underlying assumption here overlooks the point made in Burke's speech to the Bristol electors that — as a matter of both in-fact expectations and sound political principle — legislators *are* sent to "impose their will," not according to personal whim, but by exercising rational choice where it is impractical to act by town meetings.[21]

More important, Radin seems to say that, although the court should look at the language of the statute, it may treat as nonexistent any actual legislative intent that it expresses. Such a view of legislation suggests that statutes stand no higher than the finger painting allegedly done in the late 1950s by a Baltimore chimpanzee. What devastating discouragement it would heap on the legislative draftsman, who works under the illusion that he is somehow helping the legislature to communicate to the public! It is fascinating to contemplate a legislative function that could produce statutes without reflecting the will of the participating legislators. As Lord Russell said in another connection, "This is one of those views which are so absurd that only very learned men could possibly adopt them."[22] It is to Radin's credit that twelve years later, while sticking to his main guns, he made a

18. See, generally, L. Wittgenstein, Philosophical Investigations (G. Anscombe, transl. 1953). ". . . [E]ven a dog distinguishes between being stumbled over and being kicked," O. Holmes, Jr., The Common Law 3 (1881).

19. B. Stillson, Wings: Insects, Birds, Men 54 (1954).

20. M. Radin, Statutory Interpretation, 43 Harv. L. Rev. 863, 871 (1930).

21. 2 E. Burke, Works 96 (7th ed. 1881).

22. B. Russell, My Philosophical Development 148 (1959). The theory under attack may not have originated wholly with Radin. Cf. A. Lenhof, On Interpretative Theories: A Comparative Study in Legislation, 27 Tex. L. Rev. 312, 326 (1949), discussing Kohler's views. But what does he assert? That there is no such thing as legislative intent? Or merely (as with Holmes) that legislative intent, so far as it is unrevealed by statutory meaning in its fullest and most sophisticated sense, may be disregarded?

limited concession to the subjectivity of legislative purpose as revealed by legislative history.[23]

His fifth point is that legislative intent, even if determinable, cannot relate to a specific factual situation that, being nonexistent when the intention was formed, could not have been specifically foreseen.[24] Fuller calls this the "pointer theory of meaning."[25] It overlooks the elementary distinction between the connotations of words, which being general may express the general intent of the utterer, and their specific denotations, which, not being limited to denotations in existence at the time of the utterance, inevitably include denotations that not only were not then in existence but could not have been specifically envisioned.[26] Even a particular subclass of events is not excluded from a broad legislative intent merely because the legislator did not specifically advert to it.[27] Thus, a legislature's inability to anticipate the development of transistors would not necessarily exclude them from the more inclusive intended category of electronic devices.

The failure to distinguish general connotations from specific denotations, which has also plagued other writers, may be due in part to the view, already discussed, that interpretation, with which it is apparently assumed any concept of legislative intention or meaning must be coextensive, necessarily includes application, with its immediate problem of specific denotation.[28] Radin's fifth point also falsely implies that the draftsman of a

23. M. Radin, A Short Way With Statutes, 56 Harv. L. Rev. 388, 411 (1942).

24. M. Radin, Statutory Interpretation, 43 Harv. L. Rev. 863, 870-871 (1930). According to Patterson, the theory that legislative intent is a myth is based on "the psychological theory of the meanings of symbols." E. Patterson, Jurisprudence: Men and Ideas of the Law 202 (1953). Under this theory, a "term is an effective means of communication if it causes the utteree to have in mind the same referent that the utterer had in mind. . . . [It is] inadequate to explain the logical function of legal symbols, their ability to enable us to make inferences or applications to referents which the person or persons uttering them did not 'have in mind.'" Id. at 27-28.

25. L. Fuller, The Morality of Law 84 (rev. ed. 1969). Accepting the pointer theory seems to be an occupational hazard of case-hardened lawyers. See, e.g., S. Mermin, Law and the Legal System 224 (1973). See also H. Jones, Statutory Doubts and Legislative Intention, 40 Colum. L. Rev. 957, 972 (1940).

26. E. Patterson, Jurisprudence: Men and Ideas of the Law 203 (1953); Sutherland §49.02.

27. G. MacCallum, Jr., Legislative Intent, 75 Yale L.J. 754, 772 (1966).

28. See ch. 3, p. 23.

statute would, if he could, advert to specific future factual situations. Although legislation is usually prompted by specific past situations, legislative draftsmen almost inevitably address their words to classes of events. It is not only impossible for them to envision the specifics of particular future events, but wholly unnecessary. In any event, to deny that the legislature's utterance of general conditions on future behavior is a proper part of the legislative function is to deny that guidance and the establishment of workable frames of reference on which reasonable expectations can be built are among the functions of the legal order.

Radin's sixth and final point is that the traditional view that looks for subjective legislative intent is undercut by the equally traditional view that the court may not go beyond the plain words of the statute and thus needs no help from any separate concept of legislative intent. But while some of his premises may be true, Radin seems to rely on two that are both unannounced and false: first, that the words of the statute are unrelated to the subjective legislative intent that lies behind it and, second, that any supposed legislative intent stands apart from the statute and competes with it. Moreover, he ignores the fact that the "plain meaning" approach, however formulated, is at least partly a separation-of-powers device to remind judges of their prime responsibility to policy set by another branch of government.

In the meantime, the expression "legislative intent" remains professionally déclassé among many law professors and some judges. Supporting this position is the undeniable fact that it has often been used, as Landis has pointed out, to conceal judicial lawmaking. [29] That the concept has been abused does not, however, deny its importance as a fundamental presupposition of the legislative process.

That the concept of legislative intent is much more alive than the currently limited use of its normal label might suggest is revealed by the extent to which those who purport to shun it may be found resorting to euphemisms to describe it. Indeed, experience suggests that we can hardly get along without it. [30] An example is the protest of Justice Frankfurter, long an avowed

29. J. Landis, A Note on "Statutory Interpretation," 43 Harv. L. Rev. 886, 887, 891 (1930).

30. This goes especially for the scavengers of legislative history. F. Horack, Jr., The Disintegration of Statutory Construction, 24 Ind. L.J. 335, 340-341 (1949); H. Jones, Statutory Doubts and Legislative Intention, 40 Colum. L. Rev. 957, 968 (1940).

nonbeliever in subjective legislative intent,[31] that the majority of the Supreme Court in a 1958 tax case failed to take adequate account of the conference report. "Our problem," he said, "is not what do ordinary English words mean, but what did Congress *mean* them to mean."[32] Even Radin, in the article in which he partly recanted on the uses of legislative history, acknowledged the existence of legislative subjectivity when he said that the legislature may "foreclose any attempt by the administration and judiciary to displace what the legislature *regards* as the more important of the purposes to be achieved."[33] If hundreds of men can subjectively "regard" something, it may not strain credulity to conclude that they could also "intend" it.

Despite occasional protestations to the contrary, the typical lawyer or judge continues to refer to legislative intent, even though it remains a matter of inference and conjecture.[34] So long as the concept is used with reasonable restraint, the art of statutory interpretation is undoubtedly the better for it.

More than that, the concept is indispensable. The postulation of some actual, though not directly knowable, legislative intent underlies the very idea of a legislative process.[35] If legislative intent in the subjective sense does not exist in at least some degree, the legislative process is blatant nonsense unworthy of serious investigation. Even if there were no actual legislative intent, judicial deference to the constitutional separation of powers would require the courts to act as if there were,[36] be-

31. F. Frankfurter, Some Reflections on the Reading of Statutes, 47 Colum. L. Rev. 527, 538 (1947).

32. Commissioner v. Acker, 361 U.S. 87, 95, 80 S. Ct. 144, 149 (1958). (Emphasis added.)

33. M. Radin, A Short Way with Statutes, 56 Harv. L. Rev. 388, 412 (1942). [Emphasis added.] And if a legislature is incapable of "intending," how is it that a statute can "strive to attain"? Id. at 408.

34. Sutherland §45.05.

35. J. Landis, A Note on "Statutory Interpretation," 43 Harv. L. Rev. 886, 887 (1930). If legislative intent "is looked upon as a common agreement on the purpose of an enactment and a general understanding of the kind of situation at which it is aimed, to deny the existence of a legislative intention is to deny the existence of a legislative function." Note, A Re-evaluation of the Use of Legislative History in the Federal Courts, 52 Colum. L. Rev. 125, 126 (1952).

36. ". . . [A] fiction, however weak it may prove to be upon logical analysis, is created from sheer necessity." J. MacDonald, The Position of Statutory Construction in Present Day Law Practice, 3 Vand. L. Rev. 369, 371-372 (1950).

cause the concept is necessary to put courts in an appropriately deferential frame of mind. This alone would be enough to moot the general issue of its "existence."

Nor should we be deterred from postulating subjective intent by the baffling problem of finding the most practicable, most reliable, and fairest constitutional means of inferring it. Because in drawing inferences of meaning the human mind is limited to objective manifestations of intent, the problem is to choose the most appropriate means to that end. That none is completely reliable does not indicate that the job is impossible or that the attempt is fruitless. Under our system of constitutional government, the court has no choice; it must do its best. That it may often fail only increases the legislature's incentive to minimize the chances of misreading by making its legislative message as clear as possible.

If this analysis is sound, it is reasonable to talk generally about actual subjective legislative intent, so long as we realize that its scope is limited and our access to it is at best imperfect. Otherwise, we reduce the legislative process to absurdity and expose statutory law to the risk that the social views of the court will displace the constitutionally expressed social views of the legislature.

The real danger in the concept of subjective legislative intent is that too much is often claimed for it. Its limitations are discussed in the next section.

Besides putting the court in the proper deferential frame of mind, the concept of actual legislative intent furnishes the general criteria of relevance and reliability necessary to determining what specific elements in the statute and its context should be taken into account and the respective weights that they should be given. On what other basis, for example, could a court properly evaluate extrinsic materials?

E. The Limitations of Legislative Intent

That there is some actual and reasonably inferable legislative intent behind every statute does not mean that there is always, or even often, a specific legislative intent with respect to the particular issue in question[37] or, if there is only a general relevant intent, that it resolves the issue. Acting through a few legislators, a legislature, even while conscious of the broad legislative problem, usually adverts to some of its specific aspects without adverting to all. That the courts often deal with matters with respect to which specific legislative intent is either nonexistent or imperfectly revealed may explain why many persons distrust the general concept itself.

Moreover, actual intent, whether specific or general, normally cannot keep abreast of expressed intent (meaning). An author inevitably encompasses in what he says more than he has specifically in mind[38] and often encompasses even more than he has generally in mind.[39] Thus, to this limited extent we can agree with Kohler that "the idea contained [in the written text] has a life of its own independent of the person who thinks or expresses it."[40] The fact was noted in *Chapman v. Brown,*[41] a products liability case. On the other hand, the limiting force of context exemplified in *Church of the Holy Trinity v. United States*[42] fortifies the courts against the risk that this "life of its own" will carry the statute too far.

At the same time, we must read statutes as if actual intent and manifest intent coincided, because in the long run we can approximate actual intent more reliably under that assumption than under any other.[43] That short of extrasensory perception there

37. F. Horack, Jr., Cooperative Action for Improved Statutory Interpretation, 3 Vand. L. Rev. 382, 388 (1950); H. Jones, Extrinsic Aids in the Federal Courts, 25 Iowa L. Rev. 737, 742 (1940).

38. "I cannot believe that any of us would say that the 'meaning' of an utterance is exhausted by the specific content of the utterer's mind at the moment." L. Hand, The Bill of Rights 18-19 (1958). See also G. MacCallum, Jr., Legislative Intent, 75 Yale L.J. 754, 772-774 (1966); E. Patterson, Jurisprudence: Men and Ideas of the Law 203 (1953).

39. J. Kohler, Judicial Interpretation of Enacted Law, in Science of Legal Method 187, 188 (1921); E. Patterson, Jurisprudence: Men and Ideas of the Law 27 (1953); H. Hart, Positivism and the Separation of Law and Morals, 71 Harv. L. Rev. 593, 627-628 (1958).

40. J. Kohler, Judicial Interpretation of Enacted Law, in Science of Legal Method 187, 195 (1921).

41. 198 F. Supp. 78, 118 (D. Hawaii 1961) (". . . those who drafted this law may not have fully realized the extent of the exception expressly recognized by this section. . . .").

42. 143 U.S. 457, 12 S. Ct. 511 (1892).

43. It is the very nature of language to reflect prevailing usage. See also ch. 2, pp. 10-11.

appears to be no alternative compels the interpreter to presume in all cases what he knows to be true only in most. The interpreter must, therefore, assume that the actual intended meaning coincides with the manifest intended meaning until the user clarifies his message by restating it, whereupon the same kind of problem is presented in a new, and presumably clearer, form.

One reason for restraint in pursuing legislative intent is that, once the reliable manifestations of the intent behind a statute have been examined and weighed, it is idle to speculate on the sweep of actual intent in the specific instance. Although it is necessary to assume a general legislative intent to give direction and significance to statutory interpretation, the courts' bases for inferring what it presumes to be the particular intent respecting the issue before it are necessarily limited to the statute and appropriate extrinsic materials. Any residual inconsistency between manifest intent and actual intent remains one for unverifiable speculation.[44] Lawyers, who are no more capable than philosophers or psychologists in this respect, should therefore limit themselves to these significant questions: What legislative materials are entitled to what weight? What inferences of actual intent can most plausibly be drawn from those materials?

Some courts have asserted that where legislative meaning is uncertain legislative intent is useful in removing the uncertainty.[45] But if "intent" means actual specific subjective intent it can never be helpful, because it is never directly knowable. Once we assume that the statute, viewed with other reliable indicia of intent, leaves a significant, unresolved uncertainty, we have by hypothesis exhausted the only objective evidence from which any specific actual intent can reliably be inferred. Actual intent as such is no more available at this point to resolve the uncertainty than it was in the first instance. There is nothing left to examine except external manifestations of intent of doubtful reliability.

To say that in cases of uncertainty legislative intent is helpful in ascertaining statutory meaning is to put the matter exactly backwards, if "legislative intent" means actual subjective intent.

44. "Even assuming the existence in any case of an actual legislative intention different from any sensible textual meaning, it is pure speculation to attempt to say what it is. . . ." F. de Sloovère, Textual Interpretation of Statutes, 11 N.Y.U.L.Q. Rev. 538, 541 (1934). Competing inferences from other sources suffer from the same inherent uncertainty.

45. E.g., Saxon v. Georgia Assn. of Independent Ins. Agents, Inc., 399 F.2d 1010, 1015 (5th Cir. 1968).

Rather, statutory meaning is helpful in ascertaining subjective legislative intent. Indeed, there is no other way to get at such intent. The main problem is to determine what expressions of meaning it is appropriate to look at.

On the other hand, if "legislative intent" means manifest intent, there is a limited sense in which it may sometimes help to resolve a particular uncertainty of meaning. If the statute is plainly intended to deal with all of what appears to be a unified problem, some of whose aspects lie outside a literal reading of the statute and that if not dealt with in its other aspects would provide a means of undermining what the statute clearly tries to accomplish, and if the statute, read in context, is capable of bearing a meaning that covers these additional aspects, there is presumably a legislative intent to deal with the whole problem and not merely a less manageable part of it. It can also be presumed that the words were intended to carry a meaning coextensive with that intent. This, indeed, was the gist of *Heydon's Case.* [46]

However, what the tireless pursuers of legislative intent have in effect been saying is that, where some evidences of intent (usually the statute) do not clear up the uncertainty, other evidences (usually legislative history) may. The practical danger in pursuing actual legislative intent is the temptation to pursue it relentlessly, under the misapprehension that if the interpreter looks at enough evidence actual intent will sooner or later become directly knowable. [47] Thus, he is tempted to press beyond the reliable and otherwise appropriate evidences of intent to those that are so unreliable or otherwise inappropriate that, even though relevant, they should be rejected. This is the problem that haunts the scavengers of legislative history. No matter how far he wanders, the searcher always ends with having to infer actual intent from objective writings of varying reliability and accessibility. [48]

46. 3 Co. 7a, 76 E.R. 637 (Ex. 1584). P. Heymann, in Ice Cream at Harvard Square, But No Vehicles in the Park — A Study of Purposes 13, 14 (third-year paper, Harvard Law School, 1960) makes this perceptive observation: "For the context of purposes creates a field of forces in which a very unusual meaning for a word may be clearly 'meant.' 'Empty the baskets' may be clearly meant to include a pile of discarded paper on the floor next to a full waste basket." See also ch. 11, pp. 214-215.

47. E.g., Saxon v. Georgia Assn. of Independent Ins. Agents, Inc., 399 F.2d 1010, 1015 (5th Cir. 1968).

48. ". . . [S]ubjective intention must always be determined by inferences from objective manifestations. . . ." C. Nutting, The Relevance of Legislative Intention Established by Extrinsic Evidence, 20 B.U.L. Rev. 601, 607 (1940).

For purposes of cognition, there is also the problem of constitutionality. The only legally effective way to express the legislative will is to enact a statute,[49] and a court should not subvert this principle by treating as co-equal with the statute statements such as those found in legislative hearings or even committee reports, or by treating as part of proper legislative context materials that fall outside it. At best, the legislative intent that can be reliably inferred from materials falling outside proper context is appropriate only for its confirmatory value. For purposes of judicial creation, on the other hand, examining reliable materials that fall outside proper context may be helpful.

The practical issue, therefore, is not whether to infer subjective intent or not, but how to select and evaluate the available evidence. This is the significant problem of "legislative intent," and it is unfortunate that it has been obscured by misgivings over its "existence." How the selection and evaluation should be made will be considered in chapters 9 and 10.

F. Objective Versus Subjective Interpretation

It is common to classify approaches to interpreting statutes as either "objective" or "subjective."[50] This dichotomy is usually explained in terms of whether the pursuer of meaning is preoccupied with the statute itself (an objective legal writing) or with the actual, and therefore subjective, intent of the legislature. On the other hand, if we look at actions rather than claims, we find that the judicial working distinction is, instead, between disregarding legislative history and taking it into account.[51] That the latter distinction has nothing to do with whether the approach is objective or subjective becomes clear when we realize that the objective writings that comprise legislative history are

49. See ch. 2, pp. 9-10.

50. E.g., A. Ross, On Law and Justice 121-22 (1959); W. Bishin, The Law Finders: An Essay in Statutory Interpretations, 38 So. Cal. L. Rev. 1, 3 (1965); A. Lenhoff, On Interpretative Theories: A Comparative Study in Legislation, 27 Tex. L. Rev. 312, 326 (1949); H. Thornstedt, The Principle of Legality and Teleological Construction of Statutes in Criminal Law, in 4 Scandinavian Studies in Law 1960, at 209, 228-229.

51. "The difference depends on the data that are taken into consideration in the interpretation." A. Ross, On Law and Justice 121-122 (1959).

no closer to actual, subjective states of mind than the objective writings that comprise statutes.[52] Indeed, in relevance and reliability, they may be even farther removed.

The same confusion exists among those who, although forgoing any distinction between "objective" and "subjective," nevertheless identify the search for legislative intent with the examination of legislative history. For example, the California Assembly's special 1962 task group, although called the "Subcommittee on Legislative Intent," concerned itself almost entirely with analyzing legislative history.[53] This preoccupation seemed to imply that an interpreter who is dedicated to discovering legislative intent cannot successfully pursue it without consulting at least some legislative history. Ironically, such an approach means consulting interpretative materials, which, although identified with legislative meaning, are for the most part unreliable, or purposive materials, which, although more reliable, relate only indirectly to intended meaning. Legislative history will be discussed in greater detail in chapter 10.

Apart from constitutional considerations, belief in the existence and significance of legislative intent involves no commitment to examining any specific kind of evidence. It involves only a commitment to ascertaining intent by inference from an examination of appropriate text and context. There is certainly no constitutional obligation to consult inappropriate evidence.

Appropriateness has two aspects. The factual aspect involves fidelity to normal principles of communication, which are presupposed by the constitutional system.[54] The constitutional aspect involves the prescription that only a statute can carry the direct force of legislative law.[55] Other factors are excluded except so far as they qualify as proper context.

Thus, an honest and persistent search for the corporate intent

52. See note 47 *supra.*

53. Final Report of the Subcommittee on Legislative Intent of the Assembly Committee on Rules, 28 Assembly Interim Committee Reports 1961-1963, No. 1, California Legislature. ". . . [I]ntention is a residuary clause intended to gather up whatever other aids there may be to interpretation beside the particular words and the dictionary." O. W. Holmes, letter quoted in F. Frankfurter, Some Reflections on the Reading of Statutes, 47 Colum. L. Rev. 527, 538 (1947). "It is only when the language or ordinance is ambiguous that the courts should search for legislative intent." Ott v. Johnson, — Ind. —, 319 N.E.2d 622, 624 (1974).

54. See ch. 2, pp. 10-11.

55. Id. at 10.

of the legislature is a search for legislative intent only as it has been constitutionally expressed. There is no inconsistency between seeking legislative intent and refusing to look for it in places that are constitutionally off limits.[56]

G. Summary

If this analysis is correct, we may assume (1) that behind every statute and the implications that it generates there is an actual, but not wholly determinable, legislative intent that provides its impetus and significance; (2) that the best working approximation of this actual intent is the intent that it is most plausible to infer from the appropriate objective manifestation of intent, which is, in the case of cognition, the statute as read in its proper context and, in the case of creation, the statute as read in its proper context supplemented by other relevant and reliable extrinsic evidence; (3) that, although there are frequent deviations of manifest intent from actual intent, there is no known way to measure these deviations; (4) that manifest intent, in addition to deviating to an unknowable extent from actual intent, often conveys meaning to the typical reader that transcends to an unknowable extent what the legislature generally intended; and (5) that, despite this, there is no practical alternative to assuming that the manifest intent is the actual intent, until new appropriate evidence is available or the legislature enacts a corrective amendment.

From this analysis, we may also assume that the most important function of the concept of subjective legislative intent is to

56. "The courts have no institutional obligation to enforce the words of committeemen, if the words are not found in the statutory text." W. Bishin, The Law Finders: An Essay in Statutory Interpretation, 38 So. Cal. L. Rev. 1, 16 (1965). ". . . [T]hese policies of clear statement may on occasion operate to defeat the actual, consciously held intention of particular legislators, or of the members of the legislature generally. . . . [I]n other words, they constitute conditions of the effectual exercise of legislative power. But the requirement should be thought of as constitutionally imposed." Hart & Sacks 1412-1413. ". . . [L]egislative intention established by extrinsic aids is irrelevant unless reasonably consistent with the words of the enactment. . . . Certainly it is not true in practice that legislative intention is given effect wherever possible." C. Nutting, The Relevance of Legislative Intention Established by Extrinsic Evidence, 20 B.U.L. Rev. 601, 609, 610 (1940). For the incentives for good drafting that this approach provides, see ch. 12, p. 223 (esp. n. 13).

put the judge or other interpreter in a proper, deferential frame of mind *vis-à-vis* the legislature. Its second most important function is to help the interpreter select and weigh the many elements of statutory language and legislative context by giving him a general criterion of reliability. On the other hand, it is useless for clearing up statutory uncertainties that remain after the appropriate manifestations of intent have been exhausted.

8

Basic Concepts: Legislative Purpose

. . . [T]he "policy" of a statute should be drawn out of its terms, as nourished by their proper environment, and not, like nitrogen, out of the air.
— Frankfurter, J., dissenting, in D.A. Schulte, Inc. v. Gangi, 328 U.S. 108, 121-122 (1946)

A. Relation to Legislative Intent; Terminology

Whereas the concept of "legislative intent" is in disfavor with many legal writers, that of "legislative purpose" enjoys not only favor but preeminence. [1] For most, it is the touchstone of statutory interpretation. It is important, therefore, to distinguish it from legislative intent and examine it in some detail.

In their widest senses the two concepts overlap. Thus, if it may be said that when a legislature took particular action it had a

1. "Though the intention of the legislature is a fiction, the purpose or object of the legislation is very real. . . . Though real, it is not always easily discoverable. . . ." J. Corry, Administrative Law and the Interpretation of Statutes, 1 U. Toronto L.J. 286, 292 (1936). See also J. MacDonald, The Position of Statutory Construction in Present Day Law Practice, 3 Vand. L. Rev. 369, 372 (1950); M. Radin, A Short Way with Statutes, 56 Harv. L. Rev. 388, 398, 400 n. 20; J. Thomas, Statutory Construction When Legislation is Viewed as a Legal Institution, 3 Harv. J. Legis. 191, 201, 204 (1966); J. Witherspoon, Administrative Discretion to Determine Statutory Meaning: "The Middle Road": 1, 40 Tex. L. 751, 789–805 (1962). "Legislative purposes also include those at work in the field to which the statute belongs." Id. at 826. This is an aspect of general legislative context that needs further study.

range of ever-widening purposes, beginning at the inner extreme with the specific purpose of taking that action and ending at the outer extreme with the very general purpose of helping to advance the total public good, the former is coextensive with the legislative intent to effectuate the specific purpose. [2] The important fact is that lawyers tend to identify the immediate legislative purpose with "legislative intent" and to reserve the term "legislative purpose" for any broader or remote ("ulterior") legislative purpose.

Thus, in general legal usage the word "intent" coincides with the particular immediate purpose that the statute is intended to directly express and immediately accomplish, whereas the word "purpose" refers primarily to an ulterior purpose that the legislature intends the statute to accomplish or help to accomplish. Although some ulterior purposes, like the immediate purpose, tend to be fully served by the statute in the sense that compliance with its working provisions will fully carry them out, most ulterior purposes are broad enough that they can be only partly served by such compliance.

Even with these qualifications, the concept of "purpose" presents no wholly new element, because, if revealed to the legislative audience, it is part of the proper context of the statute, which must be considered in ascertaining its meaning. Indeed, as an integrating factor it is often the most important part of that context. How general context affects the meaning of a document will be considered in the next chapter. Here, we will discuss only the extent to which legislative purpose exists, how it is to be determined, and how it is related to the ascertainment of meaning.

The distinction between immediate legislative purpose and ulterior legislative purpose is both valid and useful (only ulterior purpose can be part of context). Although there is some question whether marking that distinction with the words "intent" and "purpose" does not tend to obscure their close affinity, the following analysis will honor semantic convention by using "purpose" for the most part as including only ulterior purpose.

2. See A. Cox, Judge Learned Hand and the Interpretation of Statutes, 60 Harv. L. Rev. 370, 371 (1947); J. Landis, A Note on "Statutory Interpretation," 43 Harv. L. Rev. 886, 888 (1930).

B. The Limitations of Legislative Purpose

The basic problems of legislative purpose are similar to those of legislative intent. Does the legislature have an actual legislative purpose when it enacts a statute? Is that purpose useful in clearing up uncertainties of meaning? If so, how can we reliably find out what it is?

Again, we must distinguish between the subjective and the objective; that is, between the purpose that the legislature (or at least some legislators) actually had in mind and the purpose, if any, that is revealed by the statute and the other evidence that a court may properly consider. Wherever subjectivity poses a problem of ascertaining legislative intent, it poses a problem of ascertaining legislative purpose.

So far as legislative purpose (in the literal sense) coincides with legislative intent, answers have already been given. So far as it consists (in its narrower legal sense) of ulterior purposes, the answer to the question whether subjective legislative purpose exists is that there is often a real consensus among those most closely responsible for the bill on a purpose that the bill is designed to help achieve.

There may even be a congeries of purposes.[3] For example, the legislative intent to lower the minimum age at which men may contract marriage may reflect the purposes of removing a discrepancy between men's majority for marriage purposes in that jurisdiction and their comparable status in another; of removing a discrepancy between men's majority for marriage purposes and their majority for voting purposes; and of removing a discrepancy between the rights of men and those of women. It may also include the broader and more remote purposes of achieving a better balanced social system and of attracting political support for its proponents. There may be other purposes. That these purposes may not comprise a neat and logical hierarchy reflects,

3. E. Patterson, Law in a Scientific Age 26, 52 (1963). See also Hart & Sacks 1414 ("hierarchies or constellations" of purposes); M. Radin, Statutory Interpretation, 43 Harv. L. Rev. 863, 876 (1930); J. Witherspoon, Administrative Discretion to Determine Statutory Meaning: "The Middle Road: I," 40 Tex. L. Rev. 751, 796-800 (1962).

as Lenhoff has suggested, "the compromising nature of the democratic process." [4]

Moreover, legislative purposes may or may not be shared. As between individual legislators, they may even be inconsistent. [5] In such a case, it is hard to say which is "the" legislative purpose.

The reasons for supposing an actual consensus on legislative purpose are sometimes stronger, but usually weaker, than they are on legislative intent. [6] True, it is sometimes easier for a group of persons subjectively to share the same general purpose than it is for them subjectively to share the same intent. But, although this might make the supposition of an actual legislative purpose more palatable to some of the skeptics of subjective legislative intent, there are countervailing considerations.

The disciplines of the legislative process are directed more to attaining agreement on the specific action to be taken in a bill [7] than to attaining agreement on its legislative purposes, even

4. A. Lenhoff, Comments, Cases and Other Materials on Legislation 631 (1949). Note that the purpose of equalizing age requirements is ulterior to, but not broader than, the legislative intent to lower the minimum marriage age for men, whereas the purpose of achieving a better balanced social system is both ulterior to, and broader than, that intent.

5. Sutherland §48.17. "A statute as a statement of purpose is limited in its generality by the actual and possibly conflicting purposes of the legislature. This is not very different from saying that the words of a statute express the legislature's optimum reconciliation in general terms of its positive desires and negative aversions." P. Heymann, Ice Cream at Harvard Square, But No Vehicles in the Park — A Study of Purposes 37 (third-year paper, Harvard Law School 1960). S. Wasby, Legislative Materials as an Aid to Statutory Interpretation, 12 J. Pub. L. 264 (1963).

6. "It is not much easier to learn about the general purposes of legislators than to learn about the specific intentions of legislators." G. MacCallum, Jr., 75 Yale L.J. 754, 780 (1966). Cf. Jones' statement that "the purpose or policy embodied in a statute . . . is more often discoverable than . . . an understanding of legislators as to technical meaning or specific application. A greater number of the members of a legislative body are likely to be aware of, and to put themselves on record as to, the purposes underlying a legislative proposal. . . ." H. Jones, Extrinsic Aids in the Federal Courts, 25 Iowa L. Rev. 737, 761 (1940). However, the important questions are not how many legislators are talking and how much of their talk is about legislative purposes but which ones are closest to the bill and how is their attention focused. This focus is more likely to be on the immediate legislative purpose (meaning) than on a particular ulterior purpose.

7. ". . . [W]henever a law is adopted, all that is really agreed upon is the words." J. Kohler, Judicial Interpretation of Enacted Law, in Science of Legal Method 187, 196 (1921).

when these purposes have been memorialized in the bill itself. Even those who are closest to the bill are likely to focus more sharply on the specific action taken in the bill than on any general statements of purpose. [8] Other legislators, whose knowledge of the bill tends to be general only, are likely to have their own notions of the broader or more remote purposes that it will serve and not so likely, therefore, to adopt the states of mind of others. Indeed, even those who are closely familiar with the specific terms of the bill may agree on the same specific action for a variety of reasons. [9] As a result, there is likely to be less actual agreement on specific ultimate objectives than there is on the action taken in the bill itself. This may explain why most formal statements of purpose in bills or committee reports tend to be innocuous generalities designed to offend the least number of people, a fact that destroys most of their usefulness for resolving specific uncertainties of meaning. As a general result, there are likely to be fewer reliable evidences of legislative purpose than there are to be of legislative intent. Indeed, there may be no discernible legislative purpose at all. As Radin has pointed out, a statute may have no discoverable purpose beyond what the statute itself expressly reveals and immediately effectuates. [10]

This is not to say that actual legislative purpose cannot and does not exist, or that there is no reliable basis for inferring it. Rather, it says that the elements that have made the concept of

8. Cf. W. Bishin, The Law Finders: An Essay in Statutory Interpretation, 38 So. Cal. L. Rev. 1, 21 (1965).

9. P. Heymann, Ice Cream at Harvard Square, But No Vehicles in the Park — A Study of Purposes 13-14 (third-year paper, Harvard Law School 1960). Nashville & K. R. Co. v. Davis, 78 S.W. 1050 (Tenn. 1902), involved the question whether geese were covered by a statute requiring train engineers to take evasive action when an "animal or obstruction" appeared on the track. In view of the doubt that a goose could be either an "animal" or an "obstruction," the purposes of the statute were a critical factor. If its purpose was merely to protect animals or their owners, the question whether the kind of animal in question was an obstruction was irrelevant, but the question whether or not it was a wild animal could be important. If its purpose was merely to protect passengers and employees operating a train or to protect the operators of railroads and their property, the risk that a goose or geese might derail or otherwise damage a train likewise would be important. The court decided the case on the assumption that the statute was directed only to "obstructions." Yet, the question remains: What *were* its purposes and how were they ascertained?

10. M. Radin, A Short Way with Statutes, 56 Harv. L. Rev. 388, 423 (1942).

subjective legislative intent unacceptable to many exist in many cases to an even greater degree for subjective legislative purpose. In the face of these considerations, it is ironic that the amorphous and elusive "legislative intent" has been spurned by many in favor of the even more amorphous and elusive "legislative purpose."

This raises the general question of how subjective legislative purpose is to be determined.

C. Ascertainment of Legislative Purpose

Whether we search for actual legislative purpose or for actual legislative intent, we can infer it only from external materials. Unfortunately, in the ascertainment of legislative purpose, it cannot always be assumed that there is in fact such a purpose or, if there is, that there is reliable evidence of it. For most state legislatures, there is only the statute and the backdrop of proper context. The statute normally includes no preamble or purpose clause, and there is little recorded legislative history. Even where they exist, there is no assurance that either will be relevant.

As with legislative intent, the danger in presuming an actual legislative purpose beyond what is expressly or impliedly revealed is that the interpreter will either attribute to the statute a purpose of his own contriving or search for actual purpose so relentlessly that he goes beyond the limits of the appropriate available evidence. Because the reliable indicia of any purpose are more likely to be found beyond the mere words of the statute, the temptation to scavenge among the materials of legislative history is at least as great as it is for legislative intent.

If this analysis is sound, merely to switch from "intent" in the sense of immediate legislative purpose to "purpose" in the sense of ulterior legislative purpose solves none of the problems that have been supposed to make the concept of legislative intent unworkable and untenable. Instead, the limitations and pitfalls increase. If the concept of subjective legislative intent is inappropriate, that of subjective legislative purpose is *a fortiori* inappropriate. Thus, the use of legislative purpose should be considered as an application, on a broader and less reliable front, of principles that apply with sharper focus, greater intensity, and greater reliability to the kind of immediate legislative purpose that is identified with "legislative intent."

Nor can we avoid the problem of reliable inference by pursuing objective statements or other evidences of purpose in disregard of the likelihood that they reflect actual legislative states of mind. Otherwise, we would have no adequate guide to the relevant and reliable manifestations to which a search for legislative purpose should be limited.

That the subjective aspects of legislative purpose tend to be more diffuse and elusive than those of the immediate purpose voiced by the statute itself is not critical, because in both instances they are inferable from objective evidence. The significant difference is that, however necessary, inferences of actual legislative purpose can in general be drawn with less confidence than those of actual legislative intent.

D. Judicial Bootstrap Pulling

Because the need to draw inferences of legislative purpose is less compelling and because the reliability of such inferences tends to be less, the danger of inventing fictitious and fanciful legislative purposes is correspondingly greater. This does not mean that the concept of a legislative, as distinct from a general social or judicial, purpose must be repudiated. It means only that the objective of discovering a real, nonfictitious legislative purpose must be pursued with greater caution.

In *Johnson v. United States,*[11] the Circuit Court of Appeals for the First Circuit had to decide whether R.S. 860, which provided that "No pleading of a party, nor any discovery or evidence obtained from a party or witness by means of a judicial proceeding . . . shall be given in evidence . . . against him . . . in any criminal proceeding" applied to a schedule in bankruptcy. Although Judge Holmes found that such a schedule fell outside the words of the statute, he found that it came within its purpose, which he said "was to prevent the required steps of the written procedure in court preliminary to trial from being used against the party for whom they were filed."[12]

Where did Holmes find that purpose? The statute included no statement of purpose, and the usual kind of legislative history was either unavailable or not consulted. All he had to go on,

11. 163 F. 30 (1st Cir. 1908).
12. Id. at 32.

beyond the words of the statute, was the general materials of proper context. Most helpful was the Bankruptcy Act, in the light of which the schedule in bankruptcy was seen as generally analogous to a pleading. As with legislative intent, the manifest purpose must be presumed to be the actual purpose.

Because the specific formulation of purpose was Holmes's, how could he be reasonably sure that he was stating a purpose that Congress would recognize as its own? Or was he merely creating a sensible policy, well served by the clear elements of the statute, that he could thereafter use to interpret more broadly what was otherwise narrow language? Although the result was probably sensible and fair, can it be supported as something cognitively discoverable from the statute and its proper context? Or was it in significant aspects a judicial purpose that Holmes himself assigned to the statute? So far as it may have been the latter, the result must be sustained, not as the ascertainment of statutory meaning, but as an act of judicial lawmaking.

As a result, the concept of legislative purpose, despite its frequent usefulness, provides a strong temptation to perform the bootstrap operation of formulating a "legislative purpose" with one eye on the situation to which it is to be applied. While this is an appropriate way to pour the foundation for a judicial rule of law, it is of doubtful propriety and candor when the result is supposedly controlled by the independent purposes of the legislature.

Although Judge Hand has described interpretation as the "proliferation of purpose,"[13] Justice Frankfurter notes that in the hands of "judges intellectually less disciplined than Judge Hand . . . it might justify interpretations by judicial libertines, not merely judicial libertarians."[14] On a later occasion,[15] he added that judicial construction ought "to stick close to what the legislature says and not draw prodigally upon unformulated pur-

13. Quoted in F. Frankfurter, Some Reflections on the Reading of Statutes, 47 Colum. L. Rev. 527, 529 (1947).

14. Id.

15. F. Frankfurter, Foreword, A Symposium on Statutory Construction, 3 Vand. L. Rev. 265, 367 (1950). In an apparent attempt to minimize the pitfalls of seeking actual, subjective legislative purpose, Hart and Sacks use the more objective-sounding expression "purpose which ought to be attributed to a statute" (e.g., Hart & Sacks 1414). Read literally, this suggests that they may

poses or directions." There is reason to believe that Frankfurter's fears have often been realized. [16]

E. Legislative Purpose as an Aid to Interpretation

On the necessity of legislative purpose to legislative interpretation, Llewellyn has said, "If a statute is to make sense, it must be read in the light of some assumed purpose. A statute merely declaring a rule, with no purpose or objective, is nonsense." [17] Hart and Sacks have inquired whether it is not true that *"The meaning of a statute is never plain unless it fits with some intelligible purpose."* [18]

If, as each quoted statement suggests, "purpose" is used in its usual legal sense of ulterior purpose, such statements are simply not true, because, as Radin has pointed out, a statute may have no discoverable purpose. [19] Here the meaning of the statute and its revealed legislative intent are the same thing. Nor are they necessarily obscure. That the court can, on its own initiative, view the evidence of legislative intent in the light of a *judicial* purpose does not imply that the legislature shared that purpose.

---

be supporting the assignment, in some cases, of a legislative purpose that is insupportable on any theory of cognition. If so, the approach might be rationalized as a legitimate aspect of judicial lawmaking if it is used to effectuate the most satisfactory accommodation with the rest of the legal order. However, the fact that the authors use their concept as a tool for "inferring purpose" suggests that they are talking about cognition, not creation. This, of course, presupposes a search for actual purpose.

16. "There is a danger that this emphasis on the purpose of the enactment itself might overshadow the generic purposes of legislation, which is after all designed for communication to the public at large. Thus where the terms of a statute are allowed to deviate repeatedly and significantly from their meaning in common parlance, public trust and confidence in written enactments might be hurt." G. Gottlieb, The Logic of Choice 209 (Harvard S.J.D. dissertation 1961).

17. K. Llewellyn, Remarks on the Theory of Appellate Decision and the Rules or Canons About How Statutes Are to be Construed, 3 Vand. L. Rev. 395, 400 (1950). ". . . [I]s it really ever possible to interpret a word in a statute without knowing the aim of the statute?" L. Fuller, Positivism and Fidelity to Law — A Reply to Professor Hart, 71 Harv. L. Rev. 630, 664 (1958).

18. Hart & Sacks 1157. (Emphasis in original.)

19. See note 10 *supra*.

Nor is the necessity of postulating a legislative purpose implied in the fact that for most statutes it is reasonable to suppose that the legislature in fact had a purpose ulterior to its legislative intent.

If, instead, such statements refer only to the immediate purpose embedded in legislative intent, they dissolve into tautology. A statute whose only discoverable purpose is that fully realized by the statute itself is no more or less intelligible than the revelation of immediate purpose that constitutes its meaning. The statements are therefore true, but only by hypothesis. Their main value is that they imply that all commands, prohibitions, and other legislative communications are purposive acts that should be approached as such, thus putting the court and other readers in a deferential frame of mind.

Llewellyn's statement goes beyond tautology to self-contradition, because no statute is 100 percent gibberish and every statute necessarily implies the minimum purpose of accomplishing what it purports to say. A statute without even the purpose of enacting the legal rule that it prescribes (whatever that may be assumed to be) could hardly be imagined. That what the statute says may lack clarity of meaning and thus clarity of purpose does not necessarily reduce it to "nonsense."

For legislative purpose, Lenhoff's statement seems more satisfactory: "The purpose of a statute is certainly an excellent guide for the discovery of the legislative intent." [20] This asserts, not the necessity of such a purpose, but its utility if it exists.

Immediate purpose, on the other hand, is ordinarily useless for determining legislative intent because, being coextensive with legislative intent, it is merely another way of describing the problem. However, as pointed out in the preceding chapter, [21] there is a sense in which inductively revealed immediate purpose is occasionally helpful, and this is undoubtedly what Llewellyn and Hart and Sacks were driving at. This is the case in which proper context strongly suggests that the actual legislative intent was modestly broader or narrower than what the literal meaning of the statute directly supports.

On this basis, the statements of Llewellyn and of Hart and Sacks might have been more accurate had they read, "Every statute represents an attempt to accomplish an immediate legisla-

20. A. Lenhoff, Comments, Cases and Other Materials on Legislation 630 (1949). And see case cited in n. 9 *supra*.

21. See ch. 7, p. 82.

tive purpose, presumably an intelligible one. This purpose is coextensive with the legislative intent and, so far as it is discoverable from the statute and its proper context, it corresponds also to its legislative meaning."

However, the usefulness of a particular legislative purpose for unlocking legislative intent (and thus legislative meaning) normally exists only when it is truly ulterior, because, with the exception noted, it can illumine only what is not identical with it. [22] Unfortunately, the broader the legislative purpose, the less likely that it will illumine the specific problem raised by the text. The value of an express purpose is that it reduces judicial speculation.

Once legislative purpose has been reliably ascertained, the only remaining problem is to determine the extent to which the language used in the statute can sustain a meaning that not only is coextensive or consistent with that purpose but appears to be the most plausible one under the circumstances.

F. Drafting Policy

This analysis may suggest that good draftsmanship calls for the inclusion of a general purpose clause in every statute. Although this is the practice of some draftsmen, there is usually no need in a very specific statute to include a formal purpose clause. [23] There are, however, exceptional instances in which there are significant pervasive doubts that cannot be resolved in the specific working provisions and in which, therefore, a broad statement of purpose may be helpful to the courts. These are the unusual cases in which the general thrust of even a well-drawn statute may not be apparent on its face. But if the draftsman includes such a clause, he must be careful not to create, by the omission of other legislative purposes, the misleading impression that they were not also relevant.

Because general statements of purpose serve best as antidotes to inadequate draftsmanship, the draftsman who doubts his own draftsmanship would do better to omit any such statement,

22. One aspect of legislative purpose is that it makes relevant the probable effect of the statute. Crawford 286-290.

23. A. Cox, Judge Learned Hand and the Interpretation of Statutes, 60 Harv. L. Rev. 370, 378 (1947). Despite the many adherents of formal purpose clauses, they are rarely helpful. R. Dickerson, Legislative Drafting 107-108 (1954); Professionalizing Legislative Drafting — The Federal Experience 51, 94, 154 (R. Dickerson ed., 1973).

because the deficiencies of draftsmanship that infect the working provisions of the bill are likely also to infect its statement of purpose. Instead, he should let the court draw its own conclusions about legislative purpose from the evidences provided by the working provisions and context of the statute. If, on the other hand, he is sure of his draftsmanship, he is assuming a condition in which a general purpose clause would not normally be needed.

A general legislative purpose clause may, however, be helpful where a very general statute in effect delegates lawmaking power to the courts.

Much more effective for the general run of statutes is the piecemeal approach, under which specific purpose statements are respectively prefixed, as needed, to particular commands, authorizations, or prohibitions ("For the purpose of . . . , the contractor shall. . . .").[24]

G. Discrepancies Between Purpose and Intent

Suppose that manifest legislative purpose is broader than, or conflicts with, manifest legislative intent. Which should presumably prevail? Much modern writing suggests the former. I suggest, instead, that the latter should normally prevail. For one thing, there is little basis in experience for assuming that a legislative purpose has been precisely and comprehensively articulated. Even if it has, a legislative affirmation of purpose does not guarantee that it has in fact been achieved in the working provisions of the statute; the aspiration may remain at least partly unrealized.[25] Its authors may even have recognized and accepted the fact.

24. ". . . [I]f the Bill is done properly, one does not ordinarily need a purpose clause. Let me soften that statement somewhat. The best way to do it in most cases is to fragment your purpose clause and simply say at the beginning of specific sentences, where it is helpful. 'To accomplish so-and-so, the Secretary shall' and so on, or 'For the purposes of such-and-such,' etc. These fragmented statements of specific purpose are preferable, because they are focused on specific uncertainties. For example, you might say, 'To help reduce population growth, we prescribe as follows.' " R. Dickerson, testimony before the Committee on the Preparation of Legislation, United Kingdom, December 12, 1973.

25. ". . . [A] most sensible starting point certainly is from the question 'what did the author mean.' We may perhaps conclude that he did not ac-

A statement of legislative purpose cannot be read as decreeing whatever is necessary to achieve it beyond what can be sustained by the specific working provisions of the statute when read in the context of the legislative purpose.[26] "This is what we are trying ultimately (or generally) to accomplish with the help of this act" is certainly not the same as "This is what we have in fact decreed in this act."

Suppose this statute: "Section 1. The purpose of this act is to protect the public health. Section 2. No person may dump loose garbage in the street." This statute does not apply to the contamination of drinking fountains, even though that kind of contamination frustrates the legislative purpose declared by section 1; the legislature was not trying in this statute to take every step necessary to protect the public health. Indeed, it is the essence of a broader legislative purpose that it will not be wholly fulfilled by the statute in question even if its working provisions are fully complied with.

On the other hand, the statement of broader ulterior purpose in section 1 might help resolve doubts of meaning that would otherwise arise in section 2. For example, section 1 might help the court decide whether the statute applied to refuse whose threat to health had otherwise been neutralized. Thus, it might supply the contextual basis for an implied exception or other limitation. Even here, the purpose clause would not necessarily control, because (1) legislatures often intentionally accept discrepancies between working provisions and ulterior purposes in situations where the precise matching of specific mandates to the general legislative aspirations is not administratively feasible, and (2) the intention to tolerate such discrepancies is not likely to be recited in the purpose clause. A court should not automatically assume, therefore, that a purpose clause precisely and comprehensively records the actual legislative intent of the statute.

Sometimes a specific working provision conflicts squarely with the express statement of a legislative purpose under circumstances in which it can be reliably inferred that the legislature

---

complish what he intended to accomplish." J. MacDonald, The Position of Statutory Construction in Present Day Law Practice, 3 Vand. L. Rev. 369, 372 (1950).

26. "To let general words draw nourishment from their purpose is one thing. To draw on some unexpressed spirit outside the bounds of the normal meaning of words is quite another." Justice Frankfurter in Addison v. Holly Hill Fruit Products, Inc., 322 U.S. 607, 617, 64 S. Ct. 1215, 1221 (1944).

intended such conflicts to be resolved in favor of the specific working provision. For example, in the codification of military laws culminating in the enactment of title 10, Armed Forces, of the United States Code, the codifiers made a clear-cut error in section 1333(3) [27] through a cross-reference that was improperly limited to section 1332(a)(1). So written, section 1333(3) unequivocally excluded, for the purposes of computing the retired pay of nonregular members, service performed after July 1, 1949. In thus changing preexisting law, the section failed to fulfill the legislative aspiration announced in section 49(a) of the act: "In sections 1-48 of this Act, it is the legislative purpose to restate, without substantive change, the law replaced by those sections on the effective date of this Act." [28] The question immediately arose whether section 1333(3) of title 10, which was enacted by section 1 of the act, or section 49(a) of the same act controlled. The question was submitted to the comptroller general.

Under the view, now widely held, that purpose is the touchstone of interpretation, it would be easy to conclude that section 49(a) controlled. Such an interpretation would turn a mere legislative aspiration into a guarantee of success.

Such a result, unfortunately, would be doctrinally unsound and practically catastrophic. The contrary result may be defended on the ground that section 49(a) did not exhaust the immediate general purposes of the act, because it failed to state that the act's central purpose was not only to restate preexisting law accurately but also to enact a statutory codification law that could be relied on, at least where uncertainty of meaning did not arise. Not to preserve the reliability of the clear language used (which included preserving the integrity of the codifiers' clear-cut errors) would have destroyed the effectiveness of the codification act and frustrated its central purpose, which was to establish a code whose clear language could be relied on.

Such an interpretation would have had the same effect as section 2(a) of the Act of June 30, 1926, ch. 712, "An Act to consolidate, codify, and set forth the general and permanent laws of the United States in force December seventh, one thousand nine hundred and twenty-five," the act that established the United States Code. This section provided: [29]

27. 70A Stat. 103.
28. Id. at 640.
29. 44 Stat. (Pt. 1) 1.

> The matter set forth in the Code . . . shall establish prima facie the laws of the United States, general and permanent in their nature, in force on the 7th day of December, 1925; but nothing in this Act shall be construed as repealing or amending any such law, or as enacting as new law any matter contained in the Code. In case of any inconsistency arising through omission or otherwise between the provisions of any section of this Code and the corresponding portion of legislation heretofore enacted effect shall be given for all purposes whatsoever to such enactments.

The practical effect of this provision was to reduce the act to the equivalent of a mere editorial compilation (however official), instead of an effective code. Not even its clearest provisions could be fully relied on.

During the preparation of title 10, one participant even suggested the inclusion of a saving clause that would have said, in effect: "Any substantive error that has been made in this codification is hereby corrected"! This was summarily rejected, because such a provision would have had the same devastating effect as section 2(a) of the 1926 Act.

Did the comptroller general read section 49(a) as overriding the clear mandate of section 1333(3)? Fortunately, he did not.[30]

The lesson is clear. Although specific working provisions, which carry the legislative freight, should always be read in the light of the proper legislative context, including the limitations implied by any manifest general legislative purpose, the latter should not be treated as a definitive, overriding pronouncement.

H. Summary

If this analysis is correct, the following conclusions would seem warranted:

(1) The necessity of assuming some actual subjective purpose includes only the necessity of assuming an immediate purpose exhausted by the statute. This purpose is best identified by the term "legislative intent." Being co-extensive with the problem of intended meaning, this concept normally furnishes, not a solution to, but a more helpful statement of, the problem.

(2) Beyond the immediate legislative purpose that is identified

30. B-130034, 36 Comp. Gen. 498 (1957); JAGA 1956/1908 (2/13/56).

with legislative intent, a legislative purpose, while normal, need not be assumed in every instance; actual consensus is less likely to exist in this area. If a legislative purpose is in fact discoverable from the statute and its proper context, it may or may not be useful in resolving uncertainties of meaning, if any, that would otherwise exist.

(3) Subjective purpose, not being directly knowable, can be ascertained only by inference from the external manifestations of purpose. These include the statute and the elements of proper context. The necessity of relying on inference raises problems of relevance and comparative reliability for which the concept of subjective purpose provides an invaluable guide. However, for purposes of cognition it does not warrant resorting to inappropriate manifestations of purpose or attributing to the statute meaning that the words of the statute taken in their proper context are incapable of bearing.

(4) The manifestations of legislative intent are normally fuller and more reliable than those of any legislative purpose.

(5) The manifestation of a legislative purpose does not imply that the working provisions of the statute were adopted as perfect instruments of that purpose. Therefore, if there is a discrepancy between manifest ulterior purpose and the working provisions, it does not necessarily follow that the working provisions were intended to be read as not containing the discrepancy.

(6) If neither legislative intent nor legislative purpose can be reliably inferred from the statute when read in its proper context, the court may attribute to the statute a purpose that supports the "meaning" that is most consistent with the clear elements of the statute and its related laws. This constitutes an act of judicial lawmaking.

9

Basic Concepts: The Statute and Its Context*

A statute rarely stands alone. Back of Minerva was the brain of Jove, and behind Venus was the spume of the ocean.
— J. Landis, "A Note on Statutory Interpretation," 43 Harv. L. Rev. 886, 891 (1930)

A. Introduction

In the communication of meaning there are two main elements: (1) the vehicle of communication specially created and controlled by its author, and (2) the context within which that vehicle operates. [1] No communication is complete without both. [2]

* This chapter is an edited and expanded version of the author's article Statutory Interpretation: The Uses and Anatomy of Context, 23 Case W. Res. L. Rev. 353 (1972) (used with permission).

1. Although context is constantly referred to, its structure and specific functions are only rarely discussed. The select few include E. Hall, The Silent Language (1959) and B. Shartel, Our Legal System and How It Operates 329-349 (1951).

2. ". . . [P]eople can only communicate among themselves because they share a common culture. . . . Communication never takes place in a social vacuum, but always between individuals who are part of a total social context." E. Nida, Message and Mission 35, 94 (1960). This is universally accepted by language experts. See, e.g., C. Cherry, On Human Communication 10 (2d ed. 1966) and the others cited in this chapter. Most legal authorities would hasten to agree. ". . . [A]ny serious effort on the part of judges to discover the thought or reference behind the language of a statute must be based on a painstaking endeavor to reconstruct the setting or context in which the statutory words were employed." H. Jones, The Plain Meaning Rule and Extrinsic Aids in the Interpretation of Federal Statutes, 25 Wash. U.L.Q. 3 (1939). ". . . [W]e . . . convey meaning by the aggregate of our symbols interpreted in the

The functional difference between vehicle and context is important because in the field of relevant considerations the former is central, the latter peripheral. It is perhaps best described in terms of Polanyi's distinction, made in a different connection, between the area of "focal awareness" and the area of "subsidiary awareness." [3] The simplest example is in the eye itself, where despite no discernible line of demarcation we make a crude distinction between central vision and peripheral vision. Things seen only with the former lose much of their meaning or significance. An analog with a sharper line of distinction would be the engagement ring, a precious stone in a metal setting.

Whether the line between language vehicle and context is easy or hard to draw, the distinction is important, especially for statutes. Apart from the inherent preeminence of the focal over the peripheral, constitutional provisions governing the enactment of statutes imply a vital distinction between what is enacted and what is not. [4]

B. The Statute

The role of the utterance that constitutes the written document to be interpreted is, in its general aspects, reasonably plain. As the primary source for ascertaining legislative intent, it is the key factor in directing, orienting, and organizing the total message, including the relevant elements of context. [5] The first step in interpretation, therefore, is to gather all the documents by which the author has transmitted the particular message. Before we ask, "What does this document mean?" we must ask, "What document are we interpreting?"

---

surroundings of their use." F. Horack, Jr., The Disintegration of Statutory Construction, 24 Ind. L.J. 335, 338 (1949). "Any verbal declaration, oral or written, must be interpreted against the cultural background in which it is made. . . . This background is implied in all uses of language. . . ." B. Shartel, Our Legal System and How It Operates 330 (1951).

3. M. Polanyi, The Study of Man 30 (1959).

4. See ch. 2, pp. 9-10.

5. ". . . [If communication] is to be achieved at all (and the achievement is always imperfect at best) the common words must be chosen and contextualized with discriminating suitability. Much of the context is constructed in the act and by the manner of saying forth; it is not previously given." P. Wheelwright, Metaphor and Reality 170 (1962).

In some instances, it is a part of a statute. In others, it is an entire statute, including its amendments. In still others, it is a group of statutes, or of parts of statutes, that have been found to be *in pari materia.* [6] In any event, they must all be statutory instruments. This includes available, otherwise nonstatutory instruments that have been incorporated by reference.

Where there is more than one document, it may make a difference whether the documents under consideration were intended to complement each other, and thus to constitute an integrated whole, or were uttered independently. In the latter case, the document to be interpreted is the most recent relevant one. The earlier ones are, at best, merely parts of its context.

C. Its Context

1. The Backdrop of Culture

What is the significance of the context in which a message is read? It is highly improbable that any document, considered entirely apart from the culture that it presupposes, can convey meaning, except in another culture that shares some of the same elements. [7] Indeed, to suppose an effective communication entirely apart from its cultural environment would be almost a self-contradiction. Obviously, a verbal communication must be expressed in the language appropriate to the culture in which the communication takes place. The essence of a language is to reflect, express, and perhaps even affect the conceptual matrix of established ideas and values that identifies the culture to which it belongs. [8] For this reason, language has been called a "concep-

6. "Statutes in pari materia [are] those which relate to the same matter or subject. . . . They are to be construed together as if they constituted one act." Crawford 431, 434. See also Sutherland, ch. 51.

7. R. Dickerson, The Fundamentals of Legal Drafting 21 (1965).

8. ". . . [T]he basic premise of the philosophy of language is that there is a strong relation between the form and content of language and the form and content of conceptualization." J. Katz, The Philosophy of Language 4 (1966). "The world of our experiences must be enormously simplified and generalized before it is possible to make a symbolic inventory of all our experiences of things and relations and this inventory is imperative before we can convey ideas. The elements of language, the symbols that ticket off experience, must therefore be associated with whole groups, delimited classes, of experience rather than with the single experiences themselves." E. Sapir, Language 12

tual map of human experience."[9] As with any map, it has little or no significance apart from what it mirrors.

The underlying cultural elements that provide the materials of context include (1) the pervasive network or grid of concepts presupposed by the language of that culture;[10] and (2) the coordinate fund of habits, knowledge, values, and purposes that are shared by the great bulk of the speech community of which both author and audience are members and at least some of which are taken account of in each communication. Together, the factors make up the aggregate of relevant human expectations.

The first of these two aspects of culture gives language its primary referents or meanings.[11] Besides the substance of dictionary meanings, it provides the meanings of those particular word combinations whose incidence has been high enough to

---

(1921). "We cut nature up, organize it into concepts, and ascribe significance as we do, largely because we are parties to an agreement to organize it in this way — an agreement that holds through our speech community and is codified in the patterns of our own language." B. Whorf, Science and Linguistics, in 42 The Technology Review 231 (1940). "Ordinarily, language is the chief evidence for the existence and character of thought. . . . In the category which we have generically referred to as thought, perception must be included, as well as what may be called the *conceptual organization of experience.*" P. Henle, Language, Thought, and Culture 2, 3 (1958). (Emphasis added.) "'Culture' . . . is both a condtion and a product of language." J. Dewey, Logic: The Theory of Inquiry 56 (1938). "The world can be structured in many ways, and the language we learn as children directs the formation of our particular structure. Language is not a cloak following the contours of thought. Languages are molds into which infant minds are poured." R. Brown, Language and Categories, app. in J. Bruner, J. Goodnow, and G. Austin, A Study of Thinking 304 (1956). ". . . [T]he Hopi language and culture conceals a METAPHYSICS. . . . We dissect nature along the lines laid down by our native languages." B. Whorf, Language, Thought, and Reality 58, 213 (1956). The Whorfian hypothesis, that language strongly influences the culture in which it operates, is now undergoing critical review. See S. Hook, Language and Philosophy, part 1 (1969). But, if or however they interact, there is no dispute that a language and its related culture are tightly interlocked. See also S. Ullman, Language and Style 214-215 (1964). On class formation and the philosophical implications of nominalism in this area, see, e.g., E. Cassirer, The Philosophy of Symbolic Forms, in vol. 1, Language, 278-302 (1953); J. Bruner, J. Goodnow, & G. Austin, *supra,* at 1-24; W. Quine, Word and Object, 233-276 (1960).

9. E. Nida, Message and Mission 80 (1960).

10. Id. at 70-71.

11. Id. at 58.

create identifiable habits of response. For the users of the particular language, this response to primary meanings is automatic and immediate, [12] without necessarily being behavioristic in the Pavlovian sense.

The primary or potential meanings of all utterances are inextricably woven into the second cultural aspect — the general fabric of basic knowledge and assumptions, express or tacit, that are shared by the users of the language. These cultural elements condition and color the primary or potential word meanings furnished by the first cultural aspect. [13] This is perhaps the most important function of context in the dynamics of communication.

The following examples will help to identify the two aspects at work. If Congress enacts an income tax statute requiring the taxpayer to compute his tax according to a specified formula, the psychological response habits that give meaning and significance to individual terms such as "compute," or that identify the relevant syntactical elements, are cultural elements of the first kind — the underlying network of concepts. On the other hand, the generally accepted assumption that, when figuring the aggregate cost of merchandise, fractions of a cent occurring in unit costs will ordinarily be carried to enough decimal places that the aggregate cost will be accurate to the nearest dollar exemplifies the second cultural aspect — the fund of commonly shared assumptions and knowledge. As part of the relevant surrounding context, it conditions the specified formula for computing the tax, because, unless a different rule is expressed in the statute, the normal corporate tax accountant will assume that fractions of a

12. C. Cherry, On Human Communication 11-12 (2d ed. 1966).

13. ". . . [T]he 'larger context' — the whole discourse or the whole experience of the speaker or the whole language — cumulatively colors each word as it occurs against one background after another." D. Bolinger, Aspects of Language 229 (1968). ". . . '[M]eaning' will depend upon the listener, upon the speaker, upon their entire experience of the language, upon their knowledge of one another, and upon the whole situation. . . . Words are partly known by their backgrounds, their pasts, like men; and like men they do not have their full significance when standing alone but are known by the company they keep. A word is essentially contained in a context and the full effect of the word is felt only when it appears in context." C. Cherry, On Human Communication 10, 72 (2d ed. 1966). ". . . [C]ontext 'prepares' the correct interpretation of the words by indicating at least the direction or sphere in which the topic is to be sought, and in many cases it indicates the topic much more precisely: we know what the other man is talking about." G. Stern, Meaning and Change of Meaning 144 (1931).

cent are appropriately so handled.[14] Here, the elements of context condition,[15] rather than create, primary meaning.

2. *The General Nature and Workings of Context*

Although the word "context" is sometimes used by lawyers to denote the cultural environment taken in its entirety, it is more properly used either (1) in the narrower sense of surrounding coordinate fund of relevant assumptions that the language vehicle takes into account, or (2) in the still narrower sense of internal syntactical structure. It is in these two senses that the word "context" will be used in this discussion. Environment in its total aspect is simply the cultural fund out of which specific context in each particular case is drawn.

From what has been said, it is not enough that author and audience merely share the document being interpreted. Author communicates to audience only so far as they also share the same general cultural environment and, within that environment, the same relevant habits,[16] knowledge, values, and purposes. (A geological map, for example, has little meaning for the lay motorist.) In the interpretation of the document, it must be assumed that the author has taken this necessary presupposition of communication into account.[17] Actual meaning, therefore, is

14. A more significant, though less obvious, example is found in cases such as Riggs v. Palmer, 115 N.Y. 506, 22 N.E. 188 (1889), where under one approach the interpretative issue is whether a statute that permits beneficiaries to enforce wills according to their terms impliedly excludes those who murder their testators, the implication being based on the tacit general legal assumption that wrongdoers are disqualified from benefiting from their wrongs.

15. "Communication can take place because a speaker encodes a message using the same linguistic rules that his hearer uses to decode it." J. Katz, The Philosophy of Language 102 (1966). "The speaker must know the limits within which he may assume a correspondence of imagery. When the context of the item under discussion is in the physical view of both, or is shared because of similarity of past experiences, or is implicitly present by virtue of a history of former interaction, the problem of context is largely solved. But when the context is neither so provided nor offered by the speaker, the listener is confronted with knotty problems of interpretation." L. Schatzman & A. Strauss, Social Class and Modes of Communication, in Communication and Culture 444-445 (A. Smith ed., 1966).

16. The backbone of language consists not of rules, but of "regularities." P. Ziff, Semantic Analysis 34-36 (1960).

17. "Successful communication involves a good deal of mutual adjustment, for the source must consider the backgrounds of the audience, and vice versa."

relative to particular presuppositions relating to document and context. If we are interested in communication, we must not ask, "What does this particular document, taken by itself, mean?" We must ask, "What does this document mean in its proper context?"

The importance of context in the interpretation of statutes has long been recognized by the courts. The argot of the judiciary is laced with phrases that reflect the effect of context on meaning. The canons *reddendo singula singulis, ejusdem generis,* and *noscitur a sociis,*[18] for example, relate to the meanings of words and phrases in the internal context of a sentence, paragraph, or section. The "whole statute" rule relates to the meaning of particular segments in the context of the rest of the statute. *In pari materia* relates, among other things, to the meaning of particular statutes in the context of other statutes. The rule that permits examination of legislative committee reports relates to the examination of segments in the supposed context of legislative history. The principle that permits a court to take into account what is judicially noticeable relates to the examination of segments in the total relevant social context.

Although the law may affect the factual presuppositions of document and context, it does not affect the basic principles of meaning as they apply to those presuppositions. Rules that determine *what* a court may look at, as distinct from *how* it may look at it, may be rules of law that condition or otherwise set the stage for the later process of interpretation, but they are not themselves rules of interpretation in the sense of rules that reveal meaning. For example, the restrictive plain meaning rule and the English prohibition against resort to legislative history are rules of law that help to define the object of interpretation and select part of the context, but they are not themselves principles of interpretation.

E. Nida, Message and Mission 71-72 (1960). This is the essence of the editorial point of view. But although meaning presupposes that author and audience share the essential elements of communication, it does not determine what is shared, nor does it determine what is to be considered "message" and what is to be considered "context."

18. Black defines these Latin phrases as follows: *reddendo singula singulis* — referring each phrase to its appropriate object; *ejusdem generis* — of the same kind, class, or nature; *noscitur a sociis* — the meaning of a word is or may be known from the accompanying words. Black's Law Dictionary 1442, 608, 1209 (rev. 4th ed. 1968).

It is important to note that some of the rules of interpretation relate to matters of context that are internal to the document as a whole, while others relate to matters of context that are external to it. Matters of context internal to the document — intralanguage matters normally within the control of the draftsman — are custom-tailored to the purposes of the particular communication. Here, according to Black, the "key problem is that of accounting for the *interaction* of *symbols*,"[19] a problem that philosophical grammarians and language theorists have not yet adequately solved. Matters external to the document — for the most part extralanguage matters beyond the draftsman's control — must be accepted as they are, except so far as the draftsman can compensate in the document for their inadequacies.[20] These include the matters that he assumes will be taken for granted by his audience as conditioning the message. In this sense, therefore, external context may be regarded as the part of a communication that has already been delivered.

What does context consist of in a particular case? If we look for the meaning of a statute as a whole, the context consists of related statutes and case law and the coordinate fund of shared habits, knowledge, values, and purposes external to that statute. In general, these are official or unofficial matters of which courts are willing to take judicial notice.[21] That some relate to facts and others to legal and ethical norms is neatly summarized in Jerome Hall's term "factual-normative contexts."[22] If we look for the meaning of a particular word, phrase, sentence, paragraph, or section, the context also includes the relevant factors, outside the item under examination, that are contained in the statute itself. As a general statement, then, we can say that the material of proper context is the totality of relevant factors in the general cultural environment external to the specific language being interpreted that are shared by the users of the language in the particular speech community and taken account of by the particular communication.

Despite the importance of context, however, the document remains central, because it is the main instrumentality that the author relies on to carry his message. Having received his closest

19. M. Black, Language and Philosophy 206 (1949). (Emphasis in original.)
20. See note 5 *supra*.
21. See E. Driedger, The Construction of Statutes 124-127 (1974).
22. J. Hall, The General Principles of Criminal Law 46 (2d ed. 1960).

attention, it is the strongest and most dynamic element among those on which the communication depends. Through it he controls what is relevant context and what is not. Under normal circumstances, nothing else has equal dignity or significance in marking out the content of his communication. At best, context plays a supporting, subordinate role.

Although subordinate, the role of context is highly significant. An utterance taken out of the specific context that it presupposes is at best inadequately oriented and overgeneral. Not only does the context limit the normal sweep of primary (semantical) meaning, but it often also selects among the alternative potentialities of primary meaning. [23] The elements of context that perform the latter function are usually factual assumptions or ethical norms that are either expressly recited in the document or, more usually, judicially noticed. They affect meaning by turning the potentialities of multiple, or alternative, primary meanings into the actualities of a single relevant primary meaning. [24] For example, they may resolve ambiguities ("Close the window," spoken when two windows are open but only one is creating a problem) [25] or the problem of merely selecting the appropriate alternative in a bundle of homonyms ("He means to use illegal means").

The most useful, indeed almost indispensable, function of context is to narrow the range of reference of otherwise overgeneral words. Without it, all but the simplest communications would be intolerably long. Consider Wittgenstein's famous example: [26] "Some one says to me: 'Shew the children a game.' I

23. ". . . [T]he immediate context, by canceling out those *known* meanings of a word that are inappropriate, leaves the one meaning that fits." D. Bollinger, Aspects of Language 229 (1968). (Emphasis in original.) However, "context may serve an extremely subtle function — as with puns, or *double entendre*." C. Cherry, On Human Communication 10 (2d ed. 1966). (Emphasis in original.) "The most important safeguard against homonymic ambiguity is . . . the influence of context." S. Ullman, Language and Style 79 (1964).

24. ". . . [A] word in isolation (i.e., without context) begins with a very wide area of meaning, for it may occur in many hundreds of situations and may be used as a label for scores of objects; but by means of the practical and linguistic contexts in which it is used we can 'whittle it down' to precisely that subarea of meaning which it must have in any specific utterance." E. Nida, Message and Mission 77 (1960).

25. This example comes from Professor H. L. A. Hart (in conversation).

26. L. Wittgenstein, Philosophical Investigations 33 n. (G. Anscombe, transl. 1953). See also the ashtray example in G. MacCallum, Jr., Legislative Intent, 75 Yale L.J. 754, 771-772 (1965).

teach them gaming with dice, and the other says 'I didn't mean that sort of game.'"

Although Wittgenstein was questioning whether the speaker consciously adverted, in his request, to the exclusion of gaming with dice, his example well illustrates our point. The shared expectations likely to exist in such a situation strongly imply the qualification "suitable under our common standards of value to children of their ages, abilities, and temperaments."

The benefits to communication resulting from being able to rely on habits, knowledge, values, and purposes that are already shared by the participants has never been illustrated more vividly than in Lieber's example, from which the reader is invited to pick out the underlying tacit assumptions. [27]

> Suppose a housekeeper says to a domestic: "fetch some soup-meat," accompanying the act with giving some money to the latter; he will be unable to execute the order without interpretation, however easy and, consequently, rapid the performance of the process may be. Common sense and good faith tell the domestic, that the housekeeper's meaning was this: 1. He should go immediately, or as soon as his other occupations are finished; or, if he be directed to do so in the evening, that he should go the next day at the *usual* hour; 2. that the money handed him by the housekeeper is intended to pay for the meat thus ordered, and not as a present to him; 3. that he should buy such meat and of such parts of the animal, as, to his knowledge, has commonly been used in the house he stays at, for making soup; 4. that he buy the best meat he can obtain, for a fair price; 5. that he go to that butcher who usually provides the family, with whom the domestic resides, with meat, or to some convenient stall, and not to any unnecessarily distant place; 6. that he return the rest of the money; 7. that he bring home the meat in good faith, neither adding any thing disagreeable nor injurious; 8. that he fetch the meat for the use of the family and not for himself. Suppose, on the other hand, the housekeeper, afraid of being misunderstood, had mentioned these eight specifications, she would not have obtained her object, if it were to exclude all *possibility* of misunderstanding. For, the various specifications would have required new ones. Where would be the end? We are constrained then, always, to leave a considerable part of our meaning to be found out by interpretation, which, in many cases must necessarily cause greater or less obscurity with regard to the exact meaning, which our words were intended to convey.

27. F. Lieber, Legal and Political Hermeneutics 18 (3d ed. 1880). (Emphasis in original.)

In this example, context could narrow the range of reference only because the specific communications that it conditions were founded on commonly understood purposes. The relevant assumptions that the hearer needed to make were cued by the implied purpose of the speaker's words. Understanding the role played by purpose is indispensable to understanding the interplay between a specific message and its context.

In general, the relevant context is ascertainable only with the criterion of relevance provided by the intent or purpose of the message. The latter, in turn, is discoverable in most cases mainly from the document that is itself the object of inquiry, but only as that document is conditioned by its proper context. In such cases, therefore, we can ascertain the meaning of a document only if we already know what it means! The paradox dissolves, however, when we realize that every communication has some clear elements of primary (semantical) meaning that imply shared elements in the underlying culture and specific context. Together, the clear elements and relevant context tend to show an immediate purpose or a group of purposes that the document is intended to accomplish. This, in turn, is useful in resolving the residual uncertainties.

Some effects that context has on primary (semantical) meaning are automatic. [28] Others are aided by conscious inference or deduction. Because primary meaning tends to merge with meaning attributable to context, it is hard or impossible to differentiate sharply between them in specific instances. [29]

It is arguable, for example, that the meaning of the phrase "parol evidence rule" is for the most part contextual (syntactical), because it transcends the primary meanings of the words "parol," "evidence," and "rule." The meaning of the phrase "interpretation of statutes" also is partly contextual, because the meaning of a phrase or sentence is normally a function not only

28. E. Nida, Message and Mission 63 (1960).

29. "What we now hear on every side is that the boundary between syntax and semantics is not a sharp one; that the interplay of syntactics and semantic features is a general phenomenon in language. . . . The rules constituting the meaning of a word are — up to a point — not different in principle from those establishing its 'syntactic' status." J. Nyiri, No Place For Semantics, in 7 Foundations of Language 56, 58 (1971). The extent, if any, to which these fields interact or overlap need not detain us here. Syntax is, of course, part of the microcontext.

of the primary meanings of its constituent words [30] but also of the syntactical rules by which they are combined.

On the other hand, the phrase "parol evidence rule" differs from the phrase "interpretation of statutes" in that the former has a meaning that cannot be derived from constituent primary meanings and syntactical rules. The whole transcends its parts. [31] It may be preferable, therefore, to say that the meaning of the phrase "parol evidence rule" is for the most part primary and only incidentally contextual. Conceivably, the latter might even be represented by the one word "parolevidencerule" or preferably (but for established usage) by a word whose elements did not suggest an aggregate meaning so significantly different from its actual meaning.

If this analysis is correct, contextual meaning, so far as it depends on the internal structure of a document, is the meaning that is based on the special though systematic ordering of verbal elements that have primary meaning (the smallest of which are called "morphemes"). [32] Primary meaning, on the other hand, is the meaning or potential meaning, other than contextual, that usage attaches to particular words and phrases and that persists even when the language unit is viewed apart from its context. The distinction corresponds generally to that between the implied and the express.

This differentiation does not imply that a phrase such as "interpretation of statutes," unlike the phrase "parol evidence rule," is grasped in three visual acts instead of one. Each of these phrases, having a high degree of recurrence, is normally read as an established unit, just as in the performance of music a recurrent cluster of notes is read as a unit rather than note by note. The important distinction between the two phrases is that a person unfamiliar with the unit but familiar with its constituent elements can construct its meaning in the one case but not in the other.

30. "In general, the meaning of a phrase can be determined by adding up the meanings of the constitutent parts (such phrases may be called endocentric)." E. Nida, Message and Mission 82 (1960).

31. "This type of expression may be called semantically exocentric, for the meaning of the whole is not the sum total of the parts." Id. See also G. Stern, Meaning and Change of Meaning 155 (1931).

32. E. Nida, Message and Mission 63 (1960). A "morpheme" is the smallest meaningful linguistic element, having no smaller meaningful parts; i.e., the letter "s" in the word "pins." Webster's Third New International Dictionary (P. Gove ed., 1961).

Primary meaning is also related to contextual meaning in another, and different, sense. Like all habits, the psychological response habit that constitutes the primary meaning of a particular language element exists only because of its recurrence in a succession of earlier, similar contexts. Thus, the primary meaning of a word or phrase is a continuing echo of a general theme previously heard in many specific and generally similar contexts.

Words in the isolation of a vocabulary list, says Whorf, "derive what meaning they have from the patterned 'potentials of linkage.'"[33] Any assertion that language is meaningless apart from specific context or that "Words . . . 'mean' nothing by themselves . . . ,"[34] so far as it relates to the users of the language, denies Whorf's assertion by falsely implying that language conveys meaning only through (1) current syntactical relationships (context internal to the document), and (2) the specific relationships between the language used and other relevant factors, existing in the given speech community, that are shared by the author and his audience (context external to the document).[35] It is more accurate to say that an utterance taken out of the specific context that it presupposes is at best overgeneral or uncertain.

Although primary meaning, like other habits or conditioned responses, is thus rooted in past recurrences, contextual meaning is meaning that, whether or not recurrent, flows from current configurations of words, collateral facts, and express or tacit collateral assumptions. To say that unique messages can be communicated only by unique combinations of language elements in unique surroundings is not to say, however, that the syntactical strands by which such elements are combined in a specific case are themselves unique. The meaning of a unique utterance is a function not only of established verbal patterns but also of established syntactical patterns, both reflecting the general patterns of surrounding context. Syntactical patterns result in relationships that can be said to carry primary meaning in the same

33. B. Whorf, Language, Thought, and Reality 67 n. 4 (1956).

34. E.g., C. Ogden & I. Richards, The Meaning of Meaning 9 (10th ed. 1956); A. Ross, On Law and Justice 113 (1959); C. Allen, Law in the Making 490 (7th ed. 1964); Sutherland §45.04. And see ch. 6 n. 21.

35. ". . . [A]ll familiar words carry some meaning even when uttered in isolation. . . . [T]heir meaning is potential rather than actual until they are linked to other words." J. Dewey, Logic: The Theory of Inquiry 349 (1938). See also E. Nida, Message and Mission 77 (1960), quoted in note 24 *supra*.

sense and in the same way as particular concrete verbal elements such as nouns and verbs.

In the sentence "Man bites dog," the applicable syntactical rule can be roughly described as one requiring the word denoting the actor to be placed before the word denoting transitive action and the word denoting the person affected by the action to be placed after it. Although syntactical rules are not included in the usual dictionary, they are analogous to the definitions of words or phrases. Together, the primary meanings of words and phrases and the primary meanings of particular syntactical arrangements make it possible to form unique combinations and meanings that draw their uniqueness from those contexts.

3. Sharing the Elements of Context (Availability)

As we have seen, communication is possible only when the response habits and collateral assumptions otherwise necessary to understanding it are shared by the author and his particular audience. Furthermore, in the case of a legal communication such as a statute or regulation, it cannot be officially interpreted or applied unless the underlying response habits and collateral assumptions are shared also by the enforcing or interpreting authority.[36] Author, audience, and monitoring authority must all operate within the language system presupposed by the particular communication. All three must be users of the same language and to this extent members of the same general speech community. This is important in the interpretation of statutes, particularly with respect to (1) statutes whose relevant cultural environment has changed significantly since their enactment, (2) statutes that have been enacted in imitation of statutes in other jurisdictions or otherwise use terms that have already been judicially defined, and (3) the use of legislative history and other extrinsic aids.

Unfortunately, the civilized world is not composed of discrete, mutually exclusive cultures, uncomplicated by subcultures. Rather, it is composed of vaguely defined, sometimes overlapping, and sometimes competing cultures that on closer examination subdivide into at least as vaguely defined, overlapping, and competing subcultures and sub-subcultures. Each of these progressively smaller subcultures is a congeries of partly shared and

36. See notes 2 and 15 *supra*.

partly divergent assumptions and moral attitudes, ending at the microcosmic extreme with the assumptions and attitudes shared by a single author and a single reader or listener.

Specific context, therefore, always relates to a particular audience in a particular culture or subculture identified by a particular speech community. A speech community or relevant language system is usually defined, not by a group of specific people, but by kinds of activities or fields of interests.[37] This is true both of major speech communities and languages identified with radically differing cultures and of secondary speech communities and special languages and technical dialects that exist in highly complicated cultures such as our own. The same person may participate in more than one speech community or be the user of more than one language. For example, a botanist may call a tomato a "fruit" when talking with a colleague but a "vegetable" when talking to his grocer.

For these reasons, the legislative draftsman should carefully appraise the audience or audiences to which his statute is addressed and the speech communities in which those audiences are found.[38] A statute that is addressed primarily to government officials may need to be written differently from one addressed to a part of the business community or to the public at large. As with communications generally, the nature of the author's audience affects not only his choice of language and appropriate sublanguage or technical dialect, but also his estimate of what relevant assumptions he can take for granted as already shared by the particular audience. Understanding this audience is important also for one who presumes to declare what the communication means.

The concept of "legislative audience" and the broader concept of "the users of a language"[39] are complicated by the irregularity with which habits, knowledge, values, and purposes tend to be shared even within the same speech community.[40] The con-

37. On the general concept of speech community, see L. Bloomfield, Language 42-56 (1933).

38. R. Dickerson, The Fundamentals of Legal Drafting 19 (1965).

39. M. Black, Language and Philosophy 29, 49 (1949).

40. This irregularity often goes unnoticed. "We remain unconscious of the prodigious diversity of all the everyday language-games because the clothing of our language makes everything alike." L. Wittgenstein, Philosophical Investigations 224 (G. Anscombe transl. 1953). Some writers, on the other hand, do notice and make allowances for the problem. Recognizing the fact of variant

cepts of "legislative audience" and "users of the language" are further complicated by the fact that some statutes are not normally read or intended to be read by the persons to whom they directly apply. Such statutes become known mainly through instrumentalities such as the bar or the executive branch of the government, or through private editorial services operating with legal advice. Perhaps the best example is the federal income tax laws. Although these laws affect almost everyone, few laymen understand or even become acquainted with their terms from a direct reading. Most tax information is delivered by word of mouth or through official instructions of the Internal Revenue Service, private periodicals or services, or private legal or accounting advice. Because this process is inevitable, such laws need not be couched in a form that makes easy reading for the public at large, nor need their factual presuppositions be made obvious to the public. It is enough that they are understood by the governmental and private lawyers who specialize in the field and on whom the public customarily relies. For the purpose of interpretation, such of the terminology and total relevant environment as is shared by legislature, tax bar, and tax accountants generally can be taken as shared on behalf of the general public.

At this point, it would be easy to be carried away by the desire to be "realistic" and to overemphasize the obvious fact that few members of a legislative audience ever read any of the legislative provisions that directly affect their activities, including those of a nontechnical nature that contemplate no intermediary. It would then be tempting to conclude that all references to "actual" or "true" meaning are as fictitious and baseless as the fictitious assumption that the legislative communication is in fact received in the form in which it was enacted. But we should not forget that the legislative audience is ultimately informed about the statute by the few members or intermediaries who do read it. Moreover, the legislature is concerned only with providing a reasonable opportunity to read the legislative message. If a typical member of the legislative audience chooses not to enjoy this

---

usages and individual aberrations, Black has tried to develop appropriate principles of exclusion leading to a more discriminating, if not wholly scientific, selection of the persons whose usages should be accepted in determining what particular language usages and factual assumptions should be taken in account in interpretation. M. Black, Language and Philosophy 49, 51 (1949). For the foreseeable future, however, courts will have to content themselves with having to operate on a curbstone basis.

opportunity, that is his privilege. But if he does choose to read the statute, he is entitled to read it in a manner normal to the language used and the context in which it has been presented to that audience.

To what extent is a court itself a representative member of the legislative audience, or an intermediary on behalf of that audience? Are not all statutes addressed to the courts as judicial intermediaries and the official arbiters of meaning? If so, it should be enough that in the particular case the relevant habits, knowledge, values, and purposes are shared by the legislature and the court, because this provides means by which the legislative message may be sent in clearer form to the persons to whom the statute is ultimately directed. Such a conclusion would make sense to anyone operating under the view that legislation is meaningless until it passes through a judicial filter. However, Gray's view that the court is the ultimate lawgiver [41] even in the case of statutes is not widely held, and some of its factual assumptions are false. Most statutory provisions are enacted and obeyed with no help from the courts. [42] Legislative draftsmen do not ordinarily address their legislative communications to the courts, nor do they assume that the courts are the normal channel to the legislative audience. Judges may participate in the interpretation of a statute as members of a broader professional group that, it is reasonable to suppose, the legislature took into account in framing the statute. But any special knowledge that the court may have about the circumstances of the legislation, including the reasons for its enactment, is not a part of proper context for the purposes of ascertaining the meaning of the statute, if that knowledge is not shared by the persons to whom the statute is primarily addressed.

Anyone engaged even preliminarily in ascertaining the meaning that a statute will have for the persons to whom it is

41. J. Gray, The Nature and Sources of the Law 171-172 (2d ed. 1929).

42. ". . . [Gray's] view of statutes seems narrow and misleading. First, it overemphasizes the 'trouble case' that leads to litigation. Statutes are law, are used as law by laymen and counsellors and officials . . . in many instances without the aid of judicial interpretation. When the federal income tax law is amended, most men pay their taxes without waiting to see whether, in a test case, the court will hold that John Doe has to pay." E. Patterson, Jurisprudence — Men and Ideas of the Law 199 (1953). ". . . [T]here are many parts of many statutes which have never been the subject of judicial interpretation at all, but which are unquestionably the law of the land." C. Allen, Law in the Making 502 (7th ed. 1964).

ultimately addressed must examine it against the habits, knowledge, values, and purposes that are assumedly shared with the legislature by typical members of that audience or of the intermediaries to which the audience normally looks for enlightenment. For this reason, information that is unavailable to the legislative audience, no matter how relevant and reliable it may be, and even though it may be available to the court, cannot be considered part of the proper context of the statute. To treat it as part of that context would be to subvert an essential presupposition of communication, that of shared environment. This is the problem that haunts the users of at least some elements of legislative history.[43]

Normally, context consists of information and assumptions already shared by the sender and his audience. However, to be part of context it is unnecessary that the audience have the specific material already in mind, so long as another shared assumption can reasonably be expected to lead to it. For example, the sender may use a word of established meaning, knowing that the audience is unfamiliar with the word, because it is reasonable to expect that the audience will or can consult a standard dictionary. Here, one shared assumption (that the recipient will consult an accepted dictionary) functionally incorporates another (the intended, accepted meaning of the word in question). The meaning of the word is a part of particular context, even though the recipient does not yet know what it is.

Similarly, a person may effectively communicate in code with one who cannot read the message directly, if the recipient knows about and has access to the applicable code book and shares the assumption that it will be referred to. Here, too, the meanings of the various symbols are part of the context of the message, because the means of access are shared and it is understood by both parties that those means are to be used. Context, therefore, consists of shared knowledge and the shared bridges to such knowledge.

4. "Taking into Account": The Reliance Factor

Of all the aspects of context, perhaps the most subtle is the fact that it is something that both parties to a successful com-

43. See, e.g., United States v. Public Utilities Commn., 345 U.S. 295, 73 S. Ct. 706 (1953), especially the concurring opinion of Justice Jackson (at 319), also discussed in ch. 10, pp. 148-149.

munication not merely share but subjectively take into account. Thus, relevant assumptions may remain tacit if the author is correct in assuming that he already shares them with his audience and that the express aspects of the message will be read in the light of those assumptions. Thus, communication is invariably a combination of the express and the implied. The system works so long as author and audience share not only the relevant semantic and substantive assumptions but also the habits of association that make it probable that the assumptions will have the same conditioning effect on express meaning for the audience that they have for the author.

In view of the necessary function that this aspect of communication performs, it is remarkable that it is almost never expressly recognized, at least in print. Shartel hit the matter a glancing blow while emphasizing the importance of shared context: ". . . [I]deally we hope that both legislator and interpreter act *in the light of* the same context." [44] Ross was closer to the target when he said: [45]

> The context extends just as far as one may assume that the one utterance was formulated *with another one in mind*. . . . The situation comprises all facts and circumstances which can provide an indication of what the author's intent was. This can include . . . the whole factual, physical and social situation of living *which conditioned the utterance*.

Fuller has reminded us that the parties may take tacit assumptions into account without being fully conscious of doing so; a person is not always aware of what he takes for granted. [46] But the fact in no wise lessens his actual reliance, and this is true at

44. B. Shartel, Our Legal System and How It Operates 330 (1951). (Emphasis added.)

45. A. Ross, On Law and Justice 116 (1959). (Emphasis added.) See also F. Gény, Method of Interpretation and Sources of Private Law 198 (2d ed. 1954, English transl. J. Mayda, 1963); F. de Sloovère, Textual Interpretation of Statutes, 11 N.Y.U.L.Q. Rev. 538, 543 (1934).

46. "The absent-minded professor stepping from his office into the hall as he reads a book 'assumes' that the floor of the hall will be there to receive him. His conduct is conditioned and directed by his assumption, even though the possibility that the floor has been removed does not 'occur' to him, that is, is not present in his conscious mental processes." L. Fuller, Some Fallacies in Theories About Interpretation 5 (mimeo. paper for Legal Philosophy Discussion Group, February 3, 1959).

both ends of the communication process. Being based ultimately on habit, the conditioned responses involved in the communication of meaning are for the most part automatic. That they may also be inadvertent does not weaken their effect or lessen their importance.

The concept of "taking into account" is important because, if valid, many of the elements of legislative history that some courts have been routinely taking into account under the banner of legislative "context" may need to be reevaluated. However, the problems involved in examining legislative history deserve fuller treatment than is appropriate in this chapter. The point to be emphasized here, of which legislative history is merely the most dramatic example, is that the way a particular language vehicle takes into account the appropriate elements of context determines to a large extent the success or failure of the communication. Lack of attention to this factor is the reason why so many legislative communications have failed to convey what the legislature intended or have required judicial interpretation. For example, a statute that relies significantly on collateral assumptions that are unshared, or only imperfectly shared, with the legislative audience is likely to misfire. Similarly, a statute that fails to suggest the affinity between the legislature's language and the shared assumptions that it has relied on to supplement that language may be seen off center by the legislative audience. An editorial point of view is as critical for the manipulation of the external context as it is for the manipulation of the language itself.

What if the reliance factor is missing? If a collateral statement is not taken into account by the written document, it cannot be part of the intended message, no matter how relevant, reliable, and fully shared it may be. Thus, a collateral statement of what a statute means is no part of its context, because, instead of buttressing the statute, it competes with it as an expression of legislative intent. If it has force, it can have it only as an independent legislative statement and only if it has been enacted.

5. *Compromising the Ideal*

How detailed and refined should the examination of contextual materials be? As Cherry has pointed out, "The full effect of a word upon its hearer may depend not only upon the [internal] context but upon the whole physical and psychological environment and, on many occasions, upon his experience of the culture of which the language forms an integral part." [47] This has been dramatically illustrated in the translations of the Bible, which have appeared in more than 200 languages. Here, according to Nida, "the exegetical analysis of any message consists in reconstructing, in so far as possible, all the significance of the communicative event within the totality of the cultural framework." [48] He adds, however, that it is false "to assume that in order to communicate one must reproduce all the circumstances of one culture within some isolated segment of another." [49] It is enough that he "select . . . these features which are culturally relevant. . . ." [50] What is true for the communicator is true also for the interpreter.

For a court, the attempt to reconstruct the author's relevant environment poses an additional problem. Here the aim is not so much to capture every nuance of true meaning as to maintain standards of determinability reliable enough to provide a working basis for resolving particular controversies, predicting their probable outcome, and planning generally for the future. Considerations such as these have forced the courts, and the readers of statutes generally, to be highly selective when looking beyond the document being interpreted, preferably avoiding subtleties that are hard to capture and thus minimizing the risk of great controversy. Fortunately, the reservation is not as great as might appear at first glance. The subsidiary elements in the broader context that may have to be ignored probably contribute more to the emotive aspects of language than to the nonemotive aspects of which legislative pronouncements are almost entirely composed.

The foregoing considerations are important in determining what elements, outside the statute itself, the interpreter may or should look at it in performing the cognitive function. Only by a discriminating evaluation of the materials of context can the interpreter arrive at a pronounced meaning that adequately approximates true meaning.

It is in the area of practical compromise that the cognitive rules for ascertaining legislative meaning tend to merge with the

47. C. Cherry, On Human Communication 75 (2d ed. 1966).
48. E. Nida, Message and Mission 39 (1960).
49. Id. at 58.
50. Id at 59.

creative rules for assigning judicial meaning, thus blurring the vital distinction between them. This blurring usually results when relevant information that should be rejected for the purposes of cognition may later be useful to the creative function of judicial lawmaking in supplementing the statute. By considering a factor that has been denied to the legislative audience, the court in effect supplements or changes the true meaning of the communication as enacted. Whether this is appropriate under the circumstances depends on principles other than those that govern cognition.

Whenever the House of Representatives, the Senate, or the President puts an imprimatur on an otherwise properly processed bill, that imprimatur supports, not the written document taken in isolation, but the document as conditioned by the surrounding context of relevant shared assumptions that it takes account of and that together with it comprise the total communication. On the other hand, a collateral utterance, however relevant and reliable, that is not assumed to be shared by the legislative audience is necessarily excluded. Such an element is not part of what has constitutionally been put before that audience and mere relevance cannot make it such a part. It cannot affect the true meaning of the statute being interpreted because it cannot comply with the standards of proper context. If it is taken into account, it must be handled as an aspect of judicial lawmaking subject to the principles governing that activity.

D. Intermediate Summary

Every communication that is generated by a written instrument consists of two elements that must be considered in arriving at the meaning of the communication: (1) the written vehicle, and (2) its context. Proper context, which thus completes the communication, consists only of the cultural aspects of the speech community concerned that, when considered in relation to the written vehicle, are (1) relevant to the written vehicle, (2) reliably revealed, (3) shared by the author and the legislative audience, and (4) relied on by both author and audience to complete the communication.

Here, the element of reliability (previously mentioned only incidentally) relates, not to the assumptions that comprise proper context, but to the available evidences of those assumptions. Whether a particular assumption related to legislative purpose is valid is unimportant. What is important is that the author's assumption be reliably revealed both to the audience and to the court.

E. Changes in Context: Aging Statutes; Reenactment

Suppose the customary meaning of a statutory word changes after the statute is enacted. Is the word now to be read in the light of current usage or in the light of the original usage? The question extends also to changes in general context.

According to Craies, "The sense must be that which the words used ordinarily bore at the time when the statute was passed." [51] Gény agrees. [52] Craies then refers to the doctrine of *contemporanea expositio,* "that is, seeing how the statutory words were understood at the time they were passed." [53] However, he adds, "*contemporanea expositio* ought rarely, if ever, to be applied to modern Acts." [54]

Does Craies thereby imply that modern acts should be read in the light of current usage and environment, rather than the original? Not at all. In his caveat he is talking only about an evidentiary rule, not the substantive principle of interpretation. Thus, we must distinguish between the normal meanings of the statutory words read as of the date of enactment and the interpretation generally put on the statute as of that time; that is, between true meaning and evidence of true meaning. When in 1873 Blackburn, J., said, [55] respecting the term "fancy bread" in the Bread Act of 1836, that the legislature "meant such bread as at the time the legislature passed this Act, was sold under the denomination of French or fancy bread," [56] he was supporting the view that meaning should be determined as of the date of enactment, without, however, accepting contemporaneous inter-

51. N. Bindra, The Interpretation of Statutes 266 (4th ed. 1965); Craies on Statute Law 79 (7th ed. S. Edgar, 1971); Crawford 258; Maxwell on the Interpretation of Statutes 85 (12th ed. P. Langan, 1969).

52. F. Gény, Method of Interpretation and Sources of Private Law 184-189 (2d ed. 1954, English transl. J. Mayda, 1963).

53. Craies on Statute Law 80 (7th ed. S. Edgar, 1971).

54. Id. at 81.

55. Aerated Bread Co. v. Gregg, [1873] L.R. 8 Q.B. 355.

56. Id. at 358.

pretation of the statute as conclusive evidence of that meaning. Thus, "this opinion was not intended to accept as *contemporanea expositio* a mistaken idea as to what the words meant in 1836." [57] Under the English view, *contemporanea expositio* can be justified as a rule of law only where the statute under consideration is so old that it is impossible or impractical to try to reconstruct the normal meanings of its constituent words as of the date of enactment. Whether the English courts are willing to give at least prima facie weight to such an interpretation in the case of modern acts is not entirely clear.

In the United States, the doctrine of contemporaneous interpretation has, at best, only presumptive weight [58] and thus need not be confined to ancient statutes (of which none exists beyond those inherited from England). Either way, it supports the principle that when the court performs its cognitive function the critical time is the date of enactment, not the present.

The principle that the court should focus on the date of enactment is supported also by the general judicial assumption that the orienting force in statutory interpretation is the search for legislative intent, a concept that, despite its limitations, most courts consider basic to the interpretation of statutes. [59] This means the intent, if any, of the enacting legislature, not that of a later or the current one. In the performance of the courts' cognitive function, legislative intent that does not culminate in an enactment may be generally ignored; so may postenactment changes in the relevant context.

To read statutes against current, rather than original, usage and environment would subject statutory meanings to uncontrolled and often capricious circumstance. Where the vagaries of usage and environment happened to produce results that were more congenial to current notions of public policy, a court would be tempted to take the present as a base. But what should it do where the results were less congenial? Or should the courts say that they will reflect current conditions where they like the result and reject them where they do not?

To take an extreme example, suppose the word "President," through changes in general usage, took on the meaning now carried by the word "Commission." Would such a semantic development change the form of the federal government?

57. Craies on Statute Law 81 (7th ed. S. Edgar, 1971).
58. Crawford 389; Sutherland §49.04.
59. See ch. 7.

The supposition is not entirely fanciful. Section 2 of the Act of July 20, 1942, ch. 508,[60] in authorizing the awarding of the Medal for Merit, referred to the "United Nations." Yet, the United Nations as we now know it did not come into being until 1946. What was the proper way to render this section in a codification statute enacted on August 10, 1956? One way if the interpreter liked the result, and another way if he did not? The codifiers rendered the source phrase as "the United Nations, *as then constituted*,"[61] referring to the date of original enactment (July 20, 1942), specified earlier in the new section. Not to have so qualified the term would have suggested to the reader, on reenactment, an unwarranted change in substance. Therefore, the codifiers read the phrase in its 1942, not 1956, context and translated it accordingly.

But how can law grow fruitfully so as to meet changing social needs if the meaning of every statute remains in the grip of the dead past? Fortunately, there may be more judicial leeway here for wholesome growth than first meets the eye.

For one thing, much of what we consider as comprising a statute is a judicial increment to the original document,[62] a product (not necessarily an improper one) of judicial lawmaking. Thus, we may assume that, consistently with the general principles governing the judicial supplementation of statutes, what the court is authorized to add by way of supplementary specificity it should be authorized to change or remove when circumstances warrant.[63]

The important, narrower question is not what the court may do or undo by judicial lawmaking but what it may do when performing the cognitive function of quarrying meaning from the original enactment as read in its proper context. The problem under discussion arose in *Commonwealth v. Welosky*,[64] in which the Supreme Judicial Court of Massachusetts faced the question whether a statute providing that a "person qualified to vote for representatives to the general court shall be liable to serve as a juror," which was enacted at a time when only men could vote, subjected women to jury duty upon the adoption of

60. 56 Stat. 663.
61. 10 U.S.C. §1122, 70A Stat. 88. (Emphasis added.)
62. Douglass v. County of Pike, 101 U.S. 677, 687 (1879).
63. See ch. 13, pp. 252-255, 261.
64. 276 Mass. 398, 177 N.E. 656 (1931).

the Nineteenth Amendment.[65] The court held that it did not. It said that the term "person" was to be read as of the date of enactment and that as of that time it had to be interpreted as meaning "men" and no more.[66] Accordingly, the statute remained limited to men even though the right to vote had been extended to women. Outraged at this result, Curtis cites *Welosky* as strong reason for rejecting the traditional approach of fidelity to original legislative intent.[67]

The decision seems clearly wrong, but not because it interpreted the juror statute as of the date of enactment rather than the date of the decision. Except for legal entities such as corporations, there was no need to construe "person" narrowly merely because the statute expressly qualified it. Even in that statute "person" meant no less than any natural individual of mature years and it was unnecessary to constrict its meaning further. The key term to be construed was not "person" but "person qualified to vote for representatives to the general court." A noun is not used in a restricted sense merely because it is qualified by an adjective.[68]

The court's second error lay in its failure to take adequate account of the difference between connotations and denotations. The connotations of words define their meanings, whereas their denotations consist merely of specific instances falling within those meanings. Consequently, changes in connotation are changes in meaning, but changes in denotation are not.[69] Freezing the former does not freeze the latter. The court's conclusion was surprising because the court had described very well the generally open-ended nature of denotations.[70]

65. To the United States Constitution (August 26, 1920): "The right of citizens of the United States to vote shall not be denied or abridged by the United States or by any State on account of sex."

66. 276 Mass. at 406, 177 N.E. at 660.

67. C. Curtis, It's Your Law 50-51 (1954). "The real intention of the legislature is that the courts shall interpret these words in the immediate presence of a particular occasion." Id. at 53.

68. The use of a qualifier does not imply a redefinition of the word qualified; otherwise, the provision would be redundant. "Where general words are given a restricted meaning it is their scope rather than their sense that is 'modified.'" E. Driedger, The Construction of Statutes 45 (1974).

69. Sutherland §§49.01-49.02. See also Maxwell on The Interpretation of Statutes 85 (12th ed. P. Langan, 1965). And see ch. 7, pp. 76-77.

70. 276 Mass. at 403, 177 N.E. at 659. And see N. Bindra, The Interpretation of Statutes 264 (4th ed. 1965); Sutherland §49.02.

> Statutes framed in general terms . . . may include conditions as they arise from time to time not even known at the time of enactment, provided they are fairly within the sweep of the meaning of the words and falling within their obvious scope and purpose.

The court found it "unthinkable" that the legislature "had any design that it should ever include women within its own scope" [71] and, in apparent disregard of its own observation, just quoted, concluded that the door was closed to new members of the statutory class. Was this merely because it did not have women in mind at the time of enactment? If so, a 1925 statute dealing with "news media" could not apply to television, and a 1930 statute dealing with "motor cars" could not apply to Volkswagens. Indeed, there would never be an occasion in which the quoted principle could be applied.

And how could the court find a legislative purpose to exclude women when the sole thrust of the statutory purpose was apparently to equate the conditions of the jury duty with the qualifications for voting? The court could have reached the opposite result without injecting the notion that statutes are to be read as of the date of enactment. If, on the other hand, the statute had referred to "15 good and lawful men," the interpretative problem would have been significantly different.

The confusion that plagued the Massachusetts court and such case-hardened lawyers as Gray and Radin resulted from an attitude that "conceives the mind to be directed toward individual things, rather than toward general ideas. . . ." [72] Once this fallacy is punctured, there is little cause to be outraged by the notion that the sweep of a statute's generalities is frozen as of the date of enactment. Thus, it is possible to honor the original expressed legislative intent and still, within the ranges of generality and vagueness circumscribed by that intent, allow for the play of judicial creativity in adapting the legislative plan to current needs. If this fails to produce an adequate result, the responsibility for correcting the matter is the legislature's, not the court's.

What has been said about changes in the meanings of words would seem to apply equally to changes in the tacit assumptions that comprise much of general context.

71. 276 Mass. at 407, 177 N.E. at 661.

72. L. Fuller, The Morality of Law 84 (1964). This is the "pointer" theory of meaning, discussed in ch. 7, pp. 76-77.

A practical difficulty remains: How does a court determine the connotations of a word, which mark the parameters of the concept designated by it? One solution, and apparently the one used in *Welosky,* is to combine all the characteristics that were shared by the things to which the word was customarily used to refer at the time the statute was enacted. Thus, in defining "automobile" for the purpose of a 1910 statute, we might say that it connoted at least a four-wheel passenger vehicle operating on a street or highway and propelled by a self-contained power device. Let us suppose also that all such vehicles in operation in 1910 had the additional characteristic of being black. Would blackness be one of the connotations of the term "automobile," with the result that in 1956 it would include black Edsels (a brand unknown in 1910) but exclude yellow Buicks? The answer seems clear: We should exclude commonly shared elements that had no functional relationship to the purposes that the concept served at the time of enactment.[73] Thus, blackness should be omitted as a component of the concept of automobile. Similarly, maleness seems to have been an irrelevant characteristic of the abstract concept of a "person qualified to vote." At least, it was no part of the legislative purpose to tie the matter of jury duty to the minutiae of election requirements that happened to be in effect on the date of enactment.

To the Curtises who believe that it is more wholesome to meet the needs of the future than to honor the dead past,[74] we may reply that, because legislation is almost always pointed to the future, intended future results cannot be assured unless the historical event that an enactment immediately becomes is later honored by the courts. This means honoring the legislative past. To do otherwise would substitute the courts for the legislature in the lawmaking process.

Suppose a statute whose context had changed after enactment was reenacted without any change in wording or as part of a statutory codification. Should its meaning be determined as of the date of original enactment or that of reenactment? There is a strong factual presumption in such cases that by retaining the original wording the reenacting legislature intended to retain the

73. See discussion of distinction between "essence" and "accident" in G. Williams, Language and the Law — II, 61 L.Q. Rev. 384, 396 (1945), respecting changes in the meaning of "cordial." See also E. Patterson, Jurisprudence: Men and Ideas of Law 289 (1953).

74. C. Curtis, It's Your Law 54 (1954).

substantive status quo,[75] even though as an original enactment the statute would have been interpreted differently. This result makes good functional sense and it can be supported on the ground that, although the later legislature called the substantive shots, it called them in the outworn language of the earlier one. Although this is undesirable codification practice, the substantive status quo was effectively preserved, because the relationship between the new statute and the old is a persuasive element in the context of the new statute and should, however inartistically, put the reader on reasonable notice.

On the other hand, where the later statute includes enough substantive revision to suggest the probability that the legislature had made a fresh start even with respect to the provision being interpreted, the opposite result seems appropriate.

In the performance of the court's creative function, the principle discussed here is relevant only so far as that function is conditioned by the statutory framework as revealed by examining the circumstances existing on the date of enactment. So far as there is residual leeway, the court is free to exercise its own judgment.

F. Geographical Differences in Context: Borrowed Statutes

Context may vary geographically as well as temporally. The fact may be important in cases in which the text of the statute being interpreted is based on a statute of another jurisdiction. This may come about in several ways.

The simplest situation is that in which the local jurisdiction inherited its statutes from another and broader jurisdiction of which it was once a part, the inheritance being accomplished by statute. In *Cathcart v. Robinson,*[76] Congress had indirectly adopted by reference the English statutes that before the break with England had already directly applied to the colonies. Specifically, when the District of Columbia was established, the law of Virginia was continued for the part of the original District of

75. Crawford 439. Whether reenactment enhances the evidentiary weight of contemporaneous interpretation or of intervening judicial or administrative interpretation is a different question. Id. at 438; Sutherland §49.09.

76. 30 U.S. (5 Pet.) 263 (1831).

Columbia that was carved out of that state,[77] most of whose legal system had been inherited from England. Did the resulting adoption of the statute, 27 Elizabeth, carry with it the judicial interpretations put on it by the English courts? The court held that it carried the interpretations made before adoption, but not those made after.[78]

In this instance, holding that adoption of the statute carried with it the relevant case law seems circuitous, because the congressional adoption apparently extended directly to case law as well, making it unnecessary to consider whether it came in piggyback.

Suppose, rather, a direct adoption-by-reference that referred only to statutes, a situation not likely to arise where a foreign jurisdiction is involved. The interpretative question in such a case would be whether under the circumstances the statute impliedly included the relevant case law. If so, the problem would be the same as that in *Cathcart*. If not, the question would be the same as that assumed by the court to be raised in that case: that the English interpretations came in, not by direct reference, but as an incident of adopting the underlying statute. Assuming in such a case that the legal meaning has not been expressly or impliedly adopted directly, what basis would there be for the piggyback approach? The court's rationale was not clear.

That borrowing a statute includes borrowing its true meaning may normally be taken for granted. But the official meaning declared by the foreign courts is not necessarily its true meaning. If the inclusion of the foreign interpretation thus depends on its validity, the court must independently interpret the statute in question. Once this is done, the foreign interpretation becomes superfluous, because the court already has its answer.

The problem may be seen more clearly with respect to a more frequent method of adoption. In the cases already considered, the statute of the adopting jurisdiction said, in effect, "Whatever the law is in the named jurisdiction the same rules apply in this jurisdiction." In the cases now to be considered, the adopting statute simply repeats the language of the corresponding statute of the foreign jurisdiction. The reason for such borrowing is

77. Organic Act of 1801 (District of Columbia), §1: "That the laws of the state of Virginia as they now exist, shall be and continue in force in that part of the District of Columbia, which was ceded by the state to the United States, and by them accepted for the permanent seat of government. . . ."

78. 30 U.S. (5 Pet.) at 279 (1831).

clear: In spelling out specific provisions, legislatures, like judges, prefer to work from precedent, thus creating a sort of "common law of legislation." [79]

Here, again, the question arises: When a state adopts the language of a foreign statute, which it repeats in the local statute, does the adopted language carry its foreign meaning? Again, we must distinguish official meaning from true meaning, taking into account the possibility that they may not be the same even if the foreign courts have confined themselves solely to, and adequately performed, their cognitive function. The problem is further complicated by the likelihood that the foreign courts may have also performed their creative function of engrafting appropriate additional meaning on the original enactment. Would the express or implied inclusion of the true meaning of the borrowed words also include judicial supplementation that, by hypothesis, lies beyond that meaning?

In such instances, the possibility of express direct incorporation of relevant case law is precluded by the absence of referential language. The possibility of implied direct incorporation, while not inevitably excluded, is factually slim. Accordingly, it seems realistic to discuss the problem, not in terms of direct legislative adoption, but in terms of whether the adopted text carries with it the relevant foreign interpretation.

Although it is a commonly announced "rule" that legislative adoption of the language of a foreign statute includes foreign interpretations [80] (at least to the date of adoption), such a rule cannot survive close inspection.

First, even express incorporation by reference of foreign case law is normally not intended to freeze the substance of the foreign case law but simply to give it the same status locally that it had in the foreign jurisdiction. (The better view is that judicial interpretations of statutes are subject to later judicial correction or withdrawal.) [81]

Second, even under the so-called "rule" the local court need not adopt a foreign interpretation that conflicts with local public policy. [82] (This reservation would presumably not apply where

79. See F. Horack, Jr., The Common Law of Legislation, 23 Iowa L. Rev. 41 (1937).

80. Crawford 440. See also Sutherland §52.02.

81. Girouard v. United States, 328 U.S. 61, 66 S. Ct. 826 (1946); Sutherland §49.05.

82. Crawford 442; Sutherland §52.02.

the foreign case law had been directly incorporated by reference, thus establishing new local policy.)

Third, there is no reason to subject the courts of the local state to the holdings of the highest court of the foreign jurisdiction, where the local court believes that the foreign court misinterpreted its own statute. [83]

Fourth, and most significant in the present context, the meanings of the specific language used, or the surrounding contexts, may differ between the local jurisdiction and the foreign jurisdiction. [84] In such a case, should the court read the local statute against the meanings and relevant tacit assumptions prevailing in the local jurisdiction or against those prevailing in the foreign jurisdiction from which the language was adopted?

If the court reads the statute against local usages and environment, which provide the normal basis for reading statutes and the constitutional basis for writing them, it may violate the intent of the legislature in cases where the legislature intended that the statute have the same effect locally that it had in the foreign jurisdiction. On the other hand, if the court reads the statute against the usages and environment of the foreign jurisdiction, it may violate the intent of the legislature in cases where the legislature, unaware of the geographical differences, intended the substantive result obtained by reading the language in the local context. Even if the legislature intended otherwise, it has expressed its intent in what is, to the extent of the difference, a language that is not only foreign but, because it masquerades as the local one, misleadingly so. In such cases, because the legislature had full opportunity to express the substance of statutes adopted from foreign jurisdictions in the language of its local legislative audience, it can hardly complain if the local courts interpret its utterances in accordance with the implied constitutional assumption that statutes have been written in a language familiar or otherwise accessible to those whose lives it is intended to affect. [85]

The problem of playing fair with the legislative audience is critical, because in the situation supposed there is no referential language in the statute to warn the reader either of the specific adoption or of the general fact of adoption. Accordingly, the court should not adopt an interpretation based on a foreign

83. Crawford 443; Sutherland §52.02.
84. See Craies on Statute Law 82 (7th ed. S. Edgar, 1971).
85. Ch. 2, pp. 10-11.

decision that differs from the most plausible local reading of the statute made without regard to the adoption. This reduces the net effect of the "rule" or "presumption" to a mere confirmatory one.

On the other hand, if the foreign statute has been incorporated by express reference, there is no such problem, because the statute itself provides the necessary warning and semantic bridge. At worst, there is the inconvenience of searching foreign usage and context and making the necessary translation or adjustment.

Like meanings, surrounding context may differ between jurisdictions. In *Melby v. Anderson,*[86] it made sense for the South Dakota Supreme Court to follow the Michigan Supreme Court's interpretation of the Michigan guest statute (from which the language of the South Dakota statute was borrowed), that "gross negligence" meant "wilful and wanton misconduct," because in neither state had degrees of inadvertent misconduct been recognized. On the other hand, had South Dakota otherwise recognized such degrees, the reasons for following the Michigan decision would have been much weaker, despite the identity of statutory texts.

This is another instance in which sound results depend on so many considerations that generalizations, let alone "rules" or even "presumptions," are highly unreliable. About the only useful, accurate statement that can be made here is that in cases of uncertainty the local court may find it suggestive or otherwise helpful to examine the decisions of the state from which the statutory language was adopted.[87] On this basis, the examination need not be limited to decisions predating adoption. However, decisions made after adoption should not have the weight of *stare decisis.*

Even here there may be difficulties. Suppose that at the time of enactment the text of the new law was already in effect in several or more states. Suppose, further, that the courts of the respective states have differed in their interpretations. Under the "rule" or "presumption" approach, how should the court determine which state to look at? Under the preferred looser approach recommended, the problem disappears, because the court is free to find guidance wherever it can.

86. 64 S.D. 249, 266 N.W. 135 (1936).
87. See Crawford 444.

The discussion so far has related to courts in the performance of their cognitive function of extracting meaning from the statutory text and its proper context. If it becomes appropriate to assign meaning in the performance of its creative function, the court's problems are to assign the meaning that fits most comfortably with the ascertained meaning of the statute and to avoid unfair surprise. In resolving an evenly poised uncertainty it seems appropriate, in the absence of more persuasive considerations, for the court to serve the general interest in uniformity by emulating the decisions of other courts that are addressed to the same statutory text. This is especially true of a uniform state statute developed by the National Conference of Commissioners on Uniform State Laws [88] and of a federal statute the text of which has been adopted by the state.

88. Id. at 445; Sutherland §52.05.

10

The Uses and Abuses of Legislative History

An explanatory tale should not wag a statutory dog.
— Jones, C.J., in A. P. Green Export Co. v. United States, 284 F. 2d 383, 386 (Ct. Cl. 1960)

A. Introduction

A resource often relied on in interpreting and applying statutes is "legislative history." Legislative history, in its broadest sense, includes all relevant events occurring before final enactment. [1] In its narrower, more usual, and legally most controversial sense, it refers to the relevant events comprising the enactment process. [2] Only the latter will be considered in this chapter.

Why do American judges (and therefore lawyers) consult legislative history so avidly?

One reason is the belief that it improves their access to actual legislative intent. Supporting this belief is the assumption that the authors of statutes somehow communicate more successfully outside statutes than inside them. Another reason is that many courts feel a higher fidelity to legislative intent than they do to the official, constitutional vehicles for expressing that intent.

For courts with greater sensitivity to constitutional require-

1. On history preceding the enactment process, see generally Sutherland §48.03.

2. On history during the enactment process, see generally G. Folsom, Legislative History: Research for the Interpretation of Laws (1972); Sutherland §§49.04-49.05.

ments,[3] an alternative and more appealing reason is that legislative history is part of proper context; consulting it does not involve bypassing the statute. All these reasons are psychologically fortified by the fact that it is easier, and more traditional, to read about a statute than to read the statute itself.[4]

B. Is Legislative History Part of Context?

1. In General

As one of the few writers, legal or otherwise, to have undertaken to analyze the elements of context, Shartel recognizes, in addition to the two factors of general context and legal context,[5]

> . . . a third contextual factor, the history and circumstances of the specific provision's enactment. This context . . . includes . . . the legislative history of the passage of the provision, embracing all changes in its wording from introduction to final approval; the report of the legislative committee or official agency or outside group, which prepared the draft of the provision for submission to the legislative body; the report of a committee to which the draft was referred for examination and recommendation; and statements of persons charged with steering the provision in question through the legislative processes, made during its consideration and enactment.

This excerpt summarizes the view now prevailing among liberal American jurisprudes: Context, which is part of the legislative message, includes legislative history[6] as identified with what happened in the course of enacting the particular statute.

3. See ch. 2.

4. Is there a more sinister factor at work here? ". . . [T]he lazy judge is likely to take the legislative history as an excuse for foregoing the difficult problems of statutory analysis which it is his responsibility to meet." W. Bishin, The Law Finders: An Essay in Statutory Interpretation, 38 So. Cal. L. Rev. 1, 17 (1965).

5. B. Shartel, Our Legal System and How It Operates 344 (1951).

6. E.g., Tidewater Oil Co. v. United States, 409 U.S. 151, 157, 93 Sup. Ct. 408, 413 (1972); H. Jones, The Plain Meaning Rule and Extrinsic Aids in the Interpretation of Federal Statutes, 25 Wash. U.L.Q. 2, 4 (1939).

If legislative history is part of context, a court is not merely permitted to take it into account but constitutionally obliged to do so. To do less would be to ignore an integral part of the legislative message, which under any acceptable modern theory of communication includes context.[7] But Shartel adds a note of caution:[8]

> There are practical differences between the significance of general context and legal context on the one hand, and specific conditions and origins on the other. Courts have recognized and acted on these differences in the processes of interpreting statutes; the courts have appreciated that general conditions, cultural or legal, can be taken to be commonly known, while specific historical materials cannot be supposed to be open to everyone who must act on the basis of the legislation.
>
> For the reason just stated, not all courts have been ready to resort to these "extrinsic aids" to interpretation. The English courts have, generally speaking, refused to consider them at all. The federal courts in this country make full use of these extrinsic aids. The state courts do not reject them outright, but have made much less use of them than the federal courts have done.

Many courts look at legislative history to resolve an otherwise unresolvable ambiguity (an act of judicial lawmaking), but not to determine whether such an ambiguity exists (an act of cognition), thus impliedly supporting the rarely articulated distinction between cognition and creation. Some courts observe the distinction intuitively. Either way, it emphasizes that the statutory text is normally to be read, at least initially, without benefit of legislative history. The implication that legislative history is not ipso facto part of context is supported also by the widespread tendency to use legislative history selectively by categories and not simply by sifting the relevant and reliable from the irrelevant and unreliable.

If at least some of the materials of legislative history qualify as legitimate aspects of external context, it is useful to ask whether standards exist for determining to what extent the heterogeneous materials of legislative history may be considered part of a statute's context and to ask, further, whether, if excluded from context, such materials may be appropriately used for any other purpose.

7. See ch. 9.

8. B. Shartel, Our Legal System and How It Operates 344-345 (1951).

If such standards exist, what are they? Henry M. Hart, Jr., has suggested at least three: relevance, competence, and probative value. [9] On "relevance," he says that "all aspects of the internal legislative history of a statute which were officially before the legislature at the time of its enactment are part of its context" and "may be directly relevant in determining the meaning which ought to be attributed to the statute." [10]

Aspects not officially before the legislature, says Hart: ". . . are not directly relevant in determining the meaning which ought to be attributed to it. They are relevant, if at all, only in determining the meaning which the words of the statute are linguistically capable of bearing." [11] But why with respect to relevance and to qualifying as "context" it should make any difference whether the given aspect was or was not officially before the legislature is not immediately clear. Nor is it clear whether his references to "meaning which ought to be attributed" and "meaning which the words are linguistically capable of bearing" apply to the cognitive process of ascertaining meaning, the creative process of assigning meaning, or both.

It would seem preferable to say simply that the courts should give no weight to elements of legislative history for any purpose, including the creative process, unless they are relevant under the usual standards of relevance.

As to what may be included as part of context, the main question is whether an element of legislative history is part of the legislative context of the statute and as such should be taken into consideration, if it is relevant, in ascertaining legislative meaning. An answer to this question will be developed in the course of the following discussion.

On "competence," Hart says: [12]

> All aspects of the internal legislative history of a statute which were officially before the legislature at the time of its enactment are competent to be considered in determining the meaning which *ought to be attributed to it,* unless such consideration would operate unfairly as to any class of persons by increasing as to them the burden of the statute in a way of which they were not reasonably put on notice. . . .

9. F. Newman & S. Surrey, Legislation — Cases and Materials 669-671 (1955).

10. Id. at 670.

11. Id.

12. Id. (Emphasis added.)

The tenor of this statement suggests that it is addressed primarily to the assignment, rather than the ascertainment, of meaning, because the only kind of meaning that could increase the burden of the statute, whether fairly or unfairly, would be one that was added judicially after enactment. The statement also carries a negative implication for the cognitive function of ascertaining meaning, because the capacity of an element of context to surprise suggests strongly that it is no part of the meaning of the statute as enacted. Again, the relevance of the question whether the aspect was officially before the legislature is not immediately apparent, except so far as matters officially before the legislature are more likely to gain the notoriety necessary to bring them to the attention of the legislative audience.

On "probative value," Hart says in substance that the court should not approach legislative history with a blank mind, but only after it has formulated specific questions based on an examination of the statute and the other relevant aspects of context.[13] By so deferring examination of the legislative history (an approach reminiscent of the plain meaning rule), Hart downgrades it to a position subordinate not only to the statute but to the other aspects of legislative context. This, too, suggests that legislative history is no part of context; if it were, it would be entitled to immediate weight.

Another reason for downgrading legislative history is that much of it is unreliable in the specifics of application. Conversely, its reliability increases with the "generality of its bearing upon the purpose of the statute."[14] He adds: "Evidence in the internal legislative history of a statute concerning a specific application envisaged by individual legislators should be given weight only to the extent that the application envisaged fits rationally with other indicia of general purpose."[15]

Because our immediate preoccupation is not the full sweep of judicial action with respect to statutes but only the ascertainment of discoverable meaning (the cognitive function), it seems preferable for this limited purpose to substitute for Hart's three tests the four tests of context developed in the preceding chapter: relevance, evidentiary reliability, availability, and the

13. Id.
14. Id.
15. Id. at 670-671.

extent to which the matter was taken into account. The first of these needs no special consideration here. The other three pose these respective questions: When is an element of the legislative history of a statute reliable enough that the court or other interpreter is justified in accepting it as a factor bearing on the true meaning of the statute? When is such an element sufficiently available to the legislative audience that it can be assumed to be shared with that audience by the legislature? Has it been taken into account in the writing and reading of the statute?

Together with the question of relevance, these three questions relate to the general capacity of the element to affect true meaning. But can legislative history, or any element of it, meet these standards? That it is undoubtedly part of the total legislative milieu does not necessarily qualify it.

Let us discuss these tests of context in inverse order.

2. *Taking Into Account*

The typical element of context is a related collateral assumption, coordinate to the document being interpreted, that the author has taken into account. A topical joke, for example, presumes a common knowledge of relevant current affairs. In the case of a statute, the most important of these collateral assumptions relate to its (ulterior) purposes. Strömholm calls documents that reveal legislative purpose "motivating texts." [16]

Collateral assumptions are, by hypothesis, not expressed on the face of the document and are often not expressed elsewhere. They are independent of the document and its specific history. Usually they were shared by the author and his audience even before the document was prepared. They tend to be relatively permanent or stable. Consciously or unconsciously, they are taken into account in the preparation of the document.

Contrast with "motivating" materials an assertion in a conference or committee report that language used in a statute is intended to have a specified meaning, a meaning that may diverge from its ordinary meaning. Strömholm calls such explanatory documents "expounding texts." [17] Together with similar explan-

16. S. Strömholm, Legislative Material and Construction of Statutes — Notes on the Continental Approach, in 10 Scandinavian Studies in Law 1966, at 173, 187.
17. Id.

atory materials from debates or hearings, they will be referred to in this book as "interpretative materials."

A material divergence from ordinary meaning was involved in *Commissioner v. Acker,* [18] where the conference report stated as the intended result a rule different from that apparently announced by the statute itself. Was the statement in the conference report part of the proper legislative context of the statute? If the report had accompanied the statute, we might be tempted to say simply that the two comprised the document being interpreted, that they contradicted each other, and that the problem was to determine, if possible, which was intended to prevail. Each being part of the total vehicle for conveying what was presumably intended as a single coherent legislative message, there would be no occasion to treat either as part of the external legislative context of the other.

Because even a conference report may not properly be treated as part of the enacted message itself, may such a document be smuggled into the hands of the legislative audience as an element of "proper context"? If it is context, it is context in a sense different from that in which the term is generally understood with respect to the cognitive aspects of communication.

The temptation to smuggle is strong, because a conscientious court normally respects the expressed will of the legislature and because what is expressly and clearly stated in a committee or conference report is among the most reliable collateral expressions of that will. But are reliability, relevance, and availability, by themselves, enough?

To sharpen the issue, take an even stronger case. Suppose that, when the statute involved in *Acker* was enacted, Congress had included the statement from the committee report in a concurrent resolution (a legislative action not joined in by the President). Here, we have an expression of legislative will almost as reliable and certainly as available, as the statute itself. Suppose, further, that the legislative history of the statute made clear that the actual will of Congress was the same as that expressed in the concurrent resolution and that the statute inadvertently misstated it.

Even here, a strong constitutional inhibition would deprive the collateral utterance of direct legislative force. Lacking the Presi-

18. 361 U.S. 87, 80 S. Ct. 144 (1959).

dent's signature, it could not be a legislative message with the force of law. For constitutional reasons, the ascertainment of legislative meaning necessarily focuses on the enacted statute and not on an unenacted expression of legislative will, however reliable. An unenacted utterance has force, if at all, only as part of the proper context of the statute. May it be treated as such for the purpose of ascertaining the true meaning of the statute as enacted?

The law can tell us what to interpret, but it cannot tell us what the enacted form of what we are interpreting actually means to a typical member of the legislative audience. Accordingly, it cannot extend for us the limitations of proper context. If it wishes, a court may often get away with disregarding a statute or amending it, but it cannot affect its true meaning as enacted. This is because the problem is one not of law but of principles of meaning that operate independently of the law.

The resolution or report under consideration would plainly be relevant. It would also be comparatively reliable, except that wanting the approval of the President and unless passed contemporaneously with the statute it would tend to be less reliable than the statute itself (the President may have approved the statute without reference to the resolution or report). It would also be as available (though separately) as the statute itself.

The critical objection is not that the resolution or report would be irrelevant, unreliable, or unavailable but that the statute took no account of it. A typical reader of the statute would have no reason to suppose that the true message lay in another document, especially one not recognized by the Constitution as a vehicle of legislative communication. This is true of any collateral statement that explains the meaning of the parent statute, regardless of its relevance, reliability, and availability. Although the statute and the competing collateral document might, after enactment, be editorially juxtaposed in an official publication, no such step has in fact been taken in the official media that legislative audiences are offered the opportunity of reading, nor is such a step likely to have been anticipated or contemplated by the authors of the statute. Mere after-the-fact availability, therefore, is not enough.

Because the statute is the constitutional center of focal awareness, it is not significant that the resolution or report took express account of it. Rather, the important question is whether the statute took account of the resolution or report, as it did the matters that comprise the proper context of the statute. Even as to two documents of equal dignity, one can be part of the context of the other without the converse being true. There is thus a close parallel here to incorporation by reference: If a statute incorporates by reference the existing terms of another statute, the latter is part of the former, but the former is no part of the latter.

These statements relate primarily to the relation between "being taken into account" and "affecting the meaning of." As assertions about current uses of the word "context," on the other hand, they may be harder to defend, because usage in this area may fall within the margin of vagueness surrounding the word "context." If so, they may be taken as proposals to sharpen usage to make it coextensive with the range of collateral assumptions that, because of established human expectations, affect the true meaning of the document being interpreted.

What is true of concurrent resolutions and conference reports is true, *a fortiori,* of committee reports, statements made during floor debate or in committee hearings (whether by the managers of the bill or otherwise), presidential comments, and such expressions of "non-legislative 'intention' " as may be made by the draftsman or a sponsoring administrative agency. [19] Sound communication principles prevent their being taken into account because, there being no basis for assuming that they are in fact shared by the legislative audience or its conduit group, they cannot be part of context in the sense of patterned expectations described in the preceding chapter.

The discussion so far has related only to interpretative materials, which purport to declare the meaning conveyed by the statute in question. What of collateral statements that relate, instead, to the purposes that the statute was intended to accomplish ("motivating texts")? Is a similar conclusion warranted for them?

Here, according to Jones, we should distinguish between the immediate purpose that the statute itself is intended to exhaust (which is co-extensive with legislative intent) and any ulterior purpose that it tends ultimately to serve. [20] It is doubtful that

19. See Note, Nonlegislative Intent as an Aid to Statutory Interpretation, 49 Colum. L. Rev. 676, 685 (1940). *Nonlegislative* intent becomes *legislative* intent so far as the legislature impliedly adopts the intent of the outsider.

20. H. Jones, Extrinsic Aids in the Federal Courts, 25 Iowa L. Rev. 737, 740 (1940).

the former could be part of the context of the statute when, as we have seen, the expression of the purpose that the statute itself immediately effectuates is identified with the meaning of the statute.[21]

Can a statute be part of its own context? The paradox is only verbal. A problem exists whenever the statute is intended to exhaust an immediate purpose that is imperfectly expressed in the statute and better expressed in a reliable part of its legislative history. However, such a situation is indistinguishable from the one, already discussed, in which there are two competing legislative expressions of the intended result, one of which has been enacted and the other of which has not. The latter, besides being constitutionally precluded from having direct weight, can hardly be classed as part of the context of the former, because it is unlikely that the statute took account of a statement that competes with it. Even if it did, it is likely to contain nothing even suggesting the fact.

The issue is more clearly drawn for statements in the legislative history expressing the purposes that the specific prescriptions of the statute were designed to implement. That the statute took account of the purposes that motivated its own preparation is so by tautology; to say otherwise would be self-contradiction. However, the important question is not whether the purposes themselves are part of the context of the statute but whether particular collateral expressions of those purposes are part of it. But context is normally made up of knowledge and assumptions, not documents. A document is part of context only where it is an accepted, shared source for providing or verifying that knowledge.

A collateral statement of purpose automatically meets the test of general relevance. Whether it is relevant also to the particular uncertainty in issue may pose a problem, but none that is peculiar to statutory interpretation. More difficult is the question whether there is any basis, apparent to the legislative audience, for assuming that the statute took it into account. That there is seems highly improbable. If there is none, the statement would seem to be beyond the limits of proper context.

Most of comment 9 to section 2-615 of the Uniform Commercial Code, a comment that is reliable and widely available, is clearly no part of proper legislative context, because rather than

21. See ch. 8, pp. 87-88.

clarify the section it attempts to set forth additional rules of law. Whereas the section excuses only the seller's delay in delivery or nondelivery resulting from the failure of a condition presupposed by the sales contract, comment 9 suggests that under comparable circumstances a similar excuse might extend also to the buyer. This comment fails as law, because it was never enacted. It fails as context, because it neither explains nor states the purpose of anything that was enacted. How, with respect to the specific thrust of section 2-615, could it have been taken into account?

3. *Availability*

Whether a broader or ulterior legislative purpose as revealed by a reliable element of legislative history is part of the context of the statute as viewed by a typical member of the legislative audience to which it is addressed depends largely on the availability of knowledge of that purpose, and on whether there is a shared practice of referring to it for that purpose. If the problem to which the statute is plainly addressed is one of which that audience is generally aware, knowledge of it must be considered part of the legislative context. The critical case is one in which knowledge of the purpose depends on knowledge of specific statements made as part of the legislative history. This, in turn, depends on the availability of the particular statements of purpose.

The most favorable situation for considering a statement of purpose part of external context would be one in which it appeared contemporaneously in another statute of which the statute being interpreted took account. Here the requirement of availability would be fully met. The next most favorable situation would be one in which the legislative purpose was revealed in a concurrent resolution. This would meet the test of availability, but doubts would arise, the President not having participated, as to its reliability.[22] Both supposed situations are highly unlikely.

Suppose, next, that the purpose has been stated in a committee report or revealed by the general tenor of the published debates or hearings. Apart from any question of reliability or "taking account of," would such materials be sufficiently available to the legislative audience to be part of the legislative context and thus capable of affecting actual meaning in the manner of context generally?

22. See p. 144.

The issue was nicely posed in *United States v. Public Utilities Commn.,* [23] where the problem was to determine whether the provision of the Federal Water Power Act of 1935, limiting the Federal Power Commission's regulatory authority over interstate wholesale sales of power "to those matters which are not subject to regulation by the States," referred only to the power secured to the states by the federal Constitution or included the power to regulate granted to them by federal statute. Justice Reed's opinion for the majority, which held that it included only the former, relied in part on the hearings of the House Committee on Interstate and Foreign Commerce. Although the majority result rests also on other grounds, Reed's references to legislative history ignited the volatile Justice Jackson, who had vehemently expressed himself on the same subject two years earlier in Schweg*mann Bros. v. Calvert Distillers Corp.* [24]

Jackson's main objection to Reed's attempt at "psychoanalysis of Congress" was the general inaccessibility of the legislative materials used. [25] "Neither counsel who argued the case for the State Commission nor the Supreme Court of California had access to the material used by the Court today." [26] Jackson underscored the assertion by saying that counsel for the Commission had been unable to obtain the materials from the City and County Library of San Francisco, the library of the University of California, the library of the largest law office in San Francisco, the Library of Congress, or the Harvard Law School library. Some of these institutions had had the materials but had declined to lend them. [27] Moreover, said Jackson, the legislative history was, ironically, "more vague than the statute we are called upon to interpret." [28] Even so, he concurred in the result, partly on the apparent assumption that, no civil or criminal exaction being involved, the action was in effect judicial lawmaking of only prospective force, and partly in deference to "the members of the Court who have had legislative experience" [29] and who were thus presumably capable of psychoanalyzing Congress.

Jackson's righteous indignation evoked widespread sympathy,

23. 345 U.S. 295, 73 S. Ct. 706 (1953).
24. 341 U.S. 384, 71 S. Ct. 745 (1951).
25. 345 U.S. at 319, 73 S. Ct. at 719 (1953).
26. Id.
27. Id at 319-320, 73 S. Ct. at 720.
28. Id at 320, 73 S. Ct. at 720.
29. Id. at 320-321, 73 S. Ct. at 720.

especially among those who have become alarmed by the growing tendency of federal courts to rummage, in Curtis's phrase, among "the ashcans of the legislative process." [30] More recent and more deliberate evaluations of Jackson's views, however, suggest that he may have overstated the case against the use of legislative history.

Hart and Sacks, for example, have shown that in the correspondence between counsel for the California Commission and the Harvard Law School library the former was informed of both the citations and the whereabouts of the relevant congressional reports and hearings. [31] Moreover, as a result of a longstanding congressional policy, there are today "at least three depositary libraries for such documents in each state" and that "As of September 1, 1956, there were twenty-eight depositary libraries in California alone." [32] Although many of these are concededly incomplete, at least one-fifth receive everything available for distribution, and, although committee hearings have been on the depositary list only since 1938, "committee hearings are easy to collect, and commonly collected." [33] Hart and Sacks concluded: [34]

> There was thus good reason for the Harvard librarian to assume that at least one library in California would have had the initiative and intelligence to keep up its collection of committee hearings as well as the collections of committee reports and the Congressional record which many of them are obliged by law to keep. . . . In any event, is it not apparent that Justice Jackson's criticism is beside the mark? As soon as the Supreme Court has definitively answered *its* question about the utility of the legislative materials in the interpretation of federal statutes, cannot private ordering be counted upon to solve *its* problem of making the materials available?

It is reassuring to know that the materials of federal legislative history are more widely available than many lawyers have heretofore suspected. This must be especially reassuring to those who, because of their preoccupation with case law, have had little or no acquaintance with the mysteries of the legislative process. It is also reassuring to have this expression of confidence in the

30. C. Curtis, It's Your Law 52 (1954).
31. Hart & Sacks 1279-1281.
32. Id. at 1281.
33. Id. at 1282.
34. Id. at 1282-1283. (Emphasis in original.)

ingenuity and resourcefulness of the individuals and institutions now devoting their energies to the problems of coping with today's embarrassment of legal riches. Apparently, Hart and Sacks assume that we may count on recently developed uses of microfilm, microfiche, or digital computers to solve the problem of storing and finding the vast, heterogeneous, and scattered materials of legislative history, thus making them even more widely accessible than they are today. [35]

And yet, despite such reassurances, there may be lingering doubts. The first doubt is whether mere availability to a court following a detailed search centered on a particular controversy is the kind of general availability that makes the information part of the shared context of which the statute takes account. Under the analysis of chapter 9, it is not enough that after an intensive postcontroversy search the information is shared by the legislature with a particular court. [36]

Let us assume further that the information is practically accessible also to the lawyers involved in the controversy. Is this enough to make it part of the shared legislative context, assuming that for this purpose the parties are typical members of the legislative audience? There are at least two reasons for doubting that it does.

First, it is not clear that every legislative audience is assumed to rely on the bar as an intermediary for receiving information about the statutes that are addressed to it. Second, and more important, is that even if it is, the information practically available to the individual attorney who is oriented toward the application of a statute to a particular past event is not necessarily the kind of information that is practically available to the lawyer who has the problem of advising his client generally on the broad range of the client's future activities in relation to the statute. [37] Precontroversy access is what ultimately counts.

It is hard enough to search a long, heterogeneous, and often

35. Availability as of 1959 is described in E. Finley, Crystal Gazing: The Problem of Legislative History, 45 A.B.A.J. 1281, 1283-1284 (1959). "But no library, however large or however prosperous, has a *compiled* history of every federal law." Id. at 1283. (Emphasis in original.) Where no compiled history is available, finding the relevant history "is no more work than tearing the digests apart trying to find a case in point. . . ." Id. at 1284. But suppose the lawyer wants to counsel his client without regard to specific litigation.

36. See ch. 9, pp. 116-120.

37. See R. Jackson, The Meaning of Statutes: What Congress Says or What the Court Says, 34 A.B.A.J. 535, 538 (1948). "In the application of

conflicting legislative history as it relates to a particular issue in a current controversy. It is vastly harder and usually impracticable to search all aspects of the legislative history as they relate to the myriad of potentially troublesome problems that the lawyer would like to anticipate. Of what significance to shared context is material that from a practical standpoint can be shared only after, and to the limited extent that, a particular dispute has arisen? It is no answer to say that for a few of the larger and better heeled corporate members of the legislative audience it may be feasible to make sweeping, before-the-dispute searches, at least for problems of high incidence or special significance.

It is appropriate, of course, for the law to hold the members of the legislative audience to a direct knowledge of the statute, even though such knowledge is a privilege not often enjoyed in fact. Constitutional guarantees exist only in the standards of availability that the prescribed mechanics of enactment strongly imply. If the legislature provides reasonable access to a statute, who is he to complain who freely foregoes the opportunity? But this presupposes reasonable and equal access to all significant aspects of the legislative message for any typical member of the legislative audience who wishes to exercise his constitutional privilege.

Moreover, reasonable access is for the most part objectively determinable. In any event, the notion that reasonable access to a legislative communication is being provided implies that both the statute and the collateral matters of context of which it takes account are shared or are reasonably shareable.

With the increasing reliance on legislation as an instrument of social change, the problem of finding the relevant statutes is increasing in geometric proportion. For this reason, it is all the more unrealistic to suppose, from the mere fact that some libraries in California have copies of the hearings held by a particular congressional committee, that knowledge of those hearings is shared by a typical member of the legislative audience who, we are assuming, is studying the statute in hopes of avoiding a broad range of future difficulties. There is also the risk of adding unduly to the cost of legal administration.[38]

---

statutes we have to take account of the needs of those who must advise. . . ." III R. Pound, Jurisprudence 487 (1959).

38. S. Wasby, Legislative Materials as an Aid to Statutory Interpretation: A Caveat, 12 J. Pub. L. 262, 264 (1963).

If effective legislative utterances are by constitutional implication limited to what is reasonably available to the legislative audience, it remains a question of fact whether a particular assumption complies with that standard. On this basis, items of legislative history, no matter how relevant and reliable, are no part of proper legislative context, if they are significantly less accessible than the standard of accessibility implicit in the applicable constitution requires.

In chapter 9, it was pointed out that context includes not only relevant information already shared by the legislative audience but also shared assumptions that can reasonably be expected to lead to such information. Can we not rationalize in the same way the use of legislative history and conclude that it, too, is part of context?

The answer would seem to be no. Certainly, we cannot analogize the aggregate of heterogeneous and uncoordinated materials involved in the legislative events leading up to enactment as providing the kind of reliability that a standard dictionary or code book provides. Nor can we persuasively urge that there is an agreed-on method of dealing with the materials of legislative history sufficient to develop a functional relationship between the statute itself and the collateral expressions of legislative intent, much of which is irrelevant or competitive with the statute and almost none of which has been taken into account by the authors as part of the legislative message.

It is conceivable that a habit of consulting miscellaneous collateral materials, loosely analogous to a dictionary or code book, might become sufficiently crystallized and established that both author and audience would take it into account as contextual background for the express elements of the communication. Unfortunately, such a method has not yet been developed or accepted as a basis for legislative communication. If this is true, it would seem unrealistic to treat the materials of legislative history as part of the context of the statute to which they relate. This does not exclude the possibility that a particular element might under exceptional circumstances meet the tests of availability and accountability that each element must meet before it can become part of context. But under present circumstances, this would be the rare exception.

We might argue that, because it is already fictitious in most cases to assume that the legislative audience actually reads the statute, both court and legislature may extend the fiction by assuming that the typical member of the legislative audience, in addition to reading the statute, knows such of the relevant and reliable elements of legislative history of which the statute takes account as might be found by diligent search. The answer is that the implied constitutional guarantees relating to the enactment of statutes rest, not on the fiction of an actual reading, but on the actuality of a reasonable opportunity to read, an opportunity that does not extend to even relevant and reliable elements of legislative history so long as they are significantly less accessible than what the applicable constitution impliedly requires for the statute itself.[39]

The consequence of either deficiency is not necessarily that the constitution is to that extent subverted. It is merely that the elements concerned, being no part of the context of the statute as viewed by a typical member of the legislative audience who chooses to enjoy the opportunity impliedly offered by the applicable constitution, have no bearing on its enacted meaning until made reasonably available to the legislative audience. An issue of constitutionality would seem to arise only where the court takes such an element into account in declaring a new meaning that, when applied to past events, results in unfair surprise.[40]

Even if for the purposes of cognition the materials of legislative history met the contextual tests of relevance, reliability, availability, and having been taken into account, it would still be hard to meet the requirement of availability where the collateral information necessary to evaluating who or what is reliable (for example, which legislators were the most knowledgeable and representative) was not equally available. In such a case, a typical member of the legislative audience would be likely to lack the sophistication needed to weigh and adequately balance the relevant historical elements.

If no part of the legislative history of a statute is on its own account part of the proper context of the statute, this fact can be changed, not by general legal fiat, but only by making the current pretenses of accessibility an actuality for the kind of legislative

39. "The familiar maxim of expediency that people are held to know the law becomes an instrument of injustice as to portions of the law which are essentially undiscoverable." Sutherland §48.02.

40. " 'How would those who must guide themselves by its words reasonably understand the intent of the Act, for the law must not become a snare for those who cannot know the reason of it as fully as do the Judges.' " L. Fuller, The Morality of Law 83 (1964).

audience involved. Although proper legislative context can be manufactured *ad hoc,* as the wide and systematic dissemination of the Worth Street Rules strongly suggest, several conditions must be met. Not only must the materials be made as accessible as the applicable constitution implies but they must be made so under conditions that make clear to the legislative audience that the statute takes them into account.

4. Relevance and Reliability

If accepted practice does not now provide both the adequate availability of legislative history and reliance on it by legislature and legislative audience, would it be desirable to try to establish such a practice?

Despite the happy availability of federal legislative history proclaimed by Hart and Sacks, there may still be a lingering doubt. The professional tears that it is now fashionable to shed over the paucity of legislative history for state statutes,[41] as contrasted with the supposed riches that surround federal statutes, may invite the question whether the interpretation of state statutes is in a significantly worse way for having been cut off from these resources. One way to answer this is to assess the value of currently available legislative history in resolving and shaping meaning in federal statutes.

There may be reason to temper our enthusiasm for the availability of federal legislative history when we consider how little of it below the level of general legislative purpose ever becomes relevant to the resolution of specific controversies. Potentially, the number of specific controversies involving questions of vagueness and other uncertainties is almost unlimited, no matter how skilled the draftsman. (He can hope only to push the frontiers of uncertainty into areas in which it is administratively manageable.) Of the controversies that do arise, I suspect that for only a small percentage is there anything in the legislative history that specifically deals with the particular points in issue. Even where there is, a high percentage of what is specifically relevant is vulnerable to objection on an even more serious ground.

41. E.g., E. Finley, Crystal Gazing: The Problem of Legislative History, 45 A.B.A.J. 1284 (1959); F. Horack, Jr., Cooperative Action for Improved Statutory Interpretation, 3 Vand. L. Rev. 382, 387 (1950); F. Horack, Jr., The Disintegration of Statutory Construction, 24 Ind. L.J. 335, 348 (1949); Comment, Statutory Interpretation — The Need for Improved Legislative Records in Missouri, 38 Mo. L. Rev. 84 (1973).

The greatest weakness in most legislative history is its unreliability.[42] The reliability of a particular element of legislative history varies widely according to its source and the circumstances in which it is created. Materials in hearings and floor debates are so heterogeneous and fragmentary[43] and so influenced by the tactics of promoting enactment that they have almost no credibility for the purposes of later interpretation.[44] Many of the statements made come from relatively irresponsible sources.[45] Even when they come from persons charged with having full knowledge of the purposes, contents, and prospective impact of a bill, they may be tentative[46] and are often impromptu. Even when they are made deliberately, the fact that politicians believe that bills "should be made to pass as razors are made to sell"[47] means that the statements are usually highly colored by legislative sales talk, not all of which would meet the

42. J. Kohler, Judicial Interpretation of Enacted Law, in Science of Legal Method 187, 197-198 (1921); S. Wasby. Legislative Materials as an Aid to Statutory Interpretation: A Caveat, 12 J. Pub. L. 262, 264 (1963) (this article provides perhaps the fullest explanation of why legislative history is unreliable).

43. J. Corry, The Use of Legislative History in the Interpretation of Statutes, 32 Can. Bar Rev. 624, 628 (1954); S. Wasby, Leglislative Materials as an Aid to Statutory Interpretation: A Caveat, 12 J. Pub. L. 262, 263 (1963). Incompleteness is likely to distort.

44. W. Bishin, The Law Finders: An Essay in Statutory Interpretation, 38 So. Cal. L. Rev. 1, 14 (1965); J. Corry, The Use of Legislative History in the Interpretation of Statutes, 32 Can. Bar Rev. 624, 630-632, 634 (1954). "It is always sensible to appeal from Philip drunk to Philip sober. But to appeal from the carefully pondered terms of the statute to the hurly-burly of parliamentary debate is more like appealing from Philip sober to Philip drunk." Id. at 632. And see G. Folsom, Legislative History 31 (1972); Sutherland §§48.10, 48.13. Apparently, debates are unreliable also for determining constitutionality. United States v. O'Brien, 391 U.S. 383-384, 88 S. Ct. 1673, 1682-1683 (1968).

45. "Reporting on the exchange between Senators Saltonstall and McCarran, which has several times been quoted in court opinions, Mr. Crumpacker said, ". . . [T]his colloquy is almost entirely meaningless, it being merely an exchange of pleasantries by some senators having little, if any, familiarity with the subject matter they were discussing." G. Rich, Congressional Intent — Or, Who Wrote the Patent Act of 1952?, in Patent Procurement and Exploitation 61, 75-76 (1963).

46. R. Jackson, 34 A.B.A.J. 538 (1948).

47. A. Russell, Legislative Drafting and Forms 23 (4th ed. 1938). According to J. Corry, The Use of Legislative History in the Interpretation of Statutes, 32 Can. Bar Rev. 624, 631 (1954), "The process of enacting new legislation is not an intellectual exercise in pursuit of truth; it is an essay in persuasion, or perhaps almost seduction!"

kind of minimum standards of fair play now considered by the Federal Trade Commission to be needed to protect the ears of unsophisticated consumers. Because of their usual incompleteness, even otherwise reliable statements may not be representative of the legislators generally.[48] For these reasons a court is fully justified in turning a deaf ear to all such utterances, even for the purposes of judicial lawmaking.

Least reliable are floor debates concerning what a bill means (interpretative materials). Any paraphrase of a bill is suspect even in the mouth of a knowledgeable legislator who is uncorrupted by legislative gamesmanship. Legislators, who ordinarily have little professional skill in achieving the kind of legislative definitiveness needed in statutes, speaking in circumstances that call for gross oversimplification, at best describe only their subjective beliefs about what the bill is supposed to say. Oddly enough, even the original, professional draftsman is unreliable in this respect, because he normally recites what he intended to say in the bill rather than give a coldly objective analysis of what impact the bill, taken in its proper context, will probably have on a typical member of the legislative audience.[49]

48. F. Newman & S. Surrey, Legislation — Cases and Materials 650 n. 2 (1955); A. Cox, Judge Learned Hand and the Interpretation of Statutes, 60 Harv. L. Rev. 370, 381 (1947); S. Wasby, Legislative Materials as an Aid to Statutory Interpretation: A Caveat, 12 J. Pub. L. 266 (1963).

49. "My Lords, I have more than once had occasion to say that in construing a statute I believe the worst person to construe it is the person responsible for its drafting. He is very much disposed to confuse what he intended to do with the effect of the language which in fact has been employed." Lord Halsbury in Hilder v. Dexter, A.C. 474, 477 (1902).

"I remember the time when Jim Minor and I and a half dozen others were sitting around a table in the Pentagon trying to recodify an Army strength provision from the Army Organization Act of 1950, a provision that in context almost defied interpretation. It was a landmark of obfuscation. Each of us had his view of what it meant. I had a view. Jim strongly disagreed. Then, he had his say, and finally the lawyer at the end of the table, . . . who had had enough of the arguments, said, 'Look, you guys, I know what it means.' So we said, 'What do you mean, you know what it means?' He said, 'I wrote it.' We asked, 'Then, what does it mean?', and he told us. We said, 'It can mean a lot of things, but of all the things it could conceivably mean, it couldn't mean that.' And we mowed him down in spite of his anguished protests." Professionalizing Legislative Drafting — The Federal Experience 165 (R. Dickerson ed., 1973). See also J. Kohler, Judicial Interpretation of Enacted Law, in Science of Legal Method 187, 189 (1921).

If the draftsman offered his opinion to a court, his testimony would be no part of legislative history and would normally be rejected. On the other hand,

Besides, statements that so compete with the bill itself (as a statement of legislative intent) can under no theory of communication be treated as part of legislative context. Falling outside the constitutionally prescribed vessel for conveying legally effective legislative prescriptions (a statute), they have, in addition to little or no credibility, no legal weight.

They are even constitutionally suspect, because as authoritative interpretations they would derogate from the court's prerogative to have the ultimate say as to what statutes mean. Worst of all, they lack the ordinary assurance of deliberateness and depth that the requirement of justiciability provides for judicial interpretation.

Accordingly, it is almost inconceivable that interpretative statements in floor debates or committee hearings, especially in view of the other limitations on legislative history, would in any circumstances be properly usable for the purposes of cognition and only in the rarest cases are they properly usable for the purposes of judicial lawmaking. That the courts are nevertheless relying heavily on such materials is reflected in the fact that members of Congress have occasionally found it necessary to formally amend floor comments on pending legislation. [50]

Floor debates or committee hearings concerned with the more diffuse matters of ulterior legislative purpose are only slightly more reliable. Although a person is likely to be more sophisticated in describing general purposes than in undertaking to do, impromptu, the kind of sophisticated exercise in empathy that even the most skillful judges find it hard to perform in the relatively serene atmosphere of their chambers, the disciplines of the legislative process bear less heavily on the reasons for legislative action than they do on the legislative action itself. [51] Legislators are thus inclined to acquiesce even in reasons with which they

---

if it was recorded as part of the legislative history, it is more likely to be considered, because of the greater likelihood that the legislature accepted it as its own view. Sutherland §48.12. However, it still has little or no credibility as reflecting the actual meaning of the statute and should be rejected along with other interpretative materials.

50. E.g., statement of Senator Morse clarifying, without objection, an earlier colloquy with Senator Prouty, 112 Cong. Rec. 25160 (Oct. 4, 1966). *Before* the Congressional Record is finally printed, a Member may revise his remarks without specific consent of the House, and may even introduce arguments that were no part of the floor debate.

51. See ch. 8, pp. 90-91.

disagree, so long as those reasons support the desired result. Also, the temptations of seller's puffing increase the risk that even the author of the disagreed-with reasons is himself not wholly sincere.

Some threats to reliability are lessened in the context of committee [52] or conference [53] reports, where the persons preparing the materials are usually closest to the considerations that shape the bill and less vulnerable to the exigencies of hand-to-hand legislative combat. On the other hand, other factors conspire to subvert reliability. Interpretative materials, while freer of the pressures of open debate, are likely to be diluted in specificity to becoming mere loose and largely useless paraphrases of the statutory text. [54] This is certainly true where the draftsman, who lacks the opportunity or time even to prepare an adequate statutory text, has been assigned the additional, and much less critical, job of preparing a significant section-by-section analysis. Even the relatively well-prepared comments on Uniform State Laws are vulnerable on this count.

Much more reliable are the explanations, in committee or conference reports, [55] of the purposes behind proposed legislation. [56] These are some of the very rare kinds of legislative history that can make a respectable showing on the scale of reliability. On the other hand, the element of salesmanship is present even here. These statements are comparable to the purpose or policy clauses that draftsmen often include in the text of the bills themselves. What they gain in reliability they usually lose in specific relevance, because the author is strongly tempted to use bland statements that in massaging the reader's social conscience will please the largest number of people and alienate the fewest. They are also vulnerable to the type of intellectual dishonesty that has plagued the framers of statutory short titles such as those placed on "Fair Trade" laws. But even if they are relatively honest, they are less likely to make available a reliably ascertainable

52. See Sutherland §§48.06-48.07. However, in most states committee reports include only recommendations, not reasons or explanations.

53. Id. at §48.08.

54. Professionalizing Legislative Drafting — The Federal Experience 140-141, 163 (R. Dickerson ed., 1973).

55. The difficulties of drawing conclusions even from conference reports are discussed in Note, Conference Committee Materials in Interpreting Statutes, 4 Stan. L. Rev. 257 (1952). And see note 52 *supra*.

56. A. Cox, Judge Learned Hand and the Interpretation of Statutes, 60 Harv. L. Rev. 370, 379 (1947).

legislative purpose than the statutory text itself is likely to make available a reliably ascertainable legislative intent.

Also, unless the collateral statement of purpose has been included in a concurrent resolution passed contemporaneously with the statute (a most extraordinary occurrence), the chances that it reflects a general consensus remains low. A legislator who votes for a specific bill may support it for a wide variety of reasons, and there is nothing in the present system of enacting legislation that commits him to any expression or purpose, outside the bill itself, that he has not directly participated in preparing, unless he somehow commits himself to official statements of purpose to which he does not expressly object. A skeptic who finds it hard to hypostatize legislative intent will find it even harder to hypostatize legislative purpose. Legislative purpose-by-adoption is likely to be even more highly attenuated than legislative intent-by-adoption.

It is arguable that the authoritative status that the applicable constitution withholds from unenacted expressions of legislative purpose has instead been impliedly conferred by the courts through their widespread attention to such expressions in the interpretation and administration of statutes. Does this not confer on legislative history a status roughly comparable to what the constitution confers on the statute itself? Any contention that it does would be hard to support, however, because the attention that courts in fact pay to nonstatutory but official statements of legislative purpose implies neither that they determine, nor that they affect, the actual meaning of the statute. Many or all of these instances are more satisfactorily explained as acts of judicial lawmaking.

Perhaps the strongest case for treating an element of legislative history as part of proper context exists for the uniform acts proposed by the National Conference of Commissioners on Uniform State Laws. When presented for enactment, a proposed bill is accompanied by official comments prepared by the authors. Some of these deal with textual uncertainties. For example, comment 3 to section 2-318 of the Uniform Commercial Code, which expressly removes the privity requirement in suits against retailers brought by a guest or member of the buyer's household, makes clear that the section is intended to imply nothing about the applicability or inapplicability of the privity requirement in suits against the wholesaler or the manufacturer.

Here, an argument can be made for considering comment 3 a

part of the context of the parent section. It is relevant to the possible existence of a negative implication. It is fairly reliable in that it probably came to the attention of at least some of the legislative proponents in the enacting states. It is widely available. Finally, the authors of the section undoubtedly took account of comment 3, at least in the final development of the section. If there are significant doubts, they lie (1) in the inherent unreliability of expounding texts and (2) because the official machinery for publishing statutes normally excludes collateral comments and explanations, in inadequate texts.

Although often relied on by courts for help in interpreting or applying statutes, the nonadoption or rejection of a proposed amendment to a pending bill is a circumstance that, standing alone, is normally inadequate as a basis for inferring legislative intent. [57] For the purposes of cognition, information of the fact is relatively unavailable to the legislative audience and the fact itself is nothing of which the statute takes account. But whether it is used for cognition or judicial lawmaking, its significance is usually too speculative to make it reliable even as a basis for inferring the legislative purpose behind the inaction or rejection itself. Its relevance is correspondingly speculative. This evaluation is certainly valid for legislative nonaction, because, being consistent with many possible explanations, [58] it has little probative value for any purpose.

The same is largely true also of express legislative rejection. [59] There are many reasons for saying no. One is that the legislature did not like the substantive result that the amendment embodied. Another is that the legislature, while wholly approving of that result, believed that the pending bill already embodied it, making amendment unnecessary. The legislature may have had other reasons that were unrelated to the interpretative point in issue. At best, express rejection is useful only for the purposes of judicial lawmaking and only if its inherent ambiguity has been reliably resolved by the other circumstances. Similarly,

57. "It is a delicate business to base speculations about the purposes or construction of a statute upon the vicissitudes of its passage." Holmes, J., in Pine Hill Coal Co. v. United States, 259 U.S. 191, 196, 42 S. Ct. 482, 483 (1922). See also H. Jones, Extrinsic Aids in the Federal Courts, 25 Iowa L. Rev. 737, 756 (1940).

58. See Sutherland §49.10.

59. Id. at §48.18.

the acceptance of an amendment is often ambiguous: Did it add new substance or merely clarify the old? [60]

Perhaps the most reliable type of legislative history is the commission report that culminates in the recommendation that legislation is desirable. [61] The authors of such recommendations, which provide the stuff of later legislative purpose, are likely to have their main attention directed more to substantive needs than to couching specific conclusions in legislative language or in peddling a legislative ware in a hectic political market.

There can be no doubt that the authors of a statute take into account the purposes that it is designed to serve. The problem, rather, is one of evidence. On this, three questions arise. (1) How probable is it that the specific objectives motivating the moving forces within the legislature coincided with those described in the report? (2) Are the contents of the report, and the evidence necessary to support such a probability, sufficiently available to the legislative audience to meet the minimum standards of availability to which the statute itself is subject? (3) Is there an established practice of consulting such sources for the purpose of completing the background knowledge against which both authors and audience, by tacit agreement, are expected to read the statute? Only if all three questions can be answered "Yes" is the report part of, or descriptive of, context and the court warranted in taking it into account when trying to ascertain what the statute, as enacted, means.

The more general a recommendation is, the more likely the legislature adopted it as a basis for action. Conversely, the more specific it is, the more likely the legislature deviated from it, at least in part. The draftsmen of the statute can deal with questions (1) and (3) by making it clear to what extent the statute is responsive to the report.

This is the one type of legislative history to which most English courts are willing to refer. Incidentally, English courts have been unfairly criticized for turning their backs on legislative history, when in effect they have turned their backs only on hearings and floor debates, which is not hard to justify. They have not turned their backs on committee reports, because in substance there is nothing for them to turn their backs on; as in most of the

60. Id.
61. Id. at §48.11.

states of the United States, English committee reports give results, not reasons. (Whether they should contain such materials is a legislative, not a judicial, question.)

The big risk in relying on commission reports is that the legislature may not adopt all the commission's substantive recommendations or that it may adopt them in significantly changed form. This puts a heavy responsibility on the courts to look for evidence of possible change. The risk resulting from such changes can be materially reduced by the draftsman through an appropriate allusion in the statute or statement in the committee report. [62]

But even if the high hurdle of reliability is leaped, relevance is always a formidable barrier, and in the case of cognition there are also the problems of availability and accountability.

5. *The General Case Against Legislative History*

The general case against using legislative history to find the meaning of a statute was forcefully stated by Justice Jackson in his concurring opinion in *Schwegmann Bros. v. Calvert Distillers Corp.*: [63]

> Resort to legislative history is only justified where the face of the Act is inescapably ambiguous, and then I think we should not go beyond Committee reports, which presumably are well considered and carefully prepared. I cannot deny that I have sometimes offended against that rule. But to select casual statements from floor debates, not always distinguished for candor or accuracy, as a basis for making up our minds what law Congress intended to enact is to substitute

62. See pp. 166-167.

63. 341 U.S. 384, 395-397, 71 S. Ct. 745, 751-752 (1951). Ironically, the justice may not have chosen the most appropriate occasion for his attack. If Justice Frankfurter's approach to the case was sound (it makes the best aggregate sense), the pieces of allegedly confused and contradictory legislative history fell rather neatly into place. Because state nonsigner clauses had fallen only because the federal antitrust laws had killed off the vertical price-fixing agreements to which the clauses referred, all that was needed to validate those clauses under federal law was to exempt from their operation the underlying vertical agreements. Mentioning nonsigner clauses in the federal law would have been superfluous. The same was not true of the several state "Fair Trade" laws, which had to include the nonsigner clauses to make vertical price-fixing agreements practically effective. This explains the apparent "discrepancy" between the federal and state statutes and why the sponsors of the federal statute remained generally silent on nonsigner clauses.

ourselves for the Congress in one of its important functions. The Rules of the House and Senate, with the sanction of the Constitution, require three readings of an Act in each House before final enactment. That is intended, I take it, to make sure that each House knows what it is passing and passes what it wants, and that what is enacted was formally reduced to writing. It is the business of Congress to sum up its own debates in its legislation. Moreover, it is only the words of the bill that have presidential approval, where that approval is given. It is not to be supposed that, in signing a bill, the President endorses the whole Congressional Record. For us to undertake to reconstruct an enactment from legislative history is merely to involve the Court in political controversies which are quite proper in the enactment of a bill but should have no place in its interpretation.

Moreover, there are practical reasons why we should accept whenever possible the meaning which an enactment reveals on its face. Laws are intended for all of our people to live by; and the people go to law offices to learn what their rights under those laws are. Here is a controversy which affects every little merchant in many States. Aside from a few offices in the larger cities, the materials of legislative history are not available to the lawyer who can afford neither the cost of acquisition, the cost of housing, or the cost of repeatedly examining the whole congressional history. Moreover, if he could, he would not know any way of anticipating what would impress enough members of the Court to be controlling. To accept legislative debates to modify statutory provisions is to make the law inaccessible to a large part of the country.

By and large, I think our function was well stated by Mr. Justice Holmes: "We do not inquire what the legislature meant; we ask only what the statute means." . . . And I can think of no better example of legislative history that is unedifying and unilluminating than that of the Act before us.

In view of these considerations, the courts' currently widespread use of federal legislative materials is professionally shocking, even recognizing that much of what they claim to be doing in the name of cognition can be constitutionally justified, if deferred and hedged with proper precautions, in the name of creation. In general, the practice is attributable to the lack of a coherent philosophy of judicial "interpretation," broad naiveté about the general principles of communication, and a general ignorance of the realities of the legislative process. Nowhere are courts more inept than in handling legislation. This is hardly surprising, because judges are still nurtured in a legal system that has remained case-oriented long after the great bulk of lawmaking necessary to sustain social change shifted from the courts to the legislature.

The derision that American reliance on the shabby materials of legislative history has prompted in some quarters reached its peak in the Canadian gibe that in the United States whenever the legislative history is ambiguous it is permissible to refer to the statute.[64] But even those who have become inured to American excesses were recently jolted when the Supreme Court came close to turning a piece of Canadian ridicule into a principle of American jurisprudence.[65]

As Corry has pointed out, ". . . [N]ot the least of the dangers of reference to legislative history is its tendency to draw interpreters away from hard thinking about the context and the general scheme embodied in the act in search of an easy road to learning in the legislative history."[66]

If Hart and Sacks' evaluation is correct, legislative history is valuable chiefly to verify hypotheses developed on other grounds and only with respect to the legislative purposes rather than specific points of meaning. But, although it is valuable to know the purposes behind a statute, they are largely discoverable or directly inferable from the statute itself when read in the light of the elements of proper context.

The infrequency with which the vast materials of legislative history provide a reliable statement of the legislative purposes not otherwise discoverable suggests that the occasional benefit that it provides may not be worth the effort of preserving, retrieving, and evaluating it.[67] Similarly, a prospector might wonder whether it is worth the effort to pan for gold in a stream that experience has shown will probably produce only an occasional nugget.[68]

64. J. Corry, The Use of Legislative History in the Interpretation of Statutes, 32 Can. Bar Rev. 624, 636 (1954).

65. "The legislative history . . . is ambiguous. . . . Because of this ambiguity, it is clear that we must look primarily to the statutes themselves to find the legislative intent." Citizens to Preserve Overton Park, Inc. v. Volpe, 401 U.S. 402, 412 n. 29, 91 S. Ct. 814, 821 n. 29 (1971). Cf. United States v. Bass, 404 U.S. 336, 339, 92 S. Ct. 515, 518 (1971), and see Sutherland §48.01 n. 9.

66. J. Corry, The Use of Legislative History in the Interpretation of Statutes, 32 Can. Bar Rev. 624, 636 (1954). And see n. 4 *supra*.

67. E. Bruncken, Interpretation of the Written Law, 25 Yale L.J. 129, 130 (1915).

68. The assertion, attributed to an unverifiable source, that "Only the million-dollar case makes it worthwhile to look at legislative history," seems sound.

6. *Adding Special Statutory Provisions*

Although some intermediate drafts of the Uniform Commercial Code provided that its official comments could be consulted in interpreting the Code (except that "if text and comment conflict, text controls"), the editorial board deleted the authorization in 1956.[69] Suppose that the board had left it in. Would it have constituted an express incorporation by reference? If so, the comments would in legal contemplation have become part of the Code itself. If not, what force would they have had? Would an express allusion have done more than merely solve the problem of "taking account of"? In any event, even such official comments tend to be unreliable.[70]

Suppose, instead, that a statute said, "In the interpretation of this act, reference may be made to its legislative history." This would make clear that the legislature had taken into account at least the part of the act's legislative history that preceded the insertion of the provision and that the reader was to do likewise.

What about availability? Technically, it is arguable that the constitutional requirement of reasonable availability has been met, because the generating legal force here is the adopting provision, which is in the statute, rather than the adopted provisions, which are not. Substantively, on the other hand, it is doubtful that a statutory provision that expressly adopted a document that was otherwise unavailable would meet what is implied in any constitutional grant of legislative power — the requirement of a fair opportunity to know.

Equally serious, such a provision might well create more interpretative questions than it solved. There is first the question whether such a provision was intended, through incorporation by reference, to give the incorporated material a status equal to that of the text, which would give it greater weight than it would have as a part of mere context. Presumably, it would not have been so intended.

The second question would be whether by "interpretation" the

69. R. Braucher, The Legislative History of the Uniform Commercial Code, 58 Colum. L. Rev. 798, 809 (1958).

70. R. Braucher and others, Report on Article 2 — Sales by Certain Members of the Faculty of Harvard Law School, 6 Business Lawyer 151, 152-153 (1951).

legislature had intended to cover both the cognitive function and the creative function. Despite rationalizations in terms of "interpretation," which in loose legal parlance normally includes the creative function, many courts have refused to look at extrinsic materials except where they are necessary to resolving doubts that are not otherwise resolvable by reference to the statute and its proper context, an approach that in effect limits their use to the creative function. But if the legislature intended only to bless what many courts are currently doing, it might be doubtful that the broad language of "interpretation" would be read as so limited.

On the other hand, the legislature may have intended, instead, to extend the range of proper context for the purposes of cognition. The main effect of the latter interpretation would be to turn what would otherwise be an act of judicial creativity into an act of judicial cognition. This would not necessarily affect the substantive force of the result, except that express incorporation of legislative history might in some instances reduce the threat of unfair surprise.

Thirdly, by referring to materials that are normally loaded with uncertainties, such a provision would tend to increase the general confusion now attending the widely indiscriminate use of federal legislative history. This is reason enough to consider such a broad reference undesirable. *A fortiori,* it would be undesirable to include it in a general "interpretation" statute, as was done in section 15 of the Uniform Statutory Construction Act.[71]

A less dangerous approach that has been used in some instances is to refer in the statute merely to the prior study, if any, that the statute was intended to implement. Thus, in the Animals Bill, 1969 (since lapsed), Lord Wilberforce moved to amend clause 13 by adding this provision: "In ascertaining the meaning of any provision of this Act, regard may be had to the Report of the Law Commission on Civil Liability for Animals (Law Commission No. 13)." The same approach had already been used in

71. "If a statute is ambiguous, the court, in determining the intention of the legislature, may consider among other matters: . . . "(3) the legislative history; . . ."

If "ambiguous" refers only to an otherwise unresolvable ambiguity, the provision is, at best, superfluous. If it refers also to apparent ambiguity, it tends to subvert the cognitive process by injecting matters, falling outside text and context, that are relied on for more than their confirmatory value. And see ch. 14.

European Communities Secondary Legislation. For example, European Communities Regulation (E.E.C.) No. 1612/68 of the Council of October 15, 1968, on freedom of movement for workers within the European Economic Community, began as follows:

> HAVING REGARD to the Treaty establishing the European Economic Community, and in particular Article 49 thereof; . . .
> HAVING REGARD to the Opinion of the Economic and Social Committee (2); . . .
> (2) OJ No 298, 7 December 1967, p. 10

This approach avoids many of the pitfalls of a blanket adoption of legislative history and, by referring to a specific factual study, impliedly supports the conclusion that the bill is intended to implement the objectives of that study and not some variation of them. (Where a variation has been made, its extent could be defined.) Also, having predated the legislative process and been found to be satisfactory, such a study is likely to throw light mainly on legislative purpose and not to include the type of interpretative materials, often found in committee reports, that tend to compete with the working provisions of the bill and whose self-serving aspects undermine their credibility.

Another approach is that followed by Indiana's Trust Code, which provides that "The report of the trust code study commission . . . may be consulted by the courts to determine the reasons, purposes and policies of this article, and may be used as a guide to its construction and application." [72] On the other hand, it apparently does not try to validate the interpretative materials, if any, in that report. This is fortunate, because the report was a concurrent, not merely preliminary, one and therefore capable of containing such materials. [73]

The main objection to this approach is the inadequate availability of the studies referred to. Although unavailability is not an objection for the purposes of judicial lawmaking, it is for the purposes of cognition. It is suggested, therefore, either that this approach be used, if at all, only to serve the courts' creative

72. Ind. Code 1971, §30-4-1-7, as added by Acts 1971, P.L. 416, §7, p. 1910.

73. The Report's commenting analysis on Ind. Code 1971, §30-4-3-2, recites that the section follows the Restatement of Trusts, §§152 and 153, whereas it omits several of the Restatement's provisions.

function or that the study referred to be made as available as the statute itself.

Such an approach in no wise improves the art of interpretation. Like the approach of improving the drafting of the working provisions, it seeks only to improve the extrinsic written evidences of legislative intent. However, unlike the approach of better drafting, it deals with the more diffuse and less reliable evidences of intent and in some instances it may create more interpretative problems than it solves. This fortifies the conclusion that the ultimate solution to the problems of statutory interpretation lies more in better drafting of the working provisions than in improving the materials of context or the art of interpretation.

Because the main value of legislative history lies in disclosing the purposes of the statute, and because these purposes can be better and more reliably expressed, where necessary, in the statute itself, would it not be preferable, in contrast to the present system, to include in each statute a statement of general purpose and turn our backs, as the English for the most part do, on legislative history? Although many of these statements of general purpose would be surplusage and not entirely accurate, [74] they would at least solve the problems of availability, accountability, and, for the most part, reliability, without the frustrations, interminable prolixities, blind alleys, and dismal uncertainties of the prevailing patterns of legislative history.

C. Use of Legislative History in Making New Law

So far, we have considered only the place of legislative history in the cognitive process of trying to extract whatever meaning there may be in the statute.

To condition or color a legislative communication by considering an element of legislative history outside the shared context by which the statute takes account is in effect to amend or supplement the statute by engrafting on it a meaning that cannot fairly be ascertained from it in the form in which it was enacted even when conditioned by its proper context. Although judicial lawmaking is justifiable in many situations, it should be per-

74. See ch. 8, pp. 97-98.

formed according to legal principles appropriate to that activity and not passed off as ascertainable fact quarriable from the statute when read against the background of proper context.

When a court has discharged its constitutional responsibility of cognition without resolving the issue at hand, it necessarily turns to the creative function of judicial lawmaking. Most if not all appropriate uses of legislative history may be justified, not as part of the act of cognition, where it can rarely, if ever, meet the standards of context, but as part of the act of judicial creation,[75] where the rules of the game differ. For this purpose, legislative history is examined to determine whether there is any relevant and reliable evidence of actual intent or purpose that has otherwise failed to meet the standards of context. Here there is no further need to be concerned with whether the material has been taken into account by the parties. Availability is no problem so long as the court, by selecting an appropriate effective date, avoids the threat of unfair surprise. On the other hand, relevance is still important, and so is reliability (except as it no longer depends so heavily on particular source). Beyond this, the materials of legislative history are less significant. In general there is no constitutional objection to examining any material that is helpful in filling in the gaps in the statute. The court is breaking new legislative ground and the main problem is to achieve the fairest result in the case at hand that both dovetails best with the legislative scheme disclosed by the cognitive process and creates no unfair surprise. This matter is discussed more fully in chapter 13.

Although there are frequent indications that courts are at least intuitively deferring the more substantial uses of legislative history until the cognitive process has been completed and the creative process begun, these indications, unfortunately, are not always clear-cut.[76]

75. Judge Hand sometimes used legislative history to resolve small ambiguities for which general purpose supplied no answer. A. Cox, Judge Learned Hand and the Interpretation of Statutes, 60 Harv. L. Rev. 370, 380-381 (1947).

76. E.g., "Some states have enacted statutes providing that courts may consider legislative history in determining the meaning of doubtful statutes." G. Folsom, Legislative History 6 n. 11 (1972). ". . . [T]he history of events transpiring during the process of enacting [an act] . . . has generally been the first extrinsic aid to which courts have turned in attempting to construe an ambiguous act." Sutherland §48.04. (Emphasis added.) The ambiguous word, of course, is "ambiguous." So far as the statute is only apparently ambiguous, legislative history is being used in the cognitive process. So far as the statute

D. Improving Legislative History

Britain's twin Law Commissions recently recommended what they considered a compromise position on the uses of legislative history.[77] Having been briefed on American abuses, they concluded that the door to examining legislative history should in general remain closed, partly on the ground of unreliability[78] and partly on the ground of unavailability.[79] With respect to the latter, they concluded that "the interpretative advantages which it might bring in the marginal case would be outweighed by the burden."[80]

At the same time, they considered the possibility of creating improved kinds of legislative history that met the requirements of relevance, reliability, and availability. In particular, they considered the advisability of providing explanatory materials specially prepared by the authors of the bill or under tightly controlled authorship.[81] This would help the courts in instances where the materials were not overridden by other considerations. The Law Commissions concluded that this would be advisable only on a selective basis where it was ". . . considered by their sponsors to be appropriate for this purpose. We had particularly in mind Bills giving effect to our own reports or to those of comparable bodies. . . ."[82]

Such a proposal has immediate, superficial appeal. If legislative

---

remains ambiguous even after thorough examination of text and context, legislative history is being used in the creative process.

Some courts seem clearly to have used legislative history during the cognitive process. Sutherland §48.01.

77. The Law Commission and the Scottish Law Commission, Statutory Interpretation (1969).

78. Id. at 32-34.

79. Id. at 35.

80. Id. at 37.

81. Id. at 38-43. Cf. Lord Chancellor Halsbury's comment in his introduction to the first edition of the Laws of England (1907): "A passage appears to be obscure: let it be cleared up rather by alteration than by comment: retrench, add, subtract as much as you will, but *never explain.* By the latter, certainty will generally, perspicuity and brevity will always, suffer. The more words there are, the more words are there about which doubts may be entertained," as quoted in The Interpretation of Statutes, 54 Law Guardian 11 (December 1969). (Emphasis added.)

82. Id. at 42.

history is vulnerable to serious defects, why not cure them? However, despite its appeal, the solution ironically approximates an approach that the Law Commissions initially considered and rejected. This was to improve the drafting of the statute itself.

> . . . [T]here are practical limits to the improvements which can be effected in drafting. Account must be taken of the inherent frailty of language, the difficulty of foreseeing and providing for all contingencies, the imperfection which must result in some degree from the pressures under which modern legislation has so often to be produced and the difficulties of expressing the finely balanced compromises of competing interests which the draftsman is sometimes called upon to formulate. [83]

But if the quality of the statute itself cannot be sufficiently improved, the question arises whether the quality of the written legislative history, which is likewise no more than written evidence of legislative intent or purpose, can.

The more effective the precautions to secure relevant, reliable, and available legislative history, the closer the functions involved approach legislative drafting. Reliable legislative history should be in writing and specially prepared. It should be prepared by highly knowledgeable persons who are expert in using language. It should be prepared, so far as possible, contemporaneously with the enactment of the statute. In most cases, this means turning to the draftsman.

It seems clear, however, that the authors of such documents are vulnerable to most, if not all, of the factors that inhibit the authors of statutes. What are these factors? First are the difficulties that inhere in communication itself. Some of the others were listed by the American Bar Association's Standing Committee on Legislative Drafting in a recent report to the Association's House of Delegates: [84]

> . . . Some proposals are drafted outside the Government altogether, and even by laymen. Those that are drafted inside the Government are often, if not usually, drafted by persons with inadequate training or experience. Most agencies hire lawyers without regard to their ability to draft and take inadequate measures to train them.

83. Id. at 4.

84. Professionalizing Legislative Drafting: The Federal Experience 171-172 (R. Dickerson ed., 1973).

> Even where statutes are drafted by Government lawyers as an assigned duty, many of them are asked to perform their drafting duties in addition to other substantial duties. As a result, few lawyers in the executive branch of the Government are permitted to specialize adequately in this area. Even where they are so permitted, they are usually inadequately trained. Much of this results from the fact that, for the most part, the nation's law schools do not provide training in draftsmanship.

Besides these factors, there is inadequate organizational and procedural recognition of the drafting function, with the result that draftsmen are often brought into the development of legislation too late to make a significant contribution. Even when they are brought in early, the prevalent underestimation of what is involved in good drafting has resulted in allotting insufficient time for whatever drafting skill is available to be used efficiently. Lacking an environment conducive to drafting, even the skilled draftsman is not permitted to do an adequate job. [85]

The problem is greatly exacerbated in the United States because, lacking the fusion at the top between the executive and legislative branches that exists in England, legislation sponsored by the executive agencies (which instigate the great bulk of federal legislation) has a vastly higher percentage of nonenactments than its English counterpart. The result is that the efforts of the tiny cadre of American legislative draftsmen who can claim to be professionally expert is largely squandered on unsuccessful legislation. In England, on the other hand, almost no public law is enacted that has not been drafted by the professionals in the Office of the Parliamentary Counsel, and relatively few of their bills fail of enactment. [86]

This difference makes it unrealistic to contemplate significantly improving legislative history in the federal government and in most of the states. As long as the hectic conditions now prevailing make it impossible for even the expert draftsman to draft statutes successfully, any time contemplated for using him to improve legislative history is needed much more to enhance his opportunity of improving the legislative text. Better explanatory texts are simply out of the question. On the other hand, including in the committee report a fuller description of the problem to

85. Id. at 10, 17, and see index.
86. Id. at 111-114.

which the legislation is addressed, prepared by persons other than the draftsman, may be not only more useful and reliable but more practicable because ordinarily it need not be voluminous.

The Law Commissions' proposal, however, can be fairly evaluated only in the light of the conditions prevailing in England.

If the explanatory document were included in the statute itself, which is the best guarantee of reliability and availability, the Law Commissions' recommendation would amount to adopting a watered down version of the better-drafting approach, which it initially rejected, and the essence of its recommendation would be simply that statutes should in appropriate cases include purpose clauses,[87] hardly a revolutionary proposal for revising the methods that courts should use in applying statutes that for one reason or another turn out to be uncertain.

That the analysis comes almost full circle is obscured by the fact that the report contemplates a collateral document rather than an addition to the statute. Again, attempts to develop collateral materials that are sufficiently relevant, reliable, and available inevitably tend to produce accompanying materials approaching the statute itself. The result is, in effect, a sort of "split level" statute (a good American example is the Uniform Commercial Code and its official comments), only one level of which has been subjected to the full legislative process.

Because the opportunities for effective communication are no greater for the author of an accompanying document than they are for the author of the statute itself, no communicative advantage is gained by expressing legislative intent or purpose in a separate document. Anything that can be stated helpfully outside the statute, including examples and needed explanations, can be stated as helpfully (and with greater reliability) inside the statute. The drive for better "motivating texts" thus logically become a drive for adequate purpose clauses in statutes. On the other hand, if the working provisions of a statute (which express legislative intent) are otherwise well drafted, a clause stating its ulterior purpose is rarely needed. However, because even a conscientious draftsman cannot always be sure that he has made the working provisions sufficiently clear and complete, it makes some sense to include a purpose clause, even though it is rarely useful.

Although a sound interpretative approach is helpful in re-

87. See ch. 8, pp. 97-98.

solving uncertainties of meaning, there is no conceivable system that can extract sense from a statute that has no sense in it.[88] And no range of interpretative precautions can remove the need for some later repair. In such a situation, the only available approach is judicial lawmaking, not an improved process of cognition. This is true even where there is relatively helpful legislative history. There is often a failure to communicate and, so far as the necessary evidences of meaning are missing, the courts have a problem that even the best approaches to statutory interpretation cannot fully solve. They can only ameliorate it.

It is far more important, therefore, to improve the quality of the statute itself. The United States needs fewer amateur and more professional draftsmen. It also needs to maintain an organizational and procedural environment that will permit them, as in England and in some states, to exploit their talents more adequately.[89] Among other things, this involves avoiding assignments, such as preparing materials of legislative history or writing interpretative opinions, that divert them from their main responsibility of preparing adequate legislation. The tragic irony is that almost no one, outside a small group of cloistered professionals, even recognizes the problem of draftsmanship, let alone has an answer to it.

E. Is Use or Improvement of Legislative History Worth the Effort?

It has been the sad lot of legislative history that use, whether for cognition or creation, leads usually to abuse.

The question thus remains whether it is worth the effort to find and evaluate legislative history, as it is now constituted, for any purpose, cognitive or creative. Certainly, it is hard to justify reference to congressional debates or hearings on any occasion. The legislative process is not designed to produce in debate more than a modest amount of balance, accuracy, or even honesty. Curtis's reference to "the ashcans of the legislative process" is no

88. "Nothing can ease the despairing perplexities caused by poor draftsmanship." R. Dias, Jurisprudence 149 (3d ed. 1970).

89. Professionalizing Legislative Drafting: The Federal Experience (R. Dickerson ed., 1973); R. Dickerson, Professionalizing Legislative Drafting: A Realistic Goal?, 60 A.B.A.J. 562 (1974).

mere hyperbole, and a judge would lose little if he closed his eyes entirely to the materials of legislative history, which he is constitutionally entitled to do except in those rare instances where specific material might achieve the status of context by being relevant, reliable, and reasonably available, and having been taken into account.

If legislative history is vital to statutory interpretation, how do courts manage to interpret administrative regulations without it? How do they manage to interpret municipal ordinances? Judicial opinions (or do judges include the necessary judicial history)? Law review articles and treatises? And can they square their self-righteous condescension toward the British reluctance to use legislative history with their own reluctance to refer to the "legislative history" of particular wills and contracts?

When we weigh the limited relevance and reliability of collateral legislative materials against the factors of cost and inconvenience,[90] we may well hesitate. In an era in which the growth of population and the proliferating complexity of human affairs has resulted in the clogging of court calendars, should we not simplify and shorten the trial of cases rather than complicate or lengthen them?

Even more important, in an era in which the lawyer devotes an increasing proportion of his time to counseling clients to forestall legal difficulties, can he afford to add to the burden of keeping up with the increasingly broad sweep of relevant statutes the burden of familiarizing himself with every aspect of the heterogeneous and ever so much larger mass of collateral legislative materials that may (but more probably will not) have some potential significance in future litigation?

There is even a risk that specific pieces of legislative history will sprout their own legislative history. Thus, we may have to confront not only the legislative history of statutes but the legislative history of legislative history! This is no mere speculation. The possibility of having explanations of the second or even third degree was recently illustrated by a draft of a proposed uniform state law (dealing with drug abuse) in which the draftsman provided in the bill itself a purpose and policy clause that, in

90. "The printed hearings of the 85th Congress alone (1957-1958) occupy almost seventy feet of shelf space. If complete *compiled* histories of all laws were to be undertaken, there would probably have to be a whole new agency to do the job." E. Finley, Crystal Gazing: The Problem of Legislative History, 45 A.B.A.J. 1284 (1959). (Emphasis in original.)

explaining the bill, was so extensive and elaborate that he felt it necessary to append an official comment explaining the explanation. Fortunately, the explanation of the explanation was so much shorter and more understandable that it inevitably prompted the suggestion that the explanation in the comment be substituted for the one in the bill (showing, again, that what can be said outside the bill can be said as well inside it). In the meantime, there was the chilling possibility that ultimately there might be a recorded floor debate explaining the comment's explanation of the explanation in the bill.

The possibility of using legislative history to the second degree became actuality in Leff's recent examination of the successive drafts of the comment of the National Conference of Commissioners on Uniform State Laws on section 2-302 of the Uniform Commercial Code, which it authored.[91] His purpose was to determine the meaning of "oppression" as it was used in that comment (but not in the Code itself). Although such in-depth gropings may be wholly appropriate for a legal pedagogue, one should pause before assuming that they would be equally appropriate to a judicial search for meaning. The attenuated inferences of legislative intent inherent in this situation were further attenuated by the fact that the primary legislative intent was not even that of the Conference, but of the legislature of the particular adopting state, in which primary legislative history is likely to be lacking even to support the assumption that when the state enacted the words of the Conference it automatically adopted, without reservation, the legislative intent of the Conference as reflected in its official comment.

Basing inferences of legislative intent on legislative materials that are twice removed from the ponderings of the cognizant state legislature seems not only risky but a little silly. The fact that the adopting state often publishes the Conference's official comments does not entirely close the gap; it does not even imply that the local legislature adopted the whole Conference rationale. It is interesting also to ponder the practical local consequences of the fact that in at least one state a privately published, but widely relied on, version of the Uniform Commercial Code carries only the comments of the local editors, not those prepared by the original Conference draftsmen.

91. A. Leff, Unconscionability and the New Code — The Emperor's New Clause, 115 U. Pa. L. Rev. 485, 499 (1967).

Leff's investigations can be supported as helping to satisfy a scholar's legitimate interest in legal history. And yet one may wonder whether the typical judge would readily distinguish between the researcher as pedagogue and the researcher as a judicial law clerk immediately concerned with specific litigation. Among the relevant materials that Leff unearthed was an early printed version of the section that, while widely available to the diligent, was passed over by him in favor of a mimeographed, but more revealing, version that is available to only the most dedicated researcher.[92] Was this part of statutory context? Was it even a part of the legislative history of the Code as enacted by a particular state?

In view of these considerations, we may be tempted to ask whether the race is worth the running. The possibility of improving and making more accessible the existing resources of federal legislative history suggests the appalling possibility that it may lead ultimately to the preservation and circulation of drafts and minutes not only for statutes, but also for regulations, ordinances, legal documents such as contracts, wills, and leases, and even for legal opinions. (For this last, a start has already been made!)[93] After all, how much does the interpretation of judge-made law differ from the interpretation of legislature-made law? Worse, how much would fuller and quicker access increase the intentional manufacture and manipulation of legislative history?[94]

92. Id. at 489.

93. At least two publishers offer (on microfilm or microcard) briefs or arguments, "and other documentation" related to litigation before the United States Supreme Court as an aid to understanding the reported decisions. So long as use is confined to academic research, no great harm can result, but there is always the risk that courts will use such "legislative history" to interpret earlier decisions. "Legislative history" has also appeared in music (e.g., see H. Leventhal, How the Problem Looks to the Courts, in Professionalizing Legislative Drafting — The Federal Experience 28 (R. Dickerson ed., 1973)) and painting (e.g., R. Arnheim, Picasso's Guernica — The Genesis of a Painting (1962)).

94. On contrived legislative history, see S. Wasby, Legislative Materials as an Aid to Statutory Interpretation: A Caveat, 12 J. Pub. L. 262, 267 (1963), who makes this comment:

". . . The court is not in the position of the psychologist observing subjects through a one-way glass; the legislators are all too aware that the court is there and is using legislative materials to determine what it thinks is legislative intent. . . . At other times, the legislators indulge in an excess of zeal for informing the court of spurious legislative intent, as when materials are read

Disregarding legislative history, at least during the cognitive function, impairs no substantive function of the courts. It challenges neither judicial responsibility nor judicial creativity. Deferring its use, at least until the creative function begins, fosters intellectual honesty. At least in the United States, judicial lawmaking is strong enough to move under its own power and legitimate enough to do so under its own name.

Even to support the creative function, legislative history should be used with restraint. Although we cannot criticize a judge for examining anything he can lay his hands on for this purpose, we certainly should not try to persuade him that, because it is part of "context," he is professionally obliged to consider it for the purpose of cognition or that it is desirable to do so for the purposes of creation. The only element of legislative history normally worth examining or improving is a detailed statement of the problem to which the legislation is addressed. Unless it deals with matters of common knowledge, even this should be used only for the purpose of judicial lawmaking. Whatever the court may feel is worth examining on its own for the purpose of creation, it should disclose nothing in its published opinion that would tend to make the use of such materials part of the process of advocacy or legal counseling. The social cost of the meager benefits that it promises is simply too great. [95]

So far as the cognitive function is concerned, it is burden enough that, in providing a decent opportunity to the citizen to know the law, we require the reader to find the relevant statutes and case law. With the current information explosion, we need a sense of proportion. The practical burden of locating the express elements of the law is becoming so formidable, especially in the United States, that one wonders what kind of judicial perfectionism justifies adding to this already monumental burden the

---

into the record, particularly by spokesmen for a minority position, in the hope that the court will find and use that interpretation."

See also W. Moorhead, A Congressman Looks at the Planned Colloquy and Its Effect in the Interpretation of Statutes, 45 A.B.A.J. 1314 (1959); C. Nutting, The Planned Colloquy — What Now? 46 A.B.A.J. 93 (1960).

95. "The danger of abuse of these publications is constantly greater than any utility they may have. Therefore it would be better always to let the statute be promulgated without allowing the public to see any of the preliminary reports." J. Kohler, Judicial Interpretation of Enacted Law, in Science of Legal Method 187, 198 (1921). Also, judges should not refer to them in their opinions.

burden of locating a more voluminous, more heterogeneous, less reliable, and rarely useful mass of information that has been dignified as "legislative history."

Nor have recent, generally successful developments in the use of computers to store and retrieve legislative materials, including some legislative history, materially undercut this evaluation. The addition of legislative history to the relatively small universe of statutory text would probably increase the data base at least a hundred-fold, filling it with legislative debris and not only complicating the almost overwhelming problem of developing adequate search strategies but greatly increasing today's already staggering costs of providing practical justice and counseling clients. Here, the availability of computer approaches even offers a serious threat of increasing, rather than decreasing, the problem of dealing with the important materials of the law. In the ecology of the law, misuse of the computer could easily increase, rather than solve, a serious existing problem of legislative pollution. New York and California have already taken steps to curtail the availability of unnecessary case law. The same may need to be done with the peripheral legislative materials comprising legislative history.

F. Postenactment Developments

Assuming that a statute is to be read as of the date of its enactment, what happens in a later legislative session cannot be part of its proper context in the sense of conditioning either the relevant legislative intent or the statute's meaning at the time of enactment. At best, the legislature's later actions or nonactions can in appropriate circumstances be a basis for inferring legislative intent that is likely to be that of a significantly different group of legislators, conditioned by different circumstances. No matter how reliable it is for determining current legislative intent, it is a highly unreliable basis for making a secondary inference respecting the original legislative intent.[96]

Suppose a legislature enacted a statute (concurred in by the executive), declaring the meaning of an earlier statute. This would be effective, at least prospectively, simply because, however inartistic, it could stand on its own feet as a valid enact-

96. For cases relying on such materials, see Sutherland, §§49.09-49.11.

ment.[97] Whether or not it would be reliable as a declaration of previous intent, it is effective, not as an interpretation (which might be an unconstitutional invasion of the powers of a coordinate branch of government), but as a new act of legislation. Thus, even if it were wholly inadequate as an interpretation, it could stand as an amendment of the earlier statute. But would it, or could it, have retroactive force?[98]

Suppose, instead, that the later legislature passed a concurrent resolution to the same effect.[99] Not having been approved by the executive, it could not stand as independent legislation. As an interpretation, it is arguably offensive to the constitutional separation of powers. However, even if inartistic in form, could the resolution stand, not as legislation or authoritative interpretation, but simply as a basis for inferring the actual legislative intent of the earlier legislature?

There are several questions here. The first is whether the later legislature purported to do more than merely state its own approval of the interpretation of the earlier statute, which might imply nothing about the state of mind of the earlier legislature, or could it be inferred that what is now in their minds to approve also implied an assertion about what was in the minds of the original legislature?[100] Assuming that the later legislature impliedly asserted a similar, earlier legislative intent, the second question is how reliable such an implied assertion would be.

Clearly, it could not be more reliable, and presumably would be less reliable, than a resolution concurrent with the enactment of the original legislation, depending on the lapse of time. It would not be part of legislative context.

Even so, it would be reliable as a basis for otherwise appropriate lawmaking if circumstances warranted it. For this purpose, a court would be warranted in using the later resolution as a guide when completing or clarifying the statute, even if the

97. E.g., Bryan v. Board of Education, 90 Ky. 322, 336, 13 S.W. 276, 279 (1900). And see Note, Declaratory Legislation, 49 Harv. L. Rev. 137 (1935).

98. F. Newman & S. Surrey, Legislation — Cases and Materials 657-658 (1955).

99. ". . . [J]udges have often given such documents great weight." Id. at 657.

100. Id. at 658-659. In Bobsee Corp. v. United States, 411 F.2d 231, 237 n. 18 (5th Cir. 1969), Gewin, C.J., said: "We agree . . . that these subsequent legislative statements are not part of the history. . . . However, [they are] entitled to some consideration as a secondarily authoritative expression of expert opinion."

later resolution intended no more than to present only the legislature's current thinking, unless the result was out of key with the general legislative pattern laid down by the earlier legislature. In the latter case, the court's general duty of deference to the legislature would in many cases be better served by acting consistently with the enacted will of the legislature than by acting consistently with the unenacted later will, despite the fact that the unenacted expression of intent was the more recent legislative expression.

Suppose the legislature refrains from amending a statute an uncertainty in which the courts of the jurisdiction have previously resolved. Would this constitute effective legislative approval of the judicial interpretation? The question becomes relevant whenever a court determines that it would be desirable to change the earlier interpretation. If implied legislative approval has frozen the interpretation, the court is powerless to correct what it now conceives to have been an error.

The first question is whether legislative silence can constitute effective legislative action. It seems obvious that a legislature cannot legislate effectively by not legislating at all. Assuming this to be so, would there be any basis for saying that the later legislature had expressed an intent that a deferential court ought to respect? [101]

The second question is whether legislative silence has a probative value for inferring current legislative intentions. The answer to this also seems clear. In the realities of the legislative process, almost no reliable inference of current intent could be drawn. In many cases the legislature is unaware of the relevant court decision. Even where it is fully aware of it, there are often reasons other than approval why a legislature remains silent or inactive.

Alternatively, there may be no reason beyond the fact that the legislature is busy with what it considers more important public matters, or that the legislature does not consider the matter important enough to engage the attention of the whole legislative process. Certainly, the Supreme Court's interpretation of the Mann Act in *Caminetti v. United States* [102] was considered a perversion of congressional intent, and yet political considerations intervened to head off corrective legislation. [103] There could hardly be less reputable legislative material than

101. The matter is discussed further in ch. 13, pp. 254-255.

102. 242 U.S. 470, 37 S. Ct. 192 (1916).

103. Note, Interstate Immorality: The Mann Act and the Supreme Court, 56 Yale L.J. 718, 727-728 (1947).

legislative silence.[104] And no court should feel inhibited, merely by virtue of legislative silence or inaction, in correcting what it conceives to have been a faulty judicial interpretation.[105]

Finally, even if silence constituted legislative approval, it would be desirable to differentiate "interpretation" in the sense of cognition from "interpretation" in the sense of judicial law-making. The possibility of such legislative freezing[106] exists only where the court has performed an act of cognition or, possibly, of judicial lawmaking in the sense of resolving a residual uncertainty. On the other hand, there would be no appropriate basis for a legislative freeze of earlier judicial action where the court had merely responded to a delegation of legislative power to make law on an intermediate plane of generality. In the latter case, implied legislative approval would freeze only the implied interpretation that what the court did was authorized by the statute. It would not freeze the court's exercise of discretion in electing among a number of equally authorized ways of implementing the original legislative mandate.

Suppose that, instead of remaining silent, the legislature reenacts the statute without changing the provision that created the problem. Is there a negative implication here that by changing some provisions and not changing others the unchanged provisions are not disagreed with and are, therefore, approved as judicially interpreted? Weakening the probability of such an implication is the possibility that the legislature had other reasons than agreement for letting the provision in question stand unchanged.

Suppose, in the legislative history of a reenactment, the legislature made it abundantly clear that it wholeheartedly approved

104. Sutherland §49.10.

105. Id. at §49.05. In Girouard v. United States, 328 U.S. 61, 69, 70, 66 S. Ct. 826, 830 (1946), the Supreme Court said, "It is at best treacherous to find in congressional silence alone the adoption of a controlling rule of law. . . . The silence of Congress and its inaction are as consistent with a desire to leave the problem fluid as they are with an adoption by silence of the rule of those cases." And see ch. 13, pp. 254-255.

106. Is this view consistent with the generally accepted view that, when a legislature uses a highly vague, general term with a substantial existing judicial explication, the term will normally be taken as incorporating the relevant field of legal knowledge? It would seem so. Incorporating an established field of law does not necessarily freeze each specific judicial contribution to that field. Thus, using the term "reasonable" in a statute identifies a broad patch of legal doctrine without necessarily underwriting the aptness of a particular application of it, which would preclude a court from later changing its mind.

the judicial interpretation. Would this be enough to constitute binding legislative approval?

There are several possibilities here. Either the judicial interpretation in question was correct or it was not, or it was partly correct and partly not. So far as the interpretation may have been correct, reenactment added nothing. So far as the interpretation may have been incorrect, later reenactment added nothing unless it somehow effectively removed the inaccuracy. But legislative history is not law. Could it be argued that, although the text of the statute remains unchanged its context has changed? But, on what basis? Because it is doubtful that proper context has so changed, how could mere reenactment change the statute's meaning when the only new element is the mere legislative intent to approve and adopt an intervening judicial opinion? How can the legislature amend a statute merely by generating a new legislative intent? Legislative intent can confirm a meaning already in the statute, but it could hardly introduce it for the first time.

Briefly, mere reenactment with the intent to approve a court's previous interpretation is either surplusage or ineffectual so far as controlling the force of that opinion is concerned. Ironically, the court must interpret the statute before it can evaluate the significance of this piece of evidence. The simpler and more sensible approach is for the court to look at the earlier cases merely for their suggestive value.[107] If they appear to be wrong, it should be free to correct them.

In any event, the extent to which the courts balance reenactment with other factors suggests that they have not adopted any flat reenactment rule of adoption.

The analysis here would seem to apply *a fortiori* to intervening administrative interpretations.

G. "Travaux Préparatoires"

Because the problems of legislative history are not confined to the United States and England, it may be helpful to look briefly at several other representative countries, particularly those op-

107. See Sutherland §49.09. The legislative adoption approach has been purportedly legislated away in section 38(4) of the Canadian Interpretation Act, 16 Eliz. II, c. 7 (R.C.S. 1970, c. I-23, s. 37(4)). See also Law Relating to Construction of Statutes, Ninth Report of the Law Reform Committee of South Australia to the Attorney-General 6 (1970).

erating under a code system.[108] Strömholm has surveyed the situations in Sweden, Germany, and France, none of which provides an exact parallel with the United States.[109] In Sweden, the materials of legislative history are called "förarbeten," in Germany "Gesetzgebungsmaterialien," and in France "travaux préparatoires."[110]

How legislative history is regarded in a country depends partly on what materials are available. It depends on the constitutional relationship between its legislature and its courts. It depends also on whether enactments are regarded simply as objective facts to be dealt with or as products of a volitional process. In turn, how the material is used affects how it is prepared.[111] The development of legislative history as a tool for interpretation or application became an object of systematic investigation about the middle of the nineteenth century, when in Germany ideas of positive law became the central consideration

108. What follows is suggestive rather than definitive. In general, foreign sources (even more than domestic ones) must be approached with caution, because it is easy to be beguiled by exotic congeries of concepts, similar to our own, that need serious reworking or to be betrayed by the impression that when different authorities use the same or similar terminology they operate in a jurisprudential universe of standardized concepts and standardized constitutional, political, and social assumptions. Interpreting, evaluating, and interrelating the important foreign philosophers of interpretation is too big a job for me here and I will not try to improve on what others have already done. Those who want to search further the comparative literature on legislative history, or even that on statutory interpretation generally, may want to start with the following materials, for which I am indebted to Professor Albert P. Blaustein: M. Amos, The Interpretation of Statutes, 5 Camb. L.J. 163-165, 174-175 (1934); J. Charmont & E. Chausse, Les Interprètes du Code Civil, 133, 152-155 (1904) (translation included in A. Von Mehren, The Civil Law System 59-61 (1957)); R. David & H. de Vries, The French Legal System 87-99 (1958); H. Gutteridge, Comparative Law 101-116 (2d ed. 1949); 1 M. Planiol, Treatise on the Civil Law, pt. 1, 149-164 (12th ed. 1939, transl. Louisiana State Law Institute, 1959). This includes a bibliography.

See also J. Bonnecase, The Problem of Legal Interpretation in France, 12 J. Comp. Legis. & Int. L. 79 (1930); A. Lenhoff, On Interpretative Theories: A Comparative Study in Legislation 312, 326-331 (1949); III R. Pound, Jurisprudence 467-506 (1959); M. Radin, A Short Way with Statutes, 56 Harv. L. Rev. 388, 424-426 (1942) (bibliography).

109. S. Strömholm, Legislative Material and Construction of Statutes — Notes on the Continental Approach, in 10 Scandinavian Studies in Law 1966, at 173.

110. Id. at 175.

111. Id. at 176.

of legal analysis.[112] In France, where the "law of nature" continued to be a strong consideration, only Gény and a few others studied the subject systematically.[113]

Strömholm points out that discussions of the uses and abuses of legislative history presuppose a particular method of preparing and enacting laws.[114] The necessity of choosing between theories of interpretation generally arises when expressions of legislative intent are available outside the statute itself.[115] Its development, he says, has been speeded whenever statutes have taken the form of commands rather than abstract propositions, because it implies more strongly that behind the statute is human intent.[116] The importance of the intent of the legislature has been correspondingly strengthened whenever it is assumed, constitutionally or otherwise, that the legislature is the exclusive author of positive law.[117]

In Strömholm's view, there are three kinds of legislative history: (1) "descriptive texts" (documents that record deliberations and debates), which are of uneven value because of the part played by chance; (2) "motivating texts" (documents explaining why the statute was prepared), which tend to be valuable because they show what the authors were trying to accomplish; and (3) "expounding texts" (texts that explain, section-by-section, what the statute does), which run "the inevitable risk of simplifying and standardizing conflicts which, when they come before the courts, may be attended by special circumstances not foreseen by the drafters and tending to make their solutions difficult to accept."[118]

Concepts of legislative intent make it necessary to define who is the "legislator," a concept that helps to determine the degree of remoteness of the particular document being considered. It may make a difference, for example, whether it was written by a

112. Id. at 181.
113. Id. at 180.
114. Id. at 181.
115. Id. at 182.
116. Id.
117. Id. at 185.
118. Id. at 187. This breakdown seems undesirable because it is based partly on source (deliberations and debates) and partly on content (purpose or explanation of meaning). It would seem more helpful to classify legislative history, first, by what it purports to do and, second, by source. The useful permutations here certainly exceed three.

preliminary technician or by the chairman of a parliamentary committee.[119]

Availability of the document is important, because whether it has been published or not affects the use that can be made of preliminary works. "Opinions scattered in public records not easily accessible to the judge and practising lawyer are likely to pass unnoticed, whatever their merits."[120]

After discussing in more detail the differences in legislative procedure, including what legislative history is developed and published, Strömholm summarizes the comparative situation as follows:[121]

> . . . [I]n France, *descriptive* texts — records of parliamentary debates — are the most important *travaux préparatoires* from a merely quantitative point of view; however, the legislative process also creates a number of *motivating* texts which often furnish information about the evaluations which are at the base of proposed enactments and contain certain clues to construction inasmuch as they proceed by antithetic reasoning and rule out one or several possible solutions. *Expounding* texts are unknown. In Sweden, *descriptive* documents are few, short, and uninteresting. *Expounding* texts, usually of a pragmatic character, abound throughout the legislative process; they clearly surpass the equally abundant *motivating* texts in quantity. Germany represents an intermediate position in all these respects. On the other hand, it sometimes results from the abstract technique used in Germany that the statements concerning the proposed enactment assume a wider scope and raise theoretical questions of a more general *portée* than do the pragmatic opinions found in Swedish legislative material.

Strömholm does not question the need to create most of the materials constituting legislative history, but he does question many of the arguments advanced why such materials are appropriate for interpreting statutes. The first argument for such use is that statutes are at best uncertain and that "context, including the speaker's identity and the purpose of the speech, is the safest way of arriving at greater certainty."[122] To this he replies that

119. Id. at 189.

120. Id. at 190. See also H. Thornstedt, The Principle of Legality and Teleological Construction of Statutes, 4 Scandinavian Studies in Law 1960, at 209, 211, 241.

121. Id. at 210. (Emphasis in original.)

122. Id. at 213.

it may be objected that emphasis on the speaker's identity and purpose would tend to throw the effects of context off center, because "courts have not had time to analyse other elements of the relevant social context. . . ." [123] (". . . [*W*]*hy* this particular speaker . . . ?") [124] And what of the "interventions in the subsequent parliamentary process"? [125] The main point here is reliability.

The second argument is that, because statutes are binding in that they express the will of the legislature, other expressions of that will should also be respected. Strömholm suggests this answer: "If the sovereign wants to be obeyed, he has a duty to tell his servants clearly, in the form of explicit commands, i.e., statutory provisions, how to act." [126]

Also, if this rationale is accepted, much legislative history must be rejected. ". . . [U]nder this theory, only the 'constitutional lawgiver' is of importance." [127] Motivating texts are important because they have directly influenced the lawgiver. [128] Descriptive texts are useful where if by chance "they contain unequivocal expressions of legislative intentions." Expounding texts must be rejected because "it seems obvious that only the actual legislation can reasonably be assumed to be the object of the 'legislator's will.' " [129]

The principle of selectivity implied in any "will" theory requires rejection of all preliminary materials prepared by technicians, because these materials cannot be reliably attributed to the legislators. [130] They may be used, however, to clarify ideas that have been expressed inadequately in the relevant material. [131] He concludes that the principle of selection embodied in the will theory is "irrational." [132]

Another argument is that legislative history, good or bad, helps to bring uniformity of application. [133] Strömholm replies

123. Id.
124. Id. at 215. (Emphasis in original.)
125. Id.
126. Id. at 213.
127. Id. at 215.
128. Id.
129. Id. at 215-216.
130. Id.
131. Id.
132. Id.
133. Id. at 214.

that the price of uniformity is too high; requiring courts to follow instructions in legislative history forces them to give up their independence.[134] Also, this theory implies criteria of selectivity, which, wanting uniformity themselves, cannot assure even that they will encourage uniformity of result.[135]

A stronger argument is that, because legislative history in the form of *exposés des motifs* (disclosing purpose and rationale) provides the first expert study on the new statute and therefore offers to save the judge's time, it should be given the same weight as a textbook.[136] This seems to be acceptable so long as it is assumed that it is being used as a quick avenue to social and legal facts that are generally available to the legislative audience through the same source or otherwise. This approach, while claiming less force for legislative history, enjoys the advantage that problems of selection and ranking become less important, because it shifts emphasis from *origin* to *rationality,* which among other things direct main attention to the technical, as distinct from the political, elements in the legislative history.[137]

Strömholm concludes:[138]

> . . . [T]he only reasonable approach . . . is to treat the *travaux préparatoires* as expert advice, no more and no less. If political rulers want to enforce a solution which cannot be attained by honest reasoning on the basis of the text and the general intentions of an enactment, but needs the support of hints in the *travaux préparatoires* which go further than the actual provisions, they have the power to do so, and they ought to accept the corresponding responsibility.
>
> Considered as expert advice, legislative material — particularly in the form of expounding texts drafted by "technicians" — is a valuable instrument for courts and practising lawyers. It is probable that good *exposés des motifs* are sufficiently convincing in themselves, independently of any vague ideas of the "legislator's will", to secure uniformity in the application of statutes. The French system, which leaves judges to tackle new enactments practically alone, undoubtedly possesses the advantage of giving the courts of justice a great deal of independence, but experience seems to show that under this system it takes a long time and a comprehensive body of clear precedents from the superior courts to achieve stability in the construction of statutes.

134. Id.
135. Id. at 216-217.
136. Id. at 214.
137. Id. at 217.
138. Id. at 218. (Emphasis in original.)

Strömholm's analysis loses sharpness because for the most part he voices no clear distinction between the courts' cognitive function and their creative function, even though the distinction seems to be implied in the first of his two concluding paragraphs, quoted above, which suggests that at least many of the uses of legislative history should be confined to supporting the creative function, without, however, foreclosing the use of legislative history for limited purposes in the cognitive function. ". . . [A] solution which cannot be attained by honest reasoning on the basis of the text and *the general intentions* of an enactment." [139] does not foreclose the possibility that "the general intentions" (ulterior purposes?) of the legislature may in some instances be discoverable only from legislative history. But it remains uncertain to what extent he presumes availability to the legislative audience and ultimately the qualification of the material as part of proper context.

The main lessons to be learned from Strömholm's analysis are that the issue of legislative history is not the simple one of using it or rejecting it and that a philosophy of use necessarily depends on the nature of the materials available and the use of which it is proposed that they be put. Legislative history should never be used to override statutory meaning in its proper context. It often has confirmatory value and it sometimes can clarify what is otherwise not clarifiable, in which case it is being used in the creative, rather than the cognitive, function (unless it can be rationalized as part of proper context). The question remains, under Strömholm's analysis, whether in the cognitive choice between competing plausibilities legislative history may properly be used to tip the scales against what would otherwise be the most plausible alternative.

Ekelöf observes that on "the Continent there is no more agreement than in England on how statutes should be applied in concrete cases." [140] In general, he says that there are three main approaches to the problem.

The "legislative intent" approach makes the search for intent the paramount consideration, to the point where it is proper to rely on sources of knowledge beyond the statute and to disregard how the proposed interpretation fits with legislative purpose or

139. Id. (Emphasis added.)

140. P. Ekelöf, Teleological Construction of Statutes, in 2 Scandinavian Studies in Law 1958, at 75, 78.

even the statutory language itself.[141] This sometimes results in the irony that if Sweden's Parliament disagrees with a court that has been led astray by legislative history, it may have to amend the statute even though the defect lies only in legislative history![142]

The "teleological approach," which Ekelöf espouses, tempers the use of legislative history and other evidences of intent by taking into account legislative purpose.[143]

The "plain meaning approach," which uses as its guide the language of the statute when read in context (which in Sweden includes legislative history), differs from the "legislative intent" approach in that it does not permit legislative history to override the statute.[144] It differs from the "teleological approach" in that it does not allow a meaning to be restricted by manifest legislative purpose.[145] Why context that discloses a narrower purpose cannot appropriately restrict the range of a statute, even under a meaning approach, he does not explain.

Ekelöf seems to recognize the dual role of the court when applying statutes and the principle that cognition should precede creation. "First I establish the *meaning* of the statute as accurately as I can and try to solve the problem at issue *on this basis alone*. After that I proceed to consider it in accordance with *the teleological method*."[146] How the uses of legislative history are allocated, if at all, between the two judicial functions is hard to determine, because Ekelöf defines "context" simply as the evidence that is used to determine what people-in-general would have meant by the language used.[147] Thus, context seems to depend on what the Swedish courts decide to use as evidence of usage, and not necessarily on what is shared and taken account of by both author and audience, a test that would ordinarily exclude legislative history.

Schmidt says that in applying a statute a Swedish court is subject to three kinds of directives: the statute, earlier decisions, and legislative history.[148] The latter two are "secondary direc-

141. Id. at 89-95.
142. Id. at 94-95.
143. Id. at 94.
144. Id. at 95-102.
145. Id. at 98.
146. Id. at 102. (Emphasis in original.)
147. Id. at 100.
148. F. Schmidt, Construction of Statutes, in 1 Scandinavian Studies in Law 1957, at 155, 158.

tives," which are of a lower order in that they do not have the absolute character of statutes. But although secondary directives cannot be used to override a statute, the court ordinarily feels obliged to respect them.

In recognizing, as Ekelöf does, "duality in the judicial process," [149] Schmidt seems to accept the basic distinction between cognition and creation, without, however, making clear in each instance which aspect he is talking about. On the other hand, he seems to assume that legislative history is an aspect of proper context and thus is not subject to purely optional use. As for judicial lawmaking, "*. . . [T]he decision of the court is the outcome of a choice only in those cases where the judge . . . has not been able to find his answer . . . in the three instruments of directives.*" [150]

Swedish legislative processes [151] are based on constitutional premises different from those in effect in the United States. When applying statutes, a Swedish court is not a "servant of the legislator" (i.e., with respect to lawmaking) but an "independent contractor," [152] which apparently gives it broader authority to mold statutes than its American counterpart enjoys.

On the other hand, political debates (floor debates) "are never appropriate sources of information on technical questions." [153] They are not carefully weighed and, because of the difficulty of examining the official records, the volume of legislative history should be kept within bounds.

Schmidt says that the Swedish Parliament, by using very abstract language in its prescriptions, often delegates law making authority to the courts and for this purpose may rely on supplementary explanations that are responsive to the statutory text. [154]

Directives lose force with the passage of time. [155] Also, reinforcement through adjudication by the courts includes reshaping the past into something new. Thus, "the judge will be free to disregard directives" when "the people have ceased to believe in the values on which the statute was based" and decide cases based on "the values of those who are *now* in charge of the

149. Id. at 164.
150. Id. at 166. (Emphasis in original.)
151. Id. at 168-170.
152. Id. at 196.
153. Id. at 170.
154. Id. at 174.
155. Id. at 192.

legislative process." [156] Who those people are and how their opinions are to be determined Schmidt does not specify.

Throughout Gény's analysis of the interpretation of French statutes, he distinguishes between "interpretation proper" and "free interpretation," which with one exception corresponds with the distinction made throughout this book between the cognitive function and the creative function. [157]

Concerning the former, he says: [158]

> . . . [To] interpret a statute is simply to look for the content of the legislative will with the help of the formula in which it is expressed. *As long as one stays in the sphere of statutory interpretation proper,* this search should be made without any preconceived ideas, about the more or less ideal form of the rule to be discovered, or about its more or less complete adaptation to the social environment within which it is to be applied. Of course I do not mean to say that the interpreter should eliminate these considerations from his horizon. But I insist that in this situation he can use them only to clarify his diagnosis of the legislative intent, not to dominate and correct it.

He also makes clear that reference to legislative history is a legitimate part of interpretation proper so long as it "should positively contribute to the discovery of legislative intent," and so long as the "statutory text is not in conflict with these complementary explanations." [159]

> This means that in the complex organization of modern legislative power these requirements will rarely be satisfied, at least with respect to statutes proper. And one can easily understand why the French courts, contrary to the feeling of many writers, tend to restrict more and more the role of legislative records, if they deal with a text which in itself has a clear and precise meaning. . . . Is it not . . . necessary with regard to the authentic formula of the statute, alone enacted by the parliamentary procedure and expressing officially the will of the legislator, to restrict narrowly the inferences from discussions, opinions, or simply personal chatter, which could have influenced the shaping of the legislative thought, but which do not, except under rare circumstances, reveal its definite result? [160]

156. Id. at 193. (Emphasis in original.)

157. F. Gény, Method of Interpretation and Sources of Private Positive Law 206-208 (2d ed. 1954, English transl. J. Mayda 1963).

158. Id. at 182. (Emphasis in original.)

159. Id. at 198, 202.

160. Id. at 203, 204.

Gény approves the use of legislative history also where it reliably shows a legislative intent that supports a meaning different from "the meaning suggested by the pure textual formula." The meaning so shown may be broader or narrower. "However," he adds, "because of the nature of this formal source, any modification is legitimate only under the condition that it always substantially rests on the text of which it must be considered a correction, never a negation." [161]

Here, Gény's analysis becomes mysterious. It is easy to see how a small extension of a statute might be considered only a "correction." On the other hand, how could a restriction that was not implied by the statute read in its proper context be considered as other than a partial "negation" of it?

From this it appears that the line between Gény's "interpretation proper" and his "free interpretation" is determined, not by what can be quarried from the statute when read in its proper context, but by what can be reliably based on legislative intent, whether it is determinable from the statute and its context or merely from legislative history. The difference is measured by the extent to which relevant legislative history cannot meet the criteria of proper context.

So far as free interpretation is concerned, it includes only results that are products of the courts' creative function. For Gény, this consists of judicial lawmaking (other than that based on manifest legislative intent) by analogy with the statute. [162] The first type of analogy is analogy that helps to fulfill the policy behind the statute. [163] The second is analogy that supports judicial lawmaking outside both the statute and its supporting policy. [164]

To the question why techniques (including the use of legislative history) that are excluded for the purpose of "interpretation proper" may be admitted for the purpose of "free interpretation," Gény replies: [165]

> . . . They have different authority and are employed under different conditions depending [on] whether they represent purely a development of written law or its independent elaboration.

161. Id. at 204-205.
162. Id. at 208.
163. Id. at 209.
164. Id. at 210.
165. Id. at 215-216.

> First, they do not have the same authority. . . . [J]udicial decisions which are not derived from the officially established legislative power . . . have a lesser force and are not so strictly binding on the judge.
>
> Secondly . . . , reasoning by analogy from written law amounts to borrowing from it a positive element which the interpreter of law then utilizes according to his own inspiration to arrive at an independent legal construction. . . . He has a much larger margin of discretion, limited only by the objective requirement of serving justice and social utility.

Gény's explanation applies equally to the importance of maintaining the distinction between cognition and judicial creativity not involving reasoning by analogy.

Although this investigation is hardly exhaustive, it suggests several general conclusions. In the code countries, as elsewhere, there is no consistent, unified theory of statutory "interpretation." Even so, there is wide recognition, sometimes implied, of the difference between "interpretation proper" and "free interpretation." There is not such wide (at least explicit) recognition of the principle that cognition should precede creation.

It is generally agreed that, except for legislative debates (which are inherently unreliable), the courts not only may but should consult the materials of legislative history, but not for the purpose of overriding the statute. Despite this, there seems to be wide disagreement on the force of such secondary "directives." Unfortunately, the apparently competing views are badly blurred by the failure of their adherents to specify when they are considering legislative history for the purposes of the courts' cognitive function and when they are considering it for the purposes of their creative function. Some of this results from their general lack of sophistication respecting the nature of legislative context, a prevalent condition among the theorists of meaning.

The most important differences between Continental and American approaches appear to lie in the respective constitutional relationships among the three main branches of government and in the differences in how laws are prepared. Continental courts are much freer in this respect than American courts would be if they paid more adequate attention to the implications of the constitutions under which they respectively operate. Also, Continental draftsmen appear to have a fuller opportunity to exploit their skills.

H. Conclusions

If it is true that only the million-dollar case warrants using legislative history,[166] it should be used not at all or only with the greatest restraint.

Because at least some kinds of legislative history have uses other than supporting the interpretation or application of statutes, there is little point in urging that what exists be destroyed or generated no more. However, even so drastic an approach would make good sense for kinds of legislative history, such as interpretative materials, that in the United States at least are of no legitimate use to the legislative audience. Interpretative materials compete with the constitutionally prescribed legislative vehicle or tend to infringe on judicial functions, are slovenly prepared, and, even when carefully prepared by professionals, have almost no reliability. Their total elimination, therefore, would be a net benefit.[167] Even for purely confirmatory purposes, they are so unreliable that they are not worth the effort of creating them. For legislatures, it would be a wise course never to create legislative history merely for the purpose of helping courts interpret or apply statutes.

The more realistic approach to legislative history would be to end or severely limit its judicial use. Aside from eliminating the wholly useless at its source, the most effective way to restrict use is through professional persuasion rather than fiat (even English judges have privately confessed to taking an occasional, surreptitious look at legislative history).

So long as they are needed for other purposes, records of committee hearings and house debates should not be eliminated. However, because they are highly unreliable as a basis of inferring legislative intent, a court should refuse to consult them either for the purposes of cognition or for those of judicial lawmaking. Even for confirming results reached by legitimate means, they have little value.

Another important consideration is that these kinds of legislative history tend to be very voluminous. For this reason, a court

166. See note 68 *supra*.

167. This in no wise rules out preparing a summary to help the busy legislator learn, during the course of enactment, what the proposed bill is generally about. If interpretative materials are needed for this purpose, they should be destroyed as soon as the bill is enacted.

should be careful not to use them so as to make them an element in predicting the outcome of specific litigation. Otherwise, the resulting responsibility of the lawyer to his client to make a relatively unproductive search among these materials would continue to make statutory interpretation a disproportionately costly and time-consuming operation. Certainly, a court that cannot resist the temptation to consult these aspects of legislative history (preferably for their shaky confirmatory value alone) should not mention the fact in its opinions.[168] Otherwise, the conscientious advocate will be tempted, where his client can foot the bill, to introduce these shoddy materials into the litigation process.

Even if these self-imposed restraints should produce a theoretically less refined administration of justice, society can no longer afford to treasure the few nuggets of reliable information that only occasionally result from a kind of legal research that is not only costly and time-consuming but adds greatly to the cost and length of the time spent in court.

Also, failure to restrict the use of this kind of judicial input increases the risk that computers, on which court administrators now heavily rely to speed the scheduling of cases and which have an enormous capacity to store not only existing but new kinds of legislative history, will contribute more to the problem than to its solution.

The only decently reliable materials of legislative history are the "motivating texts" found in preliminary studies or committee reports. However, because of their relative inaccessibility they should be used only for the purposes of judicial lawmaking.

The social costs of relentlessly pursuing refinement are monumental, whereas its purported benefits, whether in the form of greater fidelity to legislative intent or more equitable legal results, are, considering the general unreliability of the materials used, at best conjectural. Indeed, it is even likely that fidelity to legislative intent is better served without recourse to legislative history than with it. Rarely has expensive perfectionism been so poorly served.[169]

168. See note 95 *supra*. "At least they must not be referred to in Court." Lord MacMillan, Law and Other Things 164 (1938).

169. "Doubtless this goes too far, but it had enormous advantages over the cult of 'materials,' i.e., debates, drafts, reports, etc., which was the characteristic of the Continental approach to the understanding of statutes. This was found to be a great burden by progressive jurists and it is unfortunate that we chose just this excrescence in the systems of Continental law for invitation, when

The ultimate results of pressing judicial refinement to its counterproductive extreme are well exemplified in the push for expanded small-claims jurisdiction and in substantive approaches such as no-fault insurance. The lesson here is that when a process or doctrine becomes unrealistically complicated or expensive, ways will be found to bypass it. Ironically, the threat of ultimate judicial breakdown may result in measures less congenial to social goals than merely exercising wholesome self-restraint.

In general, one is tempted to relate the problem of overrefinement and spurious perfectionism rampant in the development, maintenance, and exploitation of extrinsic legislative materials to similar general tendencies in our society that threaten to create a proliferating array of products, services, and institutions, of dubious individual value, that are so numerous, specialized, and refined and so hard to find, evaluate, and relate, that the social structure that tries to accommodate them will fall of its own weight.

---

we were so notably and unreasonably supercilious about other elements in these foreign systems. The phrase, *la loi parle par elle-meme,* ought to be received back into its former seat of honor." M. Radin, A Case Study on Statutory Interpretation: Western Union Co. vs. Lenroot, 33 Calif. L. Rev. 219, 224 (1945).

11

Strict Interpretation and Liberal Interpretation; the Spirit or Equity of a Statute

. . . [T]he meaning of some words in a statute may be enlarged or restricted in order to harmonize them with the legislative intent of the entire statute. . . . It is the spirit . . . of the statute which should govern over the literal meaning. . . .

— Hanley, J., in Town of Menominee v. Skubitz, 53 Wis. 2d 430, 437, 192 N.W. 2d 887, 890 (1972)

A. Narrow or Broad Interpretation

How appropriate is an interpretation or application of a statute that is broader or narrower than its literal meaning?

The easy part of the answer is that, when performing its cognitive function of ascertaining what a statute means, a court should temper its reading by taking into account the proper context of the statute. The normal result of such tempering is to narrow the sweep of otherwise broad generalities. The limiting force of context is a major factor in making communication practicable.

Normally, the process works through tacit assumptions that, were they express, would appear as limitations or exceptions. The interpretative problem is to determine what relevant tacit assumptions are being made and the extent to which they impliedly limit the general language of the statute. The operative tacit assumptions are those shared by the legislature with the legislative audience. Whether or not a tacit assumption exists is closely related to the question of legislative purpose.

Riggs v. Palmer [1] provides a classic example. Here, the question was whether a legatee was entitled to take his bequest even though he had murdered the testator, the local wills statute not having expressly provided for such a contingency. Could the court find an exception implied in the statute or would its narrow application be judicial amendment of the statute? The former approach would, if successful, be unobjectionable, whereas the latter, being amendatory, would trespass on the functions of the legislature.

Because of the generally accepted common law principle that a wrongdoer should not reap legal advantage from his own wrong, the Ohio Supreme Court disqualified the legatee. In doing so, the court did not make clear whether, on the one hand, it assumed that this principle either overrode the statute or justified the court in creatively amending the law (either approach would hardly fit with legislative supremacy) or whether, on the other, it found that the principle was a tacit assumption in the light of which the legislature had enacted its general language (an approach wholly consistent with legislative supremacy).

Under the latter approach, it had been appropriate to find that a law of Bologna providing that "whoever drew blood in the streets should be punished with the utmost severity" did not apply to a barber who, following currently accepted medical practice, opened the vein of a person who had fallen into a fit in a city street. [2] Similarly, when a father says, "Show the children a game" and they are taught gaming with dice, we are not surprised when he protests, "I didn't mean that sort of game." [3]

The principle applies also where the legislature tacitly assumed and took into account the limitations in an earlier general

1. 115 N.Y. 506, 22 N.E. 188 (1889).

2. 1 Blackstone's Commentaries 61 (13th ed. 1796).

3. See ch. 9, note 26 *supra*. P. Heymann, in Ice Cream at Harvard Square, But No Vehicles in the Park — A Study of Purposes 45 (third-year paper, Harvard Law School, 1960), observes: "The servant who is told to empty the waste baskets into the rubbish should not throw away a five dollar bill found in a basket simply because, like other paper, the five dollar bill contributes to the fullness of the baskets, the sloppiness of their appearance, and the difficulty of continuing to use them."

statute. Although a statute can never directly affect a later statute, its existence can serve as the basis for an implied exception where the later legislature took it into account. Thus, the codifiers of the United States Code's title 10, which provided for military retirements for persons who attained specified ages or completed specified terms of service, felt justified in including a section providing, "The retirement provisions of this title are subject to section 47a of title 5." [4] This was based on section 1 of the Act of April 23, 1930, chapter 209, [5] which provided that federal retirements "shall take effect on the 1st day of the month following the month in which said retirement would otherwise be effective," and which predated the retirement laws on which the codification was based.

If, on the other hand, the court cannot in good faith find a probable limitation implied in fact, there would seem to be no constitutional basis for restrictive application unless the provision is wholly or partly unconstitutional. Nor would the court be justified in making law restrictively by analogy with other statute law.

In short, the only basis for applying a statute more restrictively than what a literal reading of the statutory language allows is through inferences of fact, based on a reading of the statutory language in the light of its proper context, sufficient to support one or more implied exceptions or limitations.

An interesting aspect of *Riggs* is that the court might have avoided interpreting the local wills act by applying the principles of interpretation, just discussed, to the will itself. Might not the testator have acted on the tacit (and possibly unconscious) assumption that the legatee would not do him in and that if he did the gift would be off? Under either approach, the fact that the court can do little more than balance reasonable probabilities does not invalidate the basic principle.

So much for narrower interpretations or applications. Conversely, may a court give a statute a *broader* interpretation or application than what a literal reading of the statute would support? The first question is whether extensions of the statute may be implied similarly to limitations. To a very limited extent, yes. Normally, the draftsmen of statutes do not rely on tacit assumptions or other aspects of context to significantly extend

4. §1404, 70A Stat. 108.
5. 46 Stat. 253.

the range of meaning supported by the literal reading. Generally speaking, context extends meaning only where it reveals a purpose broader than that otherwise shown by a literal reading and the literal wording has enough semantic leeway to be capable of a broader reading, although one that is not necessarily as broad as the revealed purpose.

An historic example may be *Heydon's Case.*[6] Although the statute referred to "any estate or interest for life," the court held that, in the light of the problem to which the statute was addressed, the term extended to copyhold tenure, which was technically an interest at the will of the landlord but which, assuming good behavior by the tenant, amounted in practical effect to enjoyment for life. Whether this is an accurate characterization of the court's action in that case, the generally accepted limitation that purpose cannot extend the meaning of a statute beyond what the language of the statute is capable of bearing[7] permits only a modest enlargement beyond literal meaning. This matter, which raises constitutional problems today, created no such problem in *Heydon's Case,* because in 1584 the respective functions of legislature and court were not sharply defined and courts were not so circumscribed by limitations on the elasticity of language as they are today. In any event, efforts made solely under the banner of cognition are unlikely to reveal a significantly expanded meaning. But the possibility must not be excluded. This possibility will be discussed further in part C of this chapter.

On the other hand, creative efforts by the court, which under the constitutional separation of powers offer no opportunity for restricting the play of literal language, do offer in many cases wide judicial opportunity for extending principles beyond the literal reading even to situations falling outside the statute.

The first issue in such a case is whether the legislature has excluded judicial creativity by preempting the area through negative implication. If the statute carries no such implication, the court has inherent power to apply the principles announced by the statute to situations falling outside the statute, conditioned

6. 3 Co. 7a, 76 E.R. 637 (Exchequer 1584).

7. E.g., see J. Hall, General Principles of Criminal Law 40 (2d. ed. 1960); Hart & Sacks 1412. For a possible modern counterpart of Heydon's Case, see United States v. Turley, 352 U.S. 407, 77 S. Ct. 397 (1957) ("stolen" read as including embezzlement).

only by principles appropriate to the creative art of judicial lawmaking (discussed in chapter 13).

Here, it is useful to distinguish two types of cases. The first is that in which the situation falls outside the working provisions of the statute, while remaining within its manifest ulterior purpose or underlying policy. In *Amtorg Trading Corp. v. Miehle Printing Press & Mfg. Co.*,[8] the plaintiff had contracted to buy 30 printing presses for shipment to Russia, on which it made a large prepayment. The necessary export license having been denied, the plaintiff refused to accept the remaining 20 presses, which the defendant seller then resold to a domestic buyer at a higher price. The plaintiff thereupon sued to get back its prepayment. The lower court denied recovery because under New York law the plaintiff was a "defaulting buyer." To overcome the traditional New York rule, the plaintiff claimed the benefit of section 204 of the Foreign Aid Appropriations Act, 1949, which provided that:[9]

> Whenever an export license for a commodity, the production or shipment of which to a nonparticipating country was contracted for in good faith prior to March 1, 1948, is denied or cannot be obtained . . . , the Administrator shall provide for the procurement of such commodity to transfer to a participating country in accordance with the requirements of such country, at not less than the contract price of such commodity to the producer or the exporter. . . .

Although the federal court conceded that the statute probably did not apply to the case at hand (the Administrator had not participated, there was no transfer to a "participating country," and the plaintiff might not even qualify as an "exporter"), it said:[10]

> . . . What we are interested in is whether Congress has set forth, by implication or otherwise, a theory of contract law which in this . . . particular situation makes application of the earlier assumed New York law impractical or improper. And we think this is the case. . . . [T]he primary object of congressional concern is . . . to safeguard [the American producer] from loss by the precipitate operation of the export license system before he has adjusted his business to it. . . . [A]n American corporation transshipping goods abroad . . . should

8. 206 F.2d 103 (2d Cir. 1953).
9. 62 Stat. 1059.
10. 206 F.2d at 107-108.

> not be denied the intended remedial benefits under the Act after the producer has been wholly recompensed.

Briefly, the court created a new legal rule similar to that provided by the statute and applied it to a situation that fell outside the statute while remaining within its statutory purpose. Here, the result was reached, not by interpretation in the authentic sense, but by judicial lawmaking. [11] There was no threat of a negative implication in the statute, because it was probably ruled out by, and to the extent of, the broad legislative purpose.

A similar situation arose in *Baker v. Jacobs,* [12] where the Supreme Court of Vermont awarded a new trial against an otherwise successful plaintiff who, after trial, had treated some of the jurors to cigars despite the following provision: [13]

> . . . [I]f a party obtaining a verdict in his favor shall, during the term of the court in which such verdict is obtained, give to any of the jurors in the cause, knowing him to be such, any *victuals or drink* . . . by way of treat, . . . the verdict shall be set aside and a new trial granted.

By no stretch of the imagination could cigars be classed as "victuals or drink." Thus, despite a presumably broad legislative policy against bribing jurors, it was impossible to read the specific working provisions of the statute as coextensive with that policy. Certainly, "victuals or drink" would not include a television set or money, and yet the policy behind the statute would amply justify the court in exercising its creative, as distinct from cognitive, powers in such a case in instances not already dealt with by the legislature and to do it free of any question whether the legislature had preempted the field by negative implication. The matter was well put in *Haeger Potteries, Inc. v. Gilner Potteries:* ". . . [A] legislative enactment is properly treated as a declaration of policy which serves as precedent in analogous situations not expressly covered by the statute itself." [14] The court's use of a statute for this purpose does not depend on the statute's having expressly stated the legislative policy. It is enough that the policy is reasonably inferable by the court.

11. See ch. 13.
12. 64 Vt. 197, 23 A. 588 (1891).
13. Id. (Emphasis added.)
14. 123 F. Supp. 261, 267 (D.C. Cal. 1954).

Should such a court-made rule of law be considered as engrafted on the statute by judicial attribution or as a mere common law rule that runs on a parallel track? Taking the latter approach is cleaner [15] and, where the court later determines that another result is preferable, it avoids the limitations that states following the one-shot theory of judicial interpretation [16] would otherwise impose.

The other principal situation in which courts may make law on the basis of policy expressed or implied by a statute is that in which the occurrence in question, although analogous to situations covered by the statute, falls not only outside the working provisions of the statute but also outside the legislative policy on which the statute was based.

This situation arose in *Agar v. Orda,* [17] where the buyer under an executory contract for the purchase of 200 shares of stock had refused to accept the seller's tender. The question was whether the seller could recover the purchase price of the stock or whether he was relegated to an action for damages. There was no statute on the subject, and in New York the common law on the sale of intangibles had always been that the seller might recover, at his option, either the price or damages. Although the same rule had also been applied to executory contracts to sell tangible goods, New York later enacted the Uniform Sales Act, which restricted the seller's right, where the buyer refused to accept tender of tangible goods, to a suit for damages. The court thus had to decide whether to continue to follow the established common-law rule for intangibles or to extend the new statutory rule covering tangibles to include intangibles. It did the latter. Although tangibles and intangibles differed in enough other

15. "In cases where the court enlarges a statutory rule to cover cases not reasonably within it, it is, of course, not 'interpreting' the statute but saying that the legislature had a good idea which ought to be extended by common law rules." C. Nutting, The Relevance of Legislative Intention Established by Extrinsic Evidence, 20 B.U.L. Rev. 601, 612 (1940).

16. See ch. 13, pp. 252-255.

17. Agar v. Orda, 264 N.Y. 248, 190 N.E. 479 (1934). "Since the Uniform Commercial Code . . . adopts the third-party beneficiary language in discussing the effect of express and implied warranties [in situations involving "horizontal" privity], it seems that this doctrine should be extended here to a situation where a seller makes a product for a user who is not a direct buyer, but with whom the seller has direct dealings [a situation involving "vertical" privity]." Rhodes Pharmacal Co. v. Continental Can Co., 72 Ill. App. 2d 362, 372, 219 N.E.2d 726, 732 (1966).

respects to warrant excluding the latter from the general sales statute, the court said: "No such differences exist here. . . . Every reason that might be urged against the old rule as applied to all personal property has at least equal force when urged against a narrower rule to be applied only to certificates of stock." [18]

Accordingly, the court on its own initiative changed the common law rule for intangibles to conform to the rule that the legislature had adopted for tangibles. Apparently it found no negative implication in the fact that the New York legislature had considered it undesirable to include intangibles in the Uniform Sales Act.

To summarize, applications of statutory rules that are more restrictive than what would otherwise be permissible under a literal reading of a statute are proper only so far as they result from judicial cognition. Otherwise, the court's action would subvert the act of the legislature, thereby impairing legislative supremacy in substantive policy making. On the other hand, applications of statutory rules that are more extensive than what would otherwise be permissible under a literal reading of the statute must ordinarily be justified, if at all, as an exercise of judicial creativity, because the room for a broader interpretation in the cognitive sense is generally limited to the semantic leeway inherent in established usage. This contrasts with restrictive application, in which a tacit assumption can serve as the basis for an implied exception. Thus, the creative extension of a statutory rule, in supplementing the statute, can subvert it only where the statute has preempted the area by negative implication.

B. Strict Interpretation and Liberal Interpretation

What relation, if any, exists between the principles already discussed and "strict construction" and "liberal construction?" [19] Although it is doubtful that these terms suggest useful approaches that are not already available in other conceptual form and under more satisfactory names, they are used often enough to deserve discussion.

18. Id. at 252, 253, 190 N.E. at 481.
19. See generally Sutherland, ch. 58.

The first thing to remember about the term "strict construction" is that it has been used to denote a wide variety of concepts, listed here in ascending order of "strictness":

(1) The court will not extend the law beyond its meaning to take care of a broader legislative purpose.[20] Here, "strict" means merely that the court will refrain from exercising its creative function to apply the rule announced in the statute to situations not covered by it, even though such an extension would help to advance the manifest ulterior purpose of the statute. Here, strictness relates not to the meaning of the statute but to using the statute as a basis for judicial lawmaking by analogy with it.

(2) The court will resolve an evenly balanced uncertainty of meaning in favor of a criminal defendant, the common law, the "common right," a taxpayer, or sovereignty.[21]

(3) The court will so resolve a significant uncertainty of meaning even against the weight of probability.

(4) The court will adhere closely to the literal meaning of the statute and infer nothing that would extend its reach.

(5) Where the manifest purpose of the statute, as collaterally revealed, is narrower than its express meaning, the court will restrict application of the statute to its narrower purpose. This differs from the *Riggs*[22] situation in that the narrow purpose is revealed by sources outside the statute and its proper context.

Senses (2), (3), and (4) appear to be the most common.

One commonly cited canon of interpretation is that statutes in derogation of the common law should be strictly construed.[23] "Derogation" apparently refers to any change in the common law. If this canon purports to express an observed factual tendency on the part of legislatures, it is hard to support. Except with respect to pure statutory codifications of existing common law, the rule makes little sense, because most statutes that affect the common law are enacted for the very purpose of changing it.

20. E.g., see Coral Gables, Inc. v. Christopher, 108 Vt. 414, 189 A. 147 (1937). ". . . [S]tatutes in derogation of the common law are to be strictly construed. . . . We are unable to say that the Legislature intended that the provisions of P.L. 35 should apply to cases not within its terms." Id. at 418, 420, 189 A. at 149, 150.

21. See note 34 *infra.*

22. See note 1 *supra.*

23. Sutherland ch. 61. The rationale for this canon is described in R. Pound, Common Law and Legislation, 21 Harv. L. Rev. 383 (1908).

How, then, can we plausibly assume in areas of doubt that the legislature did not intend to change the common law or that it intended to change the common law to the lesser, rather than the greater, degree? Where the uncertainty is evenly balanced, there is no need for a presumption either in favor of or against the common law, unless there is no alternative to flipping a coin. The impasse is preferably resolved on other grounds.

If a court relies on what it perceives to be an actual tendency for the legislature to make conservative changes in the common law, treating the rule as a generalized presumption and giving it no more weight than the special circumstances of the particular case seem to warrant, it is using the generalization to get at the true meaning of the statute in the particular case. Here the presumption (which is feeble at best) serves as a partial guide to the ascertainment of legislative meaning. In such a case, the presumption has no force beyond the general fact that the court should try to discover and carry out the particular legislative mandate.

If, on the other hand, the court applies the presumption blindly or otherwise in the absence of circumstances suggesting that in the particular instance the legislature intended the more conservative, rather than the more radical, change in the common law, the court is in effect making new law. This would seem to be the case whenever the court refuses to recognize what would otherwise be normally implied by the statute. Such action must be justified (if at all), not as judicial cognition, but as judicial creation.

However, creative judicial action that restricts a statute raises serious questions of judicial usurpation of the legislative function. This use of the rule is generally motivated by judicial unfriendliness, the expression of which in derogation of the meaning of the statute subverts legislative supremacy.

At best, the rule is an historical hangover from the time when judges were generally suspicious or distrustful of legislatures. In the United States, it apparently got its start in *Brown v. Barry.* [24] According to Lenhoff, Chancellor Kent applied the rule eagerly. [25] A great admirer of the common law, he resented the democratic antipathy to English jurisprudence.

24. 3 Dall. (U.S.) 365 (1797).

25. A. Lenhoff, Comments, Cases and Other Materials on Legislation 559 (1949).

Because there is little current basis for broad judicial distrust, the rule seems generally superfluous. In instances where the particular circumstances support the more conservative, rather than the more radical, change, that fact is reason enough to make the more conservative one without relying on a broad presumption that is only occasionally supportable.

The soundest approach to reading statutes affecting the common law is to look for the most plausible meaning of the statute and let it take the interpreter where it will. If this results in an evenly poised uncertainty, it may be useful, at least in preference to flipping a coin, to follow the rule of "strictness" as an act of judicial lawmaking for resolving an otherwise unresolvable dilemma. Beyond this, a rule of strictness seems insupportable.

Many states have enacted statutes designed to limit or do away with the rule. [26] Although some of these may be inartistic in seeming to tell the court how to perform its judicial function of interpreting statutes, they are nevertheless substantively constitutional, because in effect they merely tell the court to stick to its main job of ascertaining statutory meaning and to stay off applying a rule of law that tends to subvert it. Unfortunately, the judiciary has not been noticeably responsive.

There is little reason in today's interpretation of statutes for a general rule or presumption that statutes in derogation of the common law should be "strictly" interpreted. [27]

A rule of strict interpretation has been applied also to criminal statutes. Livingston Hall says that the rule emerged when courts were trying to lessen the impact of the penal laws at a time when the death penalty was imposed for the commission of many common law felonies, some of which would be considered only minor offenses today. [28] If so, the rule was a humanely inspired subversion of the legislative will under the euphemism of "interpretation." Because, even if valid, the rationale no longer applies, the rule must be sustained, if at all, on other grounds.

Other grounds have been advanced. One justification is that

26. Sutherland §61.05.

27. ". . . [W]hen the sovereignty of parliament became clear, the avowed application of rules of strict and liberal construction became impossible." J. Corry, Administrative Law and the Interpretation of Statutes, 1 U. Toronto L.J. 286, 298 (1936). And see F. Horack, Jr., The Disintegration of Statutory Construction, 24 Ind. L.J. 335, 345 (1949).

28. L. Hall, Strict or Liberal Construction of Penal Statutes, 48 Harv. L. Rev. 748, 750, 763 (1935).

the power to fix punishments lies with the legislature, not the courts.[29] This argument is directed only to judicial lawmaking (the courts should stick to their main job of interpreting statutes). But construction, even without judicial lawmaking, is not necessarily "strict" construction. The strictness would lie only in the court's forbearance to make new law extending the scope of criminality. This result can be supported on the ground that to permit judicial lawmaking in this area would condone *ex post facto* lawmaking. (The possibility of judicial lawmaking with a deferred effective date has not been adequately explored.)[30]

Another justification for the rule is that, because the state writes the rules, they should be construed against it.[31] Although an apparent parallel with private instruments may be superficially appealing, it is inaccurate to assume that the relationship between legislature and legislative audience is as partisan as that between the parties to a private instrument. The legislature ordinarily has the public interest in mind and any residual threat of legislative overreaching is at least partly reduced by the fact that the legislature is publicly elected. Even so, there is apparently some feeling that a court should protect the public against statutes that result from selfishly focused lobby interests.

The soundest rationale is that all potential violators are entitled to fair warning.[32] Here, it is useful to distinguish crimes that involve acts generally assumed to be antisocial (*malum in se*), in which a warning tends to inhere in the act itself, from crimes involving acts that are wrong only because they have been officially proscribed (*malum prohibitum*), which require independent warnings.

So long as the court performs only its cognitive function, the risk of unfair surprise is minimized, even for offenses *malum prohibitum,* because by hypothesis the court is bringing to light only what is already there. Unfortunately, what is already there may not be entirely clear. For penal statutes, this fact raises the question, how "strict" should the reading be?

29. Id. at 757.

30. See ch. 13, pp. 257-261.

31. L. Hall, Strict or Liberal Construction of Penal Statutes, 48 Harv. L. Rev. 748, 757 (1935).

32. Id. at 758-759. "The most important aspect of the rule is the presumption in favor of *mens rea* as a condition of criminal liability." W. Friedmann, Law and Social Change in Contemporary Britain 261 (1951).

According to Sutherland,[33] the rule of "strict construction" does not require that a criminal statute be given the narrowest possible meaning, which would tend to subvert expressed legislative intent. Rather, the language should be given a reasonable commonsense interpretation in the light of the manifest purpose of the legislation. Because this approach does not involve strict interpretation in the cognitive sense, Sutherland seems to imply that "strict construction" would be appropriate only where there are language uncertainties not adequately resolved by a manifest legislative purpose. If this analysis is correct, "strict construction" becomes a principle, not for reading statutes, but for limiting or prescribing the court's creative functions in cases where the quest for true meaning has met an impasse.[34] Here, the determination is not so much a choice between "strict" and "liberal" as the creative development of a rule that favors the accused.

There could be at least two kinds of opportunities for strict interpretation in the exercise of the court's creative, lawmaking function: (1) The court may refuse to extend the coverage of a criminal statute even though extending it would further the ulterior purposes of the statute. (2) The court may resolve an evenly balanced doubt as to the meaning of a criminal statute in favor of the defendant.

Either action can be justified on the ground that even a person bent on evil doing is entitled to fair warning. The second can be justified also on the ground that it encourages legislatures, which control the drafting process, to take greater pains to make sure that the occasions on which relatively severe sanctions are threatened are free from reasonable doubt.[35] Semantically, the adjective "strict" seems apt only here. In the first situation, on the other hand, the only basis for calling the court's action "strict" is that it is not "liberal"; it is simply nonextensive.

The most troublesome case is that in which, although the statute leans generally toward criminality, the meaning to the

33. Sutherland §59.06. See also United States v. Turley, 352 U.S. 407, 77 S. Ct. 397 (1957).

34. "Penal Acts are now given their 'ordinary meaning' — just like any other Act — with the exception, that in any case of doubt there is a bias in favour of the subject." J. Willis, Statute Interpretation in a Nutshell, 16 Can. Bar Rev. 1, 24 (1938).

35. See also ch. 12, n. 13.

typical reader includes a significant relevant doubt not clearly resolved by the statute's manifest purpose.

A rule of strict interpretation or application seems unjustified where the statute carries a strong probable meaning of criminality (even though it may not be entirely free of doubt) or where an independent warning is unneeded (*malum in se*). On the other hand, where an independent warning is needed (*malum prohibitum*) and there is a significant, reasonable doubt (not necessarily a 50/50 one) that persists even after the appropriate context has been taken into account, there is some ground for slightly deflecting the ordinary principles of communiction, which normally center on the most plausible meanings, in favor of the defendant. That this puts a heavier-than-normal burden of clarity on the legislature in the interests of common fairness does not seem to strain unduly the general principle of legislative supremacy. To this limited extent, a doctrine of strict interpretation of penal statutes makes sense, even today. At the same time, there is no reason to exploit every semantic or syntactic uncertainty against the state.

Because "strictness" has long been identified with unjustified judicial unfriendliness toward statutes, state legislatures have responded by enacting laws doing away with the rule with respect to penal statutes.[36] As with the strict interpretation of statutes "derogating" from the common law, these enactments have not been noticeably effective. Inartistically framed as apparent attempts to interfere with the courts' cognitive function and beset with conscious or unconscious judicial neglect, they have languished in near oblivion.

The net assessment must be that, beyond a modest role in the administration of penal statutes, doctrines of "strict construction" constitute a mixed bag of approaches that are currently invalid or are unneeded because, in the few cases in which they are justified, similar results are more directly attainable under the general approaches discussed at the beginning of this chapter.

What about liberal interpretation?[37] Here, comparable questions arise. So far as the court's cognitive function is concerned, we may ask generally whether an objective ascertainment of the

36. Sutherland §59.07.

37. ". . . [W]hy 'liberal construction'? No greater reason justifies artificial determination of meaning in favor of the statute than against it." F. Horack, Jr., The Disintegration of Statutory Construction, 24 Ind. L.J. 335, 346 (1949).

meaning of the statute as enacted should call for either "strictness" or "liberality." The general answer is no. While the court is trying to ascertain the meaning of a statute, it need not interpret it either "strictly" or "liberally." It should simply interpret it as best it can, following the general principles of ascertainment already discussed. Whatever value "strictness" and "liberality" may have, it is more properly realized, not in cognition, but in the court's creative function.

Amtorg, Jacobs, and *Agar,* discussed above, exemplify "liberal construction" only in the sense that in each case the court extended the cognizant statutory rule to situations not covered by the statute. It did this, not by stretching the coverage of the statute beyond what its language could support, but by creating a common law rule in imitation of the statute. Thus, despite the loose language of the courts, this is "interpretation" not in its normal cognitive sense but in the bastard sense that includes the resolution of otherwise unresolvable doubts and, as in the cases named, the common law extension of rules that otherwise exist in statutory form.

Within the purely cognitive function, the only room for "liberality" would seem to lie (a) in the situation, of which *Heydon's Case* [38] may be the classic example, where the language, in context, permits a broader or narrower range of meaning and the manifest ulterior purpose of the statute suggests that the broader meaning was the one intended, or (b) in the situation where the court detects a legislative fear that tricksters will manipulate the statutory terms to serve ends that subvert the intent of the legislature in enacting the statute. If this is "liberality," so be it. But the question remains: What purpose does the term serve? The art of interpreting and applying statutes seems no better for it. Indeed, this is another instance of intellectual litter that would not be missed if the term were abandoned. The normal workings of ulterior purpose seem adequate to sustain the load.

38. 3 Co. 7a, 76 E.R. 637 (1584), discussed on p. 201.

C. The Equity or Spirit of a Statute; Casus Omissus

Interpretation according to "the equity of a statute," [39] which was once in vogue and is now said to have fallen into disuse, was merely another name for some of the concepts that have already been discussed and are by no means wholly out of date. Briefly, it refers, in its expansive aspect, to an interpretation or application of a statute in which cases that are beyond the literal meaning of the statute but still within "the same mischiefe, or cause of the making of the same, shall be within the same remedie that the statute provideth; and the reason hereof is, for that the law-makers could not possibly set downe all [types of] cases in expresse terms." [40] *Heydon* [41] and *Amtorg* [42] come immediately to mind. Thus, it includes both cases in which, because of a broad manifest purpose, language with semantic leeway can be given the broader rather than the narrower interpretation and cases in which the court creates, within the broad purpose of the statute, rules for cases outside the literal meaning of the statute that are analogous to the rules prescribed by the statute itself.

The doctrine of the "equity" of a statute also had its contractive side. [43] As loosely phrased by some of the earlier courts and commentators, it was broad enough to support not only exceptions and other limitations reasonably inferable from the manifest purpose of the statute but also limitations and restrictions generated by the court on its own initiative to achieve fairness and equity. So far as the term referred to the former type of

39. See generally, Crawford 296-300; F. de Sloovère, The Equity and Reason of a Statute, 21 Cornell L.Q. 591 (1936); W. Loyd, The Equity of a Statute, 58 U. Pa. L. Rev. 76 (1909); S. Thorne, The Equity of a Statute and Heydon's Case, 31 Ill. L. Rev. 202 (1936). See also L. Hand, The Bill of Rights 19 (1958), quoting from Plowden's decision in Eyston v. Studd, 2 Plowden 459, 467, and also from Aristotle's Ethics, bk. 5, ch. 10.

40. Coke on Littleton 24^b. And see A. Lenhoff, Comments, Cases and Other Materials on Legislation 649-651 (1949); Sutherland §54.05. For the history of the concept, see S. Thorne, A Discourse upon the Exposicion & Understandinge of Statutes 44-47 (1942).

41. See note 6 *supra.*

42. See note 8 *supra.*

43. Sutherland §54.06. And see S. Thorne, A Discourse upon the Exposicion & Understandinge of Statutes 77, 79 (1942).

narrowing, the doctrine is still alive and well, although not necessarily under the banner of "equity." So far as it referred to the latter, which may have been constitutionally acceptable in England when the allocation of powers between legislature and courts was still only loosely defined, it has no place in a modern constitutional tripartite system based on a more rigorous division of powers.

If this analysis is accurate, it is hard to see what the term "equitable" can contribute today. Indeed the term is undesirable, because it tends to obscure the rationales of two different concepts: authentic interpretation based on the legislative purpose of the statute and judicial lawmaking by analogy as merely supported by that purpose. The difference is important, especially for a criminal statute, because, if the result is found in the working provisions of the statute, the accused has presumably been adequately forewarned. On the other hand, if it results from judicial lawmaking that implements otherwise unimplemented legislative policy, fair warning may be lacking. The difference is also important on the restrictive side because, unless the result can be based on factual implication, a narrower-than-literal application subverts expressed legislative intent and thus legislative supremacy.

Some of the same may be said respecting the term "spirit of the statute." [44] So far as it has been used as a mere synonym for "equity," it performs no useful function. On the other hand, so far as it has been used to denote, not the purpose of the statute (which includes legislative aspirations not fully realized by the statute), but implications strongly suggested by the total context of the statute respecting what the legislature probably intended to cover in this statute, it may be useful. This is apparently what Judge Holmes had in mind when he said, in *Johnson v. United States,* ". . . [I]t is not an adequate discharge of duty for courts to say: We see what you are driving at, but you have not [expressly] said it, and therefore we shall go on as before." [45] It is something like the smile on the cat in *Alice in Wonderland,* which was visible even after the cat, itself, was not. [46] Here, "finding the cat behind the smile" is an act of judicial cognition based on incomplete statutory language supplemented by implications sup-

44. See Crawford 291-296.

45. 163 Fed. 30, 32 (1st Cir. 1908). Similar cases are discussed in n. 49 *infra.*

46. Ch. VI.

plied by strong context. This may be one situation where a substantive result is supplied by context even though the literal wording, by itself, has insufficient semantic flexibility to sustain the result.

As between *Johnson*[47] and *Jacobs*,[48] it requires sophisticated, good-faith judgment to distinguish between a "pleading" statute that covers a schedule in bankruptcy (which is not, technically, a pleading, but in the context of bankruptcy serves the statute's immediate purpose) and a "victuals or drink" statute that does not cover cigars (which cannot be classed as food or drink) but is available to support a judicially created rule dealing with cigars.

Ultimately, the issue in these cases is not what the specific statutory language means but what it means when taken as a whole and read in its proper context. But there is a strong caveat here: When the legislature has used inadequate language, it takes powerful context to turn what would otherwise be an unrealized legislative aspiration (as in *Jacobs*) into a declaration (however inartistic) of immediate legislative intent (as in *Johnson*).

To summarize, if the context of a statute shows a legislative purpose that is broader than the literal import of the words used, the meaning of the statute is correspondingly broadened, but only so far as the words have enough semantic leeway to carry the broadened meaning. Beyond that, the legislative purpose remains unrealized. On the other hand, if the context also shows that despite the semantic limits of the words used the statute was intended to reach a still broader result, the meaning of the statute taken as a whole extends also to that result. Merely manifesting a broader legislative purpose is not enough. The critical factor would seem to be whether inapplicability to the kind of circumstances being considered would defeat the main thrust of the statute.[49]

47. See note 45 *supra*. The case is discussed in ch. 8, pp. 93-94.

48. See note 12 *supra*.

49. The statement, in J. Hall, General Principles of Criminal Law 40 (2d ed. 1960), that "the logic ('extension') of the purpose or policy of a statute must be restricted by the established ordinary meanings of words" presumably refers to the first type of situation.

Respecting the second type, suppose in the face of a case like Hoffman v. Misericordia Hospital, 439 Pa. 501, 507-508, 267 A.2d 867, 870-871 (1970), holding that a hospital that administers blood infected with hepatitis virus might be strictly liable whether or not a transfusion is a "sale" or a "service," a state legislature enacts a statute either declaring that a blood transfusion is a "service" rather than a "sale" (e.g., Cal. Health and Safety Code §1606) or killing "warranties" in such a case (e.g., Tenn. Code Ann. §47-2-316(5)). A court

Under the general analysis of this chapter, some of the courts' seeming double talk respecting the doctrine of *"casus omissus"* (the omitted case) can be explained. This doctrine tells us that, if the legislature omitted something from the statute, the court may not supply it. This, of course, is not a doctrine that helps a court ascertain the meaning of a statute, because it assumes the interpretative point in question.[50] Rather, it addresses itself to the question, what, if anything, can the court do about a gap left by the legislature? On the level of cognition, the answer is clear: The court cannot find in the statute what, by hypothesis, is not in it. Here, the doctrine is pure tautology. On the level of judicial law-making (creation), the doctrine denies the court the power to make law to supplement the statute even to fulfill the broader purpose beyond the statute. Here, it seems insupportable.

On the other hand, if the doctrine is only a paraphrase of the doctrine of negative implication — that the legislature by its language has preempted the field to the exclusion of the court — the doctrine makes some sense. Even so, a Latin tag adds nothing to the force of negative implication and it may even confuse, because it does not always make clear what concept is being invoked. Under the broad umbrella of unrealized ulterior legislative purpose, moreover, there is little basis for finding a negative implication, because such an implication would conflict with that purpose.

---

faced with such a "service" statute is likely to read it as impliedly forbidding the court to attach a warranty to the transfusion even if it is treated as a "service." Shepard v. Alexian Brothers Hospital, Inc., 33 Cal. App. 3d 606, 610, 109 Cal. Rptr. 132, 134 (1973). Similarly, a court faced with such a "warranty" statute is likely to read it as impliedly forbidding the court to impose "strict liability in tort," which many courts treat as distinct from warranty. McDaniel v. Baptist Memorial Hospital, 352 F. Supp. 690, 691 (W.D. Tenn. 1971). See also ch. 7, n. 46.

50. I.e., the question, Does the statute cover the particular kind of situation?, has already been answered in the negative.

12

How to Read a Statute (Summarizing the Cognitive Function)

> . . . [*Frankfurter's*] *three-fold imperative to students:* (*1*) *Read the statute;* (*2*) *read the statute;* (*3*) *read the statute!*
>
> — H. Friendly, Benchmarks 202 (1967)

A. The Perception of Meaning: In General

How is the true meaning of a statute to be discovered?

It would be gratifying to present for the first time a reliable, scientific method of discovery, one that built on demonstrable premises and proceeded by deductive logic to incontrovertible conclusions. Unfortunately, the reader who is looking for this must go elsewhere. All that he can find here are suggestions for developing a wholesome judicial attitude, an appropriate general approach, a miscellany of useful (but rebuttable) factual presumptions, and several rules of thumb relating to specific usages.

Despite the limited role of stipulated meaning, communication depends ultimately on an integrated resolution of habitual responses to recognized symbols; until a fund of common semantic habits is established, communication is impossible. The reception of meaning, therefore, is primarily a matter of exposure and recognition, a process of perception that is not only immediate but for the most part automatic.[1] Indeed, asking what a docu-

1. See ch. 3, note 31.

ment means is not greatly different from asking whether this picture before us, which we have not seen before, is or is not a picture of Winston Churchill. Either it is or it isn't. Either we recognize him or we don't. That the psychological processes of recognition and perception are immediate does not mean that they are necessarily simple. But whether simple or complex, and whether educated or not, they remain essentially visceral reactions to a complicated whole.

Except as they may suggest that the response that results from the repeated association of symbol and referent is necessarily behavioral (which it is not), Pavlov's dogs [2] help us to understand how meaning is developed and conveyed. They teach us that the central impact of meaning, whether or not it requires an act of intuition, is direct and immediate. Logic plays only a supplementary role.

Although a judge's response to symbols, being founded on habit, is largely automatic and thus beyond his control, his preliminary efforts to educate himself by determining what are the proper language vehicle and its proper context may be deliberate. In determining proper context, the judge tries to place himself in the position of a typical member of the legislative audience. How hard this is depends on how much of his relevant knowledge is not shared by the legislative audience and must, therefore, be suppressed and how much of the audience's relevant knowledge is not shared by him and must, therefore, be acquired.

A judge cannot always be sure that he is reading the statute through the eyes of the legislative audience. Merely guessing risks reading the statute merely against his own background of knowledge and thus in the light of his own idiosyncracies. Even if he is a typical member of the legislative audience, typical members of that audience may habitually react differently to the same language.

B. The Importance of Attitude

Although a judge can reach for perfection even while realizing that it is not fully attainable, the important thing is not to be perfect in practice but to develop a wholesome judicial attitude. [3]

2. C. Ogden & I. Richards, The Meaning of Meaning 56 (10th ed. 1959).
3. Hart & Sacks 1410.

The first essential to a wholesome attitude is the willingness to read a statute in the first instance with an inquiring mind and no axe to grind. To urge this is to urge a precaution ordinarily unnecessary outside the law. It is necessary here, because the judge's further responsibility of reaching a fair and constitutional result in the immediate controversy often requires him, in view of the inadequacies of language or legislative draftsmen, ultimately to reach a result that transcends an unbiased reading. Unfortunately, overeagerness to discharge this responsibility may lead him to develop what appear to be just and legally sound results before he has fully and dispassionately evaluated his legislative terms of reference. However, reading a statute without bias does not necessarily mean ignoring a bias normal to the legislative audience itself. If the legislature took it into account, it may simply be an element of proper context.

The main essential is a willingness to read the statute thoroughly and intensively in all its relevant aspects. Indeed, the Achilles heel of statutory interpretation has been the lawyer's and judge's widespread reluctance even to read a statute, let alone carefully exegete it. The matter had been well stated by Driedger: [4]

> . . . [T]he reader must be familiar with the subject-matter of the statute; he must not only read the statute but *study* it until he knows the content of every section and the relationship between the sections. He must try to reconstruct, from the words of the Act, the draftsman's final legislative scheme. In other words, he must reverse the drafting process.

C. The Role of Logic

Although meaning depends ultimately on shared habits, it does not depend solely on them. Although most of the symbolic elements used are ordinarily known and recognized, the rest are not. So far as the unknown elements are not determinable from the known elements, the legislative message is likely to be seen off

4. E. Driedger, A New Approach to Statutory Interpretation, 29 Can. Bar Rev. 838, 843 (1951). (Emphasis added.) "Though we may not end with the words in construing a disputed statute, one certainly begins there." F. Frankfurter, Some Reflections on the Reading of Statutes, 47 Colum. L. Rev. 527, 535 (1947).

center. When the interpreter is aware of this, he should try to compensate for it. If he cannot, he must conclude that, apart from or in addition to his own limitations, the message is incomplete as an expression of the legislature's intent.

How can a statute be dealt with when its meaning is not immediately apparent? The shared response habits in such a situation provide, on first reading, a miscellany of overgeneral, overvague, perhaps ambiguous, or even conflicting meanings. Whether real or apparent, the resultant uncertainties impair communication until they can be resolved, if possible, by a careful weighing of the relevant elements of internal and external context. At this point we appropriately turn to logic, both deductive and inductive. [5]

But what part can deductive logic, which normally deals with propositions of fact, play in a context of commands and permissions? One approach to closing the gap between commands and propositions, advanced by Hare, is to develop an appropriate deontic logic, which deals specially with obligations. A simpler, and apparently adequate, approach recognizes that every command can be converted to a proposition that asserts the existence of a legal obligation and each permission as one that asserts the existence of a legal privilege. [6] In this form, even statutory commands can be usefully analyzed by conventional deductive logic. The problem does not appear to be significant, because most statutory analysts, without making such a conversion, have intuitively sensed the applicability of conventional logic even to statutes couched in the imperative. Inductive logic may also play a part so far as a careful weighing of the evidence stimulates insight.

The use of deductive logic to supplement recognition rests on the presumption that the authors of statutes intend results that are both rational and coherent. [7] But even the results of deductive logic must be tempered with judgment.

5. E. Bruncken, Interpretation of the Written Law, 25 Yale L.J. 129 (1915).

6. E.g., the command "The director shall. . . ." may be written as the statement "The director has the duty to. . . ." without changing substance. R. Dickerson, The Fundamentals of Legal Drafting 6 n. 8 (1965).

7. "The statute ought always to be presumed to be the work of reasonable men pursuing reasonable purposes reasonably. . . ." Hart & Sacks 1157 (see also 1415).

D. Resolving Uncertainty

Uncertainties in meaning may be usefully divided into (1) apparent uncertainties, which dissolve when the relevant factors of text and context are logically appraised, and (2) residual uncertainties, which persist even after the resources of ascertainment have been exhausted and are thus resolvable only by judicial lawmaking. [8]

Whether an uncertainty can be resolved by the methods of discovery inherent in cognition depends on whether an interpretation can be selected with reasonable confidence as the most plausible alternative [9] on the basis of the text and proper context. In the determination of the most plausible alternative, a concept of legislative intent or purpose is indispensable. [10]

The search for legislative intent or purpose begins as a search for relevant and reliable tacit assumptions from which, together with the clear elements of the text, logical inferences may be drawn. What are these tacit assumptions? For the most part, they are simply tentative factual hypotheses or solid probabilities that are derivable from experience shared by the authors of the statutes with the legislative audience and that create probabilities of meaning. [11] For example, in *Roschen v. Ward,* [12] in which eyeglass dealers sought to enjoin enforcement of a statute requiring the attendance of physicians or optometrists at places where eyeglasses were sold, the United States Supreme Court

8. See J. Cohen, Judicial "Legisputation" and the Dimensions of Legal Meaning, 36 Ind. L.J. 414, 416-417 (1961); J. Montrose, Ambiguous Words in a Statute, 76 L.Q. Rev. 359, 361 (1960). See also F. Hawkins, On the Principles of Legal Interpretation, With Reference Especially to the Interpretation of Wills, in J. Thayer, A Preliminary Treatise on Evidence at the Common Law 577, at 585-586 (1898).

9. Justice Frankfurter refers to this as a "contest between probabilities of meaning." F. Frankfurter, Some Reflections on the Reading of Statutes, 47 Colum. L. Rev. 527, 528 (1947).

10. See chs. 7 & 8.

11. ". . . [A]ll interpretation, whether literal or inferential, is a process of inference or reasoning by probabilities. . . ." F. Hawkins, On the Principles of Legal Interpretation, With Reference Especially to the Interpretation of Wills, in J. Thayer, A Preliminary Treatise on Evidence at the Common Law 577, at 588 (1898). See also ch. 9, pp. 106-110.

12. 279 U.S. 337, 49 S. Ct. 336 (1929).

sustained the constitutionality of the statute on the basis of a tacit assumption, underlying the statute, that a physician or optometrist was needed to examine the customer's eyes or to determine the need for an examination.

It is here that we have an important difference between the ascertainment of legislative meaning (cognition) and the assignment of judicial meaning (creation). Although the presumptions of the former are easily confused with the rules of the latter, they differ in that, whereas the former are based on factual tendencies and thus rebuttable, the latter are independent propositions of law and thus have at least the force of *stare decisis*. In practice, however, the judge has wide discretion in applying them.

Because the true meaning of a provision may be only one in a wide range of plausible meanings arrayed between convincing certainty, on the one hand, and evenly poised uncertainty, on the other, it can be defined as the meaning that is the most plausible under the known circumstances.

Although no aspect of a written document, including the plainest, can be said to be fully certain in meaning, at least some of the elements are plain enough that the reader is confident that he knows what they mean. To this extent he simply says that the meaning is clear, and moves on. Such instances are of interest only so far as they represent the most that he can hope for in attainable certainty, and they are thus valuable as bases from which to draw logical inferences to use in dealing with the related uncertainties. Of more direct interest are elements that suffer from uncertainty, ranging from slight, but significant, uncertainty to the point at which there is no rational basis for saying that one alternative is more plausible as an expression of legislative intent than one or more of the others. At the latter extreme, the resolution of uncertainty is a pure act of judicial lawmaking, because by hypothesis there is no factor of probative force, discernible in either the document or its proper context, that is sufficient to tip the scales.

When the relevant factors point more strongly, but not conclusively, to one alternative, does the selection of the indicated alternative constitute the ascertainment (cognition) or the assignment (creation) of meaning? It is enough to characterize the total result as "cognition" or "creation" depending simply on whether the interpreter can confidently select an alternative. This at least separates the instances in which the possibility of unfair surprise is likely to be negligible from those in which it is likely to be significant.

E. The Main Materials of Ascertainment

What are the main materials of ascertainment (cognition) that the law shares with other fields generally and from which a court can determine a resultant legislative thrust?

The first principle of ascertaining meaning is that it is presumed, except as observed circumstances show otherwise, that the author of a document has reflected the basic presuppositions of communication. Because all communication rests ultimately on usage, it is presumed that the author has followed the established conventions of language, common to him and his audience, in preparing the document in question. It is presumed, more specifically, that he has used his words in senses that are normal or usual for the subject to which the statute is addressed. This is the rebuttable presumption of normal usage. Although the weight of this presumption does not bear with overwhelming force at each specific point in the text, it generally does so for the text taken as a whole. A statute the great bulk of whose terms did not generally conform to normal understanding would be hard to imagine.

This fact permits, and indeed requires, us to assume that, except as observed circumstances show otherwise, the meaning of a statute to the hypothetical typical member of the legislative audience to whom it is addressed closely approximates, and thus expresses, the subjective intent of the authors. This presumption serves notice on the author of a communication that, so far as he deviates from accepted usage, he risks failing to communicate, for which he may be penalized by the discovery that he has generated meanings that he never intended.[13]

13. ". . . [T]aking a manifestation which in itself is an expression of intention . . . may have a tendency to encourage careful and precise drafting on the part of the legislature." C. Nutting, The Relevance of Legislative Intention Established by Extrinsic Evidence, 20 B.U.L. Rev. 601, 613-614 (1940). ". . . [T]hese policies of clear statement may on occasion operate to defeat the actual, consciously held intention of particular legislators, or of the members of the legislature generally. . . . [I]n other words, they constitute conditions of the effectual exercise of legislative power. But the requirement should be thought of as constitutionally imposed." Hart & Sacks 1412-1413. But can this

Second, it is presumed that one part of a statute is not intended to contradict another part of the same statute.[14] This is the rebuttable presumption of substantive consistency. Unlike the first presumption, however, it is based not on the presuppositions of communication but on the observed fact that inconsistency almost always frustrates rather than advances human purposes, including those that motivate the enactment of statutes.

This second presumption is thus an outgrowth of a strong underlying presumption that the statute expresses an immediate, coherent purpose that in turn implements broader or more remote purposes. This underlying presumption not only orients the interpreter but makes possible the acts of induction or deduction by which he can integrate into a coherent whole what would otherwise be only linguistic miscellany.[15] This presumption, too, is rebuttable, because the authors of communications sometimes contradict themselves and, on rare occasions, intentionally.

Closely associated with the second presumption is a third, which is both separate from the second and in general significantly weaker. Because legal documents are for the most part nonemotive,[16] it is presumed that the author's language has been used, not for its artistic or emotional effect, but for its ability to convey ideas. Accordingly, it is presumed that the author has not varied his terminology unless he has changed his meaning, and has not changed his meaning unless he has varied his terminology; that is, that he has committed neither "elegant variation"[17] nor "utraquistic subterfuge."[18] This is the rebuttable presumption of formal consistency.[19]

Because legislative draftsmen vary widely in their fidelity to formal consistency, the third presumption ranges from very weak to moderately strong. Its strength in particular cases depends largely on how scrupulous the particular draftsman appears to

---

approach, which the authors support, be squared with the "flagellant" approach (id. at 99), which they strongly deplore? Apparently the authors are willing to punish the legislature for not writing clearly by holding it to the statute's apparent meaning but not by holding it to its literal meaning.

14. See Crawford 262-264.

15. The legislators "did not inadvertently add a colonial wing to a gothic cathedral." Justice Frankfurter, dissenting in I.C.C. v. J.-T. Transport Co., 368 U.S. 81, 115, 82 S. Ct. 216, 227 (1961).

16. R. Dickerson, The Fundamentals of Legal Drafting 6 (1965).

17. Id. at 11.

18. Id.

19. E. Driedger, The Construction of Statutes 74-75 (1974).

have been in drafting the particular statute. Although the interpreter can rarely be certain, after the fact, that the draftsman has written a particular provision consistently with the rest of the statute, the presumption that he has is greatly strengthened if an examination of the statute as a whole suggests that it has been carefully drawn and is generally consistent in language, arrangement, and punctuation.

This fact offers the legislative draftsman both an opportunity and an incentive. Even in a legislative environment in which drafting standards are relatively low, he can materially sharpen the tools of language by being scrupulously consistent in arranging his materials and in selecting his words, phrases, and punctuation. He can thus reassure the careful reader that when a shift of language occurs it probably signifies a shift in meaning and not a careless inadvertence. The draftsman who cries "wolf!" by carelessly shifting his terminology should not be surprised if his intended shifts in meaning are often read as mere elegant variation.

Underlying the second and third presumptions is the presumption that the statute has a single true meaning, [20] which, over the broad range of statutes, will tend to most closely approximate legislative intent. This presumption is likewise rebuttable, because the statute may have more than one actual meaning, depending on the number of evenly poised uncertainties that it contains, or, indeed, it may conceivably have no meaning at all.

The interpreter should thus begin each investigation of meaning on the assumption that what on first reading appear to be significant uncertainties of meaning can be resolved by intensively studying the internal elements of the document both in relation to each other and in relation to the materials of proper context. The concept of a "single true meaning," which is rebuttable in the ascertainment but not in the assignment of meaning, is a kissing cousin of what Llewellyn once referred to as the general concept of a "single right answer" in the adjudication of specific controversies. [21] That reasonable judges may differ on what the true meaning of a statute may be in a particular case does not

20. F. de Sloovère, Steps in the Process of Interpreting Statutes, 10 N.Y.U.L.Q. Rev. 1, 17 (1932). This does not mean that reasonable judges do not differ. It means merely that for each judge, acting by his own lights, there is presumably a single most plausible reading. Hart & Sacks 168.

21. K. Llewellyn, The Common Law Tradition: Deciding Appeals 24-25 (1960).

refute its general validity in putting each judge in a proper interpretative frame of mind.

Hart and Sacks have pointed out another important presumption. The court "should assume, unless the contrary unmistakably appears, that the legislature was made up of reasonable persons pursuing reasonable purposes reasonably." [22] In looser form, this seems appropriate to communications generally. They add that the court should also "presume conclusively that these persons, whether or not entertaining concepts of reasonableness shared by the courts, were trying responsibly and in good faith to discharge their constitutional powers and duties." [23] These twin presumptions might well be combined in a general presumption of reasonableness and fidelity to duty.

Why the former presumption should be rebuttable, while the latter need not, they do not explain. Although a conclusive presumption is appropriate for judicial lawmaking, it would seem inappropriate for the cognitive function of ascertaining meaning. It is one thing for the court to be "mindful of the nature of law and of the fact that every statute is a part of the law and partakes of the qualities of law, and particularly of the quality of striving for even-handed justice." [24] It is something else to assume in all cases that the legislature, which is likely to be fallible, intended the optimum legal result. Where, on the one hand, in an otherwise evenly poised ambiguity one alternative plainly violates the presumption while the other sustains it, experience supports the strong probability that the legislature intended the fair result. On the other hand, the presumption could hardly override clear language, extend its outer limits, or change the elements of proper context. Too many existing statutes include inequities that cannot be interpreted away through any principle of cognition.

Also, there is an important, and likewise rebuttable, presumption peculiar to statutes and other prescriptive documents. This is the presumption that the legislature has taken account of the rest of the legal order and has tried to integrate the statute with it, both fairly and rationally. [25] Unfortunately, this has only a lim-

22. Hart & Sacks 1415 (see also 1157).

23. Id.

24. Id. at 1411.

25. Crawford, ch. XXII; Sutherland, chs. 50-53. ". . . [A] court must strive to make sense *as a whole* out of our law *as a whole*." K. Llewellyn, Remarks on the Theory of Appellate Decision and the Rules or Canons about

ited factual basis to sustain it in situations in which the language used strongly suggests the contrary.

When we apply these general presumptions, should it make a difference whether the particular uncertainty is one of ambiguity or one of vagueness?

If it is one solely of ambiguity, experience supports a strong presumption that the legislature did not intend to equivocate, but to prefer one alternative over the other. The same is true of hydraheaded equivocations, which Llewellyn has called "multiguities."

Compare the uncertainty of vagueness. This differs from ambiguity in two respects:[26] (1) In the drafting of statutes, it is practically impossible not to include some vague elements. (2) Far from always being a disease of communication, some vagueness is often desirable. Accordingly, there is less reason to presume that it was not intended.

F. The Canons of Interpretation

Many efforts to ascertain meaning seem to be sustained by the forlorn hope that actual meaning can be ascertained by applying one or more of the so-called "canons" or "rules" of statutory interpretation. How useful are they in a good faith search for meaning?

It is now fashionable to repudiate all "canons of interpretation" on the ground that they largely cancel each other out.[27] Because this reason assumes that all canons are rules in the same sense and unconditioned by moderating principle, the repudiation is unrealistic and the explanation more than a little glib.

How Statutes are to be Construed, 3 Vand. L. Rev. 395, 399 (1950). (Emphasis in original.)

26. See ch. 5, pp. 48-50.

27. W. Friedmann, Law and Social Change in Contemporary Britain 243-244 (1951). "The lawyer must treat canons as tools of advocacy only. They *never* serve adequately as bases for counseling." F. Newman & S. Surrey, Legislation — Cases and Materials 654 (1955). (Emphasis in original.) See also K. Llewellyn, Remarks on the Theory of Appellate Decision and the Rules or Canons about How Statutes are to be Construed, 3 Vand. L. Rev. 395, 401 (1950). Cf. Sutherland §45.13. "What is needed in statutory construction is not more rules but fewer." F. Horack, Jr., The Disintegration of Statutory Construction, 24 Ind. L.J. 335, 351 (1949).

In general, the "canons" or "rules" of interpretation constitute a mixed bag. One group consists of rebuttable presumptions, of varying strengths, that reflect the probabilities generated by normal usage or legislative behavior. These represent either (1) lexicographical judgments of how legislatures tend to use language and its syntactical patterns [28] or (2) descriptions of how legislatures tend to behave. [29] They serve as useful presumptions of supposed actual legislative intent and are, therefore, modestly useful in carrying legislative meaning. [30]

Another group consists of rules for deciding cases that cannot be resolved by reference to the probabilities of actual meaning. [31] Representing rules of law or permissible guidelines for deciding cases that cannot be decided by searching for the most plausible meaning, they are irrelevant here.

Another group, of doubtful validity, consists of rules of law for overriding some aspect of legislative meaning. [32] These, too, are irrelevant here.

Another group, likewise irrelevant, helps neither to find meaning nor to decide cases, but classify and label results reached by other means. [33]

However, even though such "rules" relate to matters of meaning, they represent at best only probabilities based on past experience. There is no assurance that they carry persuasive weight in the case at hand either singly or in combination. Also, inasmuch as they tend to interact, it is impossible to foretell how a given presumption or possibility is conditioned by the facts underlying its fellow presumptions and possibilities. This tends to make each situation unique and the particular reader is obliged to do a delicate, complicated balancing act. [34] He must not only

28. E.g., *reddendo singula singulis,* discussed on p. 233.

29. E.g., *in pari materia,* discussed on p. 233.

30. "The so-called rules of interpretation are not rules that automatically reach results, but ways of attuning the mind to a vision comparable to that possessed by the legislature." J. Landis, A Note on "Statutory Interpretation," 43 Harv. L. Rev. 886, 892 (1930).

31. E.g., the rule, adopted in some jurisdictions, that if two provisions of the same statute unresolvably contradict each other, the later one prevails. See Crawford 263-264.

32. E.g., the severer aspects of the rule that a statute in derogation of common law must be construed "strictly," discussed in ch. 11, pp. 206-208.

33. E.g., *expressio unius est exclusio alterius,* discussed on pp. 234-235.

34. ". . . [C]anons give an air of abstract intellectual compulsion to what is in fact a delicate judgment, concluding a complicated process of balancing

develop semantic empathy with the typical member of the intended legislative audience but also calculate the unique resultant of a number of individual and differing forces. That is why little interpretative case law is controlling, or even helpful, beyond the particular provision involved.

If applied mechanically, on the other hand, the factual presumptions described here become rules of law. As such, they may be applied (in preference to flipping a coin), but only if the court has first made an honest but unsuccessful effort to balance the actual probabilities of meaning and not let mechanical application override the most plausible result. When courts forget that in seeking actual meaning they are dealing with presumptions of fact and not rules of law, there is real danger of subverting the legislative message.

Let us now consider some of the better known canons.

The "plain meaning rule" says, in brief, that if the statute is plain, the court may not go beyond it to find another meaning. [35] This well-known exclusionary doctrine was invoked in *Lake County v. Rollins,* in which the United States Supreme Court said, more specifically, [36]

> If the words convey a definite meaning, which involves no absurdity, nor any contradiction of other parts of the instrument, then that meaning, apparent on the face of the instrument, must be accepted, and neither the courts nor the legislature have the right to add to it or take from it.

On its positive side, the plain meaning rule states a tautology: Words should be read as saying what they say. The rule tells us to respect meaning but it does so without disclosing what the specific meaning is. At best, it reaffirms the preeminence of the statute over materials extrinsic to it. In its negative aspect, on the other hand, the rule has sometimes been used to read ineptly expressed language out of its proper context, in violation of established principles of meaning and communication. To this extent it is an impediment to interpretation.

The convolutions of the courts in this area have been too complicated and subtle to be detailed here. Part of the problem is

---

subtle and elusive elements." F. Frankfurter, Some Reflections on the Reading of Statutes, 47 Colum. L. Rev. 527, 544 (1947).

35. Crawford 256; Sutherland §46.01.

36. 130 U.S. 662, 670, 39 S. Ct. 651, 652 (1889).

that the plain meaning rule does not have a single, agreed-on content. It has taken many forms, most of which are ambiguous. Further confusion has resulted from the fact that there is no necessary correlation between the quality of judicial results and the quality of their judicial rationalizations. Good results are often reached for bad reasons, and the invocation of otherwise sound principles of interpretation are not always apt in the circumstances. Even where the underlying concept remains the same, terminology varies: Some substantive variations of the plain meaning rule are called the "rule of literalness" or the "golden rule" (the terms are not necessarily interchangeable).[37] Although the plain meaning rule was said to have been abrogated in *United States v. American Trucking Assns., Inc.,*[38] it is not clear which versions were disavowed.

Putting aside names, let us examine some of the substantive variations. As stated in *Lake County,* does the plain meaning rule command literalness? Not quite, because internal context is not excluded and external context may be taken into account to the extent of weighing the chances of absurdity.[39] What is not clear is whether the rule excludes taking into account all other external considerations, including relevant matters that are part of proper context,[40] or merely excludes matters outside the statute that are also outside its proper context.[41] The courts thus do not always make clear what they are excluding. Some seem to say that they are excluding everything outside the statute, even while they give weight to many of the tacit assumptions that make up much of surrounding context.

Taken at its face value, the most extreme rule of exclusion is the rule of literalness; Statutory words must be given effect according to their relevant dictionary senses.[42] So stated, the rule is simple nonsense; to exclude consideration of context would be to ignore one of the basic principles of communication. Even excluding a significant part of context risks throwing the

37. E.g., see R. Dias, Jurisprudence 131-134 (3d ed. 1970); E. Driedger, The Construction of Statutes chs. 1-2 (1974); The Law Commission and the Scottish Law Commission, The Interpretation of Statutes 15-19 (1969).

38. 310 U.S. 534, 60 S. Ct. 1059 (1940).

39. Crawford 257.

40. Sutherland §46.02.

41. E.g., see note 45 *infra.*

42. J. Willis, Statute Interpretation in a Nutshell, 16 Can. Bar Rev. 1, 10 (1938).

communication off center. Some judges have apparently approached this view and to this extent their actions should be repudiated. On the other hand, most courts that purport to take this view actually apply a more lenient rule that takes into account not only internal context but also at least some considerations of external context. The extent of including external context has varied from context relating to the simple notion of absurdity [43] to context relating also to unfairness and unreasonableness. [44]

At least one version of the plain meaning rule, on the other hand, is entirely acceptable. In *Hutton v. Phillips*, the Supreme Court of Delaware said: [45]

> . . . [Interpretation] involves far more than picking out dictionary definitions of words or expressions used. Consideration of the context and the setting is indispensable properly to ascertain a meaning. In saying that a verbal expression is plain or unambiguous, we mean little more than that we are convinced that virtually anyone competent to understand it, and desiring fairly and impartially to ascertain its signification, would attribute to the expression in its context a meaning such as the one we derive, rather than any other; and would consider any different meaning, by comparison, strained, or far-fetched, or unusual, or unlikely.
>
> . . . Implicit in the finding of a plain, clear meaning of an expression *in its context,* is a finding that such meaning is rational and "makes sense" in that context.

The court accordingly adopted what it had found to be the "plain meaning," even though it might have considered another interpretation more desirable and even though another interpretation

43. E.g., Lake County v. Rollins, 130 U.S. 662, 670, 9 S. Ct. 651, 652 (1889). This has been called the "golden rule." J. Willis, Statutory Interpretation in a Nutshell, 16 Can. Bar Rev. 1, 12 (1938). In the English and Canadian cases at least, "absurdity" normally refers to internal statutory harmony rather than to the rationality of legislative results. E. Driedger, The Construction of Statutes ch. 2 (1974). If so, how would we classify a statute that forbade shooting a gun in a public roadway "except for the purpose of killing some noxious or dangerous animal or an officer in the pursuit of his duty"? See III R. Pound, Jurisprudence 490 (1959).

44. E.g., River Wear Commissioners v. Adamson, 2 App. Cas. 743, 764-765 (House of Lords 1877). This, too, is sometimes called the "golden rule." Maxwell on The Interpretation of Statutes 43-45 (12th ed. P. Langan 1969). And see E. Hopkins, The Literal Canon and the Golden Rule, 15 Can. Bar Rev. 689 (1937).

45. 45 Del. 156, 160, 70 A.2d 15, 17 (1949). (Emphasis in original.)

might have conferred greater tax benefits on the persons whom the legislature intended to benefit by the act.

Although any version of the plain meaning rule that excludes significant elements of proper context is justifiably condemned, one that excludes only noncontextual materials, which should be considered by the court only when discharging its creative function, may be sound. *Hutton* did not exclude consideration of relative benefits; it only concluded, after considering them, that the discrepancy, if any, between the words and manifest legislative purpose was not so great as to create a presumption that the legislature intended to give the express working provision anything but its normal meaning.

The important interpretative problem is to determine, in the light of the text and its proper context, whether the facts suggesting that a normal reading of the language would produce an absurdity, an inequity, or unreasonableness create a presumption strong enough that the most plausible alternative is to conclude that the legislature did not mean what it expressly said. [46] This is a matter of judgment under the circumstances, and specific results are hard to forecast. Although the presumption against absurdity is strong, the presumptions against unfairness and unreasonableness, depending on degree, are usually weak. Normal statutes, especially long and complicated ones, bristle with at least minor inequities to the point where there is generally only a low statistical probability that the legislature intended something other than what it said.

On this basis, a plain meaning rule may be valid, even apart from excluding materials that lie beyond proper context, if it seeks to emphasize that the presumption that the legislature meant what it expressly said is not overcome merely because the result that it calls for would produce a mild absurdity, some unfairness, or less beneficial results than the manifest purpose of the statute would seem to call for. [47]

46. ". . . [W]e are to . . . [give] the words their ordinary signification, unless when so applied they produce an inconsistency, or an absurdity or inconvenience so great as to convince the Court that the intention could not have been to use them in their ordinary signification, which, though less proper, is one which the Court thinks the words will bear." River Wear Commissioners v. Adamson, 2 App. Cas. 743, 764-765 (House of Lords 1877). And see Crawford 286-290; Sutherland §46.07.

47. "To deny that the plain meaning rule has any force or validity opens the door to violation of a fundamental objective in statutory interpretation.

At best, there should be no plain meaning "rule," only a plain meaning "presumption." It may also be true that much of the judicial talk about "plain meaning" is only a device for assigning the burden of persuasion as between parties contending over the meaning of a statute.

The rule that words are to be read in context with the neighboring words in the same document (*noscitur a sociis*) [48] recognizes that in the field of communication the whole transcends the parts. The "whole statute" rule [49] is an extention of this principle, as is the rule that statutes on the same subject (*in pari materia*) are, when enacted by the same jurisdiction, to be read in relation to each other. [50] These broad principles are both relevant and valuable, because they reinforce the use of proper context.

Except for the restrictive aspect of the plain meaning rule, these rules reflect or buttress a sincere attempt by the courts to ascertain the meaning of the statute as read in its proper context. Although they unlock little or no specific meaning in particular cases, they set the stage for proper search.

Besides general principles such as these, we find authentic presumptions for ascertaining legislative meaning in factual statements about the existence of particular conventions of language. A good example is the presumption, called *reddendo singula singulis* in its legal form, that recognizes that, context permitting, the reader may properly infer that the author has intended a distributive relationship between two juxtaposed series of ideas (e.g., "men and women may become members of fraternities and sororities"). [51] Another possible presumption is that the word "or" is used in the inclusive sense of "A or B, or both," unless the context affirmatively shows that it is used in the exclusive sense of "A or B, but not both."

The same may be true of a more specialized version of

This position leads to a denial of legislative supremacy in the statutory field." Q. Johnstone, An Evaluation of the Rules of Statutory Interpretation, 3 U. Kan. L. Rev. 1, 13 (1954).

48. Crawford 325-326; E. Driedger, The Construction of Statutes 85-86 (1974); Sutherland §47.16.

49. Crawford 258-261; E. Driedger, The Construction of Statutes 69-74 (1974); Sutherland §46.05.

50. Crawford 431-439; Sutherland §51.02.

51. Crawford 332-334; Sutherland §47.26.

noscitur a sociis called *ejusdem generis*. [52] This says that if a series of more than two items ends with a catch-all term that is broader than the category into which the preceding items fall but which those items do not exhaust, the catch-all term is presumably intended to be no broader than that category. Thus, in the phrase "oaks, elms, and other vegetation," the term "vegetation" presumably means trees. One difficulty is that there may be other equally plausible categories (e.g., deciduous trees) that also meet the test. [53] Whether the presumption is lexicographically accurate is not entirely clear.

In short, every true rule or presumption of interpretation in the cognitive sense is a lexicographical assertion about general usage or behavior, because it is the basis for normal understanding. It is ironical that so few of the so-called canons of "interpretation" are usable for this purpose. [54]

Several Latin maxims masquerade as rules of interpretation while doing nothing more than describing results reached by other means. The best example is probably *expressio unius est exclusio alterius,* [55] which is a rather elaborate, mysterious sounding, and anachronistic way of describing the negative implication. [56] Far from being a rule, it is not even lexicographically accurate, because it is simply not true, generally, that the mere express conferral of a right or privilege in one kind of situation implies the denial of the equivalent right or privilege in other kinds. Sometimes it does and sometimes it does not, and whether it does or does not depends on the particular circumstances of

52. Crawford 326-331; E. Driedger, The Construction of Statutes 86-95 (1974); Sutherland §§47.17-47.22.

53. In United States v. Alpers, 338 U.S. 680, 70 S. Ct. 352 (1950), the question was whether a statute banning the interstate shipment of any "obscene . . . book, pamphlet, picture, motion-picture film, paper, letter, writing, print, or other matter of indecent character" extended to phonograph records. Although these media made their impact visually, they did not exclusively do so. Books have often been read aloud and motion-picture film was later to acquire a sound track. The phonograph record differs only in that (except for its protective jacket) it makes its impact only aurally. The court held that phonograph records were included.

54. ". . . [T]he ordinary 'interpretative process' is rather a technical language to set forth a conclusion than an organon for reaching one." M. Radin, A Case Study in Statutory Interpretation: Western Union Co. vs. Lenroot, 33 Calif. L. Rev. 219, 229 (1945). The statement is probably too sweeping.

55. See Crawford 334-337; E. Driedger, The Construction of Statutes 95-102 (1974); Sutherland §§47.23-47.25.

56. See also ch. 4, p. 41; ch. 5, p. 47.

context.[57] Without contextual support, therefore, there is not even a mild presumption here. Accordingly, this maxim is at best a description, after the fact, of what the court has discovered from context.[58]

57. If it does, the relevant omitted matters are not only outside the express grant but also impliedly denied. If it does not, they are merely outside the express grant. Even here, their status may still be in doubt, because it depends on the existence of an independent supporting statutory provision or common law rule. Thus, although there is no negative implication, the ultimate result may be the same as if there were, if there is no independent statutory provision and the court is unwilling on its own initiative to declare an analogous rule. E.g., Hochgertel v. Canada Dry Corp., 409 Pa. 610, 613-615, 187 A.2d 575, 577-578 (1963).

58. Perhaps the most difficult problem in the interpretation of statutes is that of determining whether a negative implication exists and, if so, how far it extends. A particularly baffling, yet fascinating, example exists in the warranty, disclaimer, and notice provisions of the Uniform Commercial Code and its predecessor, the Uniform Sales Act. The Code creates rights to a safe product as between immediate buyer and seller, permits disclaimer under specified conditions, and requires notice of breach of warranty, without spelling out the extent, if any, to which these rights and limitations apply with respect to third parties (other than members of the family or household of the retail buyer with respect to claims against the retailer (§2-318)). Except for an ambiguous comment that tries to head off a negative implication at least with respect to the members of the retail buyer's family or household, the possible alternative interpretations are these:

(1) UCC does not preempt any relevant field.

(2) UCC preempts the field of consumer warranties based on promise, but not those based on misrepresentation.

(3) UCC preempts the field of retailer warranties with respect to persons horizontally related to the retail buyer other than members of his family or household (i.e., the retail buyer's employees).

(4) UCC preempts the field of consumer warranties also with respect to claims against sellers other than the retailer (e.g., manufacturers).

(5) UCC preempts the field of the consumer's rights to a safe product, whether or not based on warranty, that are not dependent on the seller's culpability.

In the development of statutory products liability law, the main problem has been not so much to find answers as to recognize that a problem of negative implication even exists. See Hawkins Construction Co. v. Matthews Co., 190 Neb. 546, 209 N.W.2d 643 (1973); Markle v. Mulholland's Inc., 265 Ore. 259, 509 P.2d 529 (1972). For general discussions, see R. Dickerson, The ABC's of Products Liability — With a Close Look at Section 402A and the Code, 36 Tenn. L. Rev. 439 (1969), Was Prosser's Folly Also Traynor's? or Should the Judge's Monument Be Moved to a Firmer Site?, 2 Hofstra L. Rev. 469 (1974); M. Franklin, When Worlds Collide: Liability Theories and Disclaimers in Defective Products Cases, 18 Stan. L. Rev. 974 (1966); N. Littlefield,

The *casus omissus* "rule" is, on the surface, an aspect of the plain meaning rule: If an idea has not been stated, the reader (including the court) may not supply it.[59] This is not a rule for ascertaining meaning, but an assertion of political principle that only the legislature can legislate the particular result in a situation in which it has already been determined that the legislature has in fact not done so. Because the "rule" comes into play only after we have determined what the statute means, it merely presumes meaning; it does not determine meaning. At best, it is a way of describing an assumed limitation on the scope of judicial lawmaking with respect to an area that has been left untouched by a statute whose meaning has already been ascertained. In view of the discussion (in chapters 11 and 13) of judicial lawmaking by analogy to statutes, it is doubtful that even this assumed limitation is valid.[60]

G. Summary

Every rule or presumption of interpretation that serves the cognitive function of ascertaining the meaning of a statute as enacted represents at best a statistical judgment that, competing possibilities permitting, the meaning that it reflects is more probable than not. Other factors being neutral, it reflects favorable gambling odds. Because other factors are not always neutral, the interpreter is often faced with finding the resultant thrust of a unique complex of individually general and diverse tendencies, none of which may be controlling.

To do his cognitive job well, a judge must be unbiased, sensi-

---

Some Thoughts on Products Liability Law: A Reply to Professor Shanker, 18 W. Res. L. Rev. 10 (1966); D. Rapson, Products Liability Under Parallel Doctrines: Contrasts Between the Uniform Commercial Code and Strict Liability in Tort, 19 Rutgers L. Rev. 692 (1965); M. Shanker, Strict Tort Theory of Products Liability and the Uniform Commercial Code: A Commentary on Jurisprudential Eclipses, Pigeonholes and Communication Barriers, 17 W. Res. L. Rev. 5 (1965); H. Titus, Restatement (Second) of Torts Section 402A and the Uniform Commercial Code, 22 Stan. L. Rev. 713 (1970); J. Wade, Is Section 402A of the Second Restatement of Torts Preempted by the UCC and Therefore Unconstitutional?, 42 Tenn. L. Rev. 123 (1974).

59. Crawford 269-272.

60. Cf. E. Driedger, The Construction of Statutes 76-79 (1974).

tive to language usages and shared tacit assumptions, perceptive in combining relevant elements affecting meaning, capable of reasoning deductively, and generously endowed with good judgment. In view of these formidable demands, it is hardly surprising that judges often disagree on the true meaning of a statute.

13

How to Apply a Statute (Summarizing the Creative Function)

. . . *[I]nterpretation is inescapably a kind of legislation.*
— J. Frank, "Words and Music: Some Remarks on Statutory Interpretation," 47 Colum. L. Rev. 1259, 1269 (1947)

A. The General Problem

How does a court apply a relevant statute whose revealed meaning fails to dispose of the case at hand? The problem arises in many forms, all or most of whose solutions have conventionally been treated as "interpretation." [1]

The first type of situation, which does not necessarily involve a problem of meaning, is that in which the statutory rule is so general that sustaining the court's decision calls for a smaller-mesh network of legal concepts than the statute provides. The classic example is the Sherman Act. Here the statutory mandate is so general that the court is impliedly invited, and indeed

1. See ch. 1, pp. 1-2; ch. 3, pp. 13-15. That judicial lawmaking with respect to statutes is a many-splendored thing has been noted by J. Cohen in Judicial "Legisputation" and the Dimensions of Legislative Meaning, 36 Ind. L.J. 414 (1961). For a broad-gauged survey and analysis, see the series of articles by J. Witherspoon on the "high," "low," and "middle" roads to the Administrative Discretion to Determine Statutory Meaning in 35 Tex. L. Rev. 63 (1956), 38 Tex. L. Rev. 392, 572 (1960), and 40 Tex. L. Rev. 751 (1962). The reader is warned that Witherspoon uses the term "assignment of meaning" to include the cognitive function.

compelled, to supplement it with more specific rules. This is akin to "delegated legislation."

The second type of situation, which (like the remaining types of situation) does involve a problem of meaning, is that in which the statute remains ambiguous or vague even after the resources of meaning have been exhausted. Here, the court makes law to remove real, as distinct from merely apparent, uncertainty. It may do this by a significantly creative effort, by applying an existing rule of law for resolving an otherwise unresolvable impasse of meaning, or by attributing to the statute a purpose that is not sustained by the statute and its proper context.

The third type is that in which the situation in question falls outside the meaning of the statute and within its manifest purpose. Here, the court may make law by analogy with the statute, freed by the purpose of the statute from any risk of negative implication. [2]

The fourth type is that in which the situation in question falls outside the meaning of the statute and outside its manifest purpose. Here, too, the court may make law by analogy with the statute, but only if it has first determined that the statute carries no negative implication. [3]

The fifth type is that in which the court seeks to ameliorate what it considers to be a harsh, unfair, or otherwise undesirable result by refusing to give effect to the statute's most plausible reading. These involve the more drastic applications of "strict interpretation." Typical examples include criminal statutes and statutes "derogating" from the common law. [4]

The sixth type is that in which the court makes law by overruling an earlier interpretation now determined to have been wrong. [5] This is lawmaking that is intended only to cancel earlier judicial action that through inadvertence turned out to be lawmaking instead of mere cognition.

A possible seventh type has been suggested by Gény. [6] Where

2. Amtorg Trading Corp. v. Miehle Printing Press & Mfg. Co., 206 F.2d 103 (2d Cir. 1953), discussed in ch. 11, pp. 202-203.

3. E.g., Agar v. Orda, 264 N.Y. 248, 190 N.E. 479 (1934), discussed in ch. 11, pp. 204-205.

4. See ch. 11, pp. 205-211.

5. E.g., Girouard v. United States, 328 U.S. 61, 33 S. Ct. 826 (1946), discussed later in this chapter, pp. 254-255.

6. F. Gény, Method of Interpretation and Sources of Private Positive Law 204 (2d ed. 1954, English transl. J. Mayda 1963).

legislative history shows that the text has stated the legislative intent too broadly or too narrowly, [7] the reading of the text can be changed accordingly, but only if the change is a "correction" and not a "negation." [8] Broadening the sweep of a statutory rule can normally be handled as type 3 or 4 lawmaking, so that a seventh type is to this extent unnecessary. The more difficult type of change to rationalize is one narrowing an otherwise broader statutory meaning to conform it to a narrower legislative intent as revealed by legislative materials that, while reliable, do not meet the other qualifications of proper context. Here, there is clear fidelity to actual legislative intent. Whether there is adequate fidelity to the constitutional legislative process is another matter, and we may well wonder whether there is significant room for a narrowing "correction" that does not constitute a "negation." Because Gény does not show where or how the line should be drawn, there seems to be no adequate basis for recognizing such a category of judicial lawmaking.

Of the six types, type 5 ("strict" interpretation) may be passed over as having been adequately discussed in chapter 11. Here, the court should simply stay away from unfriendly lawmaking that would derogate from the most plausible legislative meaning.

Let us now discuss the remaining types of situation.

B. Supplementing the Very General (Type 1)

Because of the range of discretion involved, the broadest and possibly most difficult area of judicial lawmaking with respect to statutes is that of supplementing very general legislative mandates. Although this is often called "interstitial" lawmaking, it is doubtful that the term is apt. Taking the Sherman Act as the classic example, the need for supplementary lawmaking by the courts has resulted not so much from gaps in the statute as from

7. Commissioner v. Acker, 361 U.S. 87, 80 S. Ct. 144 (1959), discussed in ch. 10, at p. 143.

8. F. Gény, Method of Interpretation and Sources of Private Positive Law 205 (2d ed. 1954, English transl. J. Mayda 1963).

the two broad characteristics of generality and vagueness, with both of which this law is generously endowed.[9]

Although they often accompany each other, generality differs from vagueness;[10] only the latter involves problems of meaning. What is immediately relevant here is the kind of legislative generality that requires further implementation before the broad statutory mandate can be brought to bear on specific situations. In this limited respect there is neither a gap in the texture of the statute nor an uncertainty of meaning. The courts make the transition from broad legislative generality to judicial particularity by making legal rules on intermediate planes of generality.

Here, the common designation of "interpretation" takes on a new dimension: There is a direct delegation of legislative power, not to an administrative agency to promulgate implementing rules having the force of law ("delegated legislation") but to the courts to promulgate implementing guidelines in the form of rules of law set forth as supports for decision in a series of litigated cases. The process is similar to that performed by the courts in creating supplementary constitutional law under the guise of finding the "meaning" of the applicable constitution.

The basic problems here are, first, to resolve the relevant problems of vagueness, if any, and, second, to evolve supplementary rules of law that not only produce fair and workable results, but also operate compatibly with the general thrust of the statute read in the light of its proper context.

Here, the question arises whether the court is free to follow its own policy predilections in creating new law. On this, broad principle seems clear. The court should have free rein only so far as it is probably a matter of indifference, under the statute and its proper context, which of the available implementing alternatives it selects. So far as it is not, the court should select the alternative that it believes is the most responsive to the general tenor of the statute, whether it prefers that alternative or not.

The creativity permitted by legislative generality differs from that permitted by unresolvable legislative uncertainty. The re-

9. "If it be recognized that a judge when operating within the fringes of meaning is not interpreting a pre-existing intent but is exercising a legislative power, the conclusion ought to be that less attention should be paid to dictionary meanings and more to legislative policy." G. Williams, Language and the Law — III, 61 L.Q. Rev. 293, 303 (1945).

10. See ch. 5, pp. 51-52.

spective guidelines likewise differ. The court does not speculate on what the original legislature would have done or what a reasonable current legislature would do; nor does it proceed by projection, interpolation, or extrapolation. It simply tries to carry out what it determines to be the broad legislative mandate by conceptualizing it at a sufficiently lower level of generality to permit the rationalization of results in specific cases. Although the cognizant statute is treated as directly applying, it makes its practical impact through a network of subsidiary rules devised by the courts, which are then considered as being engrafted on the statutes itself. In this respect lawmaking power that has been delegated to the courts differs in theory from lawmaking power that has been delegated to executive agencies. Violation of an executive regulation is considered a violation of the underlying statute only because the statute expressly so provides;[11] violation of a judicial supplementation is automatically so.

If a different supplementary rule is later determined to be preferable, what the court had the power to create it presumably has the power to change. The propriety of making such a change in an analogous situation is discussed in part F.

C. Removing Uncertainty of Meaning (Type 2)

If it has been determined that, because of a persistent uncertainty, the statutory and contextual resources of meaning are inadequate to provide an answer to the issues posed by the litigation, the court must attribute a meaning to the statute that resolves the ambiguity or vagueness as it relates to the kind of situation involved in the case before it.[12] In attributing such a meaning, what approach should the court adopt? The answer is not easy.

The alternative approaches to performing the creative function in such a situation would appear to be the following:

(1) The court should adopt the rule that the original legisla-

11. E.g., Federal Trade Commission Act, 15 U.S.C. §21(*l*) (1914); Federal Power Act, 16 U.S.C. §825*o*(b) (1920); Emergency Price Control Act of 1942, title I, §4(a), 56 Stat. 28; Communications Act of 1934, 47 U.S.C. §§501-502; Federal Aviation Act, 49 U.S.C. §1487 (1958).

12. See ch. 3, p. 14.

ture probably would have adopted had it dealt with the problem at the time it enacted the statute. This would include consideration of relevant and reliable evidences of legislative intent even if they lay outside legislative context. It might include occasional items of legislative history.

(2) The court should adopt the rule that a reasonable legislature would probably have adopted. This would presumably, but not necessarily, be the rule that best fits with the statute and other related elements in the legal order, determined as of the time the statute was enacted.

(3) The court should adopt the rule that the present legislature would probably adopt if it were now dealing with the problem.

(4) The court should adopt the rule that a reasonable current legislature would probably adopt. This would presumably, but not necessarily, be the rule that best fits with the statute and other related elements in the legal order, determined as of the present time.

(5) The court should adopt what the court considers the preferable rule for the kind of situation before it, as determined without regard to legislative intent or the related elements of the legal order, including the statute under consideration.

(6) If none of these approaches succeeds, the court should apply an arbitrary rule of law.

How should the court proceed? Suppose the relevant original legislative intent, which is not disclosed by the statute when read in its proper context, is directly and reliably disclosed by the legislative history or otherwise. Here, it would seem appropriate for the court to create a rule of law consistent with that intent, unless it determined that to do so would be significantly incompatible with related statutory law. If such incompatibility appeared, it is arguable that, because a court has no duty to honor expressions of intent that fall outside the constitutional channels of promulgation, it is not foreclosed from selecting another, assumably preferable, approach.

Suppose the relevant legislative intent cannot be determined by direct reference to any reliable source. Here, it seems hazardous to speculate on what the original legislature would have done.[13]

13. Even so, this approach has been widely adopted. E.g., Aristotle, Nicomachean Ethics, E14 1137; L. Hand, The Bill of Rights 18-22 (1958); E. Bruncken, Interpretation of the Written Law, 25 Yale L.J. 129, 135 (1915); F. Horack, Jr., Cooperative Action for Improved Statutory Interpretation, 3

Another, common approach has been to speculate on how the legislature would have handled the matter had it been brought to its attention and had the legislature acted rationally and consistently.[14]

Hart and Sacks' concept of "creative elaboration,"[15] although not referring to the legislature and thus being formally more objective, would appear to reach the same substantive result, because a rational court and a rational legislature would presumably apply the same basic standard: What fits best with the rest of the statutory and legal system? Strömholm apparently agrees: ". . . If preliminary works are used . . . *as expert advice to the court* . . . it is no longer the *origin* but the *rationality* of the opinions given in the course of the legislative process which counts. . . ."[16]

The basic idea is to further the manifest legislative purpose as consistently as possible with the statute and the rest of the legal order. Where no legislative purpose is manifest, the court may find it helpful to attribute to the legislature the purpose that seems most compatible with the terms of the statute as read in the light of surrounding circumstances — a kind of court-created element of context. This approach, which is basically the second approach, appears to be preferable, because the attribution of purpose or meaning, being based on creative elaboration and less on legislative history, is more likely to produce a consistent, integrated substantive result than speculation about hypothetical subjective intent, which tends to give undue weight to the vagaries and minutiae of that history. In some instances, the latter approach could lead to a less compatible legal result.

The vulnerable spot in this analysis is that adhering to it rigidly can, in some cases, lead to judicially created legal rules that, although logically and artistically consistent with the pattern of the statute as it was conceived at the time of enactment,

---

Vand. L. Rev. 382, 390-391 (1950); F. Horack, Jr., In the Name of Legislative Intention, 38 W. Va. L.Q. 119, 129 (1932).

14. E.g., F. Horack, Jr., In the Name of Legislative Intention, 38 W. Va. L.Q. 119, 129 (1932). This seems to be the gist of Cohen's "legisputation." J. Cohen, Judicial "Legisputation" and the Dimensions of Legislative Meaning, 36 Ind. L.J. 414, 418 (1961).

15. Hart & Sacks 1417. See also C. Breitel, The Courts and Law Making, in Legal Institutions Today and Tomorrow 1, 2 (M. Paulsen ed., 1959).

16. S. Strömholm, Legislative Material and Construction of Statutes: Notes on the Continental Approach, 10 Scandinavian Studies in Law 1966, at 173, 217. (Emphasis in original.)

accomplish this result at the expense of relevant current needs that are both important and pressing. It is not enough to say that this is just too bad. In cases where the current judicial action is only remotely related to past legislative attitudes reasonably inferable from the statute and its proper context, what justification is there for subordinating current substantive needs to mere logical and aesthetic compatibility with the past?

Although the main tenets of this book make no room for serving current social needs by overriding reasonably inferable legislative intent or exploiting accidental postenactment semantic changes, in some cases there may be room, through judicial lawmaking, to strike a modest blow for wholesome modernity, so long as the result is functionally compatible, if not logically and artistically the most consistent, with the original statutory scheme. [17]

Such an approach better serves current social needs without in any significant way violating the court's constitutional duty of deference to ascertained legislative intent and without subverting it by introducing legal rules whose operation would disrupt the statutory scheme as defined by the statute or fail to include additional legal rules necessary to its adequate operation.

Accordingly, some writers have contended that the courts are at least free from control by the original legislature. Curtis, for one, has contended that, consistently with the ascertained meaning of the statute, a court should be able to shake off the dust of the past and plant its feet firmly in the present. [18]

> . . . The legislature which passed the statute has adjourned and its members gone home to their constituents or to a long rest from all lawmaking. So why bother about what they intended or what they would have done? Better be prophetic than archaeological, better deal with the future than with the past, better pay a decent respect for a future legislature than stand in awe of one that has folded up its papers and joined its friends at the country club or in the cemetery. . . .

Is this the present as seen by the current legislature, a "reasonable" legislature, or the court? Says Curtis: [19]

17. See E. Bruncken, Interpretation of the Written Law, 25 Yale L.J. 129, 135 (1915).
18. C. Curtis, A Better Theory of Legal Interpretation, 3 Vand. L. Rev. 407, 415 (1950), rephrased in It's Your Law 54, 55 (1954).
19. Id.

> . . . Let the courts deliberate on what the present or a future legislature would do after it had read the court's opinion, after the situation has been explained, after the court has exhibited the whole fabric of the law into which this particular bit of legislation had had to be adjusted.

It is not fruitful, for this purpose, to try to psychoanalyze the current legislature, the search for whose views, considering its total silence, are even more highly speculative, and thus correspondingly less fruitful, than trying to guess what the original legislature would have done had it thought about the problem. Because the current legislature probably has not spoken, even unofficially, and its views are thus highly speculative at best, the court is likely to "speculate," if at all, by adopting its own point of view, on the assumption that its point of view is also that of the current legislature. On such a fictional basis the third approach has little to commend it.

To the question whether a court should be free to follow its own policy predilections in such a case, Mishkin and Morris respond with a question of their own: "If this sort of judicial behavior were proper, how much real power would reside in legislatures, as compared to the courts?" [20] They add:

> . . . [W]here all other indicators leave the issue entirely in equipoise, the decision might well be left to the judge's view of what (consistent with the over-all statutory purpose) is wisest social policy. If the legislative choice is for practical purposes non-existent, such conscious judicial choice would seem better than mere chance. . . . [W]hile the general idea that a judge's policy views may play a role under such circumstances may be sound, it is only rarely that it should prove necessary for it to come into play. . . . Great danger exists that a judge's strongly held view on substantive policy merits may influence his determination that the indicators of the legislative choice are completely lacking.

This analysis seems to assume that the court faces two discrete alternative situations: the existence of full legislative indicators or their complete absence. Instead, it seems more likely that judges face a range of situations between the need, discussed in chapter 3, to make a minor restoration in a vase with a missing piece, at one extreme, and the need to show, by projecting a piece from another vase, how the original (second) vase may have

20. P. Mishkin & C. Morris, On Law in Courts 444-445 (1965).

looked, at the other. In these situations courts are often confronted with unresolved uncertainties with respect to which there is a significant residual area, where, after taking into consideration the limitations imposed by manifest legislative purpose, neither statute nor context provides guidance. What is rare, outside the delegation of lawmaking power provided by broad legislative generality (which does not raise a question of interpretation), is for the area of residual uncertainty of meaning to be large.

Despite modern trends in judicial activism, the approach of unfettered judicial discretion should be rejected out of hand,[21] so far as it disregards the relationship between the new judge-made rule and related law. Even if the court owes no deference to the legislature's officially uncommunicated view, if any, of the original or current legislature, it owes fidelity to the coherence of the legal order. Only if there is no guidance, by interpolation, extrapolation, or otherwise, from the rest of the legal order, including the officially expressed views of the legislature, is the court justified in going it wholly on its own.

If this analysis is correct, the principle that cognition should precede creation[22] should be supplemented by a second principle, which operates within the area of judicial lawmaking: Disciplined creation[23] should precede free creation. Thus, before a court takes off on its own, it should first make certain that there is no alternative that fits better with the statute and its related law than any other. There is often a determinably best alternative and, when there is, the court should respect it. Impatience with this step leads to judicial bootstrap pulling. Whether this responsibility of deference is of as high an order as that of respecting the determination of legislative meaning is not easy to say. The latter is a constitutional responsibility of deference to legislative supremacy in the field of policymaking, whereas the former is partly a secondary responsibility of deference to legis-

21. "Society will not long tolerate the wisest judge who, knowing no master, decides cases only according to his individual sense of justice." A. Cox, Judge Learned Hand and the Interpretation of Statutes, 60 Harv. L. Rev. 370, 373 (1947).

22. See ch. 3, pp. 19-20.

23. To suggest the disciplined nature of this kind of judicial lawmaking, Cohen has coined the term "judicial legisputation." J. Cohen, Judicial "Legisputation" and the Dimensions of Legislative Meaning, 36 Ind. L.J. 414, 418 (1961).

lative supremacy and partly a general professional fidelity to the coherent development of the existing legal system. In either case, it is a judicial responsibility that the court should try, as fully as possible, to discharge.

This concession to modernity is supportable by an analogy from architecture. In designing an addition to a Victorian house, an architect normally tries to accomplish the purposes of the addition as consistently as possible with the functions and style of the original. On the other hand, he will not hesitate to modernize style so far as necessary to make the addition serve current functional needs, if this does not destroy the original concept of the building or its functions, or violate the general principles of aesthetic unity and scale. The analogy must not be pressed to its dry extreme, because the architect has no restraints on his creativity comparable to the constitutional restraints that inhibit courts.

Taking current needs into this limited account can be supported also on the ground that the legislature is normally too busy to attend to all the areas of growth that need legislative attention [24] and that, until acute need spurs the legislature to action in the particular area, the court can serve as a modest lawmaking agency in the service of specific current needs without derogating from or otherwise undermining what the legislature has previously prescribed. Without speculating on how the legislature is currently disposed and without betraying its earlier actions, the court can thus help to lighten the legislature's heavy social burden.

Any approach that thus lessens reliance on legislative history has the additional advantage of lessening the practical burdens of research involved in preparing a case for litigation. The advantage is increased when the court applies relatively stringent standards of reliability even within the looser context of judicial lawmaking.

The more adequately a court discharges this second responsibility the less crucial the distinction between cognition and creation becomes in the particular case. Determining what the statute most probably means strongly resembles determining what judicially attributed meaning would be most consistent with

24. That this may be gross understatement is suggested in H. Friendly, Benchmarks, ch. 4 (1967) (The Gap in Lawmaking — Judges Who Can't and Legislators Who Won't).

the statute. In discharging either responsibility, the court should first defer to the enacted will of the legislature. One requires direct deference; the other indirect.

However, although fidelity to the second responsibility tends to lessen the risk of unfair surprise, it does not eliminate it, because, in discharging this responsibility even with a more limited reliance on legislative history, the court is not limited to examining materials that are equally accessible to the legislative audience; the materials examined need not be a part of proper context. [25] The difference between cognition and creation remains important also because the results are not of equal legal force: A court can overturn an interpretation only because it was wrong, whereas, subject to the appropriate regard for the principles of *stare decisis,* it can overturn lawmaking by analogy simply on the ground that the court's current conception of social policy suggests a different and more appropriate legal rule.

Suppose that the search for meaning and reliance on the methods of reasoned elaboration fail. What then? Because flipping a coin is not a jurisprudentially acceptable way of removing the impasse, the adjudicative function has produced a special group of rules or canons that assign fictitious meanings where true meanings cannot be determined and reference to manifest purpose fails to yield a most plausible alternative. Hence the rule of law, applicable in many jurisdictions, that the later statement prevails over an earlier, inconsistent statement in the same statute. [26] Also in this class are *ejusdem generis* and similar canons when they are used only as convenient fictions for deciding specific controversies. As legitimate judicial lawmaking, they should not be confused with what they caricature, measures of actual meaning. These rules are easily confused with true rules for discovering meaning, because there is some correlation between what the writers of statutes intend to do and what these rules assume to be true. However, to the wide extent that application outruns their slender factual basis and they are applied mechanically, they operate as rules of law.

The rule that a later, inconsistent statute supersedes the

25. That certainty is not necessarily the paramount value in judicial lawmaking with respect to statutes has been noted by J. Cohen, Judicial "Legisputation" and the Dimensions of Legislative Meaning, 36 Ind. L.J. 414, 420 (1961).

26. E.g., see 82 C.J.S. 718, n. 70.

earlier,[27] at least to the extent of the inconsistency, is not a rule of interpretation, but a rule of law. Like the rule relating to internal inconsistencies, it comes into play only after the meaning of each of the two pronouncements has been ascertained. It is by no means clear that, as between two successive acts whose literal interpretations clash, the earlier must yield to the later. Indeed, the later statute is often intended to defer to the earlier. Moreover, whether an intended supersession is partial or total depends on the area of express inconsistency or, if the latter is less than total, whether, and to what extent, the later statute implies the exclusion of what it does not express. Only to this extent is a true problem of ascertainment (cognition) involved. In any event, the stated rule plays no part in solving it. It merely tells which law is in effect.

D. Furthering Legislative Purpose (Type 3)

Suppose that the case under consideration involves a situation that falls outside the working provisions of the statute while remaining under its general purpose. This was the situation involved in *Amtorg Trading Corp. v. Miehle Printing Press & Manuf. Co.*, discussed in chapter 11. Here, the court may create a rule of law by analogy with the statute, free of any risk of legislative preemption.

The important issue is whether the court is constitutionally or otherwise obliged to take such action. As Witherspoon has pointed out,[28] some writers believe that once the domain of specific statutory rules (which are not necessarily express) has been left behind, the statute and its purposes may safely be ignored. A larger number apparently believe that the court should pay strong deference to legislative policy even in areas in which the legislature has not implemented its policy with statutory rules.

Witherspoon goes even farther.[29] He argues, with some

27. E.g., Sutherland §23.17; 82 C.J.S. 718, n. 69.

28. J. Witherspoon, Administrative Discretion to Determine Statutory Meaning: "The Middle Road": I, 40 Tex. 751, 753-771 (1960).

29. Id. at 822-848.

plausibility, that the reach of a statute is not confined to its working provisions and that it includes the statute's underlying policies and general purposes as conditioned or supplemented by general legislative principles resulting from the interplay between legislative purposes, statutory rules, and administrative factors. Under this approach, unimplemented statutory purpose apparently has the same authoritative grip on the courts as the statute's working provisions, except so far as the court has leeway in determining which judicial implementation is the most responsive to legislative purpose.

I cannot do justice to this important aspect of judicial lawmaking in relation to statutes, because it has never been given adequate attention free of the cognitive aspects of "statutory interpretation." This area of judicial lawmaking with respect to statutes cries for further study. One of the critical factual questions here is the extent to which courts can reliably ascertain legislative purposes not formally recited by statutes or their legislative histories. The problem of appropriate vantage point has already been discussed in connection with type 2 situations.

E. Using an Analogy Beyond the Scope or Purpose of a Statute (Type 4)

A statute may provide a useful analogy even in the broad area that lies beyond the scope of its working provisions and even beyond that of its policy or purpose. This is exemplified by *Agar v. Orda,* previously discussed in chapter 11. Here, again, a court is free to create a common law rule by analogy with a statutory rule, if that makes the best sense in light of the rest of the legal order. Unlike a type 3 situation, which lies within the policy orbit of a particular statute, the situations under discussion would seem to call for no special statutory deference. The court should select the analogy, whether statutory or common law, that best serves the matter at hand and the coherence of the legal order. Otherwise, the considerations discussed with respect to types 2 and 3 seem equally relevant here.

F. Correcting Erroneous Interpretations (Type 6); Prospective Overruling

Because judicial lawmaking involves, by hypothesis, something new, courts in the exercise of their creative function should keep in mind that giving retroactive or even immediately prospective effect to their action may in some instances unfairly surprise those who are subject to the resulting legal rule. This risk has been obscured whenever courts have pretended, through the euphemism of "interpretation," that results that they have created were discoverable from the statute itself. Unlike English courts, American courts now accept the fact that in interpreting and applying statutes they are regularly involved, however incidentally, in making law. [30]

But whether new law is made by the legislature or by a court, the problem of due notice is broadly the same. Legislatures are well acquainted with the need to give statutes appropriate, sometimes deferred, effective dates. [31] The American judiciary, however emancipated from the English view that courts only interpret statutes, has yet to become sophisticated in this area. A fuller recognition of the difference between law finding and lawmaking helps to resolve some of the problems that have plagued judges who are sensitive to the occasional need to defer the effectiveness of their actions.

One of the hardest problems is that faced by a judge who has determined that an earlier interpretation of a statute is wrong. Here, a preliminary question arises as to whether the court can or should do anything about such an interpretation.

Under the approach supported by Horack, [32] Levi, [33] and others, [34] a court gets only one chance to deal with a particular

30. E.g., ". . . [I]nterpretation is inescapably a kind of legislation." J. Frank, Words and Music: Some Remarks on Statutory Interpretation, 47 Colum. L. Rev. 1259, 1269 (1947). And see ch. 3, p. 14.

31. E. Driedger, The Composition of Legislation 134 (1956); G. Thornton, Legislative Drafting 146 (1970).

32. F. Horack, Jr., Congressional Silence: A Tool of Judicial Supremacy, 25 Tex. L. Rev. 247, 250-253 (1947).

33. E. Levi, Introduction to Legal Reasoning, 15 U. Chi. L. Rev. 501, 523-540 (1948).

34. ". . . [J]udges often state that they are specially reluctant to override a prior decision that merely construes a statute." F. Newman & S. Surrey, Legislation — Cases & Materials 653 (1955).

uncertainty of meaning. If it interprets the statute correctly, fine. If it interprets the statute incorrectly, the court must live with its mistake until the legislature corrects it. Under Horack's approach, if its initial interpretative effort aborts, the court has inadvertently created new law that automatically merges with the statute.[35] Because only a legislature can amend a statute, only a legislature can correct such a judicial error. Accordingly, for the court to correct its mistake would usurp the legislature's function. This result is assured if the legislature has, in the meantime, reenacted the statute, because reenactment is said to constitute an implied confirmation of the court's earlier interpretation.

Horack's approach seems to rest on the assumption that, whereas inadvertent lawmaking resulting from misreading a statute is essentially a judicial act because the risk of making it is a necessary incident to the court's duty to adjudicate the case before it, judicial correction of the same error, being unnecessary, would be essentially legislative and thus usurp the legislature's policymaking function. The result is ironic: The original interpretation, which by hypothesis thwarted legislative intent, did not invade the legislature's prerogative, whereas later correction, which by hypothesis supports the result originally intended by the legislature, would invade it. Does this make sense? Instead, it would seem that, subject to the principle of estoppel, if a court has power to make law by mistake, it has power to make law to correct the mistake. The fact that the deviation was accidental while correction would be intentional does not seem to be important.

Levi's justification of the one-shot approach[36] bases judicial inaction, not on a constitutional requirement to avoid usurpation of the legislative function, but on judicial self-abnegation. The main difference here is that the latter approach does not wholly foreclose overruling (". . . it still leaves open the path for judicial action if the matter is thought vital").[37]

Levi's test is whether the change to the assumedly proper interpretation would be "controversial," a test very hard to apply. Even disregarding the high degree of vagueness, it would seem that, in the absence of detrimental reliance by the persons

35. Douglass v. County of Pike, 101 U.S. 677, 686-687 (1879) says that the term "statute" includes judicial interpretations of the statute.

36. E. Levi, Introduction to Legal Reasoning, 15 U. Chi. L. Rev. 501, 523-524 (1948).

37. Id. at 540.

subject to the statute, which has nothing to do with deference to the legislative will, deference to that will, and thus the democratic process itself (which Levi seeks to protect), is normally better served by correcting past deviations from the legislative will than by freezing them. Under Mishkin and Morris' broadened rationale for Levi's approach, that "His position must . . . necessarily mean that it is better that some misconstructions go uncorrected than that a court correct its errors," [38] the one-shot approach simply dissolves into a more generalized version of the principle that established public reliance is sometimes a persuasive reason for living with an error, a conclusion with which, in the circumstances, the current legislature is not compelled by consistency to disagree.

Assuming that Horack and Levi are right, the question then arises whether their analyses would apply also to a judicial change of mind with respect to past creation as distinct from past cognition. The answer might well depend on whether we follow the public reliance approach implicit in *stare decisis* or the approach that the court should not usurp the function of determining the more significant social thrusts that belongs to the more democratically constituted institution — the legislature. Certainly, no usurpation is involved in revising judicial lawmaking of types 1-4, and it would not be involved even with respect to type 5 were a court to repent its earlier unfriendly strictness. Even under the reliance approach implicit in *stare decisis,* type 4 and probably type 3 are straight common law operations and there is no reason to adopt a stricter standard of *stare decisis* here than for the creative common law process generally. The same seems to be true even of types 1 and 2.

The better view on overruling generally has been adopted by the United States Supreme Court. In *Girouard v. United States,* [39] the Court corrected an interpretation that it believed had been erroneously made of a provision that had been reenacted in section 335(a) of the Nationality Act of 1940. The question was whether the oath that it prescribed required the swearer to bear arms to defend the Constitution. The court not only corrected the erroneous interpretation but did so in the face of the fact that Congress had in the meantime reenacted the provision without change, thus giving rise to the contention that in the reenact-

38. P. Mishkin & C. Morris, On Law in Courts 483 (1965).
39. 328 U.S. 61, 66 S. Ct. 826 (1946).

ment Congress had impliedly approved the supposedly erroneous interpretation. To this the court said, ". . . [I]t is at best treacherous to find in congressional silence alone the adoption of a controlling rule of law." [40] The reenacted oath presumably meant the same as the original oath. *A fortiori,* the Court would have decided the same way had there been no reenactment, only congressional silence. The result seems sound. [41]

In jurisdictions that agree with *Girouard,* courts that undertake to correct errors of statutory interpretation face another problem: What, if anything, can a court do where to apply the corrected interpretation retroactively to the date of the original enactment would cause hardship to those who operated in apparent reliance on the erroneous interpretation? The difficulty results from the fact that any declaration of the true meaning of a statute inherently relates back to the date of enactment.

This problem arose in 1941 in *Warring v. Colpoys,* [42] in which a person had been convicted, in 1939, of contempt for misbehavior "so near [a court house] as to obstruct the administration of justice," even though the act in question took place at some distance from the court house. He sought habeas corpus on the ground that earlier in 1941 the United States Supreme Court had held that "near" should be read geographically, not causally, thus making the statute inapplicable to the defendant's type of behavior. The United States Court of Appeals for the District of Columbia nevertheless denied relief on the ground that the Supreme Court's revised interpretation had no retroactive effect.

The doctrinal problem that the Court of Appeals faced was this: How could the selfsame statute, which had remained unchanged since 1831, have meant one thing in 1939 and another in

40. Id. at 69.

41. Sutherland §49.05. Levi argues that "the justification for the majority opinion is its oblique reference to the Constitution. . . . *Ordinarily* a principle to be great enough to justify a reversal of legislative interpretation must be a matter for the Constitution. . . . But it still leaves open the path for judicial action if the matter is thought vital." E. Levi, Introduction to Legal Reasoning, 15 U. Chi. L. Rev. 501, 539-540 (1948). (Emphasis added.) This seems to concede that even in extraordinary circumstances not involving the Constitution interpretative overruling may be justified. Naturally, a court should not overrule an earlier interpretation unless the values of overruling outweigh those underlying *stare decisis,* taking into account the possible appropriateness of prospective overruling, discussed later. See also R. Keeton, Venturing to do Justice 79 (1969).

42. 122 F.2d 642 (D.C. Cir. 1941).

1941? The answer is that it could not, if by "meaning" we mean true meaning. On the other hand, it could, if by "meaning" we mean legal meaning; the same statute can have different legal meanings on different dates. Taking as our standard the assumed correctness of the 1941 interpretation (which was not in issue), we can say that in 1939 the legal meaning of the act, which is ordinarily what counts in court, differed from its true meaning. When in 1941 the Supreme Court made the assumedly correct interpretation, it declared a meaning that, if correct, must have been the statute's meaning from the date of enactment. By that same determination it also made the true meaning, for the first time, the legal meaning. In short, the basic relevant juridical fact was that in 1941 the legal meaning of "near" had changed.

This analysis would ordinarily liberate the court from the false dilemma of having to choose between staying with a wrong legal meaning and declaring a new correct legal meaning that is necessarily effective from the date of enactment. Because only a newly declared rule of law, which now coincided with true meaning, was directly involved, the court had discretion to make the new rule effective at what it considered the appropriate time. Thus, it is arguable that the court in *Colpoys* was free to apply the new rule only prospectively, [43] if that seemed to be the most

43. Prospective overruling was first urged as an appropriate cushioning technique by George F. Canfield in 1917. It got its first official judicial blessing, from Justice Cardozo, in Great Northern Ry. v. Sunburst Oil & Ref. Co., 287 U.S. 358, 53 S. Ct. 145 (1932). B. Levy, Realist Jurisprudence and Prospective Overruling, 109 U. Pa. L. Rev. 1, 7, 12 (1960). Although occasionally used, it has not been widely and freely adopted.

On prospective overruling generally, see also P. Mishkin & C. Morris, On Law in Courts 272-317 (1965); C. Bartlett, Prospective Overruling and Property Law, 18 W. Res. L. Rev. 1205 (1967); C. Carpenter, Court Decisions and the Common Law, 17 Colum. L. Rev. 593 (1917); T. Fairchild, Limitations of New Judge-Made Law to Prospective Effect Only: "Prospective Overruling" or "Sunbursting," 51 Marq. L. Rev. 254 (1967-1968); J. Freeman, Prospective Overruling and Retroactive Application in the Federal Courts, 71 Yale L.J. 907 (1962); R. Freeman, The Protection Afforded Against the Retrospective Operation of an Overruling Decision, 18 Colum. L. Rev. 230 (1918); W. Friedmann, Limits of Judicial Lawmaking and Prospective Overruling, 29 Mod. L. Rev. 593, 602-605 (1966); A. Kocourek, Retrospective Decisions and Stare Decisis, 17 A.B.A.J. 180 (1931); N. Littlefield, Stare Decisis, Prospective Overruling, and Judicial Legislation in the Context of Sovereign Immunity, 9 St. Louis L.J. 56 (1964); P. Mishkin, Foreword: The High Court, The Great Word, and the Due Process of Time and Law, 79 Harv. L. Rev. 56, 58-72 (1965); W. Schaefer, The Control of "Sunbursts": Techniques of Prospective Overruling, 42 N.Y.U.L. Rev. 631 (1967); O. Sny-

appropriate action. Whether it would have been more appropriate in the circumstances of that case to apply the new rule retroactively raises issues of policy that are not immediately relevant to this discussion. The difficulty with applying this analysis to *Colpoys* is that the court in that case could hardly set an effective date for a change in the law that had already been made by the Supreme Court. All it could do was interpret the Supreme Court's action with respect to the time of taking effect.

Where the problem has been recognized, the issue is usually considered to be a choice between retroactive application and immediately prospective application. However, a decision not to make retroactive a newly declared legal meaning (which is now assumedly the true meaning) does not commit the court to making its new legal meaning effective from the date of its declaration or publication. The Supreme Court's segregation cases, beginning in 1954 with *Brown v. Board of Education,* [44] rest on the principle that the legal impact of a newly declared constitutional principle may, in appropriate cases, be deferred for a reasonable time to give the persons affected time to adjust to it. The same would seem to apply to changed interpretations of statutes.

A court that would like to overrule an earlier judicial interpretation thus has three basic options: (1) make the new rule appropriately retroactive, subject to the normal constitutional and judicial restrictions on retroaction; (2) make the new rule effective immediately, so that it applies to all future events or situations of the kinds described, and no past ones; or (3) defer the effective date to a future time, so that it applies only to events occurring, or situations existing, after that time.

As measured against more recent deferral cases, *Brown* was atypical in adopting, not a date certain, but a vague, in effect conditional, effective date (the date arrived at by moving with "all deliberate speed"). Most cases that have used a deferred

---

der, Retrospective Operation of Overruling Decisions, 35 Ill. L. Rev. 121 (1940); Note, Prospective Operation of Decisions Holding Statutes Unconstitutional or Overruling Prior Decisions, 60 Harv. L. Rev. 437 (1947); Note, Limitation of Judicial Decisions to Prospective Operation, 46 Iowa L. Rev. 600 (1961); Comment, Prospective Overruling — "Sunburst" Theory, 18 Baylor L. Rev. 606 (1966); Note, Prospective Overruling and Retroactive Application in the Federal Courts, 71 Yale L.J. 907 (1962); Annotation, Prospective or Retroactive Operation of Overruling Decisions, 10 A.L.R.3d 1371 (1966).

44. 347 U.S. 483; 74 S. Ct. 585 (1954).

effective date to permit adequate advance notice of the new rule (mostly cases involving property[45] law, charitable[46] or governmental[47] immunity, or civil[48] or criminal[49] procedure) have adopted either a specified date or a fixed period beginning with the date the decision is filed or published.

For present purposes, details are unimportant. The general point is that the problem of proper notice to the public attaches to all lawmaking that overturns existing law, whether it is done by the legislature or a court; and what works for legislation may work, in at least some instances, for case law. The fact that it is often hard even for a legislature to select an appropriate date, need not concern us here.

Is a current or deferred effective date for a revised interpretation to be rationalized simply as a promise not to enforce a legal requirement presumed to be in effect, thus creating an estoppel against enforcement, or as fixing the time when the new rule is to come into being? The latter approach recognizes the general parallel between case-law making and statute-law making, it is realistic, and it avoids the assumption that the court is willing, for a defined period, to condone assumed violations. The important thing is that when a court overrules an earlier interpretation it is making new law. New law must have an effective date and it is not necessarily the date when the law being interpreted was originally enacted.

Thus, there appears to be no reason why, in appropriate cases, courts may not emulate legislatures and defer the effectiveness of a new rule of law until a specified date or one based on a generally ascertainable contingency, or until the expiration of a specified period. Unfortunately, the failure to identify the creative function in the judicial application of statutes has obscured some of the reasonable options here. In any event, the area needs

45. E.g., Russman v. Luckett, 391 S.W.2d 694, 699-700 (Ct. App. Ky. 1965) (property tax; specified date).

46. E.g., Widell v. Holy Trinity Catholic Church, 19 Wis. 2d 648, 657, 121 N.W.2d 249, 254 (1963) (one-month period).

47. E.g., Carroll v. Kittle, 203 Kan. 841, 851, 457 P.2d 21, 29 (1969) (90-day period); Proffitt v. State, 174 Colo. 113, 114, 482 P.2d 956, 966 (1971) (specified date).

48. E.g., Bell v. Pedigo, 364 S.W.2d 613 (Sup. Ct. Mo. 1963) (publication in advance sheets); Swarb v. Lennox, 314 F. Supp. 1091, 1103 (E.D. Pa. 1970) aff'd 405 U.S. 191 (earlier of specified period or legislative adjournment).

49. E.g., State v. Gannites, 101 R.I. 216, 221, 221 A.2d 620, 623 (1966) (30-day period).

further study and experimentation. An appropriate use of prospective or deferred effectiveness would at least lessen the need for predictability, emphasized by continental jurists, in the area of judicial lawmaking.

Where the court determines that, although the general rule should be changed prospectively or its effective date deferred, the plaintiff can be given relief without unfairness to the defendant, courts sometimes grant him retrospective relief while granting it on a prospective or deferred basis for all others, with the result that for the latter it covers only events occurring, or situations existing, after the effective date of the change. There are undoubtedly other occasions, peculiar to litigation, for deviating from a straight legislative approach. This has been justified on the grounds that (1) the plaintiff should be given a wholesome incentive to attack questionable rules of law, by rewarding him for success, and (2) the failure to apply the new rule to the case at hand would make the announced change mere dictum. [50]

The first justification has been challenged on the ground that, so long as retrospective application remains the rule rather than the exception, there is a sufficient incentive to challenge the old law. [51] In any event, the justification fails where granting relief would unfairly prejudice a defendant who had reasonably relied to his substantial detriment on the old rule. In such a case relief must be denied altogether, unless it can be applied only to future events or situations.

Does the latter approach make the substantive pronouncement dictum? Does this make enough difference to validate the second justification for treating the plaintiff specially? This was the dilemma on which the Minnesota Supreme Court found itself impaled in *Naftalin v. King*. [52] The court said, on the one hand, that the existing interpretation of the constitution was plainly wrong. At the same time, it concluded, somewhat hesitantly, that there had been detrimental reliance and that the application of the new rule should be deferred until a case not involving such reliance arose, presumably one in which the parties concerned had had adequate notice of the prospective change.

50. For a discussion of the various rationales for applying an otherwise prospective or deferred rule to the case at hand, see Bishop v. Langlois, 106 R.I. 56, 256 A.2d 20 (1969); Molitor v. Kaneland Community Unit School District, 18 Ill. 2d 11, 163 N.E.2d 89 (1959).

51. P. Mishkin & C. Morris, On Law in Courts 311 (1965).

52. 257 Minn. 398, 102 N.W.2d 301 (1960).

The court said that under the circumstances it could only utter a "considered dictum" and predict what it or a later court would do in a future case in which a direct holding was possible. This raised the question whether an assumedly nonbinding dictum respecting future probabilities would be sufficiently binding, as a notice to future participants, that disregard of it would justify the later court in subjecting the offending party to the new interpretation. If the notice were effective, it would be hard to distinguish such a "nonbinding dictum" from a true holding.

The more straightforward approach would be to announce that the new rule will take its place prospectively[53] or on a deferred effective date. The distinguishing characteristic of a dictum is that the legal subject is moot, an unnecessary appendage to a holding on a severable matter, and thus likely not to receive the full attention of the parties and the court. The same is not true here. The new rule arises out of an actual controversy that centers on the very legal issue to which the court's pronouncement is directed. The only difference is the number of the parties affected and the timing. Whatever deficiencies give a less persuasive force to the usual dictum, they are absent here. Conversely, the elements that make a holding more reliable are present.[54] An argument against this approach is that, if it became the more usual practice, the litigant who stood to gain by adhering to the old interpretation would have little incentive to argue on its behalf. Countering this would be the risk, which no litigant could safely ignore, that the court would apply the new rule retroactively.

Some analysts of prospective overruling have urged that cau-

53. E.g., O'Brien v. Atlas Finance Co., 223 Ark. 176, 179, 264 S.W.2d 839, 841 (1954), where the court said:

". . . [W]e cannot overrule retrospectively the holding in cases directly in point which have become a rule of property; so we affirm the judgment in the case at bar, but we hereby give the public this caveat:

"In any transaction entered into after the date of this opinion we will consider a course of dealings like that in the Simpson case, the Hickingbotham case, and the case at bar to be *one transaction,* and we will test it by the constitutional mandate against usury." (Emphasis in original.)

See also Markle v. Mulholland's, Inc., 265 Ore. 259, 509 P.2d 529, 537 (1973).

54. "So long as one party argued for normal overruling of the old doctrine and the other sought to sustain it on the merits, is not the court likely to be as well informed by counsels' arguments as it is when reaching any decision squarely on a substantive issue?" P. Mishkin & C. Morris, On Law in Courts 308 (1965).

tion be exercised by limiting prospective overruling to extraordinary circumstances, mainly on the ground that the courts should play only a modest, secondary role in developing new law,[55] whereas, freed from the disciplines of applying the new rule retroactively to the immediate parties, "overeagerness to apply the concept of 'prospective overruling' can result in unnecessarily sweeping holdings. . . ."[56] Thus, judges could "change the law drastically with greater freedom than if they could only act with retroactive effect."[57]

Mishkin and Morris have met this objection by asking whether "these dangers [are] sufficient to warrant denial of judicial power to change unsound law in areas where retroactive operation would be precluded."[58] They question whether judges are so power hungry or even capable of such action in the face of continuing legislative power.

But whether generally valid or not, the objection carries no weight where the judicial lawmaking asked for involves only the correction of an error in the cognitive process. Here, there is no risk of undermining the legislature's function as prime legal innovator. Instead, the court's corrective action protects and supports a legal innovation that the legislature has already made. Such support could hardly constitute usurpation.

As for revising an earlier product of supplementary judicial lawmaking, this, too, would seem to be free of usurpation so long as the considerations outlined in this chapter have been appropriately weighed. Otherwise there would be only the usual considerations of *stare decisis*.

55. "The philosophy underlying the retrospective effective of the judicial decision can be stated somewhat as follows: It is not the function of courts to create new aims for society or to impose on society new basic directives." L. Fuller in a tentative, unpublished paper, quoted in P. Mishkin & C. Morris, On Law in Courts 305 (1965).

56. P. Mishkin & C. Morris, On Law in Courts 306, n. 11 (1965).

57. Id. at 307. Also, Patterson argues that "the precise scope of the prospective overruling may be difficult to ascertain unless the court takes time to formulate its new doctrine in statutory form." E. Patterson, Jurisprudence: Men and Ideas of the Law §5.04 (1953). But, because announced doctrine is necessary to all judicial precedent, how is its future usefulness impaired if it is not made retroactive? Also, what misfortune results if the court uses the statutory form, as the Supreme Court came close to doing in Miranda v. Arizona 384 U.S. 436, 473-474, 478-479, 86 S. Ct. 1602, 1627-1628, 1630 (1966)?

58. P. Mishkin & C. Morris, On Law in Courts 307 (1965).

14

Legislative Control of How Courts Read and Apply Statutes

Proposals for a specific legislative code of interpretative rules are not likely to meet with success.
— S. Mermin, Law and the Legal System — An Introduction 231 (1973)

A. Introduction

A close look at the specific provisions of typical interpretation acts [1] leaves no doubt that for the most part they are intended to influence or control the way courts read and apply statutes. Is this a proper legislative activity or an unconstitutional trespass on the prerogatives of the judiciary? [2] How effective are such acts? [3] To answer these questions we must distinguish among many kinds of provisions.

Every provision of the typical interpretation act appears to serve one or more of the following purposes:

(1) To codify an existing usage of words, a general principle of communication, or an otherwise tacit assumption.

(2) To change the meaning of existing statutes.

1. On interpretation acts generally, see Crawford, ch. XXXI; Sutherland §27.03.

2. Interpretation acts are probably "unconstitutional," according to J. Thomas, in Statutory Construction When Legislation is Viewed as a Legal Institution, 3 Harv. J. Legis. 191, 211 n. 85 (1966).

3. Interpretation acts are futile so far as they try to control the behavior of readers, according to K. Wurzel, Methods of Juridical Thinking, in Science of Legal Method 286, 306-307 (1921). "The laws governing interpretation are natural laws, not legal norms." Id. at 307.

(3) To provide a rule of law for deciding cases in which the ascertained statutory meaning is unresolvably uncertain.

(4) To terminate a judicial rule of law for applying statutes.

(5) To establish a new or different usage of words or a new or different principle of communication.

(6) To establish specific rules to supplement recurrent general rules.

(7) To enact legislative boilerplate.

(8) To determine the boundaries of effective legislation.

It is often hard to say where one purpose leaves off and another begins. Thus, where a provision that appears generally to record existing usage deviates from that usage, it may to that extent reflect an attempt to create a new usage or prescribe a rule of law for deciding cases. The distinction is critical because whether a particular matter is cognitive or creative determines the stage at which it may appropriately be taken into account.

Are these eight purposes legitimate? Are they attainable?

The following analysis deals with provisions drawn for the most part from the Uniform Statutory Construction Act, the most representative of the recent construction acts. This act follows the English pattern originally laid down in 1850 in Lord Brougham's Act (13 and 14 Vict., C. 21) and later crystallized in the Interpretation Act, 1889.

B. Typical Interpretation Act Provisions

1. *Codifying an Existing Usage of Words, a General Principle of Communication, or a Tacit Assumption*

Some provisions of the Uniform Statutory Construction Act are apparently intended to codify existing usages of words. Examples:

> Sec. 3 — The singular includes the plural, and the plural includes the singular.
>
> Sec. 4 — Words of one gender include the other genders.
>
> Sec. 5 — Words in the present tense include the future.
>
> Sec. 6 — The word "week" means 7 consecutive days.

Sec. 7 — The word "year" means 12 consecutive months.

Sec. 22 — If a statute refers to a series of numbers or letters, the first and the last numbers or letters are included.

Sec. 26 — [Miscellaneous definitions]

The codification of an existing usage is a lexicographical exercise. Its accuracy depends not on the authority or status of the lexicographer but on whether the codified version accurately mirrors the usage that it purports to record. Lexicographical validity, which is established by finding the significant common denominators of actual usage, is, therefore, a matter not of law but of fact.

As codifications of existing usage, the examples cited state as absolutes what are at best solid tendencies. Certainly, it is not always true that the singular includes the plural, or conversely. Sometimes it does not and whether it does or does not depends on particular context. The same is true of the pronouncements that words of one gender include other genders and that the present tense includes the future.

Unless carefully hedged, a legislative attempt merely to record existing usage risks inaccuracy and the chance that after enactment the usage will change. Consequently, what may have been intended as a mere recital of lexicographical fact may be read as a legislative attempt either to create a new usage or to prescribe a rule of law to be applied even where context suggests a different meaning. (To this extent its applicability, if any, must be deferred until the cognitive process is complete.) As insurance against this possibility, many construction acts carry the reservation "unless the context shows otherwise." Because the Uniform Statutory Construction Act does not expressly carry such a caveat, the question arises whether the authors intended to imply one or to transmute a factual tendency into a rule of law.

Suppose, on the other hand, that the legislature has been accurate in mirroring actual usage. What is the value of enacting the dictionary? Presumably, it will assure or encourage adherence to that usage. But is it useful to require or encourage people to do what, by hypothesis, they are already inclined to do? Moreover, as for future statutes, can a legislature tie the hands of future legislatures or even its own? Merely to codify an existing usage would appear to be a legislative superfluity. Because this kind of provision does nothing that general context does not do better, it would seem preferable to forego the attempt to codify existing usage. [4]

Even where it is wholly accurate, the enactment of specific lexicographical information tends to give it disproportionate weight as against other relevant factual information, of equal validity and weight, that has not been enacted. Because it impliedly plays down what has been omitted, it tends to distort the weighing and balancing of significant relevant factors that constitute the normal materials of context.

Other provisions of the Uniform Statutory Construction Act are apparently intended to codify existing principles of communication or some of the tacit assumptions that constitute the bulk of legislative context. Examples:

Sec. 2 — Words and phrases shall be read in context and construed according to the rules of grammar and common usage. Words and phrases that have acquired a technical or particular meaning, whether by legislative definition or otherwise, shall be construed accordingly.

Sec. 13 — In enacting a statute, it is presumed that

(1) compliance with the constitutions of the state and of the United States is intended;

(2) the entire statute is intended to be effective;

(3) a just and reasonable result is intended;

(4) a result feasible of execution is intended; and

(5) public interest is favored over any private interest.

Sec. 15 — If a statute is ambiguous, the court, in determining the intention of the legislature, may consider among other matters:

(1) the object sought to be attained;

(2) the circumstances under which the statute was enacted;

(3) the legislative history;

(4) the common law or former statutory provisions, including laws upon the same or similar subjects;

(5) the consequences of a particular construction of the statute;

(6) the administrative construction of the statute; and

(7) the preamble.

4. Id. at 307.

Sec. 20 — A statute which is reenacted, revised, or amended is intended to be a continuation of the prior statute and not a new enactment, so far as it is the same as the prior statute.

Sec. 21 — A reference to any portion of a statute applies to all reenactments, revisions, or amendments thereof.

Sec. 23 — If amendments to the same statute are enacted at the same or different sessions of the legislature, one amendment without reference to another, the amendments are to be harmonized, if possible, so that effect may be given to each. If the amendments are irreconcilable, the latest in date of enactment prevails.

The same analysis applies here. Principles of communication and specific tacit assumptions are matters of fact, not law, and it seems as pointless to enact them as it would be to enact the speed of light. Although section 2 is framed as a command to follow good usage and not merely as a codification of that usage, it is doubtful that the addition of the command improves its utility.

Ironically, troublesome questions of interpretation arise even for provisions intended to facilitate interpretation. Again, in the absence of the reservation, "unless the context shows otherwise," the provisions cited deviate from accepted principles of communication sufficiently to raise a question whether the authors were attempting, on the one hand, only to codify existing usage or, on the other, either to create new principles of communication or to prescribe rules of law the application of which in some instances would produce results at variance with actual meaning.

What was intended in section 2 by the phrase "whether by legislative definition or otherwise"? Was it merely to declare that the source of a usage, once the usage is established, is a matter of indifference? (The word "acquired" suggests this result.) If so, what purpose does the declaration serve? Or did the authors intend to say that where actual usage differs from a legislative definition, the latter is to be followed? This creates no problem if the special usage is limited to the act in which it is announced. But if it is intended to apply also to future acts, the provision can only represent an attempt to broaden a less-than-universal old usage, create a new usage, or establish a rule of law.

Inclusion of the examples cited in this paragraph assumes either that they are accurate codifications of existing principle or that they are mere presumptions rebuttable by particular context.

Otherwise, they go beyond principles of meaning and become rules of law that in an uncongenial context call for departures from established meaning. If this is what they are intended to mean, which seems improbable, they should be classified, as appropriate, under succeeding paragraphs.

Sections 13, 15, and 20, dealing with the materials of context, recite or reflect some of the normally tacit assumptions that tend to underlie the enactment of statutes. Such assumptions are matters of fact, not law. The respective weights to be given these and other relevant assumptions depend on the circumstances of the particular case. Being presumptions and presumably rebuttable, they serve as innocuous reminders of some of the elements that the reader should keep tentatively in mind. Because the list is incomplete, and because it is impossible to say in advance what respective weights are to be given them in a particular case, such provisions are of only modest help. Certainly, they have no controlling force.

Although superficially appealing, section 15 is a mishmash of confusion. Besides failing to deal with uncertainties of meaning other than ambiguity, it fails to make clear whether it is designed to deal with apparent ambiguities, which can be resolved by examining the various evidences of meaning (the cognitive function), or whether it is designed to provide rules of law to deal with ambiguities that cannot be so resolved (the creative function). Although on the whole the section seems better suited to the former function, the materials in clauses (3) and (6), which are not part of legislative context, seem more appropriate as helps to judicial lawmaking in those instances where a thorough, bona fide search of legislative context fails to yield a preponderate probability of meaning. (The distinction is important because it determines the stage at which the information or rule may be introduced.) Clauses such as these are more appropriately treated as examples under paragraph (3) below.

Clause (3), which opens wider the Pandora's box of legislative history, does so indiscriminately. Surely, no one should encourage resort to legislative debates whatever the purpose.

2. Changing the Meaning of Existing Statutes

Although a legislature may amend existing statutes, even on a mass basis, it is dangerous unless the legislature identifies the statutes that it may be affecting. Because in many states the computerized searching of statutes is not yet fully operational, the legislature that seeks, for example, to standardize all existing uses of the word "year" may have to operate largely in the dark. Although there is a strong risk of unintended changes and serious difficulty in later compilation, there appears to be no constitutional objection to the mass amendment of existing statutes.

Although section 1 of the Uniform Statutory Construction Act ("This Act applies to [all] statutes [hereafter enacted]. . . .") [5] offers the enacting state an option, it seems probable that most adopting states will choose to apply it only to later statutes. Where this is the case, no amendment of existing statutes is involved in adopting the Act. Although multiple amendments are occasionally attempted, as several states recently did in lowering the age of majority, there seems to be no legitimate occasion for doing this in an interpretation act. [6]

3. *Establishing a Rule of Law for Deciding Cases Where Statutory Meaning Is Unresolvably Uncertain*

Some provisions of the Uniform Statutory Construction Act are apparently intended to prescribe rules of law for supplying meaning where statutory meaning, as ascertained by the court, is unclear or incomplete. This is the case where there is an uncertainty or omission that cannot be resolved by referring to the existing evidences of meaning.

For uncertainties of meaning that remain evenly balanced even after consideration of the relevant evidences of meaning, such a statute would appear to be beyond reproach, because a legislature may instruct the courts on how to make substantive law in supplementation of statutes, even including those enacted in the future. This involves no deviation from accepted principles of communication and thus does not subvert later legislative effort. Certainly, the legislature may prescribe legal rules for disposing of cases where meaning fails to give a reliable answer. Examples:

5. In Uniform Acts as proposed for adoption by the several states, bracketed materials are intended to be optional with the particular state.

6. E.g., a number of sections of England's Interpretation Act, 1889, cover statutes "whether passed *before* or after the commencement of this Act." (Emphasis added.)

> Sec. 12 — If there is a conflict between figures and words in expressing a number, the words govern.
>
> Sec. 24 — The repeal of a repealing statute does not revive the statute originally repealed or impair the effect of any saving clause therein.

The only problem here is whether section 12 is intended to apply even where context shows a different result. If so, this section should be considered under paragraph (5).

The traditional lead-in phrase for materials designed to plug such legislative gaps is, "Unless the context indicates otherwise. . . ." Although it defers to the overriding constitutional power of future legislatures, this deference is at least formally inadequate, because it seems to impose a burden of proof on those sensitive to statutory context. (Probable general meanings are covered in section 1.) Instead, it would be more becoming to say, "In cases of doubt that cannot be reliably resolved by reference to the statute and its context, the following rules of law shall be applied, as relevant, in giving effect to the statute." Merely to say, "In cases of doubt," is not enough, because to confuse initial, potentially resolvable, doubt with persistent doubt is to risk corrupting the cognitive process through prematurely applying rules of law. Also, the suggested language makes clear that the doubt must be evenly enough balanced to leave, at most, only a weak, and thus unreliable, preponderance of probable meaning.

4. *Terminating a Judicial Rule of Law for Applying Statutes*

Some state interpretation acts have provisions, not found in the Uniform Statutory Construction Act, that are intended to prevent the courts of the jurisdiction concerned from using rules that the legislature considers undesirable. Examples:

> The rule of the common law, that statutes in derogation thereof are to be strictly construed, has no application to this code. Its provisions and all proceedings under it shall be liberally construed with a view to promote its objects and assist the parties in obtaining justice.[7]
>
> The rule of the common law that penal statutes are to be strictly construed, has no application to this title. All its provisions and all penal

7. Code of Iowa, 1939, §64. And see Crawford 766 n. 59.

> statutes are to be construed according to the fair import of their terms, with a view to effect their objects and promote justice. [8]

Assuming that the term "strictly construed" means finding a meaning at variance with how the typical member of the legislative audience would read the statute when viewing it in its proper context, such provisions can be rationalized as requests to the courts to stop subverting normal meanings under the guise of "interpretation." Rather than a legislative intrusion on the province of the courts, it is merely an attempt, in the form of a rule of law, to keep the courts from paying insufficient deference to its pronouncements in the field of policymaking, and thus from usurping the functions of the legislature.

Unfortunately, the courts to which such statutes are addressed do not always honor them.

Section 3 of Ghana's Interpretation Act, 1960, validating punctuation as a source of statutory meaning, seems to be aimed at the once prevalent practice of ignoring it. [9]

5. *Establishing a New or Different Usage of Words or a New or Different Rule of Communication*

So far as the statutory examples discussed in paragraph (1) go beyond existing usage or principles of communication (if so limited they are of little use), they can be effective only if they in fact generate the usage that they announce, or they operate as rules of law.

As for the former, a legislature could conceivably create a new usage by inducing the legislative audience to accept it, but it cannot do so by mere legal fiat. As John Locke once reminded us, even the emperor Augustus could not, by a command, create new meanings of words. [10] Whether the legislature ultimately succeeds in such an attempt depends on whether after enactment the legislative audience ultimately adopts the prescribed usage. If for any reason it does not, the legislature has failed in its attempt. In neither event does a usage change merely because of an official

8. S.D. Code, 1939, §13.0101.

9. For Canada's attempt to dislodge the legislative adoption rule, see ch. 10, n. 107. For materials on interpretation acts in the several Commonwealth countries, I am indebted to K. T. Fuad, Director, Legal Division, Commonwealth Secretariat.

10. 2 An Essay Concerning Human Understanding 14 (bk. III, ch. II) (rev. ed. 1964). See also J. Dewey, Logic: The Theory of Inquiry 47 (1938).

pronouncement. For these reasons, the authors of interpretation acts are well advised to remember that attempts to control the way in which words and phrases are actually used by the legislative audience, or even by future legislatures, are likely to be unsuccessful.

Some provisions of the Uniform Statutory Construction Act are apparently intended to change, not merely the meanings of particular terms, but established principles of communication. Example:

> Sec. 14 — A statute is presumed to be prospective in its operation unless expressly made retrospective.

One basic, well established principle of communication is that meaning is carried not only by express words but also by the factual implications that arise from particular context.[11] Any enforced presumption against the normal play of implication would tend to subvert this principle. So far as it calls on the reader to brush aside a factual implication of retroactivity, section 14 must be explained, not as an attempt to codify a principle of communication, but as an attempt either to change it or to prescribe a rule of law that disregards the actual legislative meaning supplied by discernible implication.

Here, too, changes in the elements of communication can occur only if the elements that constitute them change. Again, this cannot be done by mere legal fiat. Because the express "unless" clause makes it hard to infer the general caveat "Unless the context shows otherwise" (if the latter is implied, section 14 becomes useless), section 14 can be explained only as a command to disregard, in some instances, actual legislative meaning.

Similar attempts to blunt the force of implication are found in section 1-105 of the Uniform Probate Code and section 1-104 of the Uniform Residential Landlord and Tenant Act, each of which provides that "no part of [this Act] is to be construed as impliedly repealed by subsequent legislation if that construction can reasonably be avoided."

If a legislative prescription goes beyond merely codifying existing usage without in fact inducing the legislative audience to adopt the prescribed usage, may it nevertheless be effective as a rule of law?

11. "The implications . . . arising from the language of a statute are as much a part of it as if they had been expressed." Crawford 266 (see also 267).

So long as the court is applying the statute in which the particular definition or statement of usage appears, no problem arises. The reader has simply been put on immediate notice of how the draftsman of that statute is using his terms. Nor does a problem arise with respect to earlier statutes if the statutory definition is directed also to them; the legislature has an unquestioned power of amendment.

The only question arises as to statutes not yet enacted. May a legislature require that resolvable uncertainties of meaning be dealt with in a prescribed way or that future statutes be read differently from what established usages would otherwise dictate? Two questions arise.

Would such an enactment usurp the judicial function? Probably not, unless the legislature tried to interpret specific enactments to resolve specific justiciable issues.

More important is the question whether a legislature can prevent either itself or future legislatures from relying on accepted usages and the normal principles of communication? If there is usurpation here, it is usurpation of a different kind. The question arises only with respect to legislative attempts to deflect the normal force of language. It does not relate to legislative attempts to prescribe how otherwise unresolvable doubts or gaps in meaning are to be resolved or filled.

Because a legislature's general power to enact laws is a power that originates and is defined outside the universe of laws that the legislature itself enacts, it cannot enact substantive law, or adopt a procedural limitation, that is invulnerable to its own later amendment or inconsistent legislative action. If it later legislates inconsistently with its earlier action, it nevertheless legislates effectively, so long as it meets the minimum requirements assumed to apply to legislation generally. The legislature may always impliedly amend or repeal what it has previously undertaken to legislate. [12]

On the other hand, whether the legislature has or has not

12. N. Bindra, The Interpretation of Statutes and General Clauses Acts 10 (4th ed. 1965). ". . . [A]n Interpretation Act is not the master but the servant of the legislature." Note on Interpretation Act, 1960, i. Ghana. See, generally, R. Dias, Jurisprudence 108-125 (3d ed. 1970). For a consideration of the comparable problem relating to constitutions, see Gatewood v. Matthews, 403 S.W.2d 716 (Ky. App. 1966). There the critical question was whether "the people" had in fact adopted the new, inconsistent constitutional principles.

bound itself in fact depends on whether the courts, as the official enforcement authority, reject or accept this approach. Here, it seems justifiable to presume that, if the approach is sound, the courts will, more often than not, accept it. Certainly, the courts' constitutional duty of deference to the legislature's will seems more adequately discharged by deferring to the most recent legislative expression rather than to an inconsistent earlier one. If this assumption is true, a legislature could not effectively provide, even by express enactment, that a law enacted by it was immune from later amendment or repeal.[13]

What about the enactment of an interpretation act? Can a legislature effectively authorize a court to read legislative pronouncements differently from what the accepted principles of communication make most plausible? To take an extreme example, suppose a legislature enacted as a rule of "interpretation" the direction that in the administration of tax statutes all significant uncertainties of statutory meaning were to be resolved in favor of the state, even where the balance of probable meanings strongly favored the taxpayer. Would the courts be obliged to accept such a direction as effective legislation and administer tax statutes accordingly?

There could be little quarrel with applying such an enactment to a statute, even one in which the unconfirmed probabilities of meaning leaned strongly in favor of the taxpayer, if the statute was already in effect. Even in the face of such an inconsistency of meaning, the legislature would only be exercising, by delegation, its power of amendment. The significant doubt would lie, instead, with respect to a statute that had been enacted after the interpretation act.

An important assumption, already discussed in chapter 2, is that, unless it specifies otherwise, a constitution that establishes a system for enacting legislation impliedly adopts the principles of communication accepted on the date of enactment in the speech communities to which the legislation is directed. If this assumption is sound (no other would be tolerable), a legislature is constitutionally powerless to legislate other than by using the established principles of communication. This being so, the legislature must be taken as intending what it has said, as measured by normal standards, unless it has made clear, by the constitu-

13. Id.

tionally recognized means of communication, that it is speaking in a different tongue and has made clear what that tongue is. Similarly, it could hardly authorize the courts to subvert future expressions of its own legislative will by reading them according to standards other than those that, under the circumstances, it seems most probable that the legislature has in fact used. The legislature that tries to adopt special methods of communication cannot assure the legislative audience that later legislatures will conform to the new standards.[14]

No problem arises even here, if the later act shows that it was enacted in the light of the interpretation act and thus implies an exception or modification in favor of it. In the case of the supposed tax statute, however, such an assumption would be implausible, because the skilled legislative draftsman, knowing that certainty of meaning is impossible, normally relies on a favorable preponderance of probable, rather than improbable, meaning. If so, the application of the supposed interpretation provision to any situation in which the probabilities of meaning leaned in favor of the taxpaper would tend to undercut the current legislative will. Here, certainly, the court should decline to apply the statute, not in defiance of the legislature, but to safeguard its most recent pronouncement.

Although the example may not be typical, it is not fanciful. A comparable provision appears as section 14 of the Uniform Statutory Construction Act, already mentioned: "A statute is presumed to be prospective in its operation unless expressly made retrospective." (Here the caveat "unless the context shows otherwise" cannot be implied.) Could a court justify applying such a provision to a later enacted statute in which the purpose to have it apply retrospectively appeared, not expressly, but by clear implication? Normal implications are as much a part of the established communication process as express statements.[15] Certainly, a legislature cannot divest either itself or later legislatures of the power to use, or revert to, accepted methods of communication.

Again, under section 12, providing, "If there is a conflict between figures and words in expressing a number, the words govern," could any plausible argument be advanced for applying the section to the phrase "one (1), two (2), two (3), four (4),

14. See pp. 270-271.
15. See n. 11 *supra*.

five (5)"? Here, the context clearly implies that the figure "(3)" controls.

In some kinds of cases, on the other hand, it may be reasonable to assume that the later statute has, in fact, been enacted in the light of the earlier. For example, if the earlier statute provides that if the date of a military retirement would otherwise fall within a calendar month it takes effect on the first day of the next succeeding calendar month, there is reason to suppose that a later military retirement act that is silent on the point has been enacted in the light of the earlier one, [16] because the administrative problem to which the earlier, general law was addressed inheres as fully in the new retirement statute as it did in earlier ones and it has not otherwise been dealt with.

What about provisions, discussed above, of a conventional construction act that do more than merely recite established usage? Is it reasonable to assume that the draftsman of a later statute takes account of legislatively standardized definitions of terms such as "person" and "oath?" This would have some plausibility in England, where almost all statutes pass through the hands of the highly knowledgeable draftsmen of the Office of the Parliamentary Counsel. It is much less plausible in the United States, where centralized, sophisticated drafting is the exception rather than the rule.

Whatever the factual probabilities in specific situations, the general principle seems clear: Because the earlier legislative act cannot control the preparation of later acts as a matter of law and thus cannot prevent the draftsmen and sponsors of these acts from relying on accepted usage, it cannot by indirection accomplish the same result by controlling how such acts are to be read. At most, it can help to establish a factual presumption, rebuttable by other evidence, that the special means of expression adopted was in fact used or taken into account in a later act.

The controlling principle, therefore, is not one of legal fiat, as the construction acts strongly imply, but of factual probability: What is the most plausible meaning of the later act? From the generally available evidence, is it likely that the later act impliedly accommodated itself to the terms of the earlier? Because an interpretation act and the circumstances that surround it can do no more than establish a factual probability or rebuttable presumption, a court should feel free to disregard any amenda-

16. See ch. 11, n. 5.

tory provision of such an act that it believes was not in fact taken into account in the preparation and enactment of the later act. An interpretation act, therefore, has a practical impact on future legislation only so far as the authors of later acts are induced in fact to expressly or impliedly adopt it. In the United States at least, such efforts have been only sporadically successful. A more realistic approach is discussed in section (7).

These conclusions do not apply to provisions that merely resolve the interpretative dilemmas involved in evenly balanced uncertainties of meaning (section (3)) or to the supplementary rules of law covered in the next section.

6. *Enacting Specific Rules To Supplement Recurrent General Rules*

Some interpretation acts, not including the Uniform Statutory Construction Act, include rules of law that specify how recurrent general statutory provisions shall or may be implemented. For example, section 13(1) of Ghana's Interpretation Act, 1960, prescribes the ways in which service may be made under each statute that "authorizes or requires a document to be served on any person without directing it to be served in any particular manner." [17]

This kind of lawmaking bears a close similarity to that discussed in paragraph (3) above, except that it does not supply a meaning where an uncertainty of meaning cannot otherwise be resolved; it simply prescribes a supplementary rule of law. It also differs from the lawmaking discussed in paragraph (7), below, in that it engrafts nothing on other (including later) legislation, but operates independently of it.

A provision classifiable under this section is appropriate only where (1) the legislature can confidently assume that the rule stated will be appropriate in all instances where the implementing specifics have been, or will be, left open by the legislature, and (2) the provision does not instruct the courts to disregard legislative meanings that are left to implication.

17. Another example would appear to be §37 of England's Interpretation Act, 1889, providing that, where a statute's effective date is later than the date of enactment, its powers to appoint, issue rules, prescribe forms, or do any other thing for the purposes of the statute may be exercised during the interim for the purposes of putting the statute into operation on its effective date.

7. Enacting Legislative Boilerplate

The title of England's Interpretation Act, 1889, which crystallized the pattern for later interpretation acts, recited that it was designed "for further shortening the Language used in Acts in Parliament." Thus, one of its purposes was to create what has sometimes been called "prefabricated and standardized law" [18] or, more often, "boilerplate." This appears to be true also of the Uniform Statutory Construction Act.

The proper objective of legislative boilerplate is to provide standardized solutions, such as a severability clause, that are usually, though not universally, appropriate to highly recurrent statutory problems. Examples:

> Sec. 8 — (a) In computing a period of days, the first day is excluded and the last day is included.
>
> (b) If the last day of any period is a [Saturday,] Sunday or legal holiday, the period is extended to include the next day which is not a [Saturday,] Sunday or legal holiday.
>
> (c) If a number of months is to be computed by counting the months from a particular day, the period ends on the same numerical day in the concluding month as the day of the month from which the computing is begun, unless there are not that many days in the concluding month, in which case the period ends on the last day of that month.
>
> Sec. 10 — A grant of authority to 3 or more persons as a public body confers the authority upon a majority of the number of members fixed by statute.
>
> Sec. 11 — A quorum of a public body is a majority of the number of members fixed by statute.
>
> Sec. 26 — [Definitions]

However desirable the objectives of legislative standardization and prefabrication may be, the traditional approach of trying to impose legal boilerplate on future draftsmen has been notably unsuccessful. As pointed out in preceding sections, a legislature can neither legislate lexicography nor tie the hands of a future legislature that chooses to disregard the earlier legislative pronouncement. For this reason, legislative boilerplate has

18. R. Dickerson, FPR No. 1: An Experiment in Standardized and Prefabricated Law, 13 U. Chi. L. Rev. 90 (1945).

been useful only so far as the normal reader can assume that the later legislature in fact adopted the work of the earlier one or so far as a later court finds it useful to adopt it as a means of judicially supplementing legislative meaning that is unresolvably equivocal or incomplete. Thus, the most that a draftsman can do under this approach is to try to generate a probability that future draftsmen will in fact take his efforts into account.

Fortunately, a more realistic approach has been developed that obviates these difficulties. Instead of trying to control future legislative action in statutes of unpredictable content, this approach undertakes only to make useful legislative boilerplate available to later legislatures by enacting it for future incorporation by reference on a specific and selective basis. Such provisions have no force of their own; the generating force in each case is the later statute. This approach appears to have been fully developed for the first time during World War II. [19] It has since proved its usefulness.

For present purposes it is unnecessary to analyze the approach in detail. It is enough to say that the enactment of legal boilerplate on such a basis is a legitimate function of an "interpretation" act, except that in no sense does it deal with either the interpretation of another statute or how it is to be applied. Thus, the approach is intended to influence and facilitate the drafting of future legislation, not how it is to be read or applied. The term "interpretation act" seems wholly inapt for provisions directed to this goal.

To distinguish legislative boilerplate from the kinds of legal rules described in sections (3) (arbitrarily assigned meaning) and (6) (specific supplementing legislation), boilerplate provisions should be placed in a separate statute or title, prefaced in substance as follows: "The following provisions supplement a statute only to the extent that it adopts them by incorporation." In jurisdictions, such as the United States, where legislative authorship is highly heterogeneous, the incorporation by reference should always be express. In jurisdictions, such as England, where legislative authorship is confined almost wholly to the Office of the Parliamentary Counsel, the incorporation may be left to implication. But even in such a jurisdiction, the possibility of occasional inaptness of application makes it desirable to incorporate the apt material expressly.

19. Id.

8. Determining the Boundaries of Effective Legislation

Several provisions of the Uniform Statutory Construction Act prescribe which of several competing legislative instruments is to be taken as the statute to be interpreted and applied. Examples:

> Sec. 18 — If statutes enacted at the same or different sessions of the legislature are irreconcilable, the statute latest in date of enactment prevails.
>
> Sec. 19 — If the language of the official copy of a statute conflicts with the language of any subsequent printing or reprinting of the statute, the language of the official copy prevails.

Where there is a possible impasse between two competing legislative instruments, it may be useful to specify how the impasse is to be resolved. Such a provision does not undertake to say what either instrument means or how any uncertainty of meaning is to be resolved. Beginning with the assumption that conflicting meanings exist, it merely prescribes what the legislative audience, including the court, is to look at as the authoritative legislative utterance. This, too, may be a legitimate subject of legislation. Again, it is questionable whether the term "interpretation" adequately accommodates such a provision.

Even here practical usefulness may be in doubt. So far, for example, as section 18 is applied to irreconcilable statutes enacted by succeeding legislatures, the question arises whether the alternative of preferring the earlier, rather than the later, statute would have been constitutionally acceptable. If not, section 18 only declares the inevitable.

Some interpretation acts undertake to prescribe what is part of a statute and what is not. For example, Ghana's Interpretation Act, 1970, provides that an act's long title, preamble, punctuation, and schedules (sections 2, 3, and 6) are part of it, but that its internal headings (section 4) are not. This last provision is hard to justify, despite the looseness of most headings, because headings are physically part of the enactment (they are often specifically amended) and they have a modest one-way significance in conveying meaning through what they include, if not through what they leave out.

Section 16 of Zambia's Interpretation and General Provisions Act provides that an act includes its amendments. Here, the question arises whether this states anything that is not necessarily implied.

The boundaries of a statute may be defined temporally as well as spatially. Thus, section 8(2) of Botswana's proposed Interpretation and General Provisions Bill, 1973, prescribes when a statute "shall come into operation."

C. Summary

Statutes of the kind traditionally called "interpretation acts" are ineffectual so far as they try to codify or change the actual meanings of words and phrases, or to codify or change the general principles of communication. They are also unsatisfactory in not clearly delineating the different functions they perform, especially with reference to whether specific provisions are to be used during the cognitive process or later as rules of law.

In general, it is fruitless in a statute to try to recite or manipulate matters essentially of fact. At best, such provisions perform a modest service in reminding the reader of some of the established usages, rebuttable presumptions, and normally tacit assumptions that constitute the bulk of legislative context. Unfortunately, because their inevitable incompleteness tends to mislead, this information should be left to the appropriate reference books.

On the other hand, a legislature may appropriately instruct the courts on how to resolve impasses or other evenly balanced uncertainties of meaning by prescribing rules of law for disposing of cases that cannot be decided by weighing the available evidences of legislative meaning. By hypothesis, such rules direct the courts to assign supplementary meaning where legislative meaning is wanting; they do not try to change or deflect it.

Second, a legislature may direct the courts within its jurisdiction to refrain from using judicial rules whose application to statutes tends to subvert their meaning.

Third, a legislature may appropriately enact specific rules to supplement recurrent general ones.

Fourth, a legislature may appropriately enact statutory boilerplate provisions dealing with highly recurrent problems in the expectation that those provisions will be helpful to the draftsmen of future statutes in partly standardizing, and to the same extent shortening, those statutes. However, such provisions are effective only so far as they are adopted by later statutes, in which case it is helpful to make the fact and extent of adoption express in those statutes.

Finally, a legislature may (1) prescribe, consistently with the applicable constitution, which of several competing legislative instruments constitutes the legislative message to be read and administered or (2) define the parameters of statutes generally.

Except for the lists of usages, factual presumptions, and otherwise tacit assumptions, none of these widely differing approaches helps to solve the problems of "interpretation" in any authentic sense. The first of the remaining approaches enacts rules of law to deal with cases in which the cognitive process has broken down. The second instructs the courts to stop usurping the legislative function. The third provides specific rules to supplement what is otherwise overly general. The fourth enacts rules of law that will become effective only if later legislatures adopt them as parts of future legislation. The last merely tells the legislative audience what it is supposed to look at.

Whether these kinds of provisions can be usefully combined in the same statute and effectively titled remains a question that needs no answer here. In any event, they should be segregated by kind and prefaced so as to make clear what purposes they are respectively intended to serve, thus forestalling the possibility that they will be prematurely introduced so as to disrupt the cognitive process.

By far the most effective control that a legislature can exercise over the ways in which courts and other members of the legislative audience read and apply statutes is by drafting each statute according to professional standards of draftsmanship, being careful to use the tools of communication most familiar to that audience, and to rely only on those tacit assumptions that it, too, is most likely to make.

Appendix A
Meanings of Terms

The following terms, which are commonly misused, misunderstood, or uncertain in meaning, have been used in this book in the following respective senses, with the hope that adherence to them will help to reduce existing confusion. In each case, the sense chosen is believed to be the closest working approximation to the way in which the term is actually used.

ACTUAL MEANING — The meaning carried by language when it is read in a particular context.

AMBIGUITY — Equivocation (alternative, and not simultaneous, possibilities of meaning). It is thus to be distinguished from vagueness and generality, with which it is commonly confused. Semantic ambiguity is uncertainty of multiple meaning that tends to follow particular words and phrases (e.g., "residence," "child") into the contexts of actual use. Syntactical ambiguity is uncertainty of modification or reference (e.g., a squinting modifier). Contextual ambiguity is uncertainty as to how a statement affects or is affected by another statement with which it is inconsistent (e.g., two inconsistent contemporaneous statutes). It also includes uncertainty as to whether a particular relevant tacit assumption has been made.

APPLICATION — Use of a statute to help resolve a specific controversy.

COGNITIVE FUNCTION — The ascertainment of meaning.

CONSTRUCTION — Interpretation. Although in current usage the terms "construction" and "interpretation" are synonymous when used with respect to statutes, some writers have defined "construction" to include additional steps necessary to determine whether a statute that is otherwise clear in its express meaning should be applied to situations not clearly falling within it. The distinction thus made between "interpretation" and "construction" tends, in some applications at least, to approximate that made in this book between the ascertainment of legislative meaning (the cognitive function) and the judicial lawmaking involved in administering an incomplete or imperfect statute (the creative function). However, where the latter distinction is considered useful, it has been made in those terms and not in terms of a verbal distinction that current usage apparently rejects.

CONTEXT — That part of the environment of a statute that is known and taken account of in the writing or reading of it. The context in which a statute is written is not necessarily the context in which it is read.

CONTEXTUAL AMBIGUITY — See AMBIGUITY.

CREATIVE FUNCTION — The assignment of meaning, or judicial lawmaking by analogy with the statute.

DESCRIPTIVE TEXTS — Materials of legislative history relating to the processes of enactment. The term is unnecessary to the approach advanced in this book.

EQUITABLE INTERPRETATION — A term of no fixed meaning, used variously to refer to (1) reading a statute extensively or restrictively to give effect to its purpose as revealed by the statute and its context, or (2) extending or restricting a statute, by judicial lawmaking, to give effect to a collaterally disclosed legislative purpose that is broader or narrower than that shown by the statute when read in its proper context. In its extensive aspect, it is sometimes identified with liberal interpretation. Neither of these meanings has been selected, because the term is unnecessary to the approach advanced in this book.

EQUITY RULE — See EQUITABLE INTERPRETATION.

EXPOUNDING TEXTS — Documents (usually of legislative history) that interpret pending legislation; one form of interpretative materials.

EXPRESS MEANING — Literal (dictionary) meaning, so far as permitted by particular context.

EXTRINSIC MATERIALS — Evidence of legislative intent, purpose, or meaning that is outside the text of the statute, whether or not it is also outside the context of the statute.

GENERALITY — The capacity of a word or term denoting a class (e.g., "American citizen") to refer simultaneously to all members of the class. The term should be distinguished from "ambiguity" and "vagueness," with which it is commonly confused.

"GOLDEN RULE" — See PLAIN MEANING RULE.

IMMEDIATE PURPOSE — See LEGISLATIVE INTENT.

IMPLIED MEANING — The meaning that particular context adds to express meaning.

INTENT — See LEGISLATIVE INTENT.

INTERPRETATION — Ascertainment of the meaning of a statute (1) in accordance with established principles of communication, (2) in accordance with the meanings of language established in the speech community to which the legislative audience belongs, and (3) in the light of the tacit assumptions ordinarily made in that speech community (the cognitive function). It is also often used to include the judicial supplementation or repair of a statute necessary to apply it to a concrete controversy (the creative function). It has not been so used here.

INTERPRETATIVE MATERIALS — Documents and recorded debates or hearings (usually of legislative history) that interpret pending or recent legislation.

LEGAL MEANING — The meaning of a statute as determined by the courts.

LEGISLATIVE HISTORY — The officially documented process, from first proposal to last step of enactment, by which a bill becomes a law. In a broader, less usual sense (not used here), it also includes predecessor events and legislation.

LEGISLATIVE INTENT — What the moving parties behind a statute subjectively intended to say by the language they used. The term should be distinguished from "legislative purpose," with which it is commonly confused and which should be used to refer only to the ulterior purposes of the statute. It is coextensive, therefore, with immediate legislative purpose, the purpose that the statute is designed to immediately accomplish. The term is also used by some to refer to the intent that is objectively manifested; that is, apparent legislative intent. It has not been so used here.

LEGISLATIVE PURPOSE — One or more ulterior purposes (broader or more remote motives) that the moving parties behind a statute intended ultimately to accomplish wholly or partly, with the help of the statute. The term should not ordinarily be used to include the immediate legislative purpose of the statute, which is coextensive with "legislative intent."

LIBERAL INTERPRETATION — A term of no fixed meaning, used variously to refer to an interpretation or application of a statute that (1) extends its coverage beyond its most plausible meaning to further what the court considers to be the ulterior purpose of the statute or relies on it to support an analogous exercise of judicial lawmaking, (2) resolves an evenly poised uncertainty in favor of the government, or (3) simply refuses to ascribe, by "strict interpretation," a meaning less friendly to the government than what appears, under the relevant circumstances, to be the most plausible meaning.

LITERAL MEANING — Dictionary meaning.

MEANING — Normally (when used alone), the "true meaning"; that is, the meaning carried by language when it is read in its proper context by a typical member of the audience to which it is addressed. This coincides with legislative intent as objectively manifested. Although the term is used also in the sense of what the author intended to say or in the sense of what the particular reader (even if atypical) found in the statute, neither sense is normally used in legislative interpretation.

MOTIVATING TEXTS — Documents (usually of legislative history) that reveal, directly or indirectly, legislative purpose.

NEGATIVE IMPLICATION — The implication of fact that matters not included in a rule or proposition are governed by a different rule or proposition; also called "reverse implication," "co-implication," or "preemption." The canon *expressio unius est exclusio alterius* asserts that the implication always arises or is always presumed to arise.

OBJECTIVE INTERPRETATION — Judicial lawmaking in disregard of evidence of legislative intent in legislative history and other extrinsic materials. The dichotomy between it and subjective interpretation is not helpful for the purposes of the approach advanced in this book.

PLAIN MEANING RULE — A term of no fixed meaning, used variously to refer to (1) a rule of literalness, (2) a rule that permits no deviation from the literal meaning of a statute except as required by internal context or the need to avoid absurdity, or, in some jurisdictions, unfairness or unreasonableness, (3) a rule that permits no deviation from the meaning of a statute that is clear when it is read in its proper context. In sense (2), it is often called the "Golden Rule." None of these meanings has been selected, because the term is unnecessary to the approach advanced in this book.

PROPER CONTEXT — That part of the relevant shared environment of a statute that the typical member of the legislative audience to which it is addressed could reasonably assume the authors took into account as completing the communication.

PROPER MEANING — See TRUE MEANING.

PURPOSE — See LEGISLATIVE PURPOSE.

SEMANTIC AMBIGUITY — See AMBIGUITY.

STRICT INTERPRETATION — A term of no fixed meaning, used variously to refer to an interpretation or application of a statute that (1) the court simply refuses to extend, by "liberal interpretation," beyond its most plausible meaning to include a situation not otherwise covered, (2) resolves an evenly poised uncertainty of meaning in favor of the common law or against the government, or (3) is unfriendly in not giving effect to what appears, under the relevant circumstances, to be its most plausible meaning. Sense (3) includes cases resolving reasonable doubt in favor of the common law or against the government, refusing to give effect to implications that would otherwise arise, or refusing to give effect to a statute beyond a collaterally disclosed legislative purpose that is more restrictive than what is shown by the statute when read in its proper context.

SUBJECTIVE INTERPRETATION — Judicial lawmaking based on evidence of legislative intent in legislative history and other extrinsic materials. The dichotomy between it and objective interpretation is not helpful for the purposes of the approach used in this book.

SYNTACTIC AMBIGUITY — See AMBIGUITY.

TRUE MEANING — The meaning carried by language when it is read in its proper context by a typical member of the audience to which it is addressed.

ULTERIOR PURPOSE — See LEGISLATIVE PURPOSE.

VAGUENESS — Marginal uncertainty of application (e.g., does "vehicle" include a baby carriage?). The term should be distinguished from "ambiguity" and "generality," with which it is commonly confused.

Appendix B
A Catalogue of Popular Misconceptions

Underlying much of the current confusion respecting statutory interpretation is a large fund of popular misconceptions. For reasons that appear more clearly in the earlier chapters, the following widely held assumptions, some of which contradict others and all of which have been causing trouble, are nominated for quick oblivion.

- There is no such thing as the actual or true meaning of a statute.
- Words are meaningless in isolation.
- In any particular application, statutory language is always ambiguous or otherwise uncertain.
- Ambiguity, vagueness, and generality are roughly the same thing, and may be indiscriminately lumped together.
- Lawyers and judges have a sophisticated understanding of semantics and the principles of communication.
- The principles of communication were all stated by Stuart Chase, Hayakawa, or Ogden and Richards.
- The question, "What is the meaning of a statute as enacted?" is a question of law.
- Case law relating to the meaning of one statutory provision is materially relevant to the meaning of another statutory provision, even where the two are not *in pari materia.*
- Case law declaring the general meaning of a term or explaining how to find the meaning of a statute as enacted is authoritative.
- The problems of applying statutes in the context of specific controversies are exclusively those of ascertaining legislative meaning.
- The problems of applying statutes in the context of specific controversies are exclusively problems of judicial lawmaking.
- The true law-giver in a state is the political institution that is charged with interpreting the law.

- The court is the supreme guardian of the public good in the interpretation and application of statutes.
- In reading and applying a statute, a court is limited only by its good-faith estimate of what is best for the public good.
- In reading and applying statutes, a court is not significantly inhibited by any concept of separation of powers because the separation is, at best, neither absolute nor certain.
- The social context of a statute is all important.
- The express meaning of a statute is all important.
- The meaning of a statute when read out of context is presumed to be its true meaning.
- The interpretation of a statute and its application are the same thing. Consequently, the interpretation of a statute is a one-stage, monolithic process.
- Problems of ascertaining meaning can be solved by applying a series of specific rules called "canons of interpretation."
- "Interpretation Acts" are generally useful in determining what a statute means.
- All canons of interpretation are fictional or otherwise spurious.
- The canons of interpretation all perform the same general function.
- "Legislative intent" and "legislative purpose" mean the same thing.
- The subjective intent of the legislature is either nonexistent or undiscoverable; consequently, the idea may be ignored.
- An ulterior legislative purpose always exists and is always discoverable.
- A legislature's intent is limited to what it can specifically foresee.
- A statute's meaning is limited to what the legislature intended.
- We cannot ascertain the meaning of a statute as enacted unless we know what its ulterior legislative purpose is.
- If manifest legislative intent conflicts with manifest ulterior purpose, ulterior purpose prevails.
- Legislative intent is useful in resolving uncertainties of meaning.
- The legislature's actual intent, however ascertained, should never be frustrated by the court.
- Legislative intent or purpose is more likely to be revealed by legislative history than by the words of the statute.
- The authors of official explanations of statutes communicate more successfully than the draftsmen of statutes.

- Legislative history is part of the proper context of a statute.
- The unavailability of state materials of legislative history is a serious disadvantage in ascertaining the meaning of a state statute as enacted.
- If the states ever provide materials of legislative history comparable to those provided by the federal government, the canons of interpretation will, as a result, become useless and will die a natural death.
- In ascertaining legislative meaning, a court may take into account all relevant extrinsic materials.
- In ascertaining legislative meaning, a court may look at no extrinsic materials unless the statute is uncertain in meaning or absurd.
- "Extrinsic materials" and "external context" are synonymous terms.

Appendix C*
Referential Meaning: The Static Aspects

To clarify the relationship between a word and the thing to which it is assumed to refer, Ogden and Richards [1] constructed the following diagram (Figure 1):

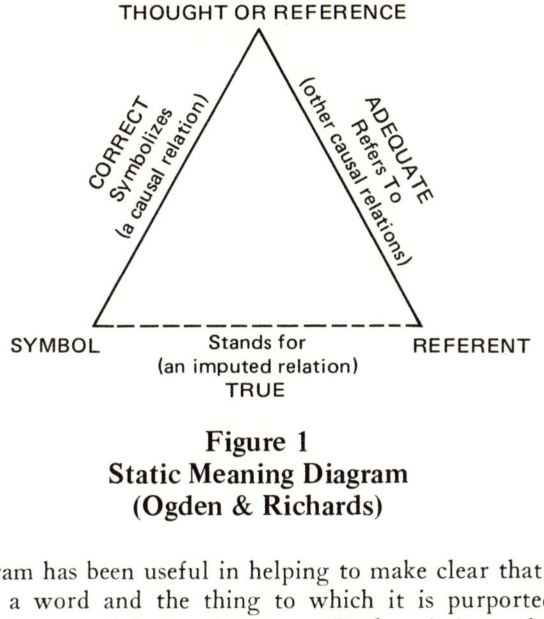

Figure 1
Static Meaning Diagram
(Ogden & Richards)

This diagram has been useful in helping to make clear that the relationship between a word and the thing to which it is purported to refer is neither God-given nor inherent in nature. Rather, it is a relationship that exists only because the members of the speech community concerned have

* This appendix is an edited version of the author's article, Referential Meaning: The Static Aspects, 10 Jurimetrics J. 58 (1969) (used with permission).

1. C. Ogden & I. Richards, The Meaning of Meaning 11 (10th ed. 1956).

habitually used the word to refer, at least indirectly, to that thing. Thus, the word "court" carries the meaning that it does only because it is habitually so used. That convention and ultimately general usage provide the connecting link is expressed by making the base of the triangle, which connects symbol with thing ("referent"), a broken line. The solid connection between the two is thus made only through thought ("reference"), which forms the apex of the triangle. The diagram also suggests that the relationship of symbol to user or hearer is, in at least some respects, a causal one.

Despite its value for these purposes, the diagram appears to have serious inadequacies. First, it suggests that the relationship between symbol and thing ("referent") is as significant as the relationship between symbol and thought of the thing ("reference"). If a symbol is viewed as ultimately designating a thing, meaning would be thwarted whenever nothing corresponding to the particular thought actually existed, unless there was a shift at that point to the assumption that in such a case the symbol designated, instead, the thought of the thing. Would it not make simpler and more consistent sense simply to say that in all cases the symbol refers to the thought, [2] even though it may seem unnatural when the object corresponding to the thought is physically observable? Certainly, the meaning of the sentence, "You will find a consumer protection act in the 1975 Session Laws" is the same whether or not such an act is included in that volume.

Second, the left side of the triangle must, as a consequence, do double duty — once for the non-causal static relationship between symbol and thought just discussed, and again for the causal. Unfortunately, the two cannot be differentiated in such a diagram.

Third, the diagram suggests that the relationship between thought and symbol, represented by the left side of the triangle, is similar to that between thought and referent, represented by the right. Whereas the relationship between thought and symbol is in one of its aspects a causal one whose direction depends on whether the thought is that of the sender or that of the receiver, the relationship between thought and thing is sometimes causal and sometimes not, and, where it is, it is a one-way relationship in which the thing provokes the thought (through the process of perception) whereas the thought does not normally provoke the thing.

Fourth, in using the right side of a symmetrical triangle to represent the relationship between thought and thing, Ogden and Richards seem to treat as coordinate with the relationship(s) between symbol and thought a relationship that falls within the area of epistemology. This relationship lies outside the field of meaning in the referential sense, and beyond the reach of the metalanguage, which is the language used to talk about language.

2. "Symbols are not proxy for their objects, but are *vehicles for the conception of objects. . . . [I]t is the conceptions, not the things, that symbols directly 'mean'.*" S. Langer, Philosophy in a New Key 60-61 (3d ed. 1957). (Emphasis in original.)

Fifth, the diagram takes no account of the relationships among symbols.

To place these elements in more useful perspective within the general theory of meaning, sometimes called "semiotic," Figure 2 is offered as an amplification of and possible improvement on that of Ogden and Richards:

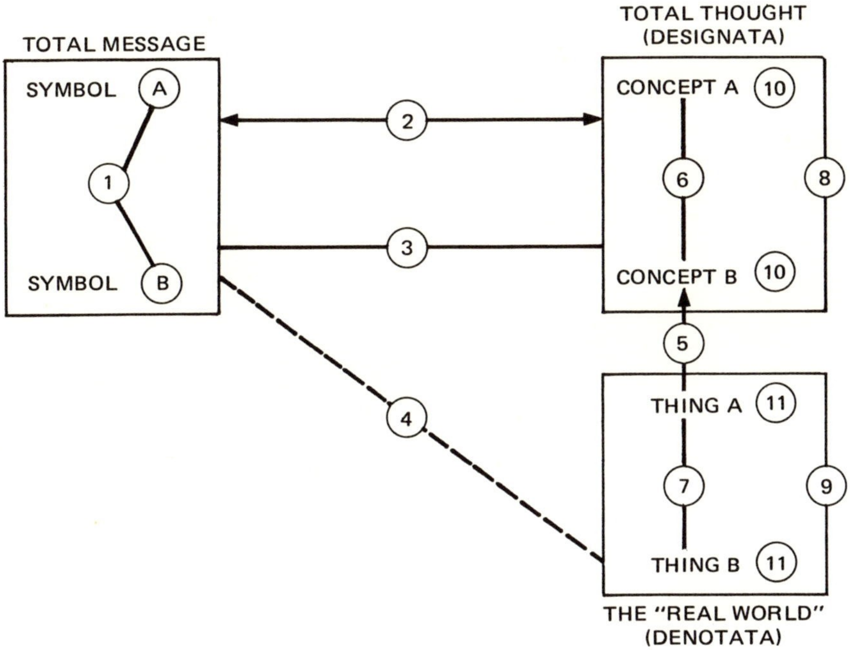

Figure 2
Static Meaning Diagram
(Revised Version)

In the terminology of the revised diagram, "concept" (designatum) replaces "thought or reference" and "thing" (denotatum) replaces "referent."

Aspect 1 is the relationship between symbols. Under the general classification developed by C.S. Pierce and his recent disciple, Charles W. Morris, [3] this is the "syntactical" dimension of semiotic. For example, the statement that "juge" is French for "judge" lies in the domain of syntactics. So does the problem of the squinting modifier and other forms of syntactic ambiguity. It is largely the area in which mathematics and deductive logic operate. It is described in the metalanguage.

Aspect 2 is the subjective, two-way causal relationship between a symbol

3. Introduction to the Theory of Signs, vol. 1, no. 2, International Encyclopedia of Unified Science 13-16 (1938).

and its corresponding concept, the tendency of minds to use or respond to particular symbols in particular ways. The tendency of minds to *use* a symbol in a particular way is based on habit. The tendency of minds to *respond to* a symbol in a particular way is based on a special kind of habit — the conditioned reflex. This is the "pragmatical" dimension of semiotic. It is largely the area in which "general semantics" operates. It is the area in which the abuse of stipulative definition, called "Humpty-Dumptyism,"[4] operates. It is described in the metalanguage.

Aspect 3 is the objective, non-causal relationship, resulting from habitual use in Aspect 2, that exists between a symbol and the concept that it refers to. This is the "semantical" dimension of semiotic, represented by the dictionary ("Bill of Attainder means. . . ."). It is described in the metalanguage. It is here that the diagram differs most significantly from that of Ogden and Richards.

Aspect 4 is the purported relationship between a symbol and the existing physical object or activity (denotation), if any, corresponding to the concept that the symbol refers to in Aspect 3. This is a bastard variant of the semantical dimension (Aspect 3). Because the existence or non-existence of the object or activity concerned is generally irrelevant to problems of meaning, the relationship adds nothing to Aspect 3. Indeed, it has no significance for semiotic and is beyond its reach.

Aspect 5 is the one-way causal relationship between an existing object or activity ("denotation") and its corresponding concept. For example, a building may generate in the viewer the idea of the state capitol; but the converse is not true. The relationship is described in the languages of psychology and philosophy (epistemology). It is beyond the reach of semiotic.

Aspect 6 is the relationship between two concepts. For example, the concept of default is closely linked with that of foreclosure. The mental relationship is described in the language of psychology. It is beyond the reach of semiotic.

Aspect 7 is the relationship between two existing objects or activities (denotata). For example, the House of Representatives and the Senate must pass the identical bill if it is to become law. The relationship is described in the object language. It is beyond the reach of semiotic.

Where concept A and concept B (designata of specific denotata) are members of the same class (which is inherently conceptual), Aspect 8 is the range of characteristics that define the class. These comprise the subjective "connotation" or "intension" of the symbol designating the class. They are ordinarily represented by a connotative definition (" 'child' means a person who has not attained his 18th birthday"). They are described in the metalanguage.

Where thing A and thing B (denotata) are members of the same class,

4. R. Dickerson, The Fundamentals of Legal Drafting 100-104 (1965).

Aspect 9 is the range of characteristics that define the class. They are the objective description of connotation or intension in the subjective sense.

Aspect 10 consists of the particular concepts (designata) that comprise the total thought expressed by the communication. They are described in the language of psychology.

Aspect 11 consists of the particular objects or activities (denotata), if any, that correspond to the particular concepts that comprise Aspect 10. They are described in the object language. They have no significance for semiotic and are beyond its reach.

Whatever its possible merits, this diagram must not be viewed as portraying all the elements that control or affect meaning. It is as much like a full-blown theory of meaning as a photograph of a garaged racing car is like the Indianapolis "500" race. It represents, in static form, basic elements that taken alone would constitute some of the tools of a very primitive language. The language of current use, on the other hand, is not confined to words that name concepts that correspond to objects. Moreover, because the conveyance of meaning depends largely on the dynamics of particular use, we must add the factors of context and its integrating force of purpose. But, despite these omissions, the diagram may help to illumine several elements basic to the total concept of referential meaning in communication.[5]

5. For a linguist's criticism of Ogden & Richards' triangle, see S. Ullman, Language and Style 17-23 (1964).

Appendix D
Modern Treatises on Statutory Interpretation

N. Bindra, The Interpretation of Statutes and General Clauses Acts (4th ed. 1965) (Allahabad)

Craies on Statute Law (7th ed. A. Edgar 1971) (London)

E. Crawford, The Construction of Statutes (1940) (St. Louis)

E. Driedger, The Construction of Statutes (1947) (Toronto)

V. Francisco, Statutory Construction (1968) (Manila)

L'Esteve and Hashimi's Interpretation of Statutes (2d ed. A. Chaudhary, 1964) (Karachi)

B. Lal, The Interpretation of Statutes (1964) (Lucknow)

E. McCaffrey, Statutory Construction (1953) (New York)

R. Martin, Handbook on Statutory Construction (rev. ed. 1972) (Manila)

Maxwell on the Interpretation of Statutes (12th ed. P. Langan ed. 1969) (London)

G. Singh, Principles of Statutory Interpretation (1966) (Allahabad)

Sutherland, Statutes and Statutory Construction (4th ed. D. Sands 1972–73) (Chicago)

Index of Names

This index includes all individuals who are discussed or quoted in the text or footnotes. It does not include authors in instances where their works are only cited.

Allen, C., 59 n.21, 119 n.42
Allen L., 47 n.11
Augustus, Emperor, 270
Austin, J., 29

Berenson, B., 43
Bishin, W., 85 n.56, 138 n.4
Black, M., 37 n.11, 50–51, 52 n.24, 62, 110, 117 n.40
Blackburn, C., 125
Bolinger, D., 107 n.13, 111 n.23
Breitel, C., 20 n.28, 28, 71
Brown, R., 105 n.8
Burke, E., 75

Cellini, B., 26
Cherry, C., 34, 107 n.13, 111 n.23, 122
Cohen, J., 26 n.53, 28, 238 n.1, 247 n.23, 249 n.25
Cohen, M., 13, 16, 25
Corry, J., 30 n.64, 87 n.1, 155 n.44, 155 n.47, 164, 208 n.27
Cox, A., 20 n.28, 247 n.21
Craies, W., 125
Crawford, E., 19, 105 n.6, 271 n.11
Curtis, C., 16, 25, 50 n.19, 54 n.2, 128, 149, 245

de Sloovère, F., 20 n.28, 29–32, 81 n.44
Devlin, Lord, 16 n.11
Dewey, J., 36 n.7, 36 n.9, 58, 105 n.8, 115 n.35
Dias, R., 59 n.21, 174 n.88
Dickerson, R., 58 n.20, 98 n.24, 156 n.49, 220 n.6, 277 n.18
Driedger, E., 128 n.68, 219

Ekelöf, P., 20 n.28, 189–190

Finley, E., 150 n.35, 175 n.90
Flesch, R., 59
Folsom, G., 169 n.76
Frank, J., 20 n.28, 24–26, 238
Frankfurter, F., 28 n.60, 77, 87, 94, 162 n.63, 219 n.4, 221 n.9, 224 n.15, 228 n.34
Friedmann, W., 5 n.7, 6, 209 n.32
Friendly, H., 217
Fuller, L., 45, 55–66, 69, 76, 95 n.17, 121, 153 n.40, 261 n.55

Gény, F., 15 n.7, 21, 125, 185, 192–194, 240
Gottlieb, G., 95 n.16
Gray, J., 14 n.4, 15, 16 n.10, 67, 68 n.4, 119, 129

Hall, J., 110, 215 n.49
Hall, L., 208
Halsbury, Lord, 156 n.49, 170 n.81
Hand, L., 80 n.38, 94, 169 n.75
Hanley, J., 198
Hare, R., 220
Hart, H., Jr., 140–142; with A. Sacks, 1, 10 n.11, 28, 85 n.56, 94 n.15, 95–96, 149–150, 154, 164, 220 n.7, 223 n.13, 226, 244
Hart, H. L. A., 45, 55–66, 111 n.25
Hawkins, F., 221 n.11
Henle, P., 105 n.8
Heymann, P., 82 n.46, 90 n.5, 91 n.9, 199 n.3
Hoadly, Bishop, 16
Holmes, O., 7, 21 n.31, 75 n.18, 75 n.22, 84 n.53, 93–94, 163, 214
Horack, F., Jr., 1, 21 n.31, 103 n.2, 211 n.37, 227 n.27, 252–254
Hughes, C., 16, 39
Hurst, J., 17

Jackson, R., 5 n.7, 148–149, 162
Jefferson, T., 31
Johnstone, Q., 232 n.47
Jones, H., xvi, 23, 30–31, 90 n.6, 103 n.2, 145
Jones, M., 137

Katz, J., 105 n.8, 108 n.15
Kohler, J., 23 n.39, 75 n.22, 80, 90 n.7, 178 n.95
Krenek, E., 24

Landis, J., 77, 103, 228 n.30
Langer, S., 292
Leff, A., 176–177
Lenhoff, A., 90, 96, 207
Leventhal, H., 177 n.93
Levi, E., 252–254, 255 n.41
Lieber, F., 112
Llewellyn, K., 22, 95–96, 225, 226 n.25, 227
Locke, J., 270

MacCallum, G., Jr., 23 n.38, 70, 73 n.13, 74 n.15, 90 n.6
MacDonald, J., 78 n.36, 98 n.25
MacMillan, Lord, 196 n.168
Merman, S., 262
Miller, A. S., 25, 43 n.1
Mishkin, P., 246, 254, 260 n.54, 261
Montesquieu, C., 9
Montrose, J., 46 n.8
Morris, Chas., 34, 63, 293
Morris, Clarence, 246, 254, 260 n.54, 261
Morse, W., 157 n.50

Newman, F., 17 n.17, 180 n.99, 227 n.27, 252 n.34
Nida, E., 103 n.2, 105 n.9, 108 n.17, 114 n.30, 114 n.31, 123
Nutting, C., 14 n.2, 22 n.32, 82 n.48, 85 n.56, 204 n.15, 223 n.13
Nyiri, J., 113 n.29

Ogden, C., 34, 37 n.13, 42, 54, 291–295

Patterson, E., 34, 76 n.24, 119 n.42, 261 n.57
Pavlov, I., 21, 218
Pierce, C. S., 293
Polanyi, M., 104
Pound, R., 17 n.19, 19 n.25, 21 n.30, 150 n.37
Prouty, W., 157 n.50

Radin, M., 9 n.8, 51 n. 23, 54 n.2, 68–78, 91, 95, 129, 196 n.169, 234 n.54
Reed, S., 148
Rich, G., 155 n.45
Richards, I., 34, 37 n.13, 42, 54, 291–295
Ross, A., 15, 83 n.51, 121
Russell, B., 37 n.12, 57, 65, 75

Sacks, A., 1, 10 n.11, 28, 85 n.56, 94 n.15, 95–96, 149–150, 154, 164, 220 n.7, 223 n.13, 226, 244
Sapir, E., 105 n.8
Schatzman, L., 108 n.15
Schmidt, F., 190–191
Scriven, M., 60
Shartel, B., 103 n.2, 121, 138–139
Silving, H., 73 n.14
Stern, G., 107 n.13
Strauss, A., 108 n.15
Strömholm, S., 142, 185–189, 244
Surrey, S., 17 n.17, 180 n.99, 227 n.27, 252 n.34
Sutherland, J., 153 n.39, 169 n.76, 210

Thomas, J., 262 n.2
Thornstedt, H., 6
Tunks, L., 20 n.28

Ullman, S., 111 n.23

Wasby, S., 155 n.43, 177 n.94
Washington, G., 31
Wheelwright, P., 104 n.5
Whitehead, A., 57, 65
Whorf, B., 58, 60, 105 n.8, 115
Wilberforce, Lord, xv, 166
Williams, G., 42 n.18, 241 n.9
Willis, J., 210 n.34
Witherspoon, J., 87 n.1, 238 n.1, 250
Wittgenstein, L., xv, 21 n.31, 37 n.13, 57, 61, 65, 75, 111–112, 117 n.40
Wurzel, K., 262 n.3

Ziff, P., 108 n.16

Index of Subjects

ABSURDITY as creating exception to "plain meaning" rule, 230–232

ACTUAL MEANING compared with literal meaning and true meaning, 38–39

ADJUDICATION as courts' main function, 13–15

ADMINISTRATIVE INTERPRETATIONS, 183

ADMINISTRATIVE REGULATIONS, 177

ADOPTION OF INTERVENING INTERPRETATION BY REENACTMENT, 182–183, 253–255

AGING STATUTES, 125–131

AMBIGUITY
- actual compared with apparent, 48, 267
- in general, 30, 43–50, 54–55, 65, 111, 139, 226, 227, 230, 239, 242–250, 267

APPLICATION
- as distinguished from interpretation, 29–32
- what is involved in, 13–21

ARCHITECTURAL REMODELING as an analogue to creative function, 248

ARMY ORGANIZATION ACT OF *1950,* 156 n.49

ASCERTAINMENT OF MEANING as component of statutory interpretation, 13–14. *See also* Cognitive function

ATTITUDE, importance of, 218–219

AUDIENCE, legislative. *See* Legislative audience

AVAILABILITY as an element of context. *See* Sharing

AVAILABILITY (SHARING) OF LEGISLATIVE HISTORY. *See* Legislative history

AVAILABILITY OF STATUTORY MESSAGE as constitutionally required, 11–12

BORROWED STATUTES, 131–136

CANADIAN INTERPRETATION ACT, 183 n.107, 270 n.9

CANONS OF INTERPRETATION
- *casus omissus,* 216, 236
- *contemporanea expositio,* 125–126
- criminal laws to be "strictly" interpreted, 208–211, 239
- *ejusdem generis,* 109, 234, 249
- *expressio unius est exclusio alterius,* 47, 228 n.33, 234
- "golden rule," 230, 231 n.43
- in general, 4, 227–236

CANONS OF INTERPRETATION (*cont.*)
in pari materia, 105, 109, 228 n.29, 233
noscitur a sociis, 233
"plain meaning" rule, 109, 190, 229–233, 236
reddendo singula singulis, 109, 228 n.28, 233
statutes in derogation of common law to be "strictly" interpreted, 206–208, 228 n.32, 239
CASES ON STATUTORY INTERPRETATION only occasionally relevant and authoritative, xvi-xvii
CASUS OMISSUS, 216, 236
CERTAINTY OF MEANING, 54–56
CLARITY, 54–55
CODE SYSTEMS, 183–194
COGNITION
as an automatic response, 21, 107, 217–218
as preceding creation, 20, 32, 190, 247
as recognition, 217–218
COGNITIVE FUNCTION, the courts'
in general, 13–33, 123, 126, 127, 136, 139, 143, 144, 153, 163, 166, 167–168, 169, 178, 182, 189, 192–194, 195, 198, 201, 205, 207, 211–212, 214–215, 217–237, 239, 248–250, 251, 252, 254, 261, 267, 280
importance of distinguishing creative function from, 2, 4, 14–15, 18, 23, 182, 214, 267
COMMISSION REPORTS as legislative history, 161–162, 166–167
COMMITTEE HEARINGS as legislative history, 145, 148–149, 155–157, 195
COMMITTEE REPORTS as legislative history, 145, 147, 196
COMMON LAW OF LEGISLATION, 133
COMMUNICATION PRINCIPLES, importance of knowing, 3
COMPETENCE OF LEGISLATIVE HISTORY, 140–141. *See also* Relevance; Reliability
COMPUTERS, 179, 196, 267–268
CONCEPTS, need to clarify, 2
CONCURRENT RESOLUTIONS as legislative history, 143, 159, 180
CONFERENCE REPORTS as legislative history, 143
CONNOTATIONS compared with denotations, 76–77, 128–130, 294–295
"CONSIDERED DICTUM" as notice of judicial intention to correct interpretation, 260
CONSTITUTIONAL REQUIREMENTS
availability of statutory message, 11–12
exclusiveness of statutory vehicle, 2, 9–10, 13, 83, 84, 143–144, 157, 240
legislative supremacy, 7–9, 10, 20, 200–201, 207, 211, 214, 245, 247
reliance on accepted means of communication, 10–11, 272–273
that cognition precede creation, 20, 32
that disciplined creation precede free creation, 247
"CONSTRUCTION" as synonymous with "interpretation," 18–19
CONTEMPORANEA EXPOSITIO, 125–126
CONTEXT
as broadening literal meaning, 200, 213

CONTEXT (*cont.*)
as narrowing literal meaning, 198–200, 213
changes in, 125–136
defined, 110
geographical differences in, 131–136
in general, 3, 10, 12, 22, 35, 36, 38–39, 44, 58–63, 64–65, 66, 80, 83, 105–136, 156, 175, 177, 183, 190, 193, 198, 200–201, 214–215, 218, 219, 225, 229, 230–232, 240, 243, 245, 249, 265, 266, 280
judicial notice as related to, 110–111
legislative history as part of, 138–162
relevance as an element of, 110, 124
reliability of evidence of, 124–125
sharing as an element of, 108, 110, 116–117, 124
taking into account (reliance) as an element of, 110, 120–122, 124
CONTEXT OF BORROWED STATUTES, 131–136
CONVENTION, language as, 36–38, 62
CORE MEANING, 54–66
CORRECTION OF ERRONEOUS INTERPRETATION, 239, 252–261
COURTS' FUNCTIONS RESPECTING STATUTES, 13–21
COURTS' INEPTITUDE IN HANDLING LEGISLATION, 163
COURTS' OBLIGATION TO CREATE NEW LAW, 14–15, 169
CREATION, disciplined, as preceding free creation, 247
"CREATIVE ELABORATION," 28, 244, 249
CREATIVE FUNCTION, the courts'
broadening statutory rule to apply to analogous situation beyond legislative purpose, 193, 204–205, 212, 239, 251
broadening statutory rule to apply to analogous situation within legislative purpose, 193, 202–204, 212, 239, 250–251
in general, 13–33, 124, 131, 136, 139, 163, 166, 167–168, 168–169, 178, 180–182, 189, 192, 193–194, 195, 201, 205, 207–208, 209, 210, 212, 214–215, 221–222, 226, 238–261, 263, 267, 268–269, 280
erroneous interpretation corrected by, 239, 252–261
performed in deference to existing statutes and rest of legal order, 248–251
range of judicial discretion in performing, 241–242, 242–250
standards for judicial performance of, 242–250
using deferred effective data, 209, 252, 256–259
CRIMINAL LAWS to be "strictly" interpreted, 208–211, 239
CULTURE as the material of context, 105–108

DEFERRED EFFECTIVE DATE, 209, 252, 256–259
DELEGATED LEGISLATION, 182, 191, 238–239, 241–242, 247
DENOTATIONS compared with connotations, 76–77, 128–130, 294–295
DEONTIC LOGIC, 220

"DESCRIPTIVE TEXTS." *See* Floor debates
DISCIPLINED CREATION as preceding free creation, 247
DRAFTING, 97–98, 118–119, 168, 171–174, 194, 210, 219, 223 n.13, 224, 225, 277–278
DRAFTSMAN'S VIEWS as legislative history, 156 n.49

EFFECTIVE DATE OF CORRECTED INTERPRETATION, 255–261
EJUSDEM GENERIS, 109, 234, 249
ELEGANT VARIATION, 225
EMERGENCY PRICE CONTROL ACT OF 1942, 52
ENGLISH EXPERIENCE, 8–9, 15, 16, 32–33, 161–162, 168, 170–174, 195, 214, 252, 275, 278
EQUITABLE INTERPRETATION. *See* Equity of the statute
EQUITY OF THE STATUTE, 8, 213–214. *See also* "Spirit of the statute"
ERRONEOUS INTERPRETATION, correction of, 239, 252–261
EXCEPTIONS, implied, 198–200, 205, 275
EXCLUSIVENESS OF STATUTORY VEHICLE as constitutionally provided, 2, 9–10, 13, 83, 84, 143–144, 157, 240
"EXPOUNDING TEXTS." *See* "Interpretative materials"
EXPRESS MEANING, 3, 40, 114, 229
EXPRESSIO UNIUS EST EXCLUSIO ALTERIUS, 47, 228 n.33, 234

"FAIR TRADE" STATUTES, 158, 162 n.63
FAIR WARNING, 209–211, 214. *See also* Unfair surprise
FEDERAL WATER POWER ACT OF *1935*, 148
FICTITIOUS MEANINGS, 249
FLOOR DEBATES as legislative history, 145, 147, 155–157, 185–187, 191, 195, 267
FOREIGN AID APPROPRIATIONS ACT, *1949*, 202
"FREE INTERPRETATION," 192–194. *See also* Creation

GENERALITY, 51–53, 198–199, 240–241, 247, 281
"GENUINE INTERPRETATION" compared with "spurious interpretation," 19, 21 n.30
GEOGRAPHICAL DIFFERENCES IN CONTEXT, 131–136
"GOLDEN RULE," 230, 231 n.43. *See also* "Plain meaning" rule

HABIT, meaning as, 37, 62, 115, 217, 219
HOMONYMS, 35, 44–45, 61, 65, 111

IMPLICATIONS OF MEANING compared with implications of formal logic, 42
IMPLIED EXCEPTIONS, 198–200, 205, 275
IMPLIED MEANING, 40–42, 114, 198–200, 271. *See also* Negative implication
IMPORTANCE OF DISTINGUISHING COGNITIVE FUNCTION FROM CREATIVE FUNCTION, 2, 4, 14–15, 18, 23, 182, 214, 267
INCONSISTENT STATUTES, later statute as prevailing, 228 n.31, 249–250
INDIANA TRUST CODE, 167
IN PARI MATERIA, 105, 109, 228 n.29, 233
INTENT. See Legislative intent

INTERACTION OF SYMBOLS, 100. *See also* Syntactical relationships
INTERPRETATION as distinguished from application, 29–32
"INTERPRETATION" as synonymous with "construction," 18–19
INTERPRETATION ACT, 1889 (ENGLAND), 263, 277
INTERPRETATION ACT, 1970 (GHANA), 270, 279
INTERPRETATION ACTS
  as attempts to change usage or principles of communication, 270
  as defining boundaries of effective legislation, 279–280
  as mediating between competing legislative instruments, 279
  effective scope of, 280–281
  enactment of facts or principles of communication as part of, 262, 263–268
  inclusion of implementing rules of law, 276
  inclusion of legislative boilerplate, 262, 277–278
  inclusion of rules for deciding cases where cognitive function fails, 268–269
  in general, 262–281
  terminating undesirable rules of interpretation, 269–270
INTERPRETATION AND GENERAL PROVISIONS ACT, 1973 (BOTSWANA), 280
INTERPRETATION AND GENERAL PROVISIONS ACT (ZAMBIA), 279–280
"INTERPRETATION PROPER," 192–194. *See also* Cognition
INTERPRETATION WITHOUT APPLICATION, 31
"INTERPRETATIVE MATERIALS." *See* Legislative history
INTERPRETER AS TRUE LAWMAKER, 16

JUDICIAL BOOTSTRAP PULLING, 93–94, 247
JUDICIAL LAWMAKING. *See* Creative function
JUDICIAL NOTICE as related to context, 110–111

LANGUAGE, as a conceptual map of experience, 105–106
LATER INCONSISTENT STATUTE as prevailing, 228 n.31, 249–250
LEGAL MEANING, 39–40, 256
LEGISLATIVE AUDIENCE, 36, 38, 64, 117–118, 124, 147, 156, 189, 195, 218, 223, 229, 249, 274, 279
LEGISLATIVE HISTORY
  as distraction, 164
  as part of context, 138–162
  availability of (sharing), 147–154, 162, 165, 167, 169, 170, 186, 189, 191
  commission reports as, 161–162, 166–167. *See also* Preliminary studies
  committee hearings as, 145, 148–149, 155–157, 195
  committee reports as, 145, 147, 196
  concurrent resolutions as, 143, 159, 180
  conference reports as, 143
  draftsman's views as, 156 n.49
  floor debates as, 145, 147, 155–157, 185–187, 191, 195, 267
  general case against, 162–164
  improvements in, 170–174
  in general, 3, 25, 82, 83, 84, 109,

LEGISLATIVE HISTORY (*cont.*)
116, 137–197, 240, 243, 267
"interpretative materials" as, 142–145, 156, 158, 172, 185–187, 195
legislative history of, 175–177
manipulation of, 177
"motivating materials" as, 142, 145–146, 157–159, 168, 173, 185–188, 196
postenactment developments as basis for inferring original legislative intent, 179–183, 245
preliminary studies as, 196. *See also* Commission reports
purpose clause as substitute for, 168, 173
of other definitive instruments, 177
relevance of, 140, 141, 144, 154, 160, 162, 169, 170
reliability of, 144, 155–164, 169, 170, 171, 186–187
taking into account (reliance on), 142–147, 160, 162, 165, 190
textual provisions in support of, 165
use of computers to search, 179, 196
use of for confirmatory purposes, 164, 189, 195
use of for counseling purposes, 150–151, 175
use of to make new law, 168–169

LEGISLATIVE INTENT
adopted (vicarious), 71–72
as distinguished from legislative purpose, 87–88
as sometimes inconsistent with legislative purpose, 98–101
corporate, 73–74
in general, 36, 37, 67–88, 126, 145, 168, 169, 176, 183, 185, 189, 192–193, 195, 196, 212, 214, 221, 223, 225, 228, 240, 243, 244, 245, 253
not necessarily co-extensive with meaning, 23, 80

LEGISLATIVE NONACTION FOLLOWING JUDICIAL INTERPRETATION, import of, 181, 255. *See also* Nonadoption

LEGISLATIVE PATHOLOGY, lawyers' preoccupation with, 17, 43, 54

LEGISLATIVE PURPOSE, absence of, 91, 95

LEGISLATIVE PURPOSE
ascertainment of, 92–93
as distinguished from legislative intent, 87–88
as sometimes inconsistent with legislative intent, 98–101
in general, 25, 57–58, 66, 87–102, 113, 145, 157–159, 169, 189, 190, 199, 201, 203, 210, 212, 213, 214, 216, 221, 224, 244, 247, 250–251
multiplicity of, 89–90
necessity of, 95–96
self-serving, 93–94

LEGISLATIVE SILENCE FOLLOWING JUDICIAL INTERPRETATION, import of, 181–182, 255

LEGISLATIVE SUPREMACY as constitutionally provided, 7–9, 10, 20, 200–201, 207, 211, 214, 245, 247

LEGISLATURE'S POWER TO BIND FUTURE LEGISLATURES, 272–276

"LEGISPUTATION." *See* "Creative elaboration"

"LIBERAL" INTERPRETATION, 8, 205, 211–212

LITERAL MEANING
compared with actual meaning and true meaning, 38–39
in general, 198, 200–201, 205, 213, 230
LOGIC
deontic, 220
role of, 218, 219–220, 221–222, 224, 237
LORD BROUGHAM'S ACT, 263

MALUM IN SE, crimes, 209–211
MALUM PROHIBITUM, crimes, 209, 211
MANN ACT, 181
MEANING not necessarily coextensive with legislative intent, 23, 80
MEANING OF "MEANING," 34–38
METALANGUAGE, 34, 292, 293
MILLER-TYDINGS ACT, 162 n.63
"MOTIVATING MATERIALS" as legislative history, 142, 145–146, 157–159, 168, 173, 185–188, 196
MUSIC as an analogue, 24–25

NATIONALITY ACT OF *1940*, 254
NEGATIVE IMPLICATION, 41–42, 47, 182, 201, 205, 216, 234. *See also* Preemption
NONADOPTION OR REJECTION OF PROPOSED STATUTORY ACTION, import of, 160
NOSCITUR A SOCIIS, 233

OBJECT LANGUAGE, 35
"OBJECTIVE INTERPRETATION" compared with "subjective interpretation," 83
OFFICE OF THE PARLIAMENTARY COUNSEL, 172, 275
OGDEN & RICHARDS' TRIANGLE, 42, 291–295
"ONE-SHOT" THEORY OF JUDICIAL INTERPRETATION, 204, 252–254
OPPORTUNITY TO KNOW THE LAW, 12, 118–120, 165

PENUMBRA OF UNCERTAINTY. *See* Vagueness
"PLAIN MEANING" RULE, 109, 190, 229–233, 236. *See also* "Golden rule"
"POINTER" THEORY OF MEANING, 76–77, 129 n.72
POSTENACTMENT DEVELOPMENTS
as basis for inferring original legislative intent, 179–180, 245
PRAGMATICS, 294
PRECEDENCE OF COGNITION OVER CREATION as constitutionally required, 20, 32
PREEMPTION, 250. *See also* Negative implication
PRELIMINARY STUDIES as legislative history, 196
PRESUMPTIONS
of adherence to normal usage, 223
of formal consistency, 224
of intended rationality and coherence, 220, 224
of reasonableness and fidelity to duty, 226
of substantive consistency, 224
that "or" is used in inclusive sense, 233
that rest of legal order has been taken into account, 226–227
PROBATIVE VALUE OF LEGISLATIVE HISTORY, 141. *See also* Reliability
PROSPECTIVE OVERRULING, 256–261
PUBLICATION OF STATUTES, 12
PURPOSE. *See* Legislative purpose

PURPOSE CLAUSE as substitute for legislative history, 168, 173
PURPOSE CLAUSES, 97–98, 168, 173

"REASONED ELABORATION," 28, 244, 249
REDDENDO SINGULA SINGULIS, 109, 228 n.28, 233
REENACTMENT, effect of, 130–131, 182–183, 253–255
REFERENTIAL MEANING, 291–295
RELEVANCE AS AN ELEMENT OF CONTEXT, 110, 124
RELEVANCE OF LEGISLATIVE HISTORY, 140, 141, 144, 154, 160, 169, 170
RELIABILITY OF EVIDENCE OF CONTEXT, 124–125
RELIABILITY OF LEGISLATIVE HISTORY, 144, 155–164, 169, 170, 171, 186–187
RELIANCE ON ACCEPTED MEANS OF COMMUNICATION as constitutionally required, 10–11, 272–273
RELUCTANCE TO READ STATUTES, 17–18
RETROACTIVE COGNITION, 252, 255, 257, 259
RETROACTIVE CREATION, 209, 252
REVERSE IMPLICATION. *See* Negative implication
RULE OF LITERALNESS, 230. *See also* "Plain meaning" rule

SEMANTICS, 294
SEMIOTIC, 293–295
SEPARATION OF POWERS, 7, 9, 11, 180, 201, 214, 262. *See also* Legislative supremacy
SHARING as an element of context, 108, 110, 116–117, 124
SHERMAN ACT, 25 n.50, 26, 27, 239, 240
SINGLE TRUE MEANING, concept of, 29–30, 53, 225
SPEECH COMMUNITY, 62, 65, 66, 110, 117, 273, 291. *See also* Legislative audience
"SPIRIT OF THE STATUTE," 214–215. *See also* Equity
"SPLIT LEVEL" STATUTES, 173
"SPURIOUS INTERPRETATION" compared with "genuine interpretation," 19, 21 n.30
"STANDARD INSTANCE." *See* Core meaning
STANDING COMMITTEE ON LEGISLATIVE DRAFTING, AMERICAN BAR ASSOCIATION, 171–172
STARE DECISIS, 135, 222, 249, 254, 261
STATUTE INTERPRETED AS OF DATE OF ENACTMENT, 125–130
STATUTES ADOPTED BY REFERENCE, 131–132
STATUTES IN DEROGATION OF COMMON LAW to be "strictly" interpreted, 206–208, 228 n.32, 239
"STATUTORY INTERPRETATION"
  as creative effort, 3
  as finding meaning, 3
  what is, 1–2, 165–166
STATUTORY VEHICLE described, 104–105
"STRICT" INTERPRETATION, 8, 205–211, 239
"SUBJECTIVE INTERPRETATION" compared with "objective interpretation," 83
SYNTACTICAL RELATIONSHIPS, 113–116. *See also* Interaction of symbols
SYNTACTICS, 293

TACIT ASSUMPTIONS, 29, 41, 60–61, 66, 69, 107, 112, 121, 129, 142, 198–201, 205, 221–222, 230, 236, 262, 265–267, 281. *See also* Context

TAKING INTO ACCOUNT (RELIANCE ON) CONTEXT, 110, 120–122, 124

TAKING INTO ACCOUNT (RELIANCE ON) LEGISLATIVE HISTORY, 142–147, 160, 162, 165, 190

TERMINOLOGY, need to clarify, 2

THEORY OF INTERPRETATION, lack of adequate, 4

TIME AS OF WHICH STATUTE SHOULD BE READ, 125–130

TITLE 10, UNITED STATES CODE, 100, 101, 127, 200

TRAVAUX PRÉPARATOIRES, 183–194

TRUE MEANING
- as extended by context beyond the limits of semantic leeway, 214–215
- as normally restricted to semantic leeway, 63–64, 200–201, 205, 214–215
- compared with actual meaning and literal meaning, 38–39
- in general, 38–39, 124, 207, 210, 217, 222, 225, 237, 255–256

UNCERTAINTIES OF MEANING, actual as compared with apparent, 48, 221, 267

UNFAIR SURPRISE, 134–135, 169, 222–223, 249, 252, 259. *See also* Fair warning

UNFAIRNESS as creating exception to "plain meaning" rule, 231–232

UNIFORM COMMERCIAL CODE, 146–147, 159, 165, 173, 176–177, 235 n.58

UNIFORM PROBATE CODE, 271

UNIFORM RESIDENTIAL LANDLORD AND TENANT ACT, 271

UNIFORM SALES ACT, 204, 235 n.58

UNIFORM STATUTORY CONSTRUCTION ACT, 166, 263–279

UNIQUENESS OF STATUTES, 28–29

UNREASONABLENESS as creating an exception to "plain meaning" rule, 231–232

"USERS OF THE LANGUAGE," 51, 62, 107, 110, 116–118

VAGUENESS, 30, 48–52, 54–55, 62, 65, 227, 239, 241, 242–250

VASE, reconstruction of, as an analogue, 26–27, 246–247

VECTOR ANALYSIS as an analogue, 27–28, 73

WORDS AS "EMPTY VESSELS," 16

WORDS IN ISOLATION, meaning of, 54, 58–59, 62, 66, 115

ADDENDUM: Too late for mention in the body of this book, *The Preparation of Legislation,* an exhaustive report to Parliament on the process of formulating statutes, prepared by the Renton Committee ("Committee Appointed by the Lord President of the Council") and published May 7, 1975, may interest the reader for its recommendations for improving explanatory materials (chapter XV) but not using them in statutory interpretation (chapter XIX).

Charles R. Priest
ATTORNEY AT LAW
31 GROVE STREET
P.O. BOX 846
AUGUSTA, ME 04330
622-3789